TECHNOLOGY IN AMERICA

A BRIEF HISTORY

SECOND EDITION

Alan I Marcus
Iowa State University

Howard P. Segal
University of Maine

HARCOURT BRACE COLLEGE PUBLISHERS

Fort Worth Philadelphia San Diego New York Orlando Austin San Antonio
Toronto Montreal London Sydney Tokyo

Publisher:	Earl McPeek
Acquisitions Editor:	David Tatom
Developmental Editor:	Margaret McAndrew Beasley
Art Director:	Susan M. Journney
Production Manager:	Diane Gray
Project Editor:	G. Parrish Glover

ISBN: 0-15-505531-3

Library of Congress Catalogue Card Number: 98-075283

Address for Orders
Harcourt Brace College Publishers, 6277 Sea Harbor Drive, Orlando, FL 32887-6777
1-800-782-4479

Address for Editorial Correspondence
Harcourt Brace College Publishers, 301 Commerce Street, Suite 3700, Fort Worth, TX 76102

Web Site Address
http://www.hbcollege.com

Printed in the United States of America

8 9 0 1 2 3 4 5 6 7   016   9 8 7 6 5 4 3 2 1

Harcourt Brace College Publishers

For Jean and for Deborah

PREFACE

It has been ten years since we wrote the first edition of *Technology in America: A Brief History*, the first single-volume study of the subject. The response has been overwhelming-so overwhelming, in fact, that Harcourt Brace has brought forth this second edition. From our perspective, the second edition is a great opportunity to increase the depth and sophistication of our treatment. And we have taken advantage of it. Where we originally had one chapter on the post–1950 era, we now have three. (We thank Harcourt Brace for giving us the additional space.) As a result, this edition is much more inclusive.

In addition to concentrating considerable attention on the post–1950 world, we have provided greater balance between what went on inside the home and what went on outside the home. Topics such as the technology of food preparation, consumer electronics, and yard maintenance merit and now receive much more consideration than they had received in the first edition. These technologies rarely seem dramatic or cutting edge as, say, spaceflight, but they are nonetheless critical and worthy of exploration.

We have retained several emphases that were received especially well in the first edition. We persist in varying the complexity with which we discuss specific technologies. We trust that the occasional, more technical explanation is written in such a manner as to serve as a model for complementary textbook sections, and, thus, will satisfy those readers with some technical training without hampering those lacking a similar background.

We also continue to reject every attempt to trivialize the history of technology or to reduce it to a series of vapid categorizations. It is bad history, an ahistorical folly, to treat technology as if it were a discrete entity and to attempt to erect laws of technological progress or development. This and other determinisms soothe the passions expressly because they merely reflect preconceived notions, but they fail to address the complexity of the past.

It is trivial, simplistic, and one-dimensional to compose a narrative that "traces" the change from preindustrial to industrial or from simple to complex in sector after sector as if those terms have meaning beyond what an author has decided or outside a particular historical context. It is equally misguided to treat technology as a force that operates outside of society and culture and has impact on or affects society and culture. The stimulus-response model erected from that framework suggests society and culture are rather like amoebas, which cringe in consistent, always reproducible fashion when faced with the same bright light or heat. But it is also much too simplistic to acknowledge that technology has good and bad implications or consequences and that such a bland analysis could pose as an investigation of the history of technology in America.

In this second edition, we have retained emphasis on technology as a multifaceted phenomenon, whose history includes material productions—techniques, structures, and apparatuses—and the organization of human activities. The history of technology is both the hardware and that hardware's relationships to American society and culture. This book concentrates on the impact of American society and culture on technology, rather than vice versa.

Instead of speculating about why something did not happen, we focus the book on explaining how something happened. What invariably made a technology acceptable and, therefore, applicable was the way it was conceptualized and the method that was explained to and understood by those who would implement it. Technologies are the products of ideas and assumptions, and their implementation also depends on ideas; persons repeatedly ask themselves a simple question: Given how we understand what we face—what we perceive as our condition or situation—is this technology a likely solution or amelioration?

Accentuating ideas may suggest elitism to some, but historical study of ideas is far from elitist. In fact, to suggest that inarticulate people—people who do not talk or write publicly—lack the capacity for formal thought is itself elitist, arrogant, and pretentious. Furthermore, if actions are guides to thought, it appears in many instances that inarticulate people do not necessarily think differently than their more articulate peers. Likewise, to insist that they in fact do think differently-that they are somehow less enlightened or that others have bamboozled them-is also elitist, arrogant, and pretentious. It is also often wrong. Social position, ethnicity, and gender are not inalterably deterministic. Culture—a series of ideas, notions, and customs—binds together diverse groups of persons in seemingly unexplainable ways and provides a common perspective from which to interpret and reason. It is from this idea of culture as common perspective that we fashion this volume.

We have identified specific, dominant cultural notions and social themes for different eras in the American past. It is these cultural notions and social themes that make a series of years a distinct era. But cultures change. In this regard, we have drawn our inspiration from more contemporary scholars who have demonstrated that culture is not simply a phenomenon of people and place. Cultures rarely emerge from the settlement of geographic areas and persist inviolate; instead, a culture has distinctive epochs, each characterized by a particular set of assumptions locked in time. In effect, American history is but a series of cultures, each of which succeeded and was markedly different than its predecessor. True cross-cultural study, then, is not only the study of different geographical units. It is also the study of the same geographical unit at different times.

The identification of cultural notions and social themes during the periods in which they predominate strikes us as a particularly useful and important way to understand America's technological past. After all, an era's social and cultural desires, opinions, ideas, themes, and notions help explain public acceptance or rejection of specific technologies. Those same factors also dictate how technologies are conceived, developed, and ultimately employed, as well as circumscribe such relative concepts as efficiency, profitability, and applicability. In that sense, what has made and continues to make technology in America distinct from technology someplace else is and are the cultural epochs through which America has passed and is passing. Technology in America is a manifestation and explication of culture-based ideas.

These latter considerations are reflected in the book's organization. The trendier designations of preindustrial, industrializing, industrial, and postindustrial America prove too limiting. Products of the impact-of-technology-on-society question, they lack the flexibility required for a systematic discussion of the influence on technology of a particular period's prevailing cultural notions and social themes. A relatively conventional American history periodization instead provides the necessary latitude. It facilitates, for example, the examination of colonial technology with reference to mercantile theory and community practice (especially the closed commercial corporation), and the investigation of late–nineteenth- and early–twentieth-century American technology in the context of that period's obsession with system, efficiency, standarization, centralization, nationalism, and the like.

We have decided to emphasize the years after the 1830s. That decision stemmed from the fact that the century after the 1830s marked America's technological heyday; with that era's extraordinary technological developments came profound social and cultural changes. Few pre–1830s technologies still seem vital today. That cannot be said of technologies fostered after those years: Americans on the verge of the third millennium continue to live with and employ variants of technologies first developed more than a hundred years ago.

ACKNOWLEDGMENTS

Many people deserve acknowledgment for their contributions to this edition. Graduate students Phil Frana, Dave Harmon, Lora Leigh Gorrell, Paul Mobley, Lester Poehner, Jason Chrystal and Dak Rasmussen, all in Iowa State University's Ph.D. program in the history of technology and science, contributed invaluable research assistance. George McJimsey, Amy Bix, Jocelyn Marcus, Gregory Marcus, and Andrejs Plakans read portions of the manuscript and offered helpful comments. Jessica Riskin, David Wilson, Daryl Hafter, Ed Layton, Joanne Goldman, W. David Lewis, Mary Ann Hellrigel, and the late Mel Kranzberg provided timely suggestions. So, too, did the late Norman Smith, former dean of the College of Engineering at the University of Maine and a longtime supporter of our efforts. Robert Bradford, who prepared the index for the first edition, also carefully prepared the index for this edition. We also acknowledge the contributions of reviewers who commented on the first edition in preparation for this revision: Jefferson D. Cavalieri, Dutchess Community College; Hamilton Cravens, Iowa State University; Elisabeth M. Infield, Iowa State University; Jeffrey L. Meikle, University of Texas at Austin; and Marc J. Stern, Bentley College. Finally, our families—Jean, Jocelyn, and Gregory Marcus, and Marjorie Marcus Schulz, Deborah Rogers, and Rick and Raechel Segal—gave us the intellectual and emotional support necessary to see us through this enterprise.

Alan I Marcus
Iowa State University

Howard P. Segal
University of Maine

CONTENTS

Part Three

10 Public and Private: Technology as a Social Question: The Later 1960s to 1990s   299

PART ONE

From the Old World to the New

1607 TO THE 1830s

Technologies were instrumental in sustaining the first permanent English settlements in North America. Established as mercantilistic ventures, the colonies mined and modified the New World's abundant resources, first to maintain themselves, and eventually for export. The success with which the colonists plied their skills, many brought with them from the Old World, seemed by the 1760s to place them in direct competition with England. Although the American Revolution broke formal connections with England, it neither lessened the New World's reliance on mercantilism nor separated America from Europe.

The United States Constitution was a product of mercantilistic notions, but Americans soon recognized that their country was a land of seemingly limitless possibilities. They endeavored to fulfill the promise of a democratic republic by rejecting aristocracies of wealth and heredity and by expanding the right to vote. By the first decade of the nineteenth century, Americans had abandoned mercantilism,

1

concentrating instead on exploring the New World's possibilities and providing the opportunity for citizens to tap them.

In this milieu, technologies became equated with the provision of individual opportunity. Governments sponsored or built turnpikes, canals, bridges, and railroads to facilitate commerce, and created an unprecedented number of corporations to take advantage of these internal improvements. A shortage of skilled and inexpensive labor plagued many of these enterprises. Entrepreneurs responded by encouraging emigration from Europe of individuals possessing special skills, by copying European production machines, and by replacing workers with machinery. They also established institutions to provide learning opportunities and to join capital with new inventions. That manufactories quickly dotted the nation's landscape was an indication that opportunity had been provided.

Manufacturing America: 1607 to 1800

THE OLD WORLD IN THE NEW

Modern vessels brought the first European settlers to the New World. Brightly colored and round-sterned, these carvel-built ships generally had several masts, a combination of square and lateen sails, and were steered by adjusting the sails or by turning a rudder-attached tiller. They were among the most sophisticated products of European technology.

Though early colonists traveled to North America in relative comfort and ease on truly seaworthy ships, they faced very different circumstances once they landed. Inclement weather, death, and disease were now their constant companions. Relations with Indians often were poor, while European shipping was frequently disrupted. Shipwrecks, pirates, and hostile natives made transport of commodities between continents unreliable, and communications difficult. The first British colonists had to rely on their technical skills just to stay alive.

Survival Through Utilization of Resources

Survival of the settlements demanded development of New World resources, and colonists quickly brought to bear their Old World technologies. Greeted by an abundance of fertile land, much of it forest, they cleared it and placed it under cultivation. Felled, trees served as the primary building material and fuel, and as a source of naval stores. The continent's plentiful rivers and streams provided water sufficient for drinking—and waste disposal—and facilitated transportation, enabling pole boats, barges, and ships to travel inland. These waterways also furnished an important source of motive power; waterwheels came to rival windmills, animals, and men as prime movers.

Through the judicious use of gears, cams, and trip-hammers, waterwheels powered bellows, and saw, grist, paper, grinding, rolling, slitting, crushing, and fulling mills. In the colonists' able hands, animal hides were converted into leather for shoes and apparel. Processed skins trimmed hats. Potash was leached from wood ashes, mixed with animal fat, and transformed into soap. Evaporation of ocean water yielded salt. Tallow—boiled fat to render it somewhat solid—and whale oil served to make candles.

But perhaps the most significant resource was the colonists themselves. Every boatload of settlers crossing the Atlantic brought knowledge of European technological processes and skills. Although English people and practices were most heavily represented, colonists also emigrated from France, Spain, the Netherlands, Poland, Sweden, the German principalities, Scotland, Wales, and Northern Ireland. They all carried with them expertise obtained in their native lands. Not all of their technical knowledge and skill was suitable to the new setting; the North American environment was different. Colonists needed to reject some European-acquired information and adapt other aspects to their new situation to fashion an existence in a harsh, sometimes antagonistic environment.

Mercantilism and Colonial Governance

Europeans carried more to the New World than practical knowledge, adaptability, and know-how. They also brought a common understanding of the nature of colonization as a corporate enterprise. Despite the physical burdens they bore, participants were unified by prospects of improving their situation, a compelling reason to accept less-than-idyllic terms and conditions.

Colonization was an investment in the near future; as a consequence, men and women endured hardships, economic and otherwise, and often put themselves in subservient positions. Each European state risked funds or granted individuals and groups exclusive privilege to settle or trade in an area to either secure a percentage of the profits or collect taxes. Individual entrepreneurs or those acting as joint-stock companies also were immediately involved. For a proportion of the settlements' anticipated profits, they covered colonists' transportation costs, supported them in the New World for specified periods, and sometimes gave them land. In return for this investment, colonists entered into agreements—sometimes tacit but always in some ways restrictive—that mandated their obligations to their benefactors.

Mercantilism and the Colonial Social Structure Colonization entailed a network of well-defined relationships and duties. Seventeenth- and eighteenth-century men and women accentuated the entire web, not any single aspect. They supposed that all parties—nation-states, entrepreneurs, and colonists—needed to benefit in order for any one party to derive benefit. Inequities were expected; it was not necessary for each participant to benefit equally. Emphasis on the whole process over, and almost to the exclusion of, the individuals who were included in it provided an attractive perspective during a period marked by an awareness that the total wealth of the world—both old and new—was limited. Pooling funds, property, and interests in return for, and according to, an established set of commitments, including guarantees of exclusivity implied in grants of monopoly, spread the risk and the burden of colonization. It allowed European states and their subjects to attempt collectively what none could effectively do separately, and participants rested secure in the knowledge that a successful venture meant that they would all reap benefits.

It bears repeating that an essential feature of this social formulation was that the world's wealth was finite. In the seventeenth- and eighteenth-centuries' mind, wealth was not created per se, but rather acquired, gathered, captured, or corralled. The sole purpose of seventeenth- and eighteenth-century governments in both the Old World and the New World was to accrue for their citizens as much wealth as possible and to guard wealth previously amassed. Government by its very definition restrained competition for wealth within its jurisdiction. Internal competition seemed wasteful, potentially a destroyer of wealth. Rather than permit each citizen to pursue his own destiny, which would presumably result in a "condition of war of everyone against everyone," governments were created and endowed with great and arbitrary powers to prevent such an occurrence. Indeed, life without government seemed hopeless: "solitary, poor, nasty, brutish, and short." Only through the formation of "commonwealths," as seventeenth- and eighteenth-century governments were sometimes known, could the common wealth—the wealth that citizens had corralled through collective activity—be protected.

A technology–government nexus became a standard manner of capturing more of the world's limited wealth. Natural resource conversion was the first step, but only through export and sale of products to a different nation-state could a commonwealth gain wealth (the British colonies were part of the English commonwealth, not a separate entity). Conversely, imports reduced wealth by removing it beyond a commonwealth's jurisdiction. As a consequence, governments rigorously encouraged exportation and just as strenuously discouraged importation of any kind.

Political economists call these beliefs *mercantilism* or *mercantile theory*. Mercantilism—especially the idea that the whole, not the individual parts, stood as the key determinant—was woven tightly within the colonial fabric. Colonists had transplanted European assumptions about the relationship among things and the nature of things to the North American soil. Arrival of subsequent settlers and the continuing European connection fortified these suppositions. The nature of local government—plantations, towns, and cities—was among the clearest expressions of mercantile thought.

The Colonial Style of Local Government Colonial cities, towns, and plantations, including New Netherlands' patroon manors, drew upon traditional European governmental practice and received charters from the crown, proprietors, or colonial legislatures that granted the right of local government. These charters were an extraordinary privilege in the seventeenth and eighteenth centuries because local governments regulated virtually all aspects of commercial and manufacturing life. Almost everyone had some government-related task. For example, a partial list of governmental posts in Boston around 1700 included

> constable, town clerk or recorder, treasurer, assessors, collectors, surveyors of highways, clerks of the market, fence viewers, hog reeves, pound keepers . . . , common drivers . . . , water bailiffs, cow keepers, town drummers and teachers of town drummers, tithingmen, perambulators, ringers and yokers of swine, sealers of weights and measures, keepers of ordinaries, town bellmen, cullers of staves, measurers of corn and of boards, corders of wood and overseers of wood corders, overseers of chimneys and chimney-sweepers, overseers of almshouses, gaugers, viewers, surveyors of casks of tar, fire wards, town criers, informers of offenders against the license laws, scalers of leather, licensors and inspectors of brick makers, cullers of fish, inspectors of hides for transportation, measurers of salt, packers of flesh and fish, inspectors of the killing of deer, deer reeves, school wardens, school teachers, truckmasters, brewers, rebukers of boys, sizers of meadows, warners of town meetings, scavengers, viewers of lands, lot layers, judges of delinquents at town meetings, judges of boundary disputes,

branders of cattle, pinders, jurymen, town cannoneers, commissioners for equalization of assessment, town fishers, town deputies, town doctors, town grubbers, and persons to keep dogs out of church.

And Boston's population at the time stood at only 6,700.

Most positions required only a small outlay of time, but their sheer number suggests the scope of local government's commercial and manufacturing involvement. Government owned the docks, markets, counting houses, warehouses, and often the vessels. It required idle persons to work. It regulated who might enter the locality, how long they might remain, and what occupations or trades they could pursue. It set prices for goods and services, fixed wages for workers, and mandated the number of persons allowed to practice each trade.

Local government was a closed commercial corporation, for its powers eliminated economic competition within its jurisdiction. Regulation of wages, prices, and number of workers placed the welfare of the plantation, city, or town above the desires of individuals residing and working there to guarantee that all citizens would share—not necessarily equally—in whatever gain resulted. A local government's influence typically extended far beyond its legal boundaries. Authority to determine who could participate in commercial endeavors enabled local government to control access to both the largest local market—the city, town, or plantation—and the European trade. Most rural artisans or agriculturists had to seek assistance of those closed commercial corporations. And that meant agreeing to abide by that local government's stipulations.

Channeling Colonial Economies Colonial governments aimed to direct or channel trade and production. Each strove to encourage its citizens to produce goods and services essential to the colony's survival, and to increase its wealth by expanding exports to other colonies and European states. The desire to approach self-sufficiency and to tap export markets to corral additional wealth—two keystones of mercantilism—led colonial governments to favor some industries, places, and people over others. Economic manipulations took several forms. For example, in the 1660s the Virginia Assembly presented premiums for the manufacture of linen thread, prizes for the best woolen cloth, and rewards based on tonnage for shipbuilding. It also prohibited the importation of salt to stimulate local manufacture. For the same reason, Pennsylvania laid an import tax on hops in 1704, and Rhode Island placed a similar duty on beer and ale in 1731. Other colonies granted land. Connecticut, Rhode Island, and Maryland offered land for establishment of saw, grist, and flour mills respectively. Monopolies were common practice. Massachusetts gave a twenty-one-year monopoly to a Boston dry dock proprietor and Rhode Island provided a fourteen-year guarantee to a Providence sawmill owner. Outright cash grants were sometimes employed. Massachusetts used a bounty to encourage papermill investors. Other enticements included tax exemptions for specified periods.

THE SEARCH FOR COMMUNITY SELF-SUFFICIENCY: THE SEVENTEENTH CENTURY

The Ubiquitous Mill

That several colonial governments encouraged mill establishment suggests its significance. Mills were crucial for large-scale production and among the first institutions erected in pioneering settlements. Unlike the Old World, which faced scarce material resources and labor abundance, the New World possessed abundant land and minerals but a shortage of labor. Tapping natural resources and cultivating lands could yield new wealth; governments and joint-stock companies profited when men and women used technical skills to develop new areas and to produce additional products. Attracting colonists to unsettled regions improved markedly when mills were established to ease work burdens.

Mills provided colonists with power generated by continuous motion. Windmills were especially common in the early 1600s, but animals or people turned the simplest mills by walking in circles or on treadmills. Neither type proved ideal, however, as both demanded heavy investment in labor or money. Watermills were cheaper and more powerful, and settlers capitalized on the New World's plentiful streams and rivers.

Colonists used three basic, ancient watermill forms that relied on differently positioned waterwheels. In the horizontal mill, the least powerful, the wheel lay flat, immersed in the water. Its chief virtues were cheapness of construction and resulting plane of rotation. It required no gearing to accomplish tasks on a plane parallel to the river. Wheels of the other two water mills—undershot and overshot waterwheels—stood perpendicular to the river and delivered motion on that plane. By means of wooden or metal gearing, that motion could be directed where it was needed, even translated to a different plane. Current turned undershot waterwheels by running beneath them; only their lower parts lay in water. Overshot wheels not only decreased the friction generated by having a portion of the wheel constantly immersed, but they also used gravity to help provide power. These wheels were placed below water courses; thus, water fell only upon the wheel's top flutes. Overshot wheels were situated in a trough and a raceway dug to channel the river there. They required the greatest capital investment, but provided the greatest power. Large-scale enterprises gravitated to overshot mills.

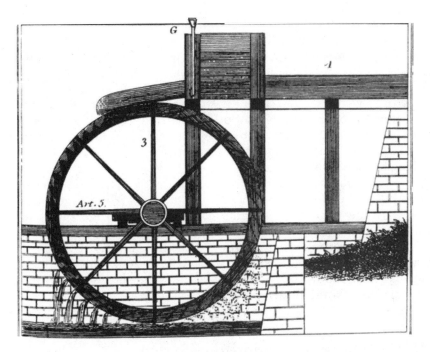

An overshot waterwheel, which combines the force of
gravity with water current to increase power

An extraordinary variety of mills dotted the colonial landscape. Gristmills appeared on plantations as early as 1617, in Jamestown in 1621, in Massachusetts in 1628, and in virtually every community, including small rural communities, soon thereafter. The earliest colonists and those lacking access to gristmills used querns, primitive handmills, to grind grain into meal, a laborious, thankless task taking at least two hours to meet a family's daily needs. Quern-ground meal yielded coarse, unpalatable bread. Gristmills were so highly prized that remote settlers willingly traveled several miles to the nearest gristmill to have their corn, rye, or wheat ground. They gave millers a portion of the milled product as payment.

Rural gristmills were generally small and usually powered by horizontal waterwheels. A structure above the wheel housed two grinding stones. The top stone was attached to the wheel by a rod in its center. The rod passed unobstructed through a hole in the middle of the lower stone, which was fixed. Movement of the top stone against the stationary lower stone milled the grain.

Rural sawmills proved nearly as desirable as gristmills. Land clearing provided colonists a ready supply of logs for fuel and shelter, and sawmills speeded and eased cutting firewood and timbers. Oak timbers, not logs chinked with wood chips, framed most colonial dwellings and other structures. Sawmills (typically horizontal water-mills) fashioned rough framing timbers, which were sometimes finished by broadax and adz before the frames were assembled on the ground and mortised a side at a time. Colonists added corner braces and vertical studs to provide the frames stability when raised. Thick clapboards were then nailed to the studs as siding to protect inhabitants from the often harsh New World climate. Roof shingles generally were not sawmill cut, but split by froes, a cleaving blade also used for splitting logs, and tapered by drawknives, two-handled bladed pulling tools for shaving surfaces.

Colonial mills numbered in the thousands. Their importance marked their builders and maintainers as the New World's most treasured artisans. These millwrights combined knowledge of wood-building crafts with smithing and surveying, a rigorous combination of skills. Émigré millwrights carried with them the latest European practice and colonial governments repeatedly enticed other European millwrights to follow. But immigration and inducements failed to relieve the New World millwright shortage.

The Colonial Master–Apprentice System

Like most other colonial artisans, New World millwrights learned their special skills and trade through the master–apprentice system. Of European origin, this system was adapted by colonists to fit a world of critical artisan and labor shortages. They blurred lines among apprentices, journeymen, and masters, and generally accelerated apprenticeships. In its most pristine and time-honored European form, the system created bonds between masters—those known for proficiency in a craft or with a process—and apprentices. Apprentices were generally pre- or early teen boys whose parents commended them to a master's service for up to seven years. Apprentices assisted masters. In addition to instructing their charges in their art, masters often clothed, shod, housed, and fed apprentices, guarded their morals, and taught them reading and writing. When apprenticeship ended, masters provided the boys with letters testifying to their adeptness in the rudiments of the art.

Rarely did these graduates move directly into the ranks of masters. That station required purchasing tools and securing a shop in which to work and live. These young men gained the necessary funding and honed their new skills as journeymen in a master's shop. Journeymen earned wages for their labors and after a period of years, could claim for themselves the mantle of master.

In Europe, guilds or local governments limited the journeymen and apprentices a master could accept at one time. These restrictions did not include kin. Masters generally welcomed sons and sons-in-law, brothers and brothers-in-law, nephews and grandchildren to learn an art. Relatives incurred a less rigid set of obligations than did formal apprentices and often were able to decrease the duration of, or even to skip, the journeyman stage. Masters sometimes lent relatives money to start their own operations.

The informality of the master–apprentice relationship in the colonies transcended even that accorded kin in Europe. Demand for artisans, especially in rural and pioneering settlements, so far outstripped supply that individuals possessing only rudimentary training and skills sometimes were looked on by desperate settlers as valuable commodities. Lack of consistent, formal stewardship produced great variation in practice among a trade's colonial artisans, which occasionally fostered beneficial experimentation and modification but more often resulted in inferior techniques.

Providing Necessities

Colonial Agriculture For much of the colonial period, joint-stock companies and proprietors armed with royal charters unsuccessfully attempted to transplant the European manorial system to the New World. Colonial America's abundant, available land undermined these efforts: with manifest alternatives, few colonists chose to live as peasants. Unlike most European rural peoples, the overwhelming majority of colonists lived on their own or rented land, grew their own food, and made their own cloth.

But it would be a mistake to conclude either that each colonial farmstead was an island unto itself or that the structure of agriculture and the tenor of agricultural life was similar in the North and South. Plantations dominated the southern scene by 1700, while small farms, usually from ten to two hundred acres, marked the Middle Atlantic and New England colonies. In the North, settlements and towns formed the basis of community; plantations served a similar function in the South. Towns and settlements provided farmers access to markets, goods, amenities, and services, while each plantation supplied its residents, as well as small farms nearby, the same advantages as towns. A full complement of artisans, many of them black slaves, lived on plantations. Most plantations were on waterways, and owners purchased or built ships to transport goods to other colonies and Europe. Dozens of people lived on each plantation, but only a handful—usually a family and perhaps a few hired hands, indentured servants, or slaves—resided on a typical northern farm. Although each plantation generally grew agricultural staples to feed its workforce, the plantation economy relied on slave labor or indentured servants and on volume production, exporting tobacco, rice, and indigo. Northern farms primarily produced grains, beef, pork, flax, and poultry; they were much less dependent on the export trade.

Northern and southern agriculture differed from each other and from England, but agricultural practices and implements of all three areas were fundamentally similar. Blacksmiths, the most common colonial metalworkers, used charcoal-fired hearths, bellows, tongs, anvils, and hammers to fashion agricultural tools. Earliest settlers did not have plows to break the soil and instead used mattocks—pickax-like devices—hoes, and spades. Plows appeared regularly from the 1640s, but many northern farmers could not afford one. Their lands often were tilled by other farmers who had purchased a plow made in the colonies—some farmers even worked as blacksmiths—or obtained from England. Towns sometimes paid bounties to plow owners to subsidize preparation of local fields. Plows manufactured in Europe proved well-crafted, but domestic plows were rather crude. Shares were almost always iron, and moldboards usually wood. To slow moldboard deterioration, farmers frequently had blacksmiths cover the wood with thin iron strips. These awkward implements required the force of several yoked oxen to pull them. Only in the mid-eighteenth century did colonists adopt a plow that cut turf more facilely. The shovel plow, its share shaped like a shovel with the convex side turned outward, cut a shallow furrow and could be pulled by a horse or mule. Southern plantations used it extensively.

Plowing was not colonial agriculture's only labor-intensive facet. Animals pulled brush harrows—small tree limbs sometimes weighed down by chains—to break cloddy soil and smooth fields. Farmers broadcast grains and covered newly sown seed with another brush harrow pass. Dibble sticks and hoes planted peas and corn: Farmers used the sticks to poke holes in the soil, dropped in several seeds, and hoed dirt over them. Corn and pea seedlings were later hand-thinned, and hoes were used for weeding. Settlers harvested crops with iron-bladed and wooden-handled sickles. Stalks were raked together with hand rakes, bound into bundles on the ground, and carried to barns for threshing.

Threshing was the only agricultural activity that was not weather-dependent. Colonists threshed indoors with a flail, two wooden sticks joined together by a piece of leather. Farmers placed stalks on floors and beat them with flails to free grain from heads. They then collected grain and chaff for winnowing. This threshing method proved much too slow for large grain-producing farms such as those of the mid-Atlantic colonies. There colonists used horses to separate the grain by spreading stalks in a circle and repeatedly walking their animals on them. Straw was then brushed away, leaving only chaff and grain, which was winnowed either by sieve or wind. For wind-winnowing, farmers placed chaff and grain in a basket and tossed them in the air outdoors or in well-ventilated barns. The heavier grain would fall straight down, while the lighter chaff would blow away.

Threshing yielded seeds for next year's crops and grain for bread. It also provided the raw material for beer, which reigned as the universal beverage for most of the seventeenth century. Colonists had numerous recipes for the brew; flavoring it with spruce, ginger, or molasses was most popular. Even the Puritan fathers approved of the drink. In fact, they converted the Great House, the official residence of Governor John Winthrop, into a tavern in the 1640s. Increase Mather best summed up the Puritan view. He argued that "drink was in itself a good creature of God," but that "the abuse of drink" came "from Satan"; alcohol was acceptable, but drunkenness was not.

Colonial beer making adapted traditional European practice and required no special skill or apparatus. Home brewers needed three barrels and a pot, and large-scale production was only slightly more complicated. Commercial manufacturers, who served seventeenth-century taverns and settlements, took barley, soaked it in water until it sprouted—germination converted some of the starch into sugar—and dried it in the sun or a kiln to produce malt. The malt was then ground or crushed in a mash tub, and heated or boiled in a copper cooker. The brewers next strained the mash and transferred the liquid—called wort—first to a cooler and finally to a fermenting tub. Yeast was added, and the batch sat. Weeks or months later, brewers strained off the yeast and transferred the beer to wooden kegs. Yeast from an especially flavorful batch was saved and used again.

Colonial Textiles Colonists transformed plant and animal products into cloth and leather. Until the late eighteenth century, North American and rural European men and women participated in the virtually identical, time-consuming process of making clothing; men commonly sheared sheep, skinned animals, and gathered fibrous material from flax, while women characteristically cleaned wool and flax fibers, and spun yarn and thread. Both sexes operated the family-owned hand loom, but the colonies occasionally employed itinerant weavers. Fulling was the only cloth-making operation ever done outside the home; fulling mills sometimes finished woolen fabric. Unlike cloth, however, leather goods were made entirely by artisans.

New Englanders favored woolen articles, and Southerners opted for cool linens (cotton did not become important until the late eighteenth century), but neither employed either fabric exclusively. Use of two materials required colonials to master different processes. Woolen yarn making began with washing wool in tubs with soap to free dirt and grease, drying it in the shade, and beating it to rid fibers of extraneous foreign material. Colonial women then carded wool by hand, using leather paddles studded with fine wire. After disentangling, sorting, and straightening wool, they spun fibers into yarn either on a distaff and spindle or on a spinning wheel. Wheels were usually hand-powered, and consisted of a cord that passed around the spindle and over the large wooden wheel.

The spinner's left hand undertook the more difficult tasks, freeing the right for turning and regulating wheel speed. Carded wool was held in the left hand and attached to the spindle. It was then drafted and elongated. The wheel was put in motion while the yarn was twisted to bind the fibers, and wound on the spindle.

Preparation of linen thread or yarn from flax took longer and demanded strength. A woody stalk surrounded the fibrous flax that would become linen. Men retted flax; that is, they prepared to remove the fiber from the stalk by either soaking it in water for two weeks or laying it on the ground for as much as a month to putrefy. The softened flax stalk was then dried and forcibly cracked in a wooden beam press called a flaxbrake. They then used a wooden knife to separate the stalk from flax fibers. A pair of thick-wired wooden paddles removed the leftover woody material. After washing and bleaching, they spun the fibers.

Spinning linen bore little resemblance to spinning wool. To make linen thread or yarn, women wrapped the raw material on a distaff and separated its fiber filaments by hand. They then fed the fibers to a foot-operated flax wheel. Each colonial family spun its own thread and yarn, and then wove it into cloth on wooden hand looms. Like spinning wheels, these looms remained similar to those built earlier in Europe. Weaving involved crossing and interlacing two distinct series of threads at right angles to one another. Warp threads fixed on the loom provided the frame for the cloth piece. The weft was wound in single threads on small spools set one after another in a movable shuttle, which was perpendicular to warp threads. The shuttle was passed alternately over and under warp threads from one side of the piece to the other, then returned in the same fashion, but on reverse sides of warp threads. This time-consuming process continued until the entire length of warp threads had become a woven piece of cloth.

Local carpenters built looms and colonists situated these large devices in barns or sheds. Loom frames consisted of four upright posts joined to form a rectangle by cross beams at the top, middle, and bottom. Looms also had cross pieces at the top to suspend heddles, movable parallel cords equipped with eyes and used to separate and guide warp threads. Pulleys and cords connected heddles to pedals called treadles. Warp threads were attached to the back center beam—the warp beam—and passed through the appropriate heddle eyes and connected to the front center beam—the cloth beam. Depressing a treadle moved the corresponding heddles and opened space in the warp threads to pass the shuttle. The loom's final major piece, the batten or beater, pressed weft threads into place after the shuttle's passage. A movable frame attached at the loom's top just in front of the heddles, the hand-operated batten was pulled forward sharply after each pass of the weft thread; its combed teeth drove the thread to its place on the cloth.

Woven linen cloth was ready to be made into garments, but fine woolens required fulling (shrinking and thickening) to provide body. Woolens, when they left looms, were uneven and unsightly in appearance, but hand fulling proved so onerous and time-consuming that early colonists fulled only woolens worn on special occasions such as Sabbath worship or holidays. Fulling removed grease (a spinning and weaving by-product), shrunk cloth, and consolidated fibers. Fabric was fulled by soaking in warm, soapy water and either beating while wet with sticks on a firm surface, or kicking the damp cloths around with bare feet for several hours. Household fulling improved the fabric's character somewhat, but fulling mills did a superior job.

Known since the Middle Ages, fulling mills were found in New England from the 1640s. Mills appeared in the mid-Atlantic and southern colonies only after 1700. Soon after their introduction they became almost as widespread as grist- and sawmills. But unlike saw- and gristmills, fulling mills were not essential to either colonial survival or easing regular daily burdens. Their rapid proliferation indicated that New England rural society in the mid-seventeenth century and mid-Atlantic and southern rural communities some sixty years later desired and could sustain enterprises not directly linked to their immediate survival.

Rural communities as well as cities and towns produced wealth enough to support fullers to operate fulling mills. These artisans placed soapy, wet bolts of cloth, tied end to end to make the process continuous, in a beating trough, where it squeezed through water-wheel-powered rollers. Later mills added trip-hammers to pound and intermesh fibers more completely. Fullers then stretched the wet cloth on frames and attached it with tenterhooks, sharp hooked nails, to maintain its shape. When it dried, they teased it, using either wire-studded paddles or the seed pods of a plant known as fuller's teasel. Teasing raised the nap, but not evenly; fullers then evened it by laying the fabric on a wooden cylinder and shearing the cloth with long-bladed shears.

Colonial Leather Making Leather's durability and flexibility were prized for harnesses, aprons, breeches, saddles, and especially shoes and boots, and its manufacture was well established in mid-seventeenth-century New World settlements. Unlike textile industries, however, leather making caused terrible smells. Colonists situated tanneries on settlement fringes far from dense population concentrations.

Skin and hide preparation took time. Tanners cut off horns, tails, and ears, and soaked the remaining parts for a day in running water. They then immersed them in vats of lime for several months to swell the skins and loosen hair. The leather was then ready for beaming. Tanners placed hides hair-side-up on an elevated log (or beam), and scraped off hair with curved two-handled knives. They then flipped the skins over to scrape away remaining flesh and fat. Hides were washed again, then stone rubbed and smoothed. One final washing made them ready for tanning.

Tanning itself was at least as time-consuming as skin preparation. Even before the skins were ready, tanners had gathered and prepared their tannin—hemlock bark in the North and oak bark in the South— as a coarse powder in animal-powered bark mills. Tanning's initial phase required dumping hides and skins into a weak solution of bark and water. Tanners gradually strengthened the infusion over several months, and regularly redistributed skins to ensure uniform tanning. Calfskin or buckskin took from four to six months to tan, but cowhides required a second treatment. They were first dried and then placed into another vat with one-inch layers of ground bark alternated with layers of hide. Tanners flooded the vat with water and repeatedly agitated the hides, which remained for as much as a year. They then washed the leather and hung it to dry. Pounding the leather with heavy clubs to compact it completed tanning.

Shoe and boot manufacture, predominantly a local enterprise, consumed much leather. Customers often took such an active interest in their footwear that they purchased leather for shoes and boots directly from tanyards and supplied it to shoemakers. Artisans reciprocated by measuring a foot in several places and whittling a last, or model, to reflect the foot's unique contours. The last provided the sole-making guide. Thick leather was cut to conform to the last, beaten to increase flexibility, and smoothed. Shoemakers also modeled the uppers, but did not build it to individual specifications. They kept several wooden patterns on hand and chose by visual inspection the appropriate form. They then fashioned the uppers in two pieces: the vamp, which covered the toe and instep and ended in a wide tongue; and the counter, which covered the heels and sides and ended in straps for either lacing or buckling.

Shoemakers next stretched the uppers over the last, allowing some material to hang over its edge, and inserted temporary tacks. Unlike modern shoes on which uppers are tucked under and sewn to soles, colonial uppers were turned out. To hold the leather in the proper position for stitching, craftsmen glued the uppers to the sole. They then cut a narrow channel in the sole to keep stitches from rubbing on the ground, and punched regularly spaced holes through the leather to facilitate sewing. Using waxen hemp or linen thread, and hog bristles

Each colonial shoemaker made a complete shoe.

needles, shoemakers joined the two parts together. They then added the heel by nailing to the sole several heel-shaped thicknesses of leather. Finally, they removed the tacks and last, pasted in linen linings, and swabbed on tallow or lampblack and wax to protect their creation.

Large-Scale Enterprise

Most seventeenth-century technical activities were small enough that they could be established even in sparsely inhabited rural settlements. Iron manufacturing and shipbuilding deviated from that pattern. The largest colonial enterprises, both manufacturing iron and building ships, were pursued in limited areas, involved a range of craftsmen, and served distant communities. Both took advantage of raw materials abundant in the New World but scarce in England. Using technologies to transform colonial ores and trees into iron and ships, these enterprises enabled England and its colonies to retain wealth that otherwise would have gone to other countries to purchase these crucial commodities; they were manifestations of an active mercantile philosophy.

Colonial Iron Manufacture Iron manufacture was perhaps the most demanding colonial enterprise. It required several types of skilled labor, copious amounts of wood, readily available supplies of flux, and plentiful sources of ore. Colonists, therefore, erected ironworks in the wilderness near resources as they found it far easier to transport finished iron bar than bulky raw materials. Unfriendly Indians and fires, however, often plagued these wilderness enclaves.

Workers required support while in residence at ironworks—a considerable expense. Colonists did not rely on supplies from surrounding settlements but organized wilderness production facilities to be self-sufficient. In that sense ironworks resembled the agricultural plantations of the southern colonists, and the patroon manors of New Netherlands. Sizable land grants usually accompanied permission to engage in iron production, which offered both the raw materials necessary to produce large quantities of iron and the means to maintain the work force. On these lands artisans, laborers, indentured servants, and slaves built houses, offices, dams, mills, stores, ovens, roads, and watercourses. They also cleared areas for orchards, grain fields, and grazing animals. They remained at the site to continue their support for large-scale production.

Iron production was among the oldest colonial technologies. Its long history stemmed from its extensive New World application and European encouragement. Britain's perennial wood shortage and the Crown's dependence on high-priced Swedish iron placed a premium on establishing colonial manufacture. As early as 1619, the Virginia Company of London sent 150 men to North America to erect three ironworks. John Winthrop, Jr., son of the Massachusetts Bay Colony governor, toured England in the 1640s and attracted new ironworks investors, which yielded no fewer than eight separate works in New England prior to 1680.

Gathering and preparing three essential ingredients constituted the first step in iron manufacturing. Workers mined ore from bogs, outcroppings, and shallow deposits; felled trees and converted wood into charcoal; and collected flux, usually limestone. Most often ores required roasting or washing to remove impurities.

Charcoal production was a highly skilled activity. Colliers, artisans skilled at making charcoal, exercised great care to burn wood slowly, evenly, and only partially. Too rapid or complete combustion ruined the wood and raised the specter of fire. Colliers controlled the combustion rate and extent by limiting the oxygen supply. They buried wood in earth-covered pits or poured dirt mounds over cone-shaped wooden stacks. In both furnace configurations, colliers eliminated air pockets by piling wood precisely—often as much as thirty cords—and filling natural gaps with smaller pieces. A chimney rested at the center of these charring furnaces. It was filled with wood chips, ignited, and then covered, the fire radiating from the chimney to the stacks underground. Colliers sometimes cut draft holes into the pile to ensure uniform charring.

The entire charcoal-making process took more than a week. Colliers stood ready at all times. They used probing rods to detect uneven burning and warily protected against open flames, gas explosions, and strong winds. The last several days were spent cooling the charcoal.

*Colliers cover a mound of wood to prepare charcoal
for smelting iron.*

They removed the outer covering of the stack slowly, a portion at a time, and kept the cooling material in small quantities away from the great mass. Only when they were sure it was cold did they carry the finished charcoal to the coal house.

The three raw materials went to a bloomery or to a blast furnace. The bloomery was a modest contraption, used primarily to furnish small quantities of iron. It consisted only of a fireplace, bellows (usually pumped by an apprentice), tongs, and a hammer. The ore, charcoal, and flux were heated in the fireplace with the aid of bellows. A spongy mass of iron—a bloom—resulted. It was lifted by tongs, reheated, consolidated by hammer, heated again, and pounded again to drive off more impurities. This wroughting process continued until refining was complete.

The blast furnace was far grander, standing roughly twenty-five feet tall—like a pyramid with its capstone removed—and devouring enormous quantities of raw materials. Thick stones mortared together formed its outer walls, which were lined with bricks or clay. Internally, the furnace had a narrow throat to accept the ore, charcoal, and flux. This passage gradually widened to a chamber with a diameter of ten feet. About three yards above the ground it tapered quickly to a diameter of roughly two feet; this sloping area functioned as a platform to support the three ingredients. This circular platform drained into the crucible, the reservoir for molten iron and liquid slag, or waste.

Attached through a porthole were huge twenty-foot-long leather bellows, inflated by means of cams on giant overshot waterwheels. Stone counterweights enabled bellows to discharge powerful blasts that generated the extreme temperatures necessary for iron-smelting.

Most activity revolved around the crucible. Usually once or twice daily, workers drew the slag off the top, opened a clay plug to tap the molten iron, and let it run into a series of sand molds to make bars. They also used iron for casting pots, kettles, and the like, ladling the liquid metal into clay molds. The draining of molten iron, however, did not signal the end of blast furnace operations; the cycle continued uninterrupted for as long as forty weeks. Ironworkers then repaired the furnace's inner lining and leather bellows and gathered materials for next season's smelting.

Only a fraction of iron went directly to produce finished goods. It lacked the tensile strength required for high-stress applications and needed further refining. Its conversion into wrought iron occurred in two stages at a forge. In the finery, where the first part of the process took place, workmen heated iron to melting in a bellows-assisted charcoal fire, stirred it several times to burn off excess carbon, and then allowed it to solidify. They next placed the red-hot metal on a stout iron anvil and beat it repeatedly with a massive waterwheel-driven triphammer. The force of the hammer's blows squeezed out many remaining impurities. The resulting iron mass resembled a flattened dumbbell. It now went to the chafery, a cooler, non-bellows-aided fire, for the final purification step. Attention there focused on the bar's ends. Both were heated and hammered. When the consolidated iron cooled, it was left in the form of wrought-iron bars.

These bars reigned as the principal form of commercial iron. In blacksmiths' shops they became axes, horseshoes, plows, wires, tools, and blades. Wheelwrights used the material to fashion chains, fittings, and iron tires necessary to outfit long-lasting wagons. For a few important products, the bars underwent further processing in special facilities. Most common were waterwheel-powered rolling and slitting mills. In rolling mills, heated iron bars were pressed several times through a pair of heavy rollers rotating in opposite directions. The resulting metal sheets were used as plate iron or sent to slitting mills, where sharp-edged discs cut the iron into uniform strips suitable for nails.

Colonial Shipbuilding Iron also played a significant role in colonial shipbuilding. Shipsmiths used iron for each ship's several anchors, for iron braces to hold the rudder to the ship, and for iron bolts to attach the keel to the rest of the ship's frame and the rigging to the hull. But wood was the most important shipbuilding material. Colonists felled oaks by broadax, then dressed them into timbers with an adz or sawed them into planks at sawmills. They selected locustwood to supply wooden dowels (treenails) for fastening together timbers and planks. Two other shipbuilding staples, sailcloth and cordage, were usually imported from England.

Abundant wood and iron in Massachusetts contributed to that colony's rapid ascent as the New World's shipbuilding center. So, too, did its concentration of people intimately acquainted with commerce—Pilgrims and Puritans—and the colony's short growing season and rocky soil, which made agriculture difficult. By the late 1630s, the towns of Boston and Salem were doing a big shipbuilding business. Their craftsmen constructed ships for English and colonial merchants primarily to carry timber and salted fish, but by the late seventeenth century they were transporting New England-produced turpentine and rum. Turpentine went to England, while rum fueled the odious "triangular trade." New England merchants traded rum in Africa for slaves, sold the slaves in the West Indies and southern colonies, and carried back molasses from which to make more rum. They also used Massachusetts-built ships to trade corn, wheat, cattle, fish, and horses for molasses in the West Indies, and rum to fishermen in the icy North Atlantic.

The shipbuilding trade relied on bulky raw materials, but it was a predominantly urban industry. Colonists found it simpler to transport iron and wood from forests than completed ships. To ensure ease of launch and low overhead, shipyards generally were located in the lowlands and coves near rivers, on inexpensive land away from dense settlement. There worked a diverse force. A shipwright and a few day laborers manned some yards, while others employed shipwrights, shipsmiths, sawyers, carpenters, joiners, and caulkers. In a highly structured shipyard, shipwrights supervised construction; shipsmiths did iron work; sawyers worked sawmills; carpenters secured planking; joiners smoothed planks, built deck rails, and finished cabins; and caulkers filled in seams with oakum, tar-covered unraveled hemp.

The ship's eventual owner initiated the shipbuilding process by providing rough specifications for the ship to the shipwright. The wright drew up detailed plans—perhaps even made a scale model—submitted them for the owner's approval, and superintended construction. Workers laid the keel first, then fastened stem and stern posts (the front and rear posts, respectively) to its ends. They then built the ribs, each composed of several smaller timbers—the floor anchor, floor, three or more futtocks, and two top timbers, one long and one short. Only by dividing ribs into sections could shipbuilders find lumber of the desired curvature. Each rib was two timbers wide, with overlapping pieces pinned together to provide the strength necessary to bear the anticipated load. After they completed the framing, ship carpenters placed the keelson on top of the floor anchors, and bolted it to them and the keel, which stiffened and fortified the frame. They

A large shipyard located on the fringe of New York City, ca. 1717

then planked the ship's interior and exterior, pausing at deck level to construct the deck. The deck beams were supported on both sides by wooden braces (knees) fastened to each rib, and in the middle by wooden columns (stanchions) attached to the keelson. The planking resumed when the deck stood in place.

All that remained was to finish the craft. Joiners dressed the rough surfaces with planes. Caulkers used wheels, irons, and mallets to pack every crevice with oakum. Sheathing the part of the ship that would rest underwater was the final operation. Shipwrights coated those planks with a mixture of tar and hair, and sometimes covered them with fir boards.

BEYOND SUBSISTENCE: THE EIGHTEENTH CENTURY

The colonial economy moved from subsistence to surplus in the eighteenth century. Several generations of immigrants had successfully applied and modified European technologies and practices to suit New World conditions and needs. As the English had hoped when they founded the colonies, colonists had converted the continent's plentiful material resources into several commodities in short supply in the Old World and had begun to export these products. After about 1700, coastal towns such as New York, Philadelphia, Boston, Providence, and Charlestown emerged as prominent commercial centers and collected raw materials and finished goods from rural settlements for shipment to Europe and elsewhere. Flourishing trade heightened demand for ships, and North American forests furnished supplies of lumber.

Shipbuilding spread to every colony; Pennsylvania, New Jersey, Rhode Island, and Delaware contested the claim of Massachusetts to colonial shipbuilding supremacy. Expansion of iron production exceeded that of shipbuilding. Each colony made some iron, but the New England colonies, Virginia, Maryland, and Pennsylvania were the heaviest producers. By 1760, colonial installations produced one-seventh of the world's annual iron output.

Colonial agricultural productivity was sufficiently great that colonists could also export some products. New York and Philadelphia became foci of the beer export trade. New York post mills (primitive windmills) and Philadelphia, Baltimore, Wilmington, and Richmond water mills powered flour mills as colonists tapped overseas markets, which demanded a more highly refined product. Colonists developed methods to clean grain, bolt (sift by sieve) meal to rid it of impurities, and cool and pack the flour to ship to the West Indies and Europe. Shoemaking also developed a made-for-export component as New England shoemakers, with as many as forty artisans working in a single place, made entire shoes and boots in standard sizes and shipped them to southern plantations and the West Indies.

Signs of New Wealth

In accordance with mercantile theory, colonial coastal merchants handled these exports and accumulated the largest portion of the wealth. A move to more expensive brick structures—houses, churches, warehouses, and counting houses—in East Coast municipalities indicated the colonies' economic success. Whitesmiths, silversmiths, coppersmiths, and pewterers rose to serve the expanding merchant class. Whitesmiths specialized in finishing imported goods by filing, polishing, and assembling iron parts—labors essential to commercial enterprise.

Only a few silversmiths worked in New York or Boston in the late seventeenth century, but they could be found in all major colonial cities in the eighteenth century. No colonial artisan rivaled the silversmith's prestige. He handled the most expensive materials and possessed direct merchant connections. His product—primarily silver plate—testified to his customers' prominence. Silver plate stood as the surest way to store wealth at a time before neighborhood banks. Unlike the silver English and Spanish coins from which it was made, silver plate was readily identifiable. Often formed to individual specifications, it always carried the silversmith's distinctive markings and consequently could be traced and retrieved. Customers generally secured the silver for their silver plate. They saved coins, took them to smiths, and discussed the type of plates desired. Silversmiths complied with these requests by melting the money in a small furnace, adding a bit of copper to form a stronger alloy, and casting the alloy as an ingot. They hammered ingots to the appropriate thickness on heavy anvils, shaped them, and used screw presses or dies to adorn them. Engraving was done by hand. Some customers sought more intricate products, such as silver teapots. Silversmiths made these devices by shaping or casting parts separately and then soldering them together.

Colonial coppersmithing also prospered in northern cities in the early eighteenth century. The metal's ability to conduct heat efficiently and to resist corrosion contributed to its attractiveness. Yet copper in colonial America was dear, and smiths were never numerous. Virtually all copper worked by coppersmiths was imported as sheets or obtained by recycling old copper goods. Copper was used, not admired. Coppersmiths fashioned pots and kettles for the home, and brewery and distillery apparati for the alcohol trade. They shaped it like silver or melted it in a foundry with lead or tin. They also mixed it with zinc to make brass for maritime and scientific instruments.

Pewterers were even scarcer than coppersmiths. Prior to 1750, there were probably fewer than twenty in the colonies. Like coppersmiths, pewterers congregated in northern cities. There they mixed and heated tin with copper, antimony, or lead, and cast the soft material as plates, candlesticks, and coffee pots. They also melted old pewter and recast it.

Emergence of popular entertainment also indicated that the question of subsistence no longer consumed colonial society. East Coast merchants sponsored subscription libraries, organizations to investigate natural history or philosophy, theaters, and especially inns, taverns, and coffeehouses. Beer remained the home beverage, but eighteenth-century colonists increasingly left the home to drink applejack, peach brandy, rum, coffee, and tea. More than ever before, tippling had become a year-round public social event. These drinking houses provided informal settings in which to discuss commercial ventures. But ardent spirits played an even greater role in colonial elections. Outcomes were often influenced by a candidate's free distribution of drink. For example, when George Washington stood for election in 1758 to the Virginia House of Burgesses, he spent thirty-seven pounds sterling, seven shillings on his campaign, "of which over 34 pounds was for brandy, rum, cider, strong beer and wine."

TECHNOLOGY AND THE REVOLUTION, 1763–1783

Printing as a Catalyst for the Revolution

The export-generated interest in extralocal affairs produced local markets for information about other settlements and areas. The mid-eighteenth-century rise of colonial presses and newspapers fed that demand. By 1763 colonial master printers operated some forty presses, published at least a dozen newspapers, and issued thousands of pamphlets. Mid-century colonial printing had become self-sufficient and Benjamin Franklin stood as a crucial figure in this event. He had financed several journeymen printers in establishing their own print shops and, more important, reigned from the mid-1730s as the largest supplier of white linen rags, colonial paper's essential ingredient. Franklin's rags went to stamping or Hollander mills and were converted into thin fibrous pulp. Papermakers dipped rectangular-framed, fine wire meshes into vats of pulp. The captured fibers became paper sheets, which were placed between felts, squeezed of excess water in screw presses—pressing also forced fibers to adhere together—hung to dry, and smoothed with stones. Indeed, Franklin's rag-collecting endeavors led to establishment of no fewer than eighteen papermills.

Franklin proved equally adept at ensuring colonial printers had ink. Printers' ink was oil-based, made from linseed oil boiled with rosin until it became viscous. Its color came from lampblack, the fine soot resulting from the incomplete combustion of carbonaceous substances. Although Franklin made some oil and mixed some ink, he specialized in lampblack. He purchased his first lampblack house in 1733. By 1756 he had several others and assumed in the ink trade a position as fully important as he had in the paper trade.

Franklin's extensive involvement in printing and the colonists' resistance to English threats to restrain their ability to communicate testified to the significance of communication. Three acts of Parliament appeared particularly menacing. The Sugar Act of 1764, which levied taxes on sugar, coffee, molasses, and wine, threatened public drinking establishments. Indeed, James Otis, recognized as the "great incendiary of New England," maintained that the Sugar Act "set the people a'thinking in six months more than they had done in their whole lives before." The Stamp Act of 1765 taxed colonial newspapers, pamphlets, almanacs, and playing cards. The Townshend Acts of 1767 endangered the colonial papermaking industry and tea houses. Colonists railed against these acts and, at Otis's behest, sent representatives to Massachusetts to formulate a united response to the Stamp Act.

The vehemence with which colonists greeted these acts opened a new chapter in the imperial relationship. To be sure, England had long imposed commercial regulations on the colonies to restrict competition between elements of the English-colonial commonwealth. Taxes, prohibitions on manufactures, and the rerouting of commodities served to retain the commercial viability, prosperity, and supremacy of England and *its* merchants and manufacturers. For example, the Crown had stipulated that colonial sugar, tobacco, rice, copper, furs, naval stores, and cotton could not be sold in Europe unless they first passed through England. It also maintained that except for salt, slaves, and wine, colonists could import no foreign products not transferred and taxed in England. Similarly, England had prohibited exports of colonial wool, woolen cloth, and hats—commodities that England itself produced in abundance—and outlawed colonial iron-finishing establishments, such as slitting mills, plating forges, and steel furnaces, to end intercommonwealth finished iron competition. To ensure that the colonies followed regulations and did not squander wealth, it had also banned all colonial joint-stock companies unless expressly approved by Parliament.

These and other edicts had hurt colonial industries. Occasionally those particularly aggrieved petitioned colonial governors or assemblies, or proprietors, Parliament, and the king for redress. Those complaints had been relatively few, their tenor mild. No doubt the colonists' ability to circumvent these regulations—smuggling was prevalent—had contributed to their docility. So, too, had the comparably small quantity of colonial exports. But the matter went deeper. At its heart lay mercantilist social theory in which colonists accepted inequalities as the "normal" state of affairs, their persistence tolerable so long as the whole seemed likely to persevere. Only when the whole— usually referred to as the "public good, order or safety"—appeared threatened did drastic action seem appropriate.

The Parliamentary Acts of the 1760s seemed to colonists to create that situation. They argued that England's attempts to regulate communication and various industries, coupled with introduction of massive new taxes, was an effort to transform the colonies from full, if unequal, partners into serfs. The Crown recognized the problem differently. It asserted that colonists had not paid their fair share of the British Empire's costs and that the time had come to correct that imbalance; the colonists flourished while the English were burdened with increasing sums for their colonies' defense (for example, during the French and Indian War).

These varying perceptions of the commonwealth's well-being produced an impasse in which each subsequent dispute exacerbated tensions. England cracked down on colonial communication—it temporarily dissolved the New York and Virginia Assemblies and the Massachusetts General Court—regulated aspects of colonial commerce and manufacturing, and levied and collected heavy taxes. Colonists persistently objected to Crown policies and refused to purchase English goods. The English boycott fortified many colonial industries and spawned new ones. The New World's first type foundries were an attempt to ensure communications would flow during nonimportation agreements.

The economic relationship between England and the colonies could not long withstand a situation in which its constituents perceived only disadvantages. Economic skirmishing gave way to a full-blown conflagration, and the colonies declared their independence from Britain on July 4, 1776. Ironically, each newly emancipated republic initially pursued its own course against their common foe. To be sure, the Continental Congress and army existed, but the states contributed to them secondarily, almost as an afterthought. Each state sought to ensure its own defense and to encourage within its borders production of a full range of war supplies. Most offered inducements—bounties, land, freedom from taxation—for the manufacture of gunpowder, cannons, and guns; and all exempted from military service gunsmiths, cannonmakers, shot- and shell-casters, papermakers, and gunpowder manufacturers. Only with the Articles of Confederation's passage and ratification did the states concede that in the war their interests were virtually indistinguishable, and only then did they begin actively to provide for the common defense. Congress's creation of armories and manufactories for ordnance at Carlisle, Pennsylvania; Springfield, Massachusetts; West Point, New York; and New London, Virginia, stood as testament.

Manufacture of Arms

Of the necessary war ordnance, colonists were most familiar with firearms manufacture. Gunsmiths quickly geared up for the conflict. Two types of firearms predominated: the smooth-bore flintlock and the Pennsylvania long rifle. They had similar firing mechanisms and operated in the same fashion. Pulling the trigger caused the hammer's flint to strike a serrated metal plate, which sparked and touched off powder in the priming pan. This ignited the main charge. The dense smoke generated by rapid combustion of gunpowder increased dramatically the pressure behind the ball, which together with a sealing patch had been jammed down the barrel's bore with a heavy iron ramrod—sometimes assisted by a small mallet—and the ball shot from the barrel.

As suited its name, the Pennsylvania rifle's barrel was longer than the smooth bore—five feet rather than three and one-half or four—and its bore was rifled with spiral grooves. The increased barrel length and rifling produced greater range and accuracy. Despite design and performance differences, however, barrels of the two guns were made in much the same way. Smiths heated long wrought-iron bars to white heat a section at a time, and hammered them around mandrels. After completing this forging and welding process, artisans made apertures uniform with a hand-operated boring device. Another boring machine added the Pennsylvania rifle's characteristic grooves.

A typical large firearm manufactory might include three barrel forges, a similar number of lock forges, a casting shop for brass fittings, forges for bayonets and the like, watermills for grinding and

Using a handful of mobile artillery pieces, the rebels surprise the British at the Battle of Princeton on January 3, 1777.

polishing gun parts, and an assortment of files for finishing the locks' various parts. It would employ more than one hundred men and produce several thousand weapons a year.

Colonists also had extensive experience producing gunpowder, but only two of its ingredients, charcoal and sulfur, were plentiful in America. The third, saltpeter, was generally purchased from France, although Americans made approximately one-eighth. Heaps of animal and vegetable refuse, mixed with limestone and wood-ashes and moistened periodically with urine, were left to decompose. The noxious matter was then leeched with water, which was collected and evaporated. The crystalline residue, saltpeter, went to gunpowder mills where a hundred parts by weight were usually mixed with fifteen parts of sulfur and eighteen of charcoal. Water helped form a paste-like concoction. A water-powered stamp mill replicated the action of mortar and pestle, grinding coarse materials as finely as possible to ensure even combustion. The powder was then air-dried, run through a fine sieve, and loaded into rotating wooden kegs, a final guarantee against incomplete mixing.

In contrast, Americans were relatively unacquainted with cannons. These important devices served the military as artillery for sieges and field battles, as weapons for harbor and coastline defense, and as the primary means for conducting naval engagements. Nor was there an established American cannon-making industry. Most cannons were cast from brass, an amalgam of copper and zinc, and copper was dear in the New World. Unable to produce brass cannons, and compelled by the war to develop an alternative, the states encouraged iron manufactories to cast cannons. These iron armaments were used only defensively because they were difficult to move; they required thicker walls than their brass counterparts and weighed roughly three times as much. But Americans did not have to do without brass cannons completely. They seized British armaments and (especially after 1777) purchased French cannons. These two sources provided Americans a sufficient supply of mobile artillery.

THIRTEEN COMMERCIAL NATIONS, 1776–1789

Ironically, the Articles of Confederation extended only to pursuing the war. In other spheres states cooperated little. Each colony had declared its independence, framed a governing document, and become its own commonwealth. All new state constitutions embraced mercantile theory; new states granted their governments extensive powers to regulate commerce and manufacturing within state borders.

Interstate Commerce

In true mercantilist fashion, each state discouraged importation and encouraged exportation. The nascent states applied the policy to each other as well as Europe; in commerce and manufacturing they stood as separate, competing entities. State governments exempted lands from taxation; lent entrepreneurs money; purchased interests in ventures; passed laws prohibiting the export of manufacturing tools; granted land, monopolies, and bounties; and enacted tariffs to defend home manufactures. For example, North Carolina, Connecticut, and New Hampshire exempted rod and nail works from taxes. Pennsylvania lent £300 to erect a steel furnace, while Massachusetts loaned Aaron Burr £200 at no interest to build carding and spinning machines. Pennsylvania fined "ill designing persons" who exported manufacturing tools and machines as well as those guilty of "seducing" manufacturers to leave the state. It also bought one hundred shares (valued at £1,000) in a failing cotton mill. North Carolina granted 5,000 acres of land to anyone establishing a successful ironworks, while New Jersey gave a bounty of six shillings per hundredweight for wool, flax, or hemp raised in the state. The bounty in New York was eight shillings for the same quantity of hemp, while Connecticut excused forty shillings from hemp growers' taxes for each crop acre. Rhode Island put a twenty-five-percent tariff on ready-made garments, canes, and watches produced out of state.

State governments concentrated on decreasing imports, but efforts to step up exportation and to bring additional wealth into a state received only a modicum of governmental assistance. Enterprising traders, especially merchants, were generally left to their own devices, and sometimes revised established practice. Such was the case with the "putting-out system" in late–eighteenth-century Massachusetts footwear and cloth manufacture. Desire to increase the volume of production undercut the traditional role of artisans as financiers and producers. Essential to extralocal trade and the wealthiest Americans, merchants alone had money enough to bankroll ventures of this magnitude. They used their funds to purchase large quantities of leather, wool, and linen, then hired shoemakers, spinners, and weavers for a fee to make shoes, boots, and cloth. These artisans worked in their own homes or home-shops, then returned the products to the merchants, who marketed the goods in other states and overseas. That this new practice engendered little comment testified to the persistence of mercantilistic notions even after independence; the state, not England and its colonies, had become the commonwealth.

Although the states remained economic adversaries, the war had led them to conclude the Articles of Confederation as a mutual defense pact. This agreement looked both east to Europe and west past the Appalachian Mountains; approval had been delayed until states had ceded their often-conflicting claims to western lands north of the Ohio River. The presence of unfriendly Indians, coupled with the vacuum that would be left in the West if the English were driven from North America—a vacuum that some other European nation might seek to fill—made the orderly development, consolidation, and control of the interior a top priority. The confederation also recognized the West's economic significance; its sale would help pay war debts. Since 1776, land speculators had clamored to buy large chunks of the West and to resell them as small parcels to homesteaders at considerable profit.

Linking the East and West

It appeared crucial to link the West to the East. That meant establishing not only an administrative relationship and rational settlement procedure—realized in the Land Ordinance of 1785 and the Northwest Ordinance of 1787—but also commercial ties, which required adequate transportation.

To be sure, Conestoga wagons carried some freight between East and West. Developed by Pennsylvania's Palatine Germans about 1750, the large, high-wheeled wagons had a floor that was curved upward

*Heavy, sturdy Conestoga wagons led the settlement
of the trans-Appalachian West.*

at its ends to prevent cargo from shifting on steep grades. But climbing
the Appalachians with these vehicles was problematical. Other entrepreneurs attempted to create improved forms of transport. George
Washington was the most illustrious.

Soon after his retirement from the army, Washington promoted
Potomac River transportation to join East and West. From a source
near the Ohio River, the Potomac ran through a gap in the Appalachians, past Washington's Mount Vernon estate, and into the Chesapeake
Bay. (The river's attractiveness for linking the West commercially and
politically to the East would later lead Washington to designate its
southernmost point the new nation's capital.) By the mid-1780s Washington considered circumventing the river's waterfall and rapids no
problem; short canals, such as those common in England, could be
dug around them. But Washington remained puzzled about how to
get vessels upstream against the stiff current. James Rumsey, a mill-
wright familiar with the blacksmith's art, offered him in 1784 what
seemed an answer. Rumsey had built a model paddlewheel-powered
pole boat—essentially a floating undershot watermill geared to poles
that pushed on the river bed. He demonstrated his invention to Washington, and with the general's support, received late that winter ten-
year monopolies on the use of his device in Virginia and Maryland,
the two states bordering the Potomac.

Washington was not alone in applauding Rumsey's invention. Thomas Jefferson and John Marshall also endorsed it. But Rumsey did not build a full-scale pole boat as steam power intrigued him. Steam pressure would force water through a narrow cylinder at the stem to propel a boat. Although Rumsey's plan to employ steam to power a craft was unusual, moving of water by steam engine was not. All American steam engines (there were but a handful), as well as the vast majority in Europe, raised water—either to clear mines, to provide cities with drinking water, or to power waterwheels during hot weather when streams dried up. These engines generally operated on principles different from that proposed by Rumsey. Their power stemmed from the atmosphere's weight forcing down a piston in a cylinder in which the swift condensation of steam had created a partial vacuum; Rumsey's device used steam at high pressure as its motive power.

Before Rumsey had made headway, he gained a competitor, John Fitch. Apprenticed as a clockmaker, Fitch had worked in brass and as a silversmith. He was familiar with the Newcomen engine—an atmospheric steam engine in which steam was cooled in the cylinder—and proposed to connect this engine to an endless belt and to attach to the belt a series of paddles; steam power would row the boat upstream. Franklin and the ubiquitous Washington offered Fitch encouragement.

Washington also acted on his own behalf. In early 1785, he helped secure Virginia and Maryland charters establishing the Potomac Company to make the river navigable as far west as possible, and to build a wagon road from that terminus to the Ohio River. Washington was the company's president. No doubt he expected either inventor to produce a craft soon, yet he made provisions if they failed. He intended to fasten iron chains to rocks and trees on the banks so boatmen could pull vessels upstream. Washington hired Rumsey to superintend construction, and purchased slaves as well as indentured Irishmen to do the heavy labor.

Rumsey worked on a steam-powered craft as he superintended construction. He quickly decided that the massive spherical boilers usually associated with steam engines took up too much space for steamboats, were too heavy, and required great amounts of fuel to keep the water heated. A small pipe-shaped boiler, containing only enough water to produce the steam necessary to fill the cylinder, overcame objections. Rumsey found, however, that the highly pressured, superheated steam in these vessels melted solder connections, causing leakage or explosions.

While Rumsey grappled with this problem, James Madison and Patrick Henry offered Fitch support, and he received a New Jersey steamboat monopoly. Fitch attached paddles to cranks and tried to power his boat with a horizontal, double-acting Newcomen engine.

He finally settled on a vertical, single-acting Watt engine—an atmospheric engine with a separate condenser for cooling steam—with modest success. Fitch's heavy mechanical vessel could travel upstream, but only at about three miles per hour, far too slow to justify the device's considerable expense. Construction of a truly functional steamboat lay in the future, but Fitch was justifiably proud of his creation, which he demonstrated during the Constitutional Convention.

FRAMING AND IMPLEMENTING A COMMERCIAL PACT, 1787–1800

Few Convention members witnessed Fitch's demonstration as they hammered out a new relationship among states. Competing trade policies of the thirteen sovereign states had caused problems; the Convention call specifically urged modifications in the Articles of Confederation "to take into consideration the trade and commerce of the United States." Each state's emphasis on home manufactures had seemed to some wasteful, even menacing. In 1785 the Massachusetts Legislature placed a protective tariff on all state products. The commonwealth conceived of this act as defensive, to avoid an influx of "foreign" goods, and it urged other states to enact similar laws until Congress gained power to regulate trade. Delaware and South Carolina agreed, but the outspoken Pennsylvania Assembly feared that unless Congress soon regulated trade, the confederation would dissolve. James Madison explained the situation graphically with particular reference to the plight of New Jersey and North Carolina. "New Jersey," he wrote, "placed between Philadelphia and New York, is likened to a cask tapped at both ends; and North Carolina, between Virginia and South Carolina, to a patient bleeding at both arms. Most of our political evils," he concluded, "may be traced to our commercial ones."

The Constitution: A Commercial Document

The new document, the Constitution of the United States of America, provided the general government the "power to lay and collect . . . duties, imposts and excises" so long as they "shall be uniform throughout the United States." It also granted Congress authority "to regulate commerce with foreign nations, and among the several states, and with the Indian tribes." Both the Constitution's proponents and opponents recognized its commerce clauses as liberating and not restrictive. Experience had proved that the states constituted an economic whole—they made up a commonwealth—and that pursuit of separate, overlapping commercial and manufacturing strategies merely created waste; each state's ability to corral wealth suffered from the competition. Even the Constitution's opponents felt it mandatory for the states to unite in economic matters. In classic mercantile fashion, they argued that commercial and manufacturing regulation was the federal government's sole justification and the only reason for a union. Aware that "all the states have local advantages," these men and women urged them "to supply each other's wants" and maintained that Congress must have power to carry out the program. "A diversity of produce, wants and interests, produces commerce," they asserted, "and commerce, where there is a common, equal and moderate authority to preside, produces friendship." Such a broad consensus about managing commerce and manufacturing overcame objections about the potential abuses of power, and the states ratified the Constitution in 1789.

No matter how later generations would interpret it, the Constitution established a government that differed from the preceding confederation primarily in its power to regulate trade. Congress moved quickly to place customs duties on all imports and a tonnage duty on all shipping. It designed these measures to raise revenue and to encourage domestic manufacture while decreasing importation. The 1790 enactments by Congress pointed directly to technology's role in advancing the new nation's mercantile interests. Congress created a patent board to rule on priority of inventions and to grant true inventors monopolistic rights for specified periods; established the United States Mint; and sought to develop a standard of weights and measures.

Action on patents had come at President Washington's request. Like his compatriots, Washington believed that government guarantees of exclusivity were essential to stimulating public disclosure of new devices and processes. Without that assurance, inventors would conceal their inventions, which would impede the public interest by hampering American manufacturing and commerce. The new nation's secretaries of state and war and its attorney general—Thomas Jefferson, Henry Knox, and Edmund Randolph, respectively—constituted the patent board, but Jefferson dominated. He scrupulously examined every application and rigorously tested every device. His criteria proved so demanding that the board issued only three patents during its first year.

The third of those patents went to Oliver Evans. Apprenticed as a wheelwright, Evans left that trade to work with his brothers, who were Pennsylvania millers. During the mid-1780s, he received monopolies from Maryland and Pennsylvania for a water-powered grain mill. Evans' mill wheel powered a modified chain of pots to raise grain, which was delivered to the mill's upper floor. There an Archemedian screw turned a conveyor that carried the grain through water-powered drying, grinding, spreading, cooling, and sorting until it reached the ground as flour. When the federal government received patent authority, Evans immediately approached Jefferson, who took rapid notice of his device. Jefferson even built a similar flour mill at his Monticello plantation, taking care to pay Evans a licensing fee for the right to use his patented invention.

Hamilton's Call for Federal Assistance

That Congress should regulate commerce and manufacturing went without question. But what were the just and proper limits of federal involvement sparked great debate. Alexander Hamilton, treasury secretary, was the most notable advocate of large-scale, direct federal intervention. His "Report on Manufactures," submitted to Congress in December 1791, outlined his plan.

The report contained three main sections: a survey of American manufactures; a defense of their utility for the nation as a whole; and suggestions of ways that the federal government might encourage them. Much of Hamilton's analysis compared manufactures to agriculture. He argued that both remained critical, but that manufacturing held some wealth-accruing advantages. Manufacturing required each artificer to master only a single task, which increased skill; allowed women and children to participate, which expanded the number of producers; relied on extensive use of machinery, which reduced the drudgery associated with heavy labor; permitted children to choose from a larger store of occupations, which increased happiness; fostered recognition of talent and enhanced productivity; encouraged immigration, which brought America new wealth-transforming skills; and created a larger and stable demand for the nation's agricultural products, which ensured farmers a consistent, fair price for their goods.

Hamilton's arguments for federal aid proved equally compelling. American entrepreneurs needed assistance to combat what he saw as their countrymen's natural resistance to change, as well as foreign governments' active support of their own manufacturing. Hamilton's recommendations about the federal government's encouragement of domestic manufactures were in line with established mercantile theory and reminiscent of the states' policies under the Articles of Confederation. He favored protective tariffs, exclusion of designated goods, bans on the export of certain processes and equipment, bounties to stimulate production, and premiums and exemptions from taxes to reward production. But he also developed several innovative measures. Hamilton wanted to extend patent law to cover inventions of foreign origin introduced into America; mandate inspection of certain exportable products to ensure quality (this would build the new

*Late–eighteenth-century agricultural tools
commonly used on American farms*

country's reputation and allow certified producers to expand exports); create a single, nationwide paper money; and finance a system of internal improvements such as roads, bridges, canals, and harbors. His final proposition was even more imaginative: he urged Congress to finance a board to promote American manufactures by defraying immigration expenses of artificers in specified fields, paying rewards to inventors of designated processes or devices, and soliciting for and securing machinery unavailable in America.

This last proposal smacked of industrial espionage, but all Hamilton's suggestions were intended to garner and preserve wealth for the new country. Import duties would yield the necessary revenue, and he looked to the National Bank as a financial source. This suggestion, like much of his report, horrified many Americans, including Jefferson and Madison, who generally championed manufacturing and machinery. Jefferson, for instance, served on the patent board, applauded water-powered grist mills, and operated carriage, furniture, and nail manufactories on his Monticello plantation. He also invented several devices, such as a copying machine and automatic door-openers, and designed numerous others, such as a horizontal windmill, an improved plow, a fulling machine, and a spinning jenny. Although an avid supporter of mercantile theory at this point in his life, Jefferson detested the huge European manufactories and the teeming industrial cities they bred, likening their contributions to virtuous government to sores on the body politic. Fear that Hamilton's scheme would reproduce the corrupt European system in America fueled Jefferson's hostility.

Dispute between the two camps rested on the question of whether the policy would benefit the whole nation. Hamilton's antagonists considered his program flawed because it favored manufacturing interests over agricultural and commercial ones. Federally sponsored inducements to establish and encourage American manufacture, including tariffs and import prohibitions, would surely be met by a wave of European protectionism—a move that would damage American agriculture and commerce. To his antagonists Hamilton's program seemed a product of faction, of the desire of the few to further themselves at the whole's expense. Only private investors—speculators—would benefit; others would lose. Government would enable "the few to increase the inequality of property, by an immodest, and especially unwritten, accumulation of riches." In short, those opposed to Hamilton contended that his program did "not appeal to the understanding and to the general interest of the community."

Private Development of Manufacturing

Although the anti-Hamiltonians offered no formal alternative to the treasury secretary's report, their strength in Congress effectively removed the federal government from actively fostering manufacturing. Initiative rested on private citizens, and even before Hamilton submitted his report, Americans had formed local associations to promote manufacturing. The Pennsylvania Society for the Encouragement of Manufacturing and the Useful Arts (established in Philadelphia in 1787) was the most wide-ranging, but similar organizations were created in Boston (1786), New York (1788), Baltimore (1788), Wilmington (1789), Burlington (1791), Morristown (1792), and Newark (1793). Although their members might engage in manufacturing, these groups themselves generally sought only to inspire it. They held meetings to discuss possible legislation, gathered and exchanged information about new manufacturing techniques, and published their deliberations. They also rewarded inventors and provided financial aid to those claiming special knowledge about manufacturing processes.

Only the Pennsylvania society went further. Under stewardship of Tench Coxe, who would later become Hamilton's assistant secretary and help develop the manufacturing report, it raised through public subscriptions a fund to establish cotton textile manufactories. Coxe understood that American textile manufacturing success depended on competition with the sophisticated British; it required the new late-eighteenth-century inventions—the water frame and carding machine, the spinning jenny, and the mule (a machine for simultaneously spinning thread and winding it onto tubes called caps)—as well as experienced operators. Coxe himself hired an agent and, "for the good of the

United States of America," sent him to England both to secure "models and patterns" of textile machinery and to induce mechanics to emigrate to America. When the British uncovered the scheme, the society's agent fled empty-handed.

The society remained undeterred. It employed several hundred women to spin yarn, and by August 1788, its weavers worked twenty-six looms. In its first year, the manufactory had made more than seven thousand yards of cloth. A fire closed the plant in 1790, but its example apparently encouraged others. Associations to manufacture textiles were organized in Beverly, Massachusetts (1787); Hartford (1788); Baltimore (1789); and New York (1789). Each aggressively recruited European workmen; the New York organization gave Samuel Slater, who brought knowledge of the new European textile machines, his first American position. But these manufacturing entities pale when compared to the grand design of the Society for Establishing Useful Manufactures. Chartered in New Jersey just prior to Hamilton's report, the society was the treasury secretary's and Coxe's brainchild. It hoped to create "the National Manufactory" to demonstrate the utility and feasibility of American industrial development. Funded primarily by a consortium of Hamilton's well-to-do friends and located at what is now Paterson, New Jersey, the national manufactory echoed colonial plantations and foreshadowed late nineteenth-century factory towns. Its stockholders envisioned it as the home of an extraordinary number of diverse establishments, including mills to make paper, pasteboard, sailcloth, stockings, ribbons, blankets, carpets, textiles, women's shoes, earthenware, brass and iron wire, and beer. The society would own the entire complex, but would sell workers plots to erect dwellings. A European émigré skilled in production of that product would supervise each manufactory. For example, Thomas Marshall, who claimed to have directed installation of Richard Arkwright's cotton mills, controlled textiles. The society also pledged to secure from abroad "such machines and implements as cannot be had here in sufficient perfection."

As befitted a site aspiring to become the "capital scene of manufactures," the society hired Pierre L'Enfant, architect of the new federal capital, to design the physical plant. Among L'Enfant's contributions were a great aqueduct to carry Passaic River water to power the mills' waterwheels, and a canal to transport society products to the river. The national manufactory became the largest eighteenth-century American manufacturing venture. Prior to 1796, the society had facilities to make cotton goods, brass and iron wire, and stockings, and machines to spin hemp, flax, and wool. It also established a drying and bleach works, sawmill, gristmills, and waterworks and constructed houses for fifty workers. Some production facilities were quite large. For instance, the cotton mill was built of stone and stood four stories high, ninety feet long, and forty feet wide, while its stone carding and roping house was two stories tall, sixty-four feet long, and thirty-six feet wide.

The society's recruitment of European factory operatives was somewhat successful. In addition to those European émigrés who came to America on their own, the society had attracted several French wire-makers, roughly a dozen Scottish stocking workers, and two hundred Manchester cotton mill employees. Though impressive, the European influx did not begin to fill the society's skilled worker needs. It was also beset by a continuous lack of funds. Its investors became increasingly restive when returns failed to materialize. By 1796, many had withdrawn, and the society's manufacturing activities stagnated.

The case of the national manufactory demonstrated American manufacture's difficulties. Competition from Europe, a dearth of skilled workers trained in the newest techniques, ignorance about manufacturing apparatus, a lack of financing, debates over the merits of large-scale manufacturing, and modest governmental assistance combined to place America at a severe disadvantage. Nonetheless, the nation had emerged as a serious economic rival to Europe less than 200 years after the first permanent English settlement. North American inhabitants had combined New World abundance and Old World technologies to go beyond subsistence, to enter the export trade, and by the late eighteenth century, to begin to frame larger (albeit still modest) commercial and manufacturing objectives. These successive transformations each had occurred within the context of a rigid mercantilistic philosophy in which society as a whole accrued wealth while its members reaped benefits differentially. The Constitution brought the beginnings of a modicum of political equality, but the notion of similar socioeconomic equality waited until the first decades of the next century.

FOR FURTHER READING

Baron, Stanley. *Brewed in America: A History of Beer and Ale in the United States* (1962).

Bishop, J. Leander. A *History of American Manufactures from 1608 to 1860*, 3 vols. (1868).

Bridenbough, Carl. *The Colonial Craftsman* (1950).

Cole, Arthur Harrison. *The American Wool Manufacture* (1926), vol. 1.

Cooke, Jacob E. *Tench Coxe and the Early Republic* (1978).

Davis, Joseph Stancliffe. *Essays in the Early History of American Corporations*, 2 vols. (1917).

Flexner, James Thomas. *Steamboats Come True* (1944).

Goldenberg, Joseph A. *Shipbuilding in Colonial America* (1976).

Gordon, Robert B., and Patrick M. Malone. *The Texture of Industry: An Archaeological View of the Industrialization of North America* (1994).

Hartley, E. N. *Ironworks on the Saugus* (1957).

Haynes, Williams. *American Chemical Industry* (1954), vol. 1.

Hazard, Blanche Evans. *The Organization of the Boot and Shoe Industry in Massachusetts Before 1875* (1921).

Hofstadter, Richard. *The Idea of a Party System: The Rise of Legitimate Opposition in the United States, 1780–1840* (1969).

Hunter, Louis C. *Waterpower* (1979).

Hurt, R. Douglas. *American Farm Tools: From Hand-Power to Steam-Power* (1982).

Lutz, Donald S. *Popular Consent and Popular Control: Whig Political Theory in the Early State Constitutions* (1980).

McGaw, Judith A., ed. *Early American Technology: Making and Doing Things From the Colonial Era to 1850* (1994).

Mulholland, James A. *A History of Metals in Colonial America* (1981).

Storck, John, and William Dorwin Teague. *Flour For Man's Bread: A History of Milling* (1952).

Teaford, Jon C. *The Municipal Revolution In America: Origins of Modern Urban Government, 1650–1825* (1975).

Tunis, Edwin. *Colonial Craftsmen and the Beginnings of American Industry* (1965).

Van Gelder, Arthur Pine, and Hugo Schlatter. *History of the Explosives Industry in America* (1927).

Welsh, Peter C. *Tanning in the United States to 1850: A Brief History* (Washington: U.S. National Museum, 1964), Bulletin 242.

Wroth, Lawrence C. *The Colonial Printer* (1938).

York, Neil Longley. *Mechanical Metamorphosis: Technological Change in Revolutionary America* (1985).

Young America and Individual Opportunity: 1800 to the 1830s

BEYOND MERCANTILISM

Americans found mercantilism an acceptable socioeconomic form in a world of limits, but in the late 1790s a growing number began to question whether wealth was in fact limited. Oliver Evans and Thomas Ellicott, two noted millwrights, were among the earliest Americans to hint otherwise. Published in 1795, their *The Young Mill-Wright and Miller's Guide* was ostensibly an American water-milling text. But its concentration on flour milling and other large, complex milling operations not normally associated with contemporary American enterprises suggested a quite different vision of America. Through technology the nation could create and sustain virtually limitless growth. America's abundant resources, in conjunction with technical processes, could produce unprecedented plenty. Rather than the creation of a single or even several national manufactories, Evans's and Ellicott's volume promised the establishment of as many wealth-producing manufactories as Americans desired. Technology in America would foster almost inconceivable material prosperity.

These views characterized early–nineteenth-century America. Americans surveyed their abundant lands and natural resources,

41

threw off the yoke of mercantilism, and emphasized progress, development, and growth. Watermills increased from fewer than ten thousand in 1800 to well over fifty thousand by 1830. The country's population more than tripled, creating a ready demand for additional goods. Scores of new cities were established as citizens moved west. New roads, canals, bridges, and railways, most built with governmental assistance, joined settlements. Steamboats carried goods on waterways, and steam locomotives began to bring them over land. Congress established the Army Corps of Engineers and the United States Military Academy to provide a ready supply of military engineers. Mechanics' institutes blossomed in Philadelphia, Cincinnati, Boston, Baltimore, New York, and elsewhere.

Extending Europe

America seemed poised to open a new chapter of world civilization, potentially the greatest. Its defenders championed it as a free land with free institutions in which Old World aspirations would be played out, unencumbered by European traditions and trappings. They looked to Europe for inspiration, but considered themselves Europeans freed of their chains, as Old World people in a New World setting.

Americans tempered their reverence for Europe with democratic notions, heralding their country as "the great experiment in democracy." The new nation's citizens repudiated some European customs, such as a hereditary aristocracy, as inconsistent with a democratic republic, and debated the suitability of others, such as secret, restricted organizations. But infatuation with democratic notions ran far deeper than mere custom. To early–nineteenth-century Americans, the idea of privilege, special rights granted only to some citizens, seemed an anathema in a nation marked by plentiful resources. They identified privilege as a vestige of an authoritarian political system (in a sense, the product of mercantilistic ideas), and defined it as a barrier that hampered individual opportunity—including the awarding of unjustified competitive advantage by the government. They sought to eliminate privilege. The assault on privilege was to protect and provide opportunity for success, not a guarantee that all individuals would succeed. Opportunity for success for all constituted America's promise.

The Ascendancy of the Individual

Early–nineteenth-century Americans rarely agreed on who received privilege, or what constituted privilege, and many disputes turned on these points. In that sense, privilege in the new century was reminiscent of eighteenth-century faction. But crucially different premises lay under the two concepts. Eighteenth-century faction was deprecated because a group pursued its own agenda at the whole's expense; faction was a crime against society. Nineteenth-century privilege was attacked because recipients gained advantages unavailable to others. Pursuing one's own ends was not the problem—competition was welcomed—but rather, unfair or unwarranted assistance; privilege hindered other individuals' opportunity to compete. Put simply, the eighteenth century focused on the whole while nineteenth-century counterparts concentrated on the parts.

The individual—the part—was the fundamental unit of early–nineteenth-century American society. Organization, conduct, and explanation of technological enterprises manifested this social calculation. It served as appraiser of propriety and adjudicator of efficacy. A new kind of business entity, the corporation, which with family partnerships became the predominant form of large-scale manufacturing and commerce, reflected the new emphasis. Unlike the previous centuries' joint-stock companies, plantations, and town governments (each regulating a whole spectrum of activities, creating total environments, and in effect replicating society in miniature), early–nineteenth-century corporations functioned as individuals. They assumed in law the status of individuals, and generally were permitted to tackle only one or a handful of closely related tasks. Their mandates were neatly circumscribed by state legislatures precisely because of their potential to impinge on the opportunity of others if left unchecked. Prohibitions against engaging in banking—congregating and controlling wealth unnecessarily—were almost always included in corporate charters. Corporations were created because of some obstacle to individual opportunity and received only the authority necessary to overcome that barrier; the grant of additional extraneous powers constituted privilege, and would likely result in hurdles for others.

BUILDING THE NATION'S INFRASTRUCTURE

A building boom swept early–nineteenth-century America; its citizens engaged in a spate of turnpike, canal, bridge, and railroad construction. New routes linked the West securely to the East, connected seaboard cities with those inland, and generally facilitated travel, commerce, and communications. Americans recognized that individual opportunity and economic development went hand in hand, and that both required creation of an "infrastructure"—roads, bridges, canals, and so on—to join producers and markets.

The federal government played a crucial role in this infrastructural revolution. As part of its constitutionally mandated provision for the national defense, it improved harbors and seacoast fortifications, built the National Road, and provided numerous topographical surveys. The Army Corps of Engineers, stationed at West Point and constituting a military academy, planned and executed these works. Created by the federal government in 1802, the Corps recruited French engineers to teach and direct many projects. These professors used French texts (French was the academy's military language), maps, and instruments. The Corps' dependence on the French persisted beyond its earliest years. It solicited French engineers for American projects, and in 1815 conducted a survey of French fortifications and engineering schools—a move that led to West Point's being remodeled after the acclaimed Ecole Polytechnique. Not until the late 1820s did the Corps free itself from French influence.

From its inception, several prominent Americans hoped to enlarge the Corps' functions. As early as 1806, Jefferson called for a constitutional amendment allowing the Corps to plan and direct nonmilitary improvements, an approach seconded by Treasury Secretary Albert Gallatin's 1808 report on roads and canals.

President Madison also urged permitting the Corps to undertake those internal improvements that required "a national jurisdiction and national means" to bind "more closely together the various parts of our extended confederacy." John C. Calhoun went a step further. His bonus bill, passed by Congress in 1817, would have appropriated $1.5 million to the states to fund road and canal construction. Madison vetoed the measure.

Madison's veto message said that Congress lacked authority to fund canal and road planning in cases other than the national defense. His sentiments were outdated; the Corps already provided localities direct and indirect assistance. Its experienced officers surveyed numerous turnpikes and canals for states and cities, and several resigned their commissions or took leaves of absence to direct local projects. President Monroe acknowledged the new reality in his 1822 veto of a measure to collect tolls on the National Road when he argued that Congress could fund internal improvement plans, but lacked jurisdiction over their construction and operation. The General Survey Act of 1824, which authorized the president to employ the Corps and others to conduct road and canal surveys considered of national importance, institutionalized that view. During John Quincy Adams's presidency, the Corps surveyed thirty-four canal routes, eighteen roads, forty-four river and harbor projects, and six railroads. Nor did Andrew Jackson's election end federal involvement in internal improvements; he signed an 1836 measure to distribute all but $5 million of the federal surplus to plan and finance internal improvements in each state.

The Panic of 1837, fueled by rampant land speculation, negated the act's significance. Funding of nonmilitary internal improvements remained with states and cities. Indeed, state and city governments had participated in most construction projects, although they rarely undertook ventures alone. They worked through mixed corporations, which joined public and private capital. Chartered by states—most often at some entrepreneur's request—each mixed corporation constructed a single project that linked two points, and followed certain guidelines in return for public support. In most cases, the charter prescribed the project's exact specifications—for instance, the type and depth of surfacing, maximum grade, and drainage requirements for roads—and a state or local board was created solely to oversee its planning and implementation. Public funding usually came as land grants or subscriptions to specified amounts of stock, but sometimes it merely consisted of the right to charge tolls or of an award of exclusivity.

These transportation projects had economic implications far exceeding the investment. New routes raised the value of adjoining lands, fostered creation of new cities and towns, and increased the scope of nearby settlements' economic influence. But new transportation pathways also placed municipalities at a competitive disadvantage. Many died or declined as their citizens moved closer to the new routes, while others demanded the same advantages and called on the state to undertake projects in their vicinity.

These political considerations often increased construction difficulty and expense; straight routes with few grades or hollows were of course cheapest and simplest to build, but they rarely satisfied everyone. Ease of land clearing also remained a factor, as did suitable building materials. Rarely did technical questions take precedence, however, and few projects paid investors dividends as construction costs frequently surpassed the corporation's ability to pay. But few projects were ever abandoned. New investors, an increase in state or local support, or total state or municipal ownership completed the work, and citizens reaped improved transportation benefits.

Building Turnpikes

Early–nineteenth-century Americans continued colonial precedents and improved travel overland and on the nation's waterways. Most colonial roadways were essentially unimproved pathways where only traffic volume kept underbrush from growing over, while river transport upstream was limited to pole boats and rowed vessels. Adaptation of a common European roadway, the turnpike, constituted a major commercial innovation. By the mid-1810s, Americans had built several hundred-mile or longer for-profit tollways. A decade later turnpikes joined eastern cities to the tramontane West. Early–nineteenth-century American commercial vehicles had no standardized form, so wide turnpikes with plenty of room for passing accommodated different kinds of traffic traveling at unequal speeds.

Unlike European turnpikes, American tollways traversed sparsely settled areas and generally were built on inexpensive land. Often twenty-eight feet wide, turnpikes were slightly raised in the center and sloped outward to encourage water runoff, and generally abutted by drainage ditches. Surfacing material and depth varied considerably. Earth, clay, or timber composed the primitive surfaces, but broken granite, slate, or limestone paved heavily trafficked ways. These broken-stone surfaces usually ran between nine and eighteen inches deep. Milestones marked the distance from the road's point of origin, and guideposts indicated the termini of intersecting ways.

Strength was a prerequisite for those who built turnpikes, but specialized knowledge was not. Only surveyors, who laid out routes, possessed even a cursory technical competence—geometry and trigonometry. The turnpike contractors were selected because of their local prominence as only their reputations guaranteed that specifications would be followed. Each contractor organized and superintended construction of a road section and employed local farmers to do the work. Using shovels, rakes, and hoes to move earth, and two-pound hammers to break rocks, the farmers/laborers cleared trees, stumps, and large stones, then dug drainage ditches, piling dirt from ditches in the center to form a raised road bed. The bed was then tamped down and sculpted in preparation for surfacing.

Builders of the earliest American stone turnpikes followed the then-current European practice. Stones of five to eight inches in diameter constituted the surface's bottom layers, and those with diameters of between one-and-one-half and two-and-one-half inches composed its top. Stone dust, gravel, or sand enhanced surface binding. Americans adopted even newer European techniques around 1820. The beds, not the surfaces, of these new macadam turnpikes bore the traffic's weight. Named after Scottish road-builder and inspector John McAdam, these roads cost less because of their thinner, readily maintained surfaces. Keeping the bed dry was crucial. Earlier surfacing with large and different-sized stones permitted water to percolate to the bed. Macadamizers advocated use of stones two inches in diameter throughout, cleansed of all moisture-trapping or gap-creating material, to allow them "to unite their own angles into a firm, compact, impenetrable body." The initial layer was rammed into the bed, and each successive layer was compacted by traffic before the next was laid. Regular rut filling was usually the only maintenance necessary.

Building Bridges

American turnpike-builders faced a recurring problem rarely confronted by their European counterparts; the New World's numerous rivers and streams required construction of many bridges to transport turnpike traffic. Bridge construction was expensive, so Americans made those structures to last. States generally created different corporations to build bridges, but occasionally authorized turnpike companies to build their own. Separate tolls were usually charged for bridge travel.

American bridge-building was virtually identical to classic Roman practice; like turnpike construction, it required no special skills. Laborers created a watertight enclosure by driving wooden piles through river mud to reach bedrock, removed water and silt, and built masonry arches resting securely on the river bottom. These arches supported the span—generally stone—but timbers occasionally formed the roadway. Wooden superstructures often protected timbers from the elements.

Improved River Travel—Building Steamboats

Improved river travel entailed a new prime mover. Fitch and Rumsey had attempted to adapt steam power to the river trade, but neither was alive when steamboats became operational. Rumsey had died suddenly in 1792; a despondent Fitch committed suicide a few years later. Evans experimented with a high-pressure steamboat in 1802, but ultimately placed the engine in a sawmill. John Stevens, a Hoboken mechanic, failed to build a working vessel until late 1807. By that time, Robert Fulton's *North River* (often incorrectly called the *Clermont*) was steaming on the Hudson River between New York City and Albany.

A jeweler's apprentice and a cameo painter, Fulton had gone to England in 1788. There he learned of Fitch's work and met Rumsey, but apparently neither man made an immediate impression on him. Canals captivated Fulton, and during the 1790s he offered his unsolicited views on canals to George Washington, Napoleon, and Parliament. He also proved something of a mercenary, building for the French an underwater bomb-attaching submarine. Fulton failed to destroy the English Navy, but he gained Robert Livingston's attention. Although he was then ambassador to France—Livingston held a New York steamboat monopoly, and had employed Nicholas Roosevelt, a New Jersey steam-engine-maker, to design a craft (that proved to be unsuccessful)—Livingston told Fulton of his steamboat experiments, and decided to finance the young man in that endeavor.

Fulton began work quickly. By 1802 he had determined that paddlewheels delivered steam power adequately and that a long, narrow boat with stem and stern cut sharply at sixty degrees would best slice through water. He also concluded that the boat should have an atmospheric engine, and directed England's Boulton and Watt to build the

Notice the careful gearing from the engine to the paddlewheel of the North River.

engine and ship it to America. England had learned of Fulton's under-water vessel, however, placed a lien on the engine, and prohibited its export—a procedure called "attachment"—until he designed another submarine to attack the French fleet. Although Fulton again failed to produce a successful submarine, the Crown relented and released the engine in November 1806. In August 1807, Fulton gave Livingston's friends their first public demonstration, and the next month began commercial runs.

Livingston and Fulton made a $16,000 profit in 1808, and they hurried to capitalize on the western trade. The Louisiana Purchase of 1803 had opened the port of New Orleans to Americans, and the Mississippi, Missouri, and Ohio Rivers seemed to provide a natural means to tap and settle the nation's interior. With the exception of the Orleans territory, however, western states and territories favored competition for their trade and refused to grant Livingston and Fulton monopolistic privileges. Two technical problems also plagued the New Yorkers. First, western rivers' swift currents often destroyed Fulton's angular steamboats. A return to conventional hulls resolved that problem. The second problem proved more difficult; his steamboats lacked power to move effectively upstream. Although Fulton tried larger atmospheric engines, he died in 1815 without solving the problem. His boats operated on western rivers after his death, but they met stiff competition from, and were soon superseded by, high-pressure steamboats.

Henry M. Shreve, a steamboat captain disappointed by atmospheric engine performance, introduced the first working high-pressure steamboat in 1816. Although Shreve first adapted high-pressure engines to western steamboats, these engines had appeared in the region from about 1805. Evans had shipped numerous high-pressure engines to power western saw- and gristmills, and in 1805 his son George opened an engine-building manufactory in Pittsburgh. Shreve learned high-pressure steam engine technology there and in his spare time adapted it to navigation. Shreve's engine employed four boilers, each with separate flue, and dominated the deck. Its single cylinder turned two side paddlewheels through connecting rod and crank. As had Evans, Shreve stressed the need for effective valves to release dangerous steam and prevent explosions when boiler pressure reached critical levels.

Shreve began service in 1816, but the unthinkable happened. A boiler explosion in his boat, the *George Washington,* killed nine passengers and knocked him unconscious. He attempted to re-establish his line but no passengers would travel with him. Virtually alone, he made it to New Orleans where he was immediately arrested for violating the Fulton/Livingston steamboat monopoly. Shreve turned down overtures to place his invention under the monopoly and a lawsuit ensued. The judge argued that monopolies for river transport hampered the jurisdiction's interest by preventing competition.

Others would shy away from developing improved transportation forms and the individuals living in a place would be put at a competitive disadvantage; they would suffer unfairly from the monopoly. Yet that doctrine had little legal standing, so the judge overturned the Fulton/Livingston monopoly on a technicality; neither man was a resident of New Orleans and therefore could not receive a monopoly there.

Almost immediately steam engine and steamboat manufacture blossomed. Three times as many engines and vessels were started during the panic years of 1817–18 as there had been in the previous years. In less than a decade, more than two-thirds of the western steamboats used high-pressure steam engines, which were much lighter and as much as ten times more powerful than atmospheric engines. By 1830 some two hundred steamboats operated in the West. Cincinnati, Louisville, and Pittsburgh entrepreneurs built about two-thirds of American steamboat engines.

Building Canals

Canals were perhaps the most spectacular early–nineteenth-century internal improvements. America built its first canals in New England in the 1780s. Patterned after the English canals of the 1760s, these

Horse-drawn canal boats make their way on the Erie
Canal, the largest early–nineteenth-century
American canal.

first few artificial waterways traversed short, straight, level distances. Towpaths bordered the first canals, as well as those of the nineteenth century, and horse or mule teams drew special flat-bottomed canal boats.

The steamboat's success did not lessen the country's interest in canals. In fact, the American canal era flourished after steamboats were already coursing the nation's rivers. Although Americans had built fewer than one hundred canal miles prior to 1815, during the next twenty-five years they spent more than $125 million on nearly thirty-one hundred canal miles. New York, Pennsylvania, and Ohio accounted for more than half that amount.

States and corporations retained canal-building authority, but responsibility for technical matters and daily operations usually rested with each canal's superintendent. His recommendations were generally accepted on technical questions, such as the canal's width and depth, number of locks necessary to keep channels level, type of lock mechanism, and whether locks should be made from wood or stone. He was expected to oversee surveyors, rodmen, chainmen, and axmen, as well as other workers. English or French canal builders were usually first choices to be superintendents, but often these men refused to come to America. Americans with European canal-building experience or who had already headed an American canal project were solicited, as were those currently working in the upper echelon of an ongoing canal venture. Experience was equated with, and was the test of, competence.

New York's decision to build the Erie Canal joining Albany to Buffalo on Lake Erie sparked the canal boom. Constructed between 1817 and 1825, but proposed over a decade earlier for New York to counter New Orleans' growing Western commercial influence, it dwarfed all preceding American canals. Its channel was 363 miles long and four feet deep, with bottom and surface widths of twenty-eight and forty feet respectively. The canal contained eighty-four locks, the largest of which was 110 feet by 18 feet, for a total lift of 689 feet. Its towpaths stood about three feet above the channel's surface and were fourteen feet wide. Although the towage rate averaged less than two miles per hour, and the canal cost more than $7 million to build, it reduced freight charges to one-twentieth the overland price.

It was the Erie Canal's economic and technological potential, as well as its subsequent success, that fueled canal construction nationwide. Seaboard cities such as Philadelphia and Baltimore, already threatened by New Orleans' rise and the western river trade, saw the canal as further threatening their economic viability: it provided New York City (connected to Albany by the Hudson River) with a tremendous competitive advantage in the west. Goods would flow to and from New York City or New Orleans, while Baltimore and Philadelphia would become secondary cities with limited markets. Other cities urged their legislatures to grant them the same advantages as New York City; they wanted competing canals. Western states and cities looked to the Erie Canal as an opportunity to expand their eastern trade, and constructed canals linking them to Lake Erie. The various Ohio canals, Indiana's Wabash Canal, and the Illinois Canal were testimony to that thrust.

Men who had worked on the Erie Canal often built these western canals. The magnitude and difficulty of Erie seemed the supreme American test of engineering mettle, particularly in the fifteen years after 1817. During that period, former Erie employees directed far more nonmilitary construction projects than West Point graduates and Corps of Engineers members combined. Only when canal building waned in the late 1830s did the Erie men lose preeminence.

Constructing level, watertight channels was a most demanding aspect of canal building. Grades or currents, consequences of poor surveying, would strain boat-pulling beasts. The absence of grades was so critical that canal companies constructed stone aqueducts, similar to turnpike bridges, over even small streams. Variations in water level also produced difficulties. Surface drainage into channels raised water levels precipitously and played havoc with locks, while seepage, often the result of channel-burrowing animals, caused boats to run aground. Canal workers lined channel walls and floors in two ways. Workers called puddlers mixed tempered clay with sand and gravel, kneaded it by hand, and applied it to channels in layers three inches

Operational view of the Erie Canal at Lockport

deep, roughening surfaces to promote adhesion. In the Erie Canal, and many later ones, a limestone-based hydraulic cement replaced puddling. Laborers kiln-heated the distinctive limestone, broke it, and mixed two parts' lime with one part sand. They spread the pasty mixture in the empty channel and then flooded it.

Locks permitted various level stretches of the canal at different altitudes to be joined. They varied considerably in shape, size, and material, but all worked according to a similar principle: boats could be raised or lowered simply by raising or lowering the water level, like a water elevator. Situated in cutouts parallel to channels, timber or masonry long and wide enough to accommodate the largest boats framed the locks' chambers. Their walls were tall enough to reach the canal's upper level and thick enough to secure the water necessary to raise boats to the desired height. Heavy swinging gates sealed their ends and made them watertight. Once boats entered chambers, lock operators closed the gates and pumped water in or out to achieve the appropriate end.

Building Railways

Railways were the final early–nineteenth-century transportation initiative. The first American railways replicated those in Britain a century earlier. Like the earliest British railways, Massachusetts's Quincy

Railway (1825) and Pennsylvania's Mauch Chunk Road (1827) were horse-drawn, single-purpose railways. The British railways transported coal from mines to ironworks, while the American railways carried large granite blocks from quarries. Not until 1827 did a state legislature charter a general-purpose railway. Again, the British example was crucial. George Stephenson's Stockton and Darlington Railway (1825) and the Liverpool and Manchester Road (construction began 1826) helped convince recalcitrant state legislatures to approve similar plans in America.

These initial American general-purpose railways mimicked canals and turnpikes in route, purpose, organization, and design. Citizens treated them as common roads, open to anyone who paid tolls and used proper cars as specified in the way's charter. Advocates boosted them as faster than canals and more reliable; no freezing in winter, as well as flood- and drought-resistant. States and municipalities sponsored railways to match commercial advantages available elsewhere. For example, Baltimore initiated the Baltimore & Ohio Railroad (chartered in 1827 to run over 250 miles from the Monument City to the Ohio River) both to combat New York City's western trade domination and to prevent Washington, Georgetown, and Alexandria from exploiting their Chesapeake and Ohio Canal advantages. Boston's 308-mile railway from Boston harbor to the Hudson River was designed to siphon off the New York City trade; instead of erecting a competing line, Bostonians tapped into an existing one.

Railway methods and materials dominated these early years. Designers and builders experimented with rails of stone, wood, and iron-plated wood before settling on iron. Even then they debated rail shape and whether to cast them (casting rails straight in lengths greater than five feet was difficult) or to use wrought iron. They also considered flanges to hold wheels on the track, whether railway bridges should be stone- or wood-constructed, how best to provide horse teams with a smooth walking surface, and whether to construct double- or single-tracked ways, the latter with periodic cutouts to facilitate two-way traffic.

Building railways required a curious combination of turnpike- and canal-construction skills. Making the bed level, dry, and firm was the most important task. Ironically, few canal engineers superintended railway projects. The Corps of Engineers' current and former members surveyed the great majority and directed many, sometimes after a fact-finding English tour. They situated drainage ditches, laid the way to avoid abrupt curves, and kept grades to less than one-eighth-inch per yard. Following this procedure reduced costs. Curves could involve deep ground cuts and expensive embankments. Steep grades required stationary steam engines to pull cars up the rails; horses could pull heavy loads on level ground, but contemporaries assumed that the frictionlessness of iron wheels running on iron rails prohibited them from surmounting significant grades. Even with these problems, railways grew dramatically: from twenty-eight operating miles in 1830 to more than twenty-three hundred in 1839.

A new prime mover, the steam-powered locomotive, fueled the spate of railway construction in the 1830s. Locomotives were of British origin, first introduced to carry South Wales coal in 1804. Powered by high-pressure steam generated from spherical boilers, which housed fireboxes and flues, these early locomotives' drive wheels slipped continuously on the rails, which rendered them useless. Only in the 1810s did the British recognize that abundance of power produced slippage, not contact, between frictionless surfaces. Still, horses remained ascendant until the 1829 Rainhill Trials. Sponsored by the Liverpool and Manchester Road's directors and held on a flat, one-and-a-half-mile track, the trials tested the locomotive's practicality. Entrants had to pull twenty tons at least ten miles per hour for sixty miles. Stephenson's Rocket exceeded the directors' conditions and demonstrated that a large, complex prime mover could be dependable.

The trials also captured the American imagination. The first locomotives arrived from Britain later that year, and a year later, Peter Cooper, a Baltimore mechanic, built America's first. Eager businessmen quickly put these engines in service, and determined almost as quickly that they failed to meet American needs. The British locomotive's driving wheels turned on axles rigidly attached to the engine's frame. Such an arrangement proved disastrous in America, where uneven ground and long, winding, lightly used routes would be the rule.

Two major innovations gave American locomotives a characteristic form. Albany's John B. Jervis, who had begun as an Erie Canal rodman, designed in 1833 the swivel truck—a second frame and a double set of smaller wheels under the boiler's front end—to enable locomotives to follow curves, while Philadelphia's John Harrison added the equalizer lever in 1838 to distribute shocks evenly to all drive wheels.

Other American innovations were no less important. Cow-catchers appeared in 1833 to remove obstructions from tracks and prevent derailments caused by freely roaming animals. Long-distance travel through thinly populated environs on irregular schedules also gave rise to railroad bells, which by 1835 were required in several states. These same lengthy routes led to frequent night motoring and to headlights, soon with parabolic reflectors. Smokestacks also received attention. British locomotives burned coal cleanly, but American wood-burning engines produced large sparks, which injured passengers and set fires along routes. As early as 1832, Americans employed crude, wire-mesh devices as primitive spark arresters.

Nor was that all. In 1836, William Norris, owner of a Philadelphia engine-building establishment, conducted a public demonstration of locomotive practicality as significant as the Rainhill Trials. He demonstrated that a locomotive could run easily up a grade as steep as 363 fcct per mile; grades were no longer debilitating. Eliminating the expense of precision leveling and stationary steam engines to pull locomotives and cars over even modest grades made the locomotive's potential appear unlimited.

CHANGES IN MANUFACTURING AND LABOR

New transportation routes and forms provided a commercial infrastructure, served as immigration pathways, and determined settlement patterns. European immigrants streamed into New York, New Orleans, Boston, and other coastal cities, but generally moved beyond their port of first call. The overwhelming majority of immigrants resided near a site blessed by improved transportation. These men and women produced and purchased goods. America's abundant natural resources promised, when modified by technical or technological endeavors, to yield unprecedented growth, and material prosperity seemed within reach of anyone whose opportunity remained unchecked.

Immigration, technologically engineered production, and increased consumption heightened demand for material goods and quickened America's manufacturing pace. Small manufacturing ventures remained the rule. Establishments generally perpetuated shop-based, master–apprentice relationships, but with less formal master–apprentice connections. These manufactories flourished from Boston to Baltimore and in the newer cities in the West. Urban manufactories generally served outlying areas with easy access to the city. Competition surfaced for rural and village markets situated between two or more manufacturing centers as each wanted to extend its influence and penetrate the others' hinterlands.

Manufacturers borrowed heavily from European technology. Immigrants and industrial espionage brought European practices and techniques, especially machinery, to America, but Americans used waterwheels, not steam engines, to power the great preponderance of manufacturing machines. Lack of cheap labor led some American industries, such as clockmaking, to rely even more heavily on machinery than their counterparts in Europe, but this early machine-based production usually failed to duplicate the skills of artisans. Yet the scope and diversity of early–nineteenth-century manufacturing interests was truly impressive. For example, Cincinnatians had created before 1820 foundries for casting copper, brass, and iron; a manufactory for textile machinery and cotton gins; a steamboat works; a manufactory for white and red lead; and a chemical works. By 1830, the city housed

*A modest ironworks in the 1830s combined machine
shop and foundry operations.*

more than three times as many chemical and steamboat works and
foundries and had added several machine shops, gunpowder and
paper mills, steam engine and casting manufactories, a sugar refinery,
and manufactories of tallow candles and soap.

Machine Shops as Adjuncts to Mills

At the heart of water-powered, machinery-based manufacturing were
mills, millwrights, and machine shops. The explosive growth of mills
testified to the proliferation of manufacturing, while their relatively
small power output—generally less than one hundred horsepower—
indicated the modest size of most manufacturing establishments. Demand for millwrights far exceeded that of the colonial period, and
early–nineteenth-century millwrights needed to understand the sophisticated linkages often required between mills and machines. But
machinery-dependent production also required a new type of crafts-
man/manufacturer—one who worked in a machine shop. These ma-
chine-makers fashioned devices from wood and metal to fit individual
specifications and repaired broken machines. Because completed machinery was often unwieldy to transport, machine shops were located
near manufacturing complexes and on transportation routes; they
served localities. The number of machine shops increased markedly
during the century's first three decades, but their form remained essentially unchanged. These single-room operations employed fewer
than fifteen men, were fitted with hand- or foot-powered lathes, contained workbenches with vises and grinding stones, and included tool

chests filled with assorted hammers, chisels, and files. Only a few larger shops before the mid-1830s housed water-driven lathes, screw-cutting engines, or boring, drilling, milling, and planing machines.

Metal-working machine shops depended on foundry castings, rods, and sheet metal. Establishments, often called works, combined a machine shop and foundry and generally included a drafting room to prepare plans on paper, a pattern room to store wooden casting patterns, a blacksmith shop, and an assembly room to assemble finished articles. Works sometimes employed as many as fifty hands in machine shops and produced large items such as steam engines.

Use of Machinery in Textiles

Textile manufacture was the most significant consumer industry to embrace machinery. Carding engines, spinning jennies, water frames, mules, throstles, and power looms were integral parts of American textile manufacturing. Although most Americans continued to sew their own clothing, a lesser number wove their own cloth. As they shifted to machine production, textile manufacturers reduced labor costs by replacing skilled workers with less-skilled or unskilled workers, or even children.

Much cloth was produced for local domestic markets, but imports by the heavily mechanized Europeans remained formidable. American manufacturers repeatedly protested that European authoritarian regimes kept labor costs artificially low, an unfair advantage. In labor-short America, the free labor market and comparably profitable endeavors such as farming forced manufacturers to compete for workers with relatively high wages: American textile workers received wages from 30 to 50 percent higher than their European counterparts. The Jeffersonian Embargo and the War of 1812 dramatized the new nation's dependence on European textiles, and led some to conclude that American security required the country to foster a sustainable domestic textile manufacture. Increasingly they turned to the national government for assistance. The term "American System," popularized by Henry Clay, came from these pleas, as did protective tariffs, as high as 45 percent, imposed on imported textiles in 1816, 1818, 1824, and 1828.

Part of the American textile manufacturers' difficulties in competing stemmed from the fact that the transformation from skilled labor to machinery occurred neither all at once nor at the same rate in cotton and woolen textiles. Mechanization of spinning preceded changes in weaving, and changes in cotton fabric manufacture predated those in wool manufacture. Despite these differences, early textile mills assumed a characteristic configuration. Individual operations generally were housed in separate buildings or rooms. In cotton spinning, for example, raw cotton first went to a picker house where machines clawed apart bales, removed impurities missed by cotton gins, and shaped it into clean batting sheets for carding. In another location, rotating wire-toothed cylinders called carding engines sorted out fibers and laid them parallel to form loosely twisted cotton ropes, which water frames roved. At their next destination rovings were drawn, twisted, and wound on bobbins or spindles by throstles (for strong, coarse yarn) or mules (for fine yarn). Both machines employed mechanical rollers or plates to do work formerly done by fingers, and both used flyers to guide yarn onto bobbins and spindles.

Textile machinery manufacture also occurred in textile mills. Machine shops were in basements of new mills, where mechanics built mill machinery while carpenters and masons completed the mill's structures. Rarely did mills sell machinery to competitors, but trading them was common, as was leasing inventions. The ad hoc prohibition of machinery sales helped restrict the industry to those already in operation, while trading and leasing protected inventors' rights and spread improvements among industry participants. Only with the industry's tremendous expansion in the 1820s did textile manufacturers regularly sell machines. These textile machine shops then were spun off to separate quarters, and also began to make other wares such as machine tools.

But development of textile machine shops was possible only after the introduction of British textile machines invented some decades earlier. Indeed, that was the crucial step. Americans pirated English textile machines almost as soon as they were created. Prior to 1790, British precautions had proven adequate: Americans failed to reproduce machinery that yielded cotton yarn suitable for weaving. Samuel Slater, a former English cotton-spinning mill manager, was the first in America to produce workable devices. He arrived in the United States in 1789, and was working for a New York corporation when William Almy and Smith Brown of Pawtucket contacted him about building cotton-spinning machines. Slater agreed, but only after he received a half-interest in the anticipated textile mill. The manufactory opened in 1790 and children seven to twelve years old ran the equipment. The machines were so productive and child labor so inexpensive that by 1795 raw cotton costs amounted to two-thirds of the mill's operating expenses, and it produced more than enough yarn to keep one hundred weavers occupied.

The Scholfield brothers did somewhat later for woolens what Slater had done for cotton. Experienced wool-spinners, John and Arthur left England for New England in 1793 and were joined by James in 1802. They produced an impressive series of water-powered woolen textile machines (each of which was already in operation in Britain). These included carding machines (1793), spinning jacks

(1802), machines to loosen matted wool for carding (1806), spinning jennies (1809), and mules (1810).

But neither the Scholfield brothers' success nor that of Slater stimulated a rash of textile-mill construction. As late as 1808, the brothers were virtually alone in establishing woolen manufactories, and just fifteen cotton mills operated in America; Slater owned eight. Not until they recognized their English cloth supply dependence, and the southern plantation economy's dependence on British raw cotton purchases, did Americans strive to establish their own mills. By 1814, 243 cotton-spinning mills dotted the nation. Most new cotton mills copied Slater's manufactories as Slater-trained men left Pawtucket to erect their own mills or build machinery for others.

American textile manufacturers, especially cotton-spinners, faced renewed English competition after the War of 1812. National security concerns and power loom introduction into America permitted many war-generated cotton mills to survive its conclusion. Common in England before 1810, cotton power looms initially appeared in America in 1813 at Francis Cabot Lowell's Boston Manufacturing Company, located in Waltham, Massachusetts. A wealthy entrepreneur without a technical background, Lowell had planned a textile manufactory some years earlier and in 1810 went to England, presumably for his health. There he observed power looms and returned capable of building them, assisted by local mechanics. These water-powered looms replicated hand loom action, and dominated the industry after 1820. Woolen power looms were introduced in 1816 and met general acceptance in the 1820s. Noisier but much swifter than conventional looms, power looms created a woolen and cotton yarn demand while simultaneously reducing cloth manufacturers' single greatest expense—weavers' wages.

Social Experiment at Lowell Lowell and other Boston merchants planned to erect a huge textile manufactory on the lower Merrimac River near Pawtucket Falls, twenty miles from Boston and connected to it by the Middlesex Canal. Its location on the river provided its mills with 10,000 horsepower. These men faced an awesome challenge of harnessing a forceful river system, even at flood level. Dams and races of unprecedented size and scope required construction.

These men also experimented with social technology. Lowell had visited Robert Owen's New Lanark cotton mills in Europe. That visit persuaded him that large manufacturing ventures could provide sizable profits for entrepreneurs, and character-building opportunities for workers. He convinced his associates of this curious democratic utopian combination, and the Lowell mills were the result. Opening in 1823, six years after Lowell's death, and employing almost exclusively rural New England women between the ages of seventeen and

*Women operate banks of power looms in large textile
manufactories such as Lowell Mills.*

twenty-four, the mills reflected a belief that individual success rested
on mental discipline and moral management—character—and that
repetition and regimentation taught those behaviors. Working in the
Lowell Mills provided that education. Matron-supervised dormitories
to house all the women were the scheme's linchpin. Mostly widows,
the matrons ensured that mill women dressed and acted properly;
they enforced a code that prohibited immodesty, impropriety, dishon-
esty, idleness, intemperance, profanity, dancing, and gaming. Dormitories were locked at 10 p.m. Regular church attendance was required.
Violation of regulations was grounds for dismissal.

Idleness was hardly a problem; women ran textile machinery at
least eleven and a half hours daily. Despite this commitment, Lowell
women established a school, created a broad range of morally uplift-
ing organizations, and edited a literary magazine, the Lowell *Offering.*
These activities and the dormitory situation refined Lowell women.
Mill work provided them dowries. After a stay of about four years,
many married, moved West, and became schoolteachers. The constant
turnover, lack of advertising, long hours, and severe regimen never resulted in a labor shortage. Rural women recognized that Lowell offered them opportunities for advantageous matches. Eligible men
flocked to the place to meet, court, and marry these virtuous young
women.

Prominent Europeans and Americans as different as Andrew Jackson, Edward Everett, and Davy Crockett visited these mills and applauded the experiment. Crockett summed up in 1835 the prevailing

view. He discovered at Lowell "thousands, useful to others, and enjoying all the blessings of freedom, with the prospect before them of future comfort and respectability." The Lowell social experiment was abandoned shortly after Crockett's visit as not financially profitable enough. Mills even larger than Lowell, but without its costly democratic, utopian pretensions, would become common in the mid-nineteenth century on rivers in Massachusetts, New Hampshire, and Maine.

Reducing Labor Costs

Early–nineteenth-century entrepreneurs dramatically lowered labor costs in other ways. For example, modification of the putting-out system, accompanied by decreasing skilled labor, cut shoe and boot workers' wages. No entire shoe or boot was made under a single roof or by a single individual. The rise of main shops, at which leather for uppers were cut, became the critical organizational factor. Workers carried pieces cut in the main shops to their homes, sewed seams and bindings, stitched counters and straps, and returned completed uppers. These uppers and roughly cut soles were put out to another group, makers, who would last and then sole boots and shoes at home. They then deposited the goods at main shops for inspection and sale.

Replacement of high-waged artisans with lower-paid, semi-skilled labor, much of it female, reduced costs drastically and made American shoes and boots highly competitive in the world market. South America and the West Indies imported much American footwear, and northeastern shoemen further expanded sales in the southern states.

Cost-cutting moves did not always go smoothly. Particularly in traditional craft industries such as shoe and boot manufacture, early–nineteenth-century American workers vehemently protested employers' efforts to replace artisans with less-skilled laborers, to keep wages low, and to lengthen workdays. Workers occasionally demonstrated by withholding their labor; journeymen turned out on masters and workers struck owners. Wage-earners justified their actions in a characteristic early–nineteenth-century American manner: they portrayed employers as establishing themselves as an aristocracy of wealth, and maintained that this aristocracy destroyed individual improvement opportunity.

City workers most actively protested. Groups of artisans formed local trade associations mimicking the European guild system. These secret societies, many in existence by 1800, established rules for members, wage scales, and conduct codes; they attempted to regulate the labor supply, and to maintain or boost wages. Agreements not to work in shops not employing association members, or failing to follow association guidelines, were their weapons, and they sometimes shut down manufacturers refusing their demands.

This power threatened manufacturers, who sought legal redress. In a series of decisions between 1806 and 1815, courts upheld the right of laborers to associate but defined trade-association activities as an attempt "to create a monopoly or restrain the entire freedom of trade." These rulings maintained that trade-association policies hampered individual opportunity in two senses. First, they served "to injure those who do not join their society" by making it impossible for nonmembers to work. Second, employers had "rights as precious as" those of associations and that combinations "to deprive their fellow citizens" of these rights constituted illegal conspiracies.

Outlawing closed shops left moral suasion as the trade associations' sole legal right, and association influence declined. Removal of property qualifications for voting in the early nineteenth century led workers instead to politics. Newly enfranchised laborers (virtually any white male citizen over the age of twenty-one) established workmen's political parties in the late 1820s and 1830s; political power, not economic clout, would secure equal opportunity.

These parties railed against a wealthy, nonproductive aristocracy bulwarked by special privilege and government favor and argued that their candidates' election alone could repair the situation. Workingmen's parties demanded termination of special privilege, especially banking monopolies; imprisonment for debt; and mechanics' lien laws in which a mechanic's tools (and by extension his livelihood) were seized until payment of all outstanding debts. They advocated equitable taxation, direct election of public officials, and free public education. The last would provide workers' children with advantages formerly reserved for the rich.

Workingmen's parties disappeared almost as suddenly as they began. Internecine warfare marred them as various elements battled for control, and more traditional parties co-opted many of their proposals. By 1840 they ceased to exist.

PREPARING AMERICA'S YEOMANRY

The agitation of workingmen's political parties hardly constituted a rejection of the work ethic. Those who labored were glorified: early–nineteenth-century Americans lionized Eli Whitney, Robert Fulton, and Oliver Evans. Commentators considered these American inventors the archetypal American workingmen, compared them favorably to Europe's best and brightest, and celebrated their lives and technical achievements. The two seemed closely related: lofty attainments reflected a high state of individual cultivation, which included

temperance, morality, moderation, cleanliness, godliness, and indus-
triousness. Both lofty attainments and a high state of individual cultivation seemed natural products of the American political system.
These technological stalwarts' careers reaffirmed democracy's virtues;
they demonstrated what individuals, lacking Europe's institutional
advantages but freed of social restraints, could accomplish. Their successes were natural, not the result of secret organizations, special
training unavailable to others, or hereditary advantage. Their tri-
umphs seemed analogous to those of the Founding Fathers and Andrew Jackson. That Whitney, Evans, and Fulton worked with their
hands confirmed their freedom from aristocratic pretensions. Celebration of these technologists was celebration of young America's
promise, the promise of opportunity.

A closer examination of the lives of Whitney, Evans, and Fulton
would have revealed considerably less nobility than contemporaries
maintained. Evans, for example, repeatedly lobbied Congress to expand patent protection on his devices to twenty-one years. In 1808, it
granted him an additional fourteen years on one flour mill invention,
but the next year Bushrod Washington, a federal judge and the
nephew of George, ruled that Evans's patent extension violated public
rights; it enabled Evans to maintain a monopoly to the detriment of society's members. In a fit of pique, Evans burned his entire cache of
documents and technical drawings. He refused to share any material
with his countrymen without patent protection and rejected the federal judge's designation of him as a public pariah simply for seeking
patents. Destruction of his documents ended Evans's patent quests.
His 1816 explanation of why he failed to develop a working steamboat
was telling. Evans maintained that it was not lack of ingenuity but
government's failure to provide his standing patents with ironclad en-
forcement. Instead of inventing a steamboat, Evans devoted his time
and resources to fighting lawsuits to maintain his already established
patent positions and bringing suits to stop ill-designing men from
plundering his inventions without recompense.

Whether Evans and the others were as virtuous as their countrymen articulated was certainly beside the point. The issue is not
whether those lives truly merited praise, but that early–nineteenth-
century Americans found themselves with so few lives to celebrate.
America's early promise remained largely unfulfilled, an issue of great
immediacy after about 1820 as America approached the Declaration of
Independence's fiftieth anniversary. The nation had had a half century
to prove itself. And when judged by the relative paucity of individuals
worth celebrating, America seemed disappointing.

To be sure, Americans recognized that they had begun to exploit the nation's abundance and to provide a modicum of material prosperity. But a properly functioning democratic republic in

early–nineteenth-century American terms should have yielded more than increased wealth and a handful of celebratory figures. For example, James Fenimore Cooper detected an alarming tendency among Americans to abandon democracy's principles, and to imitate European aristocracy and its privileges. That America failed to measure up to expectations also implied that it did not generate a virtuous yeomanry, the base upon which democracy presumably rested. A virtuous yeomanry must include nearly everyone to achieve America's promise. A virtuous yeoman would be self-reliant, content, healthy, educated, not necessarily wealthy but certainly not destitute, and possess character. Character would ward off material and aristocratic pretensions—the pretensions of Europe—and perpetuate democratic sentiments and interests.

Signs of aristocratic bearings appeared at a distressingly high rate. Secret societies, especially Masonic organizations, offered special privileges based solely on membership. Curiously, even something as seemingly innocuous as canning food came under scrutiny. Developed by Nicolas Appert in France and Peter Durand in Britain, the canning technique was brought to the United States by Durand's former apprentice, William Underwood, in 1817. Underwood moved to Boston in 1819. There Thomas Kensett learned the technique and in 1825 received the first American canning patent.

Kensett's methods were hardly controversial. He made a tin can from an oblong piece of tin, which he bent in the form of a cylinder and soldered the joint. Two circular pieces to be the top and bottom were cut by tin snip. Each was bent around a circular mandrel. The bottom was soldered in place as was the top, but only after a hole was cut out. This hole allowed canners to fill the vessel but also to heat it to kill bacteria and to preserve the food. After heating, but while the can was still warm, canners soldered over the hole.

Although Kensett's canning technique raised few eyebrows, what American canners, generally based from Maine to Baltimore, initially sold drew criticism. Kensett and the others canned lobster, oysters, crab, and the like; gourmet seafood for sale in the nation's interior. They quickly added seasonal fruits and vegetables to their menu, also quite expensive. A number of Americans complained that canners catered to the gastronomic pretensions of an aristocracy. They offered expensive food year-round at a high price, only because some wanted to parade their material wealth in front of their countrymen. Critics objected less to the canners' tapping the market than despairing that such a market could exist in what was supposed to be a democratic republic.

This apparent failure struck at the very heart of the idea of America. It signaled a lack of individual opportunity; those artificial barriers that prohibited more from achieving the notoriety of an Evans,

Whitney, or Fulton also seemed to prevent a far greater number from developing the character on which America's present and future depended. This fear spawned several attempts to remove obstacles through creation of increased access, including self-culture campaigns. Americans produced a massive literature to supply the crucial information, and formed a dizzying variety of new character-building associations. These organizations provided additional opportunities for individuals to associate, furnished knowledge, and fostered appropriate habits among members. Mechanics' institutes, established during the mid-1820s, exemplified that thrust.

Mechanics' Institutes

American mechanics' institutes scarcely resembled their British predecessors. Americans identified as mechanics almost all urban workingmen except merchants and bankers. Knowledge to all seeking it served as the institutes' motto; it reflected a commitment to a large segment of the population, dissatisfaction with colleges as privilege's bastion, and an attack on guilds as restrictive societies. These mechanics' associations conceived of knowledge broadly, not limited to workplaces. Evening public natural history and philosophical lectures such as "The Wisdom and Goodness of God as Evinced in the Natural History of Water" were their chief educational forays. Sometimes institutes provided more formal, although hardly more technical, schooling; they established postcommon schools that taught drawing, mathematics, Greek and Latin, rhetoric, and some science to offer participants advantages similar to college attendees.

Mechanics' institutes also furnished three important technically related services. Their boards of control created yearly prizes or premiums for solutions to specific technical problems or questions of local economic interest. Institutes also housed libraries and artifactual collections. As important, they held annual exhibitions; inventors displayed their productions, while manufacturers and merchants examined them and perhaps purchased patent rights. The exhibitions thus joined mechanics with capital.

Agricultural Societies

Contemporary agricultural societies served farmers in the same ways. Early–nineteenth-century agricultural organizations offered prizes for specified technical innovations as well as for improved fertilizing and cropping methods, and held contests to adjudicate rival claimants' contentions. Field trials placed implement-makers in conjunction with capital and consumers. Agricultural societies also catered to their members' self-culture. Presentations extolled the farmers' national position and provided guidelines—temperance, cleanliness, godliness, and the like—for farmers to prepare themselves for it.

Technical Education for the Yeomanry

Other institutions also addressed cultivation of virtuous yeomanry—sometimes from an unusual angle. The Rensselaer School, founded in 1824 by New York patroon Stephen Van Rensselaer and his associate Amos Eaton, sought to create an educated yeomanry by teaching "sons and daughters of farmers and mechanics" the philosophical underpinnings of their lives' work. Instruction in the "common purposes of life" was not to establish new facts or procedures, but to imbue future yeomen with moral discipline, responsibility, and understanding—traits essential to life's virtuous conduct.

The school's goal of an improved yeomanry led it not to teach yeomen directly but rather train persons to teach them. Although it attracted well-to-do students, the school's educational thrust mimicked master–apprentice relationships. Eaton served as master in an extraordinary variety of areas within the general rubric of "agriculture, domestic economy, the arts and manufactures." He tutored each student in teaching a particular calling, such as land surveying. Eaton performed demonstrations of various skills, and explained the scientific principles upon which these exhibitions rested. Students practiced these demonstrations and explanations before Eaton and their peers, and were graduated when they could flawlessly execute and elucidate them to the school's examining board.

Few students attended Rensselaer during its early years, and fewer graduates engaged in teaching. Eaton tried to increase the school's utility by repeatedly petitioning the New York state legislature to fund one student per county to prepare there. He also applied what he preached, using his demonstration—explanation technique in public lecture courses given directly to farmers and mechanics. His series entitled "Technology," first offered in 1830, met twice-weekly in ninety-minute sessions over a period of four months, and provided learning opportunities to its three hundred participants.

Eaton's technology lectures closely approximated Josiah Holbrook's lyceums. Holbrook reportedly witnessed the burgeoning lyceum movement among English mechanics, thought America fertile ground for such a democratic institution, and adapted it in 1826. These "associations for the purpose of mutual education" quickly proved popular; by 1834, Americans operated roughly 3,000. Like Eaton's lectures, lyceum addresses were usually open to the public and depended on scientific apparatuses—Holbrook manufactured these lyceum apparatuses—to show principles on which commonplace occurrences were based. But the substance of Eaton's series was more nearly akin to the lectures that Harvard's Jacob Bigelow had given in the Boston area since the mid-1810s. The self-proclaimed "leading exponent of technology," Bigelow helped popularize the term in America. He divided technology into elements—separate fundamental units designating categories of human productions—and maintained that these elements were bound together by a particular mode of thought. To Bigelow, technological advances depended on creative but formalized thinking, the consequences of rationality, of inductive, not empirical, thought.

Bigelow claimed that the number of American inventions indicated that this reasoning had gained a New World foothold, but he worried about its lack of pervasiveness. His lectures and writings were attempts to ensure its diffusion by making audiences aware of the rational mode of thought's significance.

MACHINERY, PRODUCTION, AND DEMOCRACY

American concern for a virtuous yeomanry produced initiatives to create it. Americans worried little about the mechanization of industry. That was not the case in England. There groups of protesters called Luddites broke machines, and others decried machinery's effects. The noted English student of German romanticism, Thomas Carlyle, framed in 1829 the question for his generation. He attacked the "mechanical philosophy," which had become "a sign of the times." Mankind's moral and aesthetic future hung in the balance as "mind will become subjected to the laws of matter" and "efforts, attachments [and] opinions" will be solely "of a mechanical character." The "external and physical is now managed by machinery," and Carlyle predicted that "the internal and spiritual" would soon yield. "In our rage for machinery, we shall ourselves become machines."

Timothy Walker, a young Cincinnati lawyer, challenged Carlyle's conclusions in a characteristically American way. He asserted in 1831 that "mechanical enterprise, . . . far from being unfavorable to our spiritual growth, is the one thing needful to furnish the freedom and leisure necessary for intellectual exercises." The mind depends on the body, he contended, and "if machines could be so improved and multiplied" to gratify all corporeal requirements, then all mankind could become "philosophers, poets and votaries of art. The whole time and thought of the whole human race could be given to inward culture, to spiritual advancement." Walker surveyed past civilizations to discover how they achieved the leisure necessary for intellectual activities and found that freedom "from the bondage of perpetual bodily toil" always involved tremendous moral costs. Past civilizations operated on the "barbarous principle that one nation may purchase itself leisure ... by aggressions upon the rest"; they provided their citizens opportunities "by levying tribute upon all other nations, and keeping slaves to perform their drudgery at home." Walker claimed that such drastic measures were no longer necessary. "Force did for [the past] what machinery does for us."

The Walker–Carlyle dialogue reflected European and American differences. Carlyle's critique stressed the approach's creative and aesthetic consequences, a predominantly European concern. It suggested to Americans an unseemly preoccupation with things generally reserved for the aristocracy and appeared a plea to perpetuate aristocratic privilege. Walker accentuated the body, arguing that machinery expanded spiritual growth opportunities by providing corporeal needs. Americans debated machinery's implications among themselves, but discussed its relation to democracy, to individual opportunity. Daniel Webster, for instance, championed material prosperity as democracy's natural result. Others feared that fondness of machines approached materialism, a glorification of wealth and material possessions. John Adams and Lyman Beecher claimed that production caused temptation, and despaired that many Americans lacked the moral strength to withstand temptations to adopt aristocratic pretensions. Matthew Carey argued more optimistically that "prosperity generally expands the heart, and leaves it accessible to the suggestions of benevolence and beneficence."

FOR FURTHER READING

Bathe, Greville and Dorothy. *Oliver Evans: A Chronicle of Early American Engineering* (1935).

Calhoun, Daniel H. *The American Civil Engineer* (1960).

Cole, Arthur Harrison. *The American Wool Manufacture* (1926), vol. 1.

Cravens, Hamilton, Alan I Marcus, and David M. Katzman, eds. *Technical Knowledge in American Culture. Science, Technology, and Medicine Since the Early 1800s* (1996).

Dilts, James D. *The Great Road. The Building of the Baltimore and Ohio, 1828–1853* (1993).

Dublin, Thomas. *Transforming Women's Work: Women's Lives in the Industrial Revolution* (1994).

Flexner, James Thomas. *Steamboats Come True* (1944).

Gibb, George S. *The Saco–Lowell Shops* (1950).

Handlin, Oscar and Mary F. *Commonwealth. A Study of the Role of Government in the American Economy: Massachusetts, 1774–1861* (1969).

Hartz, Louis. *Economic Policy and Democratic Thought: Pennsylvania, 1776–1860* (1948).

Hill, Forest G. *Roads, Rails and Waterways: The Army Engineers and Early Transportation* (1957).

Hunter, Louis C. *Steamboats on Western Rivers* (1949).

Kasson, John F. *Civilizing the Machine: Technology and Republican Values in America, 1776–1900* (1976).

McAllister, Ethel M. *Amos Eaton, Scientist and Educator, 1775–1842.* (1941).

Meyers, Marvin. *The Jacksonian Persuasion: Politics and Belief* (1957).

Roe, Joseph Wickham. *English and American Tool Builders* (1916).

Scheiber, Harry N. *Ohio Canal Era: A Case Study of Government and the Economy* (1969).

Sinclair, Bruce. *Philadelphia's Philosopher Mechanics: A History of the Franklin Institute, 1824–1865* (1974).

Smith, Billy G. *The "Lower Sort": Philadelphia's Laboring People, 1750–1800* (1990).

Smith, Merritt Roe. *Harpers Ferry Armory and the New Technology* (1977).

Thomson, Ross. *The Path to Mechanized Shoe Production in the United States* (1989).

Tucker, Barbara M. *Samuel Slater and the Origins of the American Textile Industry, 1790–1860* (1984).

Wallace, Anthony F. C. *Rockdale* (1978).

Ward, John W. *Andrew Jackson, Symbol for an Age* (1955).

Way, Peter. *Common Labour: Workers and the Digging of the North American Canals, 1780–1860* (1993).

White, John H., Jr. *A History of the American Locomotive. Its Development: 1830–1880* (1968).

PART
TWO

Uniformity, Diversity, and Systematizing America

LATE 1830s TO THE 1920s

By the late 1830s, Americans eschewed identification with the Old World and began to define themselves in a new way, as a people exhibiting a distinctive and unique character. Identifying themselves as a singular collection of people who shared the same values, manners, and ambitions had profound implications for established technologies and for the creation of new ones. Rather than as providers of individual opportunity, technologies now were championed as unifying and homogenizing the nation. Uniformity and coherence became the new sine qua non. Mid-nineteenth-century Americans adopted those technologies that measured the distinctly American character, furnished the nation's citizens with a common material experience, or enhanced the country's standing within the world of nations.

Yet identification of America as a distinctive social collection with its idyllic crusade for nationwide coherence and homogeneity did not long persist. It had collapsed in the decade following the Civil War.

Unlike their mid-nineteenth-century counterparts, late–nineteenth- and early–twentieth-century Americans routinely made distinctions among peoples, places, or things. Moreover, they treated these distinctions as real and crucial, the categories as static and discrete, and the elements in categories as both representative of those categories and fixed within them. Creation of these rigid divisions produced strife; Americans disputed what constituted legitimate categories and where those categories ended. As important, they realized that their categories did not stand alone, but instead were parts of systems, a notion that accentuated ordering the diverse categories as well as determining the appropriate locus of each system. This process of ordering—of systematizing the various categories—itself caused disagreements and consternation, but all agreed that establishing a "true" hierarchy based on objective methods and criteria was critical, because only in that manner could a system operate at optimum efficiency. In the social sphere, for example, the mid-century discussion of an American behavior or character was supplanted by the late–nineteenth-century reduction of the nation to a hierarchically arranged socioeconomic and political system.

During this fifty-year period, Americans in all walks of life developed allegedly nonpartisan strategies and techniques to measure what constituted a category, to standardize the elements of those categories, and to place them in their proper place, position, role, or the like. This systems thinking had profound technological implications. Potential new processes and technologies as well as long-standing ones were subjected to scrutiny and dissected into their component parts; new technologies were conceptualized according to this precept and old technologies were reconceptualized in a similar fashion. Indeed, it would not be incorrect to state that in the fifty years after about 1870 Americans made over their nation. "System" was the touchstone of late–nineteenth- and early–twentieth-century America, and it influenced virtually every aspect of American life.

American Nationalism: A People and Common Material Experience, late 1830s to 1870s

THE SEARCH FOR A UNIQUELY AMERICAN CHARACTER

Concern about the effects of glorification of wealth on a democratic republic receded in the late 1830s. Americans had begun to realize that their pursuit of individual objectives had, in fact, produced a civilization fundamentally dissimilar to Europe. Technology had helped foster that new civilization: it produced the transportation and communications that tied together the country's diverse settlements; produced several self-reliant, burgeoning industries; and developed a national infrastructure. Mid-century Americans sought to consolidate and build upon the fruits of their immediate past. They saw their nation as a unique social unit, marked by a people exhibiting, and defined by, a character unlike that of any other country.

A full and precise definition of the uniquely American character proved elusive, however. Mid-nineteenth-century residents of the United States repeatedly asked such questions as, what is an American? or, what do specific acts or lack of action say about Americans? but rarely did they achieve absolute consensus. Everyone recognized that Americans should love their families, go to church, be compassionate, believe passionately in democracy, and be generous but

73

thrifty as well as neat, clean, orderly, and moderate in all things. Similarly, most agreed about what an American was not. The majority of citizens thought Blacks, Mormons, some other religious groups, and the poor lacked the uniquely American character. Beyond those broad categorizations and platitudes, however, or whenever a particular situation emerged, disagreements, sometimes heated, usually surfaced. (The question of slavery—the treatment of people as property—stood as the most explosive issue.)

Yet absence of an explicit, commonly held definition of the uniquely American character is and was beside the point. What focused the attention of mid-nineteenth-century citizens was that they perceived there was or ought to be a distinctly American character, and that the nation's inhabitants exhibited that character in their behavior and activities. Mid-century Americans acted on those notions.

The Break from European Society

An explicit repudiation of Europe and a conscious distancing of America from the Old World accompanied recognition of the nation's distinctiveness. Americans saw little in Europe worth imitating, and rejected not only Europe's artificial and arbitrary privileges but also its manners, morals, and arts. Calling for creation of "a distinctly American school of good manners," they wanted a body of knowledge appropriate for the United States. In 1837, Ralph Waldo Emerson spoke for his generation. He claimed that "we have listened too long to the courtly muses of Europe," maintained that "our long apprenticeship to the learning of other lands draws to a close," and called for the emergence of a new type of person, the American Scholar. Emerson's American Scholar would come from American soil and reflect American civilization; this new person would serve a new people.

Emerson's plea reflected a subtle yet profound change in how Americans defined themselves. Other commentators took for granted America's distinctiveness, and concentrated on identifying the common character-producing mechanisms. Rarely did anyone point to technological change. The European lyceum, ironically designated as a "curiously American invention," was usually given the credit; to many mid-century Americans the lyceum provided common experience, which served as "powerful social ligaments, binding together the vast body of people" to produce a unique civilization.

No matter what explanation was offered for this new American distinctiveness, the notion highlighted the idea of nationwide coherence, and Americans labored in the 1840s and after to achieve and maintain this coherence. They embraced technology to further unify and homogenize America. Improved transportation and communication technologies helped to achieve this unification: Railroad expansion, coupled with telegraphy, bound city and country, state and nation. Clipper ships joined ports, steam commuter railroads connected cities and distant suburbs, and omnibuses and horse-drawn street railways linked city sections. Mid-century technologies also permitted Americans to tap the nation's natural resources in new ways, at new locations, and on a grander scale. Coal- and wood-fueled steam power began to challenge waterpower and freed enterprising manufacturers from dependence on rivers and streams. Manufactories spread into previously impractical areas and soon blanketed the nation; manufacturing became a process to which few Americans remained unexposed. Some entrepreneurs recognized that a unified, homogenized America would create a nationwide demand for similar goods—a common material experience—and geared up their establishments to milk that demand. They introduced new production techniques, established the factory as the quintessential industrial locus, and distributed their products nationwide. They also devised new promotional strategies to convince a sometimes skeptical public the intrinsic American quality of themselves, their products, and their production methods.

American distinctiveness did not mean that the Old World ceased to influence American affairs. The nation repeatedly sparred economically with Great Britain, and passed twelve additional tariff measures to control the influx of European goods. Irish, German, and Swedish immigrants flocked to America in unprecedented numbers—more than five million between 1850 and 1870—bringing skills and expanding the labor force. Europe remained a fertile ground for inventions, furnished much-needed railroad and industrial capital, and sympathized with the Confederacy during the Civil War. Yet the nation's distinctive destiny, whether manifest or not, captured the American imagination. It fueled geographic expansion and the Mexican War, a nativist movement, competition between the industrial North and agricultural South, and a persistent argument about slavery. Ironically, this same thrust led Americans to interact with and challenge Europe—even as they repudiated the Old World—as the nation strove to achieve what its citizens considered the country's rightful place as a leading and vital member of the world of civilizations.

Using Technology to Find America—Photography

The way that Americans manipulated and employed the European invention of photography provides a graphic representation of how the notion of a distinctive American character influenced technology. In August 1839, the Frenchman L. J. M. Daguerre announced the first photographic process, the daguerreotype. Polished silverplated copper sheets, subjected to iodine vapor, constituted his film. Daguerre shielded the light-sensitive plate in a box with a lens. His simple camera had no shutter: Daguerre simply removed the lens cap to expose the plate. He developed the image by subjecting the plate to mercury vapor, and fixed (stopped development and stabilized the image) with sodium thiosulfate. Daguerre had conceived of his process as an extension of the then-popular diorama—an enormous painting, which gives the appearance of three-dimensionality—and used it to photograph landscapes. A long exposure time (a minimum of fifteen minutes at high noon in the summer sun), suitable only for reproducing inanimate objects, caused him no concern.

That was not the case in America. Within months of Daguerre's announcement, several Americans, including Alexander Wolcott, a New York manufacturer of dental supplies; Samuel F. B. Morse, a chaired professor of sculpture and painting at New York University; and John William Draper, Morse's NYU colleague, modified the process. Unlike Daguerre, these Americans attempted to adapt photography to portraits. Although Morse failed to improve upon Daguerre, his contemporaries were more successful. By October 1839, Wolcott had produced his first portrait. Draper followed two months later. Draper decreased his lens' focal length, sharpening the picture and speeding the process. Wolcott adopted the astronomical technique of a concave mirror concentrating the image on the plate. These two modifications reduced daguerreotype exposure time considerably. Indoor portraits now took from forty seconds to two minutes, while the sitting time for outdoor portraits varied from a scant twenty to ninety seconds.

Portraits captivated mid-century Americans. By 1841, most principal municipalities had daguerreotype studios, often decorated like elegant parlors. A decade later, an estimated 2,000 American daguerreotypists took more than three million portraits annually. More than 100 studios operated in New York City alone. These portraits were expensive, generally costing between one and two dollars. Wooden cases with velvet, metal foil, and glass layers protected the copper plates' fragile image, adding to the price.

The daguerreotype's popularity was even more remarkable because it competed with another simpler, much less-costly technique, the calotype. Developed by Britisher William Henry Fox Talbot around 1840, calotypes were well known in America. Calotypists used cameras similar to those employed by daguerreotypists, but finished calotypes dispensed with expensive cases. Calotypes used a paper film, not copper plates. A photosensitive silver salt was spread on translucent paper, exposed, developed with gallic acid, and fixed, producing a negative. Similarly treated paper was placed under the negative and exposed to the sun. The result was a positive, a replication of the initial image. And each negative yielded any number of nearly identical positives.

Americans considered the calotype's fatal flaw to be that light diffused through the translucent, sensitized paper and created a somewhat fuzzy picture. (Europeans viewed it as desirably "stylized.") Daguerreotypes more exactly recorded a subject, and Americans paid for a faithful representation of their appearance. Appearance seemed an outward manifestation of character, revealing the inner self. Comparison of portraits taken some time apart enabled subjects to check character development, and to measure how closely their character approximated the distinctly American archetype. That American daguerreotypists often were phrenologists (examiners of skull shape to determine character), physiognomists (examiners of body conformation to determine character), or portrait painters, was no accident. To the overwhelming majority of mid-century Americans, daguerreotypes, portraits, and phrenologic and physiognomic analyses revealed the critical element of character—to be held up to the new American ideal.

Although daguerreotypes remained popular through the 1860s, a new photographic process challenged them in the mid-1850s. Reported in 1851 by Frederick Scott Archer, an English sculptor, collodion photography used guncotton dissolved in sulfuric ether—collodion—as a binder/carrier of the photoactive chemicals. It was spread on a glass plate, impregnated first with bromides and then silver nitrate to produce a photoactive surface, and inserted in a camera. Photographers developed the image with gallic acid, then fixed it. Glass negatives made paper positives.

At first few chose collodion because of image migration. Not until the late 1850s, when the diffusion problem was resolved and accurate portraits could be produced, did the inexpensive positive collodion-paper prints become common. American photographers printed the image on salted, unsensitized albumen covering the paper, not the paper itself, which did not blur images because neither light nor chemicals migrated.

PROVIDING A COMMON MATERIAL EXPERIENCE

Setting the Stage

Daguerreotypes and collodion photography took America by storm because they recorded and measured character. Several industries also capitalized on the growing nationalist sentiment, and marketed and distributed their products nationwide. Their pitch incorporated the notion that a homogeneous, unified, and distinct America demanded a characteristically American material experience.

Demand for a common American material experience proved so compelling that consumers welcomed nationally distributed goods even as local manufactories were destroyed. National distribution was pronounced in mid-nineteenth-century food industries. Buffalo and Rochester became national flour-milling centers, and Baltimore, then Cincinnati, and finally Chicago dominated the American hog-slaughtering trade. The demand was likewise evident in manufactured products. For example, New England emerged as the nation's textile headquarters. Cyrus McCormick and Isaac Singer successfully marketed nationwide reapers and sewing machines respectively. Yet those with national marketing aspirations did not adopt identical distribution or manufacturing techniques. Production techniques and sales strategies differed drastically among manufacturers, as generally did the quality—and sometimes even the style—of goods produced by a single firm and distributed nationally under a single name. Indeed, furnishing a common American material experience required industrialists only to convince purchasers of the uniformity of productions. It did not necessitate producing identical goods.

Several mid-nineteenth-century initiatives facilitated national production, marketing, and distribution. Reassessment of the corporation's place within American society increased corporate numbers and size, unleashed capital by making corporations attractive investments, and accentuated the role of technical capabilities of corporate managers. The Supreme Court's Charles River Bridge decision (1837), among the earliest expressions of that corporate reassessment, was not immediately recognized as a potent agent of change. The Court found corporate charters neither inviolate, perpetual, nor exclusive, and permitted states to modify or revoke charters whenever the public interest dictated.

The Court's ruling mollified states establishing public interest as distinct from and superior to private, and society as superior to the individual (because corporations continued to be treated as individuals in law). But the Court's affirmation of state power made states generally confident enough to relax corporate supervision, and loosen the corporate mechanism. The states' ability to revise corporate charters, coupled with the demise of mixed corporations implicit in the public/private separation, led state governments to create numerous new corporations, to become less immediately involved in corporate activities, and often to cede their oversight authority. Creation of general state laws of incorporation to replace special legislative acts to form corporations reflected both state optimism in its capacity to rein in renegade corporate entities and recognition that corporations, especially manufacturing and commercial enterprises, furthered the public interest. Often framed during the spate of mid-century state constitution redrafting, general incorporation laws required only that individuals follow generalized guidelines, file incorporation articles with state secretaries, and issue annual reports.

The states' lenient exercise of power made corporate investment attractive, which produced more corporations and more capital for technological endeavors. Large corporations freed themselves of state-mandated sets of particularized regulations. Absence of these restrictions made investors more directly accountable for a corporation's commercial or manufacturing success. Profit depended on corporate initiatives, not state-specified procedures, and investors placed their firms under control of people well-versed in their corporations' technical activities. These technicians understood the business's complexity, which investors gambled would yield larger returns. Conversely, freedom from day-to-day corporate cares and reporting permitted investors to back a wider assortment of enterprises, which insulated them from the periodic business fluctuations. Unlike the early nineteenth century, when fortunes were routinely made and lost, mid-century capitalists frequently retained their wealth because they diversified their economic activity.

Mid-century governmental activities and policies helped create and stabilize fortunes. They supported some corporate ventures—the public/private distinction seldom was equated with absolute government/corporate separation—though not as partners but as contractors. These limited-duration wares or service contracts did not impinge on investors' abilities to set corporate priorities, missions, or activities, but provided favored entities additional operating capital and guaranteed markets. Government contracts, then, enabled investors to gain, without sacrificing autonomy, secure minimum returns on their investments, which they could use to capitalize other projects. This policy, however, like diversification of assets by the wealthy, was to begin in America rigid and permanent socioeconomic inequities at the very moment that people paraded their newfound national coherence.

Railroads Ascendant

Railroads quickly outstripped canals as the nation's primary overland transportation mode. In the two decades after 1840, Americans laid track totaling 26,000 miles. During the same period almost as many canal miles were abandoned as built. Prewar railroad construction focused in the Northeast and Old Northwest, and many new roads supplanted established canal routes.

Railroads offered entrepreneurs the virtues of speed, all-weather dependability, and flexibility as well as larger cargo capacities. Huge capital and maintenance costs for rails, locomotives, and rolling stock

*Mid–nineteenth-century railroads were complex
enterprises that were instrumental in catering to
national markets.*

were drawbacks. Despite these expenses, Americans built and maintained the overwhelming majority of prewar railroads with no or little
governmental assistance. The East's and Old Northwest's relatively
dense population, their comparatively many manufactories, and the
earlier success of turnpikes and canals made railroads attractive investments. But the massive sums of money necessary to construct and
keep up lines required arrangements more substantial than ad hoc
consortiums of local citizens. New York City merchants and their
bankers funded large enterprises. The city's fine harbor had brought
them much of the European trade—establishment of packet lines to
England and the cotton-rich South also provided crucial assistance—
while its Erie Canal connection captured considerable western trade.
These men had experienced improved transportation's financial benefits and ventured significant amounts on railroads, especially with the
new state corporate policy.

Mid-century railroad capitalization pioneered new ground, but
railroad hardware underwent no similar revision. Only the mid-century railroads' scale separated them from their predecessors. That was
no small matter. National or regional transportation businesses created logistical problems. Larger railroad lines operated over unprecedented distances, employed huge, diverse staffs, and became America's biggest iron consumers. They encountered a wide array of
difficulties and hazards as each coordinated its internal affairs. Profits
depended on a line's smooth function; iron shortages, insufficient or

mispositioned rolling stock, mechanical breakdowns and accidents cost investors money. Investors confronted these issues in three ways. First, investors selected men with broad practical, technical, railroad-related know-how to oversee company activities. These railroad generalists had considerable experience—a few had formal training at West Point or elsewhere—and could anticipate and resolve problems, assess situations promptly, and develop efficient operations plans. Second, investors demanded that railroads keep detailed records. Meticulous record-keeping produced data for rational choices; it was the technology for managers to make sound decisions. Exact records also furnished investors information to adjudicate managerial effectiveness. Third, railroads embraced electrical telegraphy.

Railroads and Telegraphy Telegraphy offered almost instantaneous communication over long distances; its judicious use permitted railroads to prevent situations and conditions from becoming problems, to remedy unanticipated difficulties, and to synchronize operations. This American telegraph–railroad nexus flowered after 1850, but electrical telegraphy was much older, a predominantly European invention. Early telegraphs were quite cumbersome. They expressed reception of electrical impulses through electrolysis or deflection of galvanometer needles and required multiple circuits to represent the entire alphabet. Samuel F. B. Morse adapted the telegraph to American conditions; the country's great size made multiple-circuit transmission prohibitively expensive. His practical high-speed devices were single-circuit telegraphs in which long-distance transmission was accomplished by relay.

Morse had begun his telegraphic musings in 1832. An artist and portrait painter who, like Fulton, had studied in Europe with Benjamin West, Morse was an inveterate mechanical dabbler and had tinkered with fire pumps and marble-cutting machines. Simplicity marked his early telegraphic speculations. Morse initially conceived of using coded type to transmit words. A unique series of spaces and teeth characterized each type letter. Telegraphers would arrange letters on composing sticks and draw them past a contact. The electrical circuit would open at spaces and close at teeth, transmitting words as dots and dashes. Morse's receiver/recorder was similarly elegant. Incoming signals tripped an electromagnet, which activated a pen that moved across paper advanced by clockwork. Operators then translated recorded dots and dashes.

Morse had considerable difficulty in producing a working line, but Leonard D. Gale, professor of geology and mineralogy at New York University, alerted him in 1836 to Joseph Henry's 1831 paper. It argued that long-distance electromagnetic transmission required high voltages (many battery cells connected in series) and powerful

*The key with the sounder speeded and simplified
telegraphy.*

electromagnets (using many turns of wire). Their empirical understanding of what would become Ohm's Law enabled Gale and Morse
to transmit a signal ten miles. Morse further extended the telegraph's
range with a relay (a distant electromagnet), which, upon receiving the
original signal, automatically engaged and disengaged an independent battery replicating the message. He then acquired another partner, Alfred Vail, an NYU graduate who built instruments from
Morse's designs.

In 1838, the group gave demonstrations at Vail's father's Speed-
well Ironworks in Morristown, New Jersey; at NYU; and at the
Franklin Institute. They also exhibited the device to President Van
Buren and his cabinet, and the House Committee on Commerce, but
not until 1843 did Congress grant Morse $30,000 to string an experi-
mental line. By that time, Morse had replaced composing sticks and
type with his famous key. Substitution of sounders for recorders came
several years later.

The experimental line was completed a year later, followed the
Baltimore & Ohio Railroad's tracks, and connected Baltimore and
Washington. Locating the nation's first telegraph line along a railroad
proved prophetic. Even before the wire was strung, some Americans
championed telegraphy's potential to create a "most speedy inter-
course ... between the most distant parts of the country" and predicted that "space will be, to all practical purposes of information,
completely annihilated." It would become yet another means to
achieve and maintain national coherence.

Business immediately recognized telegraphy's advantages. The
postal service and military quickly adopted it, and newspapers and

traders soon followed. By September 1846, American telegraph companies had strung hundreds of miles of wire, and had joined New York to Boston and to Harrisburg, Pennsylvania, and Washington, D.C., to Mobile. The Ohio River cities were added the next year and New Orleans a year later.

Establishing telegraphic connections to New Orleans corresponded to the beginning of a five-year period (1848–1853) of particularly rapid railroad expansion during which small, independent lines were consolidated to form the four great railroad corporations operating east–west trunk lines: the Baltimore & Ohio, Erie, New York Central, and Pennsylvania Railroads. These trunk lines each traveled without disruption between the eastern seaboard and western river cities. Independent lines before consolidation lacked uniformity; each had used tracks of different gauges (or distances between rails). Trains could run only where gauges for locomotive, rolling stock, and track matched. Each time a line with track of a different gauge was encountered, goods had to be unloaded from one train and reloaded on another. Formation of trunk lines, each with a uniform but different gauge, saved time, money, and equipment costs, and rendered national distribution of products more attractive.

Not until 1852 did a trunk line—the Erie—employ telegraphy extensively. But once that precedent had been set, a railroad–telegraphy nexus became a foregone conclusion. Railroad managers recognized the telegraph's significance to efficient railroad operations, and telegraphers realized the convenience of using their largest customers' rights of way. Between 1852 and 1860, Americans built 23,000 miles of telegraph lines, and railroads stretched to Burlington, Iowa, and St. Joseph, Missouri.

Telegraph companies confronted economic questions in the mid-1850s not unlike those fostering formation of railroad trunk lines several years earlier. To be sure, telegraph lines were cheaper to erect than railroads, but telegraphic instruments, receiving stations, batteries, poles, and wires required substantial capital. Most early telegraph companies failed; competition over routes meant duplicate lines and low revenues. In 1857, the six largest remaining companies reduced expenses by dividing the nation into six sections, using each other's lines in their respective sections and sharing profits on intersectional messages. Three companies did not survive competition from smaller companies in their sections, and were absorbed by the remaining three. These survivors further pooled resources in 1866 to create Western Union. This giant company then turned to New York for additional capital to expand operations, destroy competition, and dominate the telegraphic industry nationwide. Like the railroads, Western Union was superintended by men with extensive practical experience.

Governmental Investment in Railroads Telegraphic expansion continued after Western Union's formation. About 25,000 new miles were added from 1860 to 1868, and a line first joined the coasts in 1861, beating the more expensive railroads by nearly a decade. Rail construction had slowed during the Civil War but reached unprecedented rates immediately upon the war's conclusion. Over 35,000 miles were laid between 1865 and 1873. Some new mileage in the East went to creating single-gauge express lines on high-volume, profitable runs. Rather than compete for this business, the new trunk lines pooled expenses, rights of way, and equipment. They laid out these lines to not interfere with the partners' other runs, placed them under a single manager, and shared profits. The West and South received the remainder of the new railroad mileage—the majority. In 1869 the Central Pacific and Union Pacific Railroads met at Promontory Point in the Utah territory to form the nation's first transcontinental railway. This event both symbolized national unification and linked the East Coast commercial center, New York City, with its West Coast counterpart, San Francisco.

Tying the West and South to East by railroad was essential for establishing nationwide distribution of goods, but New York City-based capitalists remained leery of investing in them. Neither the South, devastated by the Civil War, nor the sparsely settled West promised the high-volume runs necessary for quick monetary returns. Citing an explicit national purpose—military defense and settlement of the nation's interior—the federal government frequently interceded when private sources refused to furnish capital. As it had occasionally prior to the Civil War (such as the Illinois Central, linking Chicago and Cairo), Congress granted public lands to states to turn over to railroad companies as they completed laying sections of track. Congress itself handled these transactions in the territories. These free lands usually abutted lines and thus were prime real estate. Railroads would sell these parcels at premium prices, then use revenues to build further.

These measures were sometimes insufficient, especially in the western mountains where relatively few people chose to live, and Congress shouldered the financial burden further by lending railroads money. Such was the case with the Union Pacific and Central Pacific, a move justified by the idea that a transcontinental railroad was a matter of compelling national interest.

Railroads and the Iron Industry Expansion of railroads and introduction of telegraphy to form nationwide transportation and communication linkages depended on a ready supply of iron. So, too, did development of other industries; nails, suspension-bridge cables, steam engines, stoves, line shafting, and structural elements such as construction beams devoured large quantities of the metal. American iron industry's explosive growth before the Civil War was caused by these demands, and the nation produced an impressive 821,000 tons in 1860. Americans relentlessly promoted their product, claiming that the country's ores gave American iron a distinctive "character" that was "superior . . . in its strength and purity" to European irons. Yet patriotic blustering and statistics paint a somewhat misleading picture; American iron demand exceeded American supply, and the country remained an iron-importing nation. The country's production lagged far behind the British total of 3.8 million tons in 1860, which subjected American industrial development to higher prices and periodic shortages.

Dependence on foreign iron had long galled Americans, but the nation's abundant forests argued against adoption of European coal-based smelting practice. As late as 1830, the large majority of American iron was produced in a manner similar to colonial iron. But the situation changed rapidly soon afterward. By 1860, over half was smelted using anthracite coal in or near eastern Pennsylvanian cities.

Americans had known of northeastern Pennsylvania's large anthracite deposits from the 1810s, and had roasted the coal in large iron retorts to generate gas for illuminating cities late in the decade. But difficulties igniting the hard, almost-pure carbon substance, coupled with American skepticism about coal's value for smelting (Europeans dealing with bituminous, or high-sulfur coal, had found that this impurity, unless removed, yielded a brittle inferior iron), and the nation's ubiquitous forests precluded use of coal in iron manufacture. The nation's initial period of railway construction placed sudden, severe strains on the Eastern charcoal-iron industry, however, and new avenues were explored to lessen pressure. Americans turned to anthracite in the late 1820s, but only to reheat wrought or cast iron for final product manufacture. This low-temperature process of brief duration did not subject iron to possible contamination. Hoping to develop a substantial coal market, Pennsylvania coal-mine operators seized upon this precedent to introduce anthracite in the more challenging conversion of pig iron to wrought iron. Pig iron was melted in an anthracite-fired reverberatory furnace (success in igniting the coal and controlling furnace temperatures were the most formidable tasks), which kept the metal from direct contact with coal and its impurities. An iron bar stirred the molten metal, exposing its carbon to the air and causing some to burn off. The iron was taken from the furnace, allowed to stiffen somewhat, and squeezed through rollers to drive off additional carbon.

Use of anthracite coal in the primary iron smelting phase began after 1840. Eastern mine operators, confident that their anthracite contained virtually no iron-ruining sulfur, adopted the hot-air-blast method, first patented in Britain in 1828 to ignite hard Scottish coal by heating the air before a steam-powered bellows blew it into the furnace.

Hot-air blasts solved the anthracite ignition problem, and because anthracite, unlike the friable charcoal, could withstand enormous weight, smelters built huge new furnaces. These new furnaces operated year-round; steam engines freed smelters from dependence on often-frozen rivers to power their bellows. Further, use of anthracite liberated them from highly paid colliers and slow, costly charcoal production. By 1849, sixty anthracite furnaces were located in eastern Pennsylvania, employing an average of eighty persons and capitalized at an average $83,000. Just four years later, forty new furnaces had sprung up.

Anthracite iron made few inroads west of the Appalachian Mountains. Transmontane shipment of anthracite, heavy iron goods, or ore were impractical. A great coal seam ran near Pittsburgh, but this coal was high-sulfur bituminous coal, not anthracite. Pittsburgh ironmen had employed this material in rolling mills quite early, shipped finished goods down the Ohio River, and created the leading western iron city. But Pittsburgh iron had been smelted in country-situated, charcoal-powered blast furnaces, and refined in similarly fueled and located forges. Not until the late 1840s—about a decade later than the East—did reverberatory furnaces, in this case bituminous coal-driven ones, secure a Pittsburgh foothold. By 1850, their domination was nearly complete. Eighty-five percent of Pittsburgh rolled-iron was made from city-refined iron (using bituminous coal) smelted in country furnaces (which had used charcoal).

Pittsburgh coal and coal technologies traveled the Ohio with finished iron products and took root at Wheeling, Cincinnati, and Ashland, Kentucky. These nascent ironworks, like Pittsburgh itself, depended exclusively on charcoal-smelted iron until just prior to the Civil War. Bituminous coal-fueled smelting furnaces gained significance in the postwar decades. Rendering coal into coke (heating coal in an oxygen-deficient atmosphere) rid it of much sulfur and produced a purer, easily ignited, hotter-burning material. Britain had been coking since the early eighteenth century, and this imported technology ultimately transformed Pittsburgh into America's iron smelting capital.

Railroads and the Steel Industry Bituminous coal-smelted iron became as important to the nation's railways in the 1860s as bituminous coal-refined iron had been to the Old Northwest's railroads from the 1840s. But in the mid-1850s, several railroad owners and rail manufacturers had worried about the rate at which huge locomotives wore out the finest iron rails—sometimes in less than two years—and investigated steel as an alternative.

Until then, virtually all American steel had been blister steel. Thin wrought-iron strips were sealed with charcoal dust in clay vessels and baked at high temperatures for up to ten days. This long process cemented carbon from the charcoal dust to the iron's surface to form a thin steel layer, which blistered under the great heat. This expensive, superior-strength material was used primarily for springs and fine cutlery, and railroad men understood that blister steel's cost and performance would not suit their needs. Instead, a new English steel-manufacturing technology captured their attention.

Henry Bessemer, an English inventor, had determined that air blown through molten pig iron would ignite the carbon in the iron and fuel the metal's refinement. If combustion could be controlled and terminated before all carbon was consumed, the superior form of iron known as steel would result. Bessemer designed a pear-shaped converter to regulate the reaction, and received a U.S. patent for his process and converter in 1856.

Yet Bessemer's patent did not result in a rapid railroad shift to steel. William Kelly, a Kentucky ironmaster who maintained that he earlier had refined pig iron through combustion of its carbon, challenged the patent almost immediately. Although Kelly had failed to develop a commercial process, the patent office was persuaded by his documentation and awarded him patent rights to the idea; Bessemer retained his converter patent. The situation was muddled further by a U.S. patent issued to England's Robert Mushet, who could not stop carbon combustion at precisely the proper point. He circumvented that problem by decarbonizing the iron completely, then introducing spiegeleisen, a compound of iron, manganese, and carbon, to impart an exact amount of carbon to form nearly uniform steel.

Large-scale commercial steel production depended on these three patents. No American organization controlled them all until after the Civil War. As late as 1865, Americans produced a paltry 15,000 tons of the material, nearly all of it blister steel. That was soon to change. In the early 1860s, a Wyandotte, Michigan, group had purchased the Kelly and Mushet patents, while entrepreneurs from Albany and Troy, New York, had obtained Bessemer's rights. Although both consortiums built steel-manufacturing facilities, they avoided possible protracted legal battles and pooled their patents in 1866 to form the Pneumatic Steel Company. The pool also limited the output of each licensee to ensure a high price for the material. Even these restrictions did not dampen American steel's meteoric rise. In 1876, the nation's producers made 470,000 tons of steel, a thirty-one-fold increase in eleven years. Almost all of this Bessemer steel went to manufacture rails.

Furnishing Uniform Goods

Attempts to provide a common American material experience encouraged manufacturers to expand production capabilities and to accentuate regularized production; money was to be made by producing nearly uniform goods for a nearly uniform people. Mid-century production for the masses required neither that finished products be identical nor that their parts be interchangeable. Uniformity—similarity or certainty that products were similar (even when they were not)—generally satisfied customers. Achievement of uniformity was accomplished in several ways. Establishment of brand names (a company's reputation as guarantor of similarity) and identification of product type (familiarity of nomenclature as guarantor of similarity) were common means to achieve uniformity, as was machine-based production itself.

The New American Factory A characteristically American locus of large-scale production, the factory, was identified during this period. Generally located on cities' fringes near railroad terminals, mid-century factories differed in both form and function from artisans' shops and, according to contemporaries, from European manufacturing establishments. These large industrial facilities contained batteries of machines, foundries, or furnaces; employed large numbers of operators; and were driven by central power sources (either waterwheels or steam engines). Power was transmitted from prime movers to upright iron shafts (shafting was wooden in some of the earliest American establishments), then throughout buildings by iron horizontal line shafts. Located near ceilings, line shafts were supported by lubricated journals, which preserved motive power. In early American factories, wooden and cast-iron gears and pulleys carried power from line shafts to individual machines, but this millwork could not withstand the stress of the higher shaft speeds of the late 1830s and after. The English developed a rigid system of precision, toothed, wrought-iron gearing suitable for the task, but Americans lacked a highly refined gear-cutting industry. They pioneered instead the use of leather belts. Joined in endless loops and stretched over pulleys or drums fastened to line shafts, belts ran around pulleys on machine drive-shafts. Belts were quieter, performed more smoothly, cost less than metal gears, and were readily installed and repaired. Load dictated machine arrangement in factories; machines requiring the greatest amount of power were placed at beginnings of lines.

American belting provided a flexible power train when compared to European gear-based practices—a fact that did not escape American notice. Cone pulleys permitted some change of speed ratios at individual machines, and clutches engaged and disengaged machines independently. In European manufacturing plants, engagement of prime movers usually produced continual operation of all individual machines, each at only one speed. But this relative American flexibility, although championed by American millwrights as a tribute to American ingenuity, also had its costs. Millwrights fretted about changes in belt tension and slippage, as well as lubrication problems. The first two caused uneven and undependable performance—and therefore less uniform products—while inadequate lubrication resulted in power loss, excessive wear, breakage, overheating, and fires. Indeed, American belting was so complicated and so troublesome that at least eight different American millwrights published volumes of rules to govern power train construction and care.

Several economic factors might have given mid-century Americans pause in their desire to establish factories. Factory power trains were very expensive to build and maintain, and securing production machines and erecting appropriate edifices required great capital investment. Manufacturers made a profit on their investment only as machines replaced skilled workers, reduced labor costs, and increased production. That these economic calculations were rarely formally considered before entrepreneurs made decisions to begin factory construction indicates that factory establishment was a matter not simply of economics, but also, for want of a better term, of style. In mid-century America, machine-based production was equated with uniform production. In shoe and boot manufacture, for example, adoption of steam-powered pegging and sewing machines and binding and punch presses, promised production of more nearly uniform footwear.

The New American Factory Worker But mid-century factories manufactured more than uniform goods. The routine of factory life, which accompanied uniform production, also yielded American factory workers who were more uniform than their predecessors. A common work experience was "manufactured" by employee-regulating work codes, which stressed responsibility, morality, and cleanliness. Those most adept at demonstrating their adaptation to these codes rose from the ranks to assume supervisory positions, working as foremen on factory floors.

Establishing a Brand Name—I. M. Singer Uniform products were the result of something more than uniform American factory workers. Character formed the basis of evaluation in mid-century America and, in manufacturing, it served as proof of a firm's dependability. Character provided consumers security by emphasizing predictability, precision, and time-tested production techniques—all of which echoed uniformity. But character was an inward trait, and Americans usually equated it with the more public reputation (or appearance, as in daguerreotype photography). Reputation and character were not necessarily synonymous, however. Reputations could be created and marketed. Recognition by some entrepreneurs that they could create and advertise reputations for themselves, their products, and their companies catapulted their corporations into the first rank.

I. M. Singer and Company was perhaps the most notable example of the reputation marketing. Singer never claimed to have invented the sewing machine, only to have perfected it—a claim he reiterated whenever he modified its design. His participation in the pooling of rival claimants' patents in 1856 indicates the degree of Singer's indebtedness: to Walter Hunt for his lock stitch, to Elias Howe for his grooved, eye-pointed needle and second-thread shuttle, and to Allen B. Wilson for his four-motion-cloth-feeding mechanism, among others. Presser-foot and needlecam-bar patents and use of a straight, vertical needle were Singer's most noteworthy contributions.

But the 1856 agreement merely ended patent infringement suits among litigants; it did not mark the beginnings of sewing-machine production. As early as 1850, several manufacturers had made machines. All promoted their product. Tailors in eastern cities quickly integrated these machines into the manufacture of "ready-made" clothing. Rather than fit each individual, tailors from the 1830s had made set patterns, cut cloth according to those patterns, and then contracted out the stitching, first to seamstresses, now to persons with sewing machines. These inexpensive batches of uniform clothing were loose-fitting, coarse productions, purchased in great number by plantation owners for slaves, by church groups for the urban poor, and by bachelors. But while sewing machines were catching on, only Singer showed a true genius for promoting himself. Identifying himself as a "self-made" man in "a country of self-made men," Singer barnstormed the nation with his machines. He gave demonstrations at carnivals and fairs and sometimes even rented halls. He regularly advertised in the penny press, circulated pamphlets, hired agents, and in 1855 published his own periodical, the *I. M. Singer and Co. Gazette,* which he distributed free of charge.

Singer and Company proved even more inventive after the 1856 patent accord. As competitors concentrated on developing a superior, more elegantly manufactured product, Singer focused on spreading the company name. For instance, Wheeler and Wilson Manufacturing Company produced interchangeable-part sewing machines by 1863, and Willcox and Gibbs had adopted that production technique even earlier. But Singer still persisted in manufacturing machines requiring fitters, even though he sold his less-precisely manufactured product at prices comparable to others. Singer machine owners could not replace broken parts with company-supplied ones, but had to pay artisans to fashion and install substitute parts or purchase new machines. Advertising compensated for Singer's technical deficiencies. The company claimed to use "precision in the application of mechanical means" to make the "universal sewing machine"; Singer created a reputation for precision production rather than engage in it.

Singer's marketing strategy forged a reputation for the company as archetypically American, the sewing-machine company that demonstrated most nearly those characteristics thought to define the

An elegant atmosphere characterized Singer
showrooms such as this one in New York City.

distinctly American civilization. The company advertised itself as generous, benevolent, reverent, and family-oriented. In 1856, for example, it held a "Grand Invitation Ball" for Singer machine owners and operators as well as company employees. More than three thousand people attended. It later sold machines to church pastors at half-price, leased machines to individuals with options to buy, and established a trade-in policy in which owners traded Singer their machines, whatever make (the company destroyed these "inferior" articles), for a $50 credit toward purchase of new Singers.

The American family received the company's most sustained attention. Trumpeting its products as "the most important labor saving machines of the century," Singer marketed the idea that ownership of Singer machines ought to characterize the nation's families. Establishment of sewing emporiums in large and medium-sized towns was essential to the plan. Kept clean, proper, and cheery to encourage women to enter, Singer emporiums furnished refreshments and some-times presents. Agents personally demonstrated machines to each visitor, commented on their superiority to hand-sewing, and maintained that they reflected the highest quality workmanship. That Singers lightened a mother's load rested at the heart of the agent's pitch: time saved sewing freed women for other familial activities and duties; conversely, women without Singers were implicitly culpable of neglecting more crucial familial responsibilities. Singer's emphasis on the family culminated in 1873 with introduction of its "New Family" model. That machine dominated the market. Singer produced about five hundred thousand a year by 1880. The brand name had become synonymous with sewing.

Other Technologies and the Distinctly American Woman Singer was hardly alone in targeting the distinctly American woman. Americans agreed with Catharine Beecher, author of the classic *Treatise on Domestic Economy*. It was the American woman's job to mold the family's character to create the new American family. Anything that raised the family's morals and eased woman's burden was desirable. Introduction of cast-iron plate stoves from the late 1830s promised to do both. Unlike the open hearths they replaced, stoves were variable, the use of dampers permitting several things to be cooked at several different temperatures at once. Manufacturers marketed these relatively inexpensive devices in large illustrated newspaper and magazine advertisements, complete with claims about how stoves would free women from mundane tasks and enable them to devote more time to their children and husbands. Manufacturers also hired agents to demonstrate their product at county fairs, often in competition with other brands. These agents were permitted to give stoves to prominent citizens in return for testimonials and to induce women to purchase these marvels by including attractive perks such as a complete set of pots and pans or installment buying.

Refrigerator use also helped define the new American woman. A rather simple form proved the most popular. Refrigerators, essentially tin- or zinc-lined wooden boxes, had shelves and food compartments. The earliest refrigerators placed the ice on the bottom, but the later devices moved it to the top. Heat rose and cold air sunk. Placing ice at top led to natural circulation and more even cooling. Steam-powered saws and other cutting devices, along with huge versions of these new domestic refrigerators, enabled northern icemen to harvest great amounts of their ware, and store and ship it throughout the United States year-round to power the new home refrigerators.

The incredible power granted the New American woman to dictate familial customs and arrangements also extended to sex. For the first time in American history, wives dictated terms of sexual interaction. Abstinence and self-denial were two technologies frequently employed, but wives also controlled fertility. They used spermicidal douches—solutions of white oak or hemlock bark, strychnine, iodine, lemon juice, alcohol, and green tea were common—diaphragms, and cervical caps, sponges with rubber pads to hold tightly onto the cervix.

Establishing a Common Nomenclature—The Pork Industry An established nomenclature could also suggest uniformity. A familiar nomenclature gave nonidentical or even dissimilar goods the appearance of similarity and promoted consumer confidence. Americans then shared a common material experience, even as they consumed different products. Mid-century examples were legion, particularly in industries relying on hand rather than machine labor. Midwestern hog slaughtering and packing operations provide an especially apt example. Distribution of their goods required that local butchers and wholesalers nationwide be familiar with a common nomenclature.

Prior to about 1840, hog slaughtering was a local activity, confined to the cooler months, and packing generally was unnecessary. After that date, however, new capital from New York, New Orleans, and Europe enabled Midwestern pork merchants to finance expansion and to send products across America. Cincinnati became the center of the new nationwide pork trade. The city had the ideal winter temperature, cold enough to hinder meat spoilage but warm enough to prevent freezing (fermented lager beer, introduced from Germany about 1840, required similar temperatures, and Cincinnati dominated the lager trade too). Cincinnati was also located near great deposits of salt for curing and pickling pork and hardwoods for smoking the meat; uncured pork spoiled too fast for long-distance shipment.

The new national pork-slaughterers and packers divided their product into general categories: fancy hams, common hams, bacon, shoulders, and four grades of bulk pork—clear, mess, prime, and cargo. A potential market for mechanical refrigeration now existed—for keeping the meat at uniform temperature and therefore in uniform condition—and American inventors secured over four dozen refrigeration patents before 1870. None proved commercially applicable. Pork slaughterers and packers were more successful introducing uniform operations. As early as 1840, hog slaughtering followed a regularized procedure. Animals were confined in small pens on slaughterhouse roofs. There they were knocked unconscious or killed by a head blow with a two-pointed hammer, then dragged inside to sticking rooms where their throats were cut and they were hung to bleed. When bleeding ceased, carcasses were scalded in caldrons of boiling water and tossed on scraping tables for hair and ear removal. They were then hung in front of gutters, who removed the entrails and sent the carcasses to basement cooling-rooms. The next day cutters severed feet

*The labor-intensive hog slaughtering and packing
industry was an apt example of a common-
nomenclature-derived uniformity.*

and heads, and divided remains first into hams, shoulders, and sides. Those parts were then butchered more finely, and the meat was distributed in graded tubs "with the exactness of machinery." It was finally smoked, pickled, or salted, then packed.

Regularized slaughtering yielded a more-uniform product. Different hog breeds complicated matters, but packers in Cincinnati and other large slaughtering centers appointed a single individual to visit area abattoirs to confirm that butchered meat conformed to packers' categories. Indeed, the packers' reputations and ultimately their markets depended on each barrel's accurate characterization. Introduction of more sophisticated slaughtering tools and techniques in the 1860s, such as animal-shackling and cutter teams, steam-powered saws, lifting machines, and scraping apparatuses, failed to dissuade packers. They continued to protect their reputations by area-wide slaughterhouse inspections.

Regularized hog-slaughtering produced not only more uniform meat cuts but also more nearly similar wastes, which helped foster and regularize a host of slaughterhouse by-product industries. In the late 1830s, for instance, two Cincinnati entrepreneurs, James Gamble and William Procter, used these wastes to form Procter and Gamble, which produced oil for lamps and machinery as well as a variety of soaps. Other manufacturers tanned hides; converted hair, hooves, offal, and blood into prussiate of potash, which textile workers used to make Prussian-blue dye; transformed offal, hooves, horns, and bones into glue; and used blood, offal, and bones for fertilizers. Pig heads, feet, backbones, ribs, and fat were rendered into lard (through use of superheated steam at pressures of five to seven atmospheres for several hours), which formed the basis of the lard oil, tallow, and stearin industries. Hog bristles became brushes. By-products were big business; as early as 1851, four Cincinnati hog-bristle processing firms employed nearly 200 workers.

Providing Interchangeable Goods—Armory Practice Perhaps the least characteristic mid-century way to provide a common material experience was through truly identical items. Interchangeable parts manufacture had been a dream of eighteenth-century French military men, and was embraced by the American military early in the nineteenth century. This dream was realized in mid-century American armories. Well before American military men could manufacture interchangeable parts for their armaments, they had attained "the grand object of uniformity." This technique using similar, but not interchangeable, parts reduced expensive and time-consuming fitting and filing. Prior to 1840, armory men had adopted drop- and die-forging to make roughly similar pieces, which were filed and fitted when soft, checked by gauges, tempered or hardened, and finally fitted, filed, and

Assembling Colt firearms was a time-consuming task. Notice the large number of fitters and filers.

gauged again. But achieving uniformity was much less complicated and costly than interchangeability. As developed in the army's Springfield Armory, interchangeability generally depended on drop- or die-forging, but it also demanded special-purpose milling and/or planing machines, rationally designed jigs and fixtures, precision gauges, and employees capable of and willing to apply the most exact standards. Interchangeability found its initial grand-scale application in the fully interchangeable Model 1841 percussion rifle and the Model 1842 percussion musket, both produced by the armory in 1847.

High armory practice—interchangeability—required an exceedingly large capital investment and tight quality control. It originated from a governmental agency—the army—which did not need to be profitable or accountable; profit was no object. Most private arms manufacturers, including Samuel Colt in his famous Hartford arms factory, did not use armory practice. Nor did this technique find much employment in other mid-century production spheres or outside New England. A handful of companies, especially machine-tool firms such as the Providence Tool Company, adopted high armory practice, but they proved most exceptional. Its lack of application did not stem from ignorance. Armory workers carried knowledge into private enterprise when they left government employ. But the precision-based technology did not easily transfer to the private sector, although some armory-designed hardware did; fitting and filing were increasingly mechanized. For the overwhelming majority of manufacturers, interchangeability was economically ludicrous. It raised production costs prohibitively and rendered companies nonncompetitive. Uniformity, not interchangeability, ruled the day.

UNIFORM AGRICULTURE

A similar emphasis on uniformity pervaded mid-nineteenth-century agriculture. Contemporaries advocated a new kind of farming—a machine-based agriculture, which mimicked machine-based manufacturing—to regularize farming. Mid-century agricultural societies sponsored thousands of farm-implement competitions, and agricultural publications were awash with advertisements for similar tools. These plows, drills, cultivators, and harvesters generally required animal or steam power and were constructed of iron or steel rather than wood. They eased farmers' burdens and enhanced users' reputations by facilitating row cropping. Neat, clean farms with rowed fields and soils prepared to a proper, nearly uniform texture were identified as the domain of the "improved farmer." The mid-century diffusion of uniform agricultural implements encouraged regularized-row agriculture (or, in the case of grains, regularized stands) and created more nearly uniform production. Use of these tools defined the distinctly American farmer.

These implements enabled agriculturists to secure and harvest greater yields from their lands, and to cultivate additional fields, while national and international marketing possibilities promised handsome returns for whatever quantities they could produce. Those economic prospects, coupled with the new tools, fortified eastern farmers and inspired others to tap the prairie lands of Illinois, Iowa, Minnesota, Nebraska, and Kansas. Located far from sizable cities, farmers there worked the rich black land and sent their huge bounties to the East.

Equipment for a Uniform Agriculture

Mid-century manufacturers bombarded farmers with a dizzying variety of agricultural implements from which to choose. All equipment manufacturers issued the same claim that their product would best improve farming and farmers. Although some implements certainly worked more proficiently than others, the relative merits of each for the physical act of farming were hardly ever clear. Farmers often selected their farm equipment the way that they, and Americans generally, chose other manufactured products: they equated how well a piece would perform with who manufactured it and how it was supposedly manufactured.

McCormick's reaper exemplified the marketing of reputations.

The McCormick Reaper Such was the case with reapers. The reaper boom began in the 1830s when Cyrus H. McCormick and Obed Hussey independently patented workable devices. By 1850, more than thirty American companies manufactured different reapers. But McCormick's firm consistently led reaper sales. In 1876 it produced 14,000 machines, a testament to the importance of marketing reputations.

McCormick certainly never produced the finest article. His reapers mowed poorly, operated unsatisfactorily in tangled fields, and broke down frequently. Similarly, McCormick production techniques were anything but uniform. In the 1830s, McCormick made all reapers in the family's Virginia blacksmith shop. During the next decade he allowed companies across America to manufacture reapers under the Mc-Cormick name; no two firms produced the same McCormick reaper. Beginning about 1850, he discontinued that practice and opened a steam-powered factory in Chicago, but it did not signal a major change in production techniques. The Chicago plant only assembled reapers; Mc-Cormick provided several contractors with specifications and depended on them to supply parts. The Chicago facility enabled McCormick to produce roughly similar reapers each year, but no two years' models were alike; McCormick redesigned the machine annually. Even in Chicago, the company used no jigs, fixtures, or precision gauges. It did not drop-forge fittings, but cast them. It relied entirely on skilled crafts-men—blacksmiths, machinists, and woodworkers—not special purpose machinery. Fitters and filers far outnumbered other employees.

The factory emerged in mid–nineteenth-century America. Above is McCormick's factory soon after the firm moved to Chicago.

McCormick nevertheless established his reputation for precision manufacture of a superior product in much the same way as would Singer and countless others. In the late 1830s and early 1840s, McCormick himself gave demonstrations at farms, participated in formal field trials, and secured testimonials from satisfied users. He also claimed that he had created the "perfect reaper" even as he altered its design, and that his product was "manufactured in the best manner." He collected endorsements from agricultural societies and newspapermen, and warranted his machine's performance because "I have a reputation to maintain."

McCormick stepped up his campaign beginning in 1843. He hired several agricultural newspaper editors to display his reapers locally. He engaged in a bit of "honest graft" by selling reapers to officers of agricultural societies and distinguished farmers—particularly those holding judgeships—at reduced prices. At the same time, he championed the motto "one price to all, and satisfaction guaranteed." He also spoke to farmers in a way different from other manufacturers. McCormick published an agricultural newspaper, the *Farmers' Advance*, which he distributed free to more than 100,000 farmers. His advertisements showed reaper-owning farmers working their machines dressed in top hats and waistcoats. McCormick sold machines on credit to permit those strapped for cash to purchase them, and so to achieve the gentlemanly state to which his advertisements suggested they were entitled. He also gave his product annual names, such as the *Reliable* and the *Advance*, to signify quality and progress.

McCormick's policy of establishing local agencies was his most effective strategy. Begun in the early 1840s and in full force by 1850, McCormick agents received sales commissions and had exclusive company contracts forbidding them from working with other reaper concerns. Unlike Singer operatives, McCormick employees had no citified emporiums. Their display rooms were local courthouse and county-seat lawns, or their own barns and wheat fields. These men traveled throughout their territories, often taking sample machines. Their responsibilities also included delivering reapers, instructing purchasers in reaper final-assembly and operation, and stocking spare parts—each McCormick reaper came to agents with a full complement of replacement parts. Agents needed sufficient mechanical skill to do repair work and render field service. Indeed, agents generally fulfilled the McCormick warranty's terms, a warranty of dependability based on the company's allegedly superior production techniques.

New Plows The McCormick name was synonymous with reapers, but three different plows shared the mid-century limelight. Cast-iron Eagle plows led the more generalized onslaught of cast-iron plows with wrought-iron shares in both the North and South during the late 1830s and 1840s. At least 25,000 of these plows (with elongated, radically curved moldboards to facilitate plowing on rough, heavily stubbled ground) were purchased yearly in the two decades prior to 1860. But Eagle plows were unsuitable for western grasslands. The region's heavy, sticky soil clung to the cast iron and required farmers to stop periodically to clean their moldboards. The Prairie Breaker, a huge plow with a 125-pound wrought-iron strap-plated moldboard, a 15-foot beam, and a wrought-iron share, was the first important western plow. Reigning through the 1840s, the Prairie Breaker's enormous weight required as many as seven yoke of oxen to pull it, but cut furrows only two or three inches deep.

Neither the Prairie Breaker's power requirements nor the shallowness of its furrows satisfied farmers, who expressed interest in a plow made by John Deere in Illinois. Deere popularized agricultural steel use when he built a steel-shared plow with a highly polished, cling-resistant cast-iron moldboard that needed only half the Prairie Breaker's draft. Deere offered his plow for sale in 1841. Although farmers were immediately impressed with its performance and durability, its cost gave them pause. Deere's price was double that of the expensive Prairie Breaker, because he hammered his shares from steel ingots imported from Germany. In 1846, Deere began to melt ingots and cast shares, and by the mid-1850s also had cast steel moldboards. Casting reduced the price somewhat, and western farmers began to purchase Deere's plows in increasing numbers.

Other Farm Implements Few other farm implements or equipment manufacturers achieved the market share of the aforementioned plows, or the notoriety of McCormick. Nonetheless, harrows, drills, and cultivators underwent changes in design, materials, and construction even more significant than those of plows and reapers. These three implements emerged as the staples of uniform row agriculture, and manufacturers designed products to further that approach to farming.

For example, square- and A-framed wooden harrows with fixed, regularly spaced iron teeth appeared in the early 1840s and persisted virtually unchanged for two decades. Later modifications dealt with materials, not design; sturdier steel teeth were substituted for iron, and iron frames replaced wood. Not until after the Civil War were harrows redesigned, but their new form did not de-emphasize row agriculture. In these new flexible-disk harrows, revolving cast-steel disks, each a foot in diameter, did the work of teeth. Farmers could adjust distances between disks, which cut several inches deep, and often used disk harrows for plowing.

Iron also replaced wood in seed drills, but increased usage of these sowing machines after 1840 was itself critical. Enabling farmers to deposit specific seed quantities at regular intervals, drills superseded broadcasting grains; they reduced waste, produced crops with more nearly uniform stands, and enhanced mechanized harvesting. They also supplanted dibble sticks and hoes for planting corn, peas, and beans, freeing farmers from the constant bending associated with those hand implements and facilitating a more nearly perfect row agriculture. Adjustable, precise mechanisms allowing farmers to use drilling techniques on uneven ground were marketed in the 1860s.

Mechanical cultivators rapidly replaced hoes as weeding implements after 1840. Farmers had initially adapted shovel plows, and harrows with the appropriate teeth removed, to the task. But by the mid-1850s several manufacturers were advertising straddle-row cultivators, which weeded both sides of a row at once. Essentially iron-shovel plows connected by arching bars that permitted cultivator bodies to pass above rows of plants, straddle-row cultivators were pulled by horses, but required farmers to walk behind and adjust the shovel depth. Sulky cultivators of the 1860s allowed farmers to ride when weeding, because sulkies were situated directly over shovels, which were engaged by a series of foot-operated levers.

Mid-century manufacturers also designed two steam-powered agricultural implements. The success of one, the steam thresher, testified to the relationship between national and international markets and farm size. Steam threshers appeared about 1850 as replacements for horse-powered devices that threshed grain, separated straw, and winnowed. Principles for both machines were the same. Fluted threshing-drums beat grain from their heads, while conveyor belts or vibrating canvases carried straw, grain, and chaff away from the drums. Grain and chaff then were separated from straw by vibration as they dropped through spaces between slats on endless belts, or through holes in agitating pans. Fans winnowed the material as it fell. By 1870, conveyor-belt elevators had been added to lift straw to stacks, and steam threshers had become grain-farm staples.

But it was the device that failed to secure a mid-century market, the self-propelled steam plow, that most captivated farmers. These ponderous vehicles with large boilers and cylinders carried their own fuel and water and moved by channeling some engine power to drive wheels. Self-propulsion required great power. The steam plow's enormous weight caused it to sink in soft soils; dynamometer tests estimated that it took thirty-five times as much power to propel engines in loose dirt as it did on rails. Inventors tried to increase traction by enlarging wheel surface area, but that approach also added weight. High capital, fuel, and maintenance costs also contributed to the steam plow's lack of utility. The first such device was not even marketed until 1873. It sold poorly.

THE CREATION OF INTERNATIONAL MARKETS

America's awareness of European events and products even while it expressed contempt for things European symbolized the nation's relationship to Old World civilizations. The country certainly had not withdrawn into itself. Fortified by its citizens' conception of their country as a distinctive culture, the nation pursued its destiny aggressively within the world of nations. The Mexican War, repeated disputes with the British, Seward's Folly, and other foreign-policy forays indicate that Americans deemed their nation fit to lead, not follow. With America's natural abundance and distinctive civilization, it seemed the country's duty to assert itself in world affairs.

International commercial expansion appeared natural within this chauvinistic context. A supposedly superior America would inevitably gain significant new markets, which would secure great wealth for Americans and improvements for the nation's trading partners. Spurred by this explanation of why international commerce would prove profitable (and finding that it exceeded expectations), Americans tripled their exports in the two decades after 1840, both increasing trade with Europe and establishing markets in Russia, China, India, Latin America, and Japan.

Mid-Century Shipping

During the early burst of American international trading enthusiasm in the late 1830s, most of the nation's products were carried overseas on

*Clipper ships joined the East and West coasts and
America to Europe and Asia.*

American-built and designed clipper ships. These long, sleek-hulled ships
had concave bows, convex sides, and rounded sterns. Smaller than earlier
packet ships, the speed generated by their tall masts and enormous can-
vas spreads compensated for reduced cargo space; some clippers covered
more than 400 miles a day. Clippers regularly sailed around Cape Horn
to Asia as well as operated on packet runs to Liverpool and California.
But the labor-intensive clipper's heyday was short-lived.

By the mid-1850s, oceangoing steamships proved superior in
speed and cargo capacity. Pioneered by the British in the mid-1830s,
the wooden, paddlewheel-driven ships made packet runs as early as
1840. American steam vessels challenged the British in the mid-1840s,
bolstered by federal transatlantic mail subsidies, but never matched
their European counterparts. They fell further behind in the 1850s
when the British introduced swift, iron-hulled steamships powered by
screw propellers. By 1860, these ships averaged less than ten days
crossing the Atlantic. The clipper record was thirteen and a half days.

The International Industrial Exhibition

American clippers lost out to British steamships, but Americans capitalized in the 1850s on a new British-inspired institution, the international

industrial exhibition, to penetrate further into world markets. The first international exhibition was proposed by Prince Albert, president of England's Royal Society of Arts and Queen Victoria's husband, to "afford a true test of the point of development at which the whole of mankind has arrived" and was held in London in May 1851. The British erected a remarkable building to house the event: a single huge structure made from a modular iron frame covered with glass, named the Crystal Palace. Despite Prince Albert's lofty sentiments, his exposition was clearly big business; he expected the Exhibition to create new markets and appreciation for the highly regarded British. But other nations also embraced the opportunity to have their products testify to their own level of development, and to open new trade vistas. The Exhibition's organizers heightened competitive aspects by organizing exhibits by nation, not product.

American manufacturers quickly recognized the Exhibition's twin significance, and the federal government established a commission to represent America. Headed by President Millard Fillmore, the commission included Joseph Henry; Thomas Ewbank, Commissioner of Patents; and other national leaders. Their work paid off. America did not embarrass itself in London. It displayed about 500 exhibits—less than three percent of the total—and received roughly three percent of the 170 council awards, the Exhibition's highest honor. Another 102 American products, or about 3.5 percent, received one of the 2,918 prize medals. American agricultural implements, firearms, and safes attracted the most notice; the McCormick reaper, Colt revolver, Robbins and Lawrence rifle, and Day and Newell safe received public acclaim. McCormick's reaper also won a council award. Other American council-award winners were Charles Goodyear's vulcanized rubber products; Gail Borden's nutritious dried-meat biscuit, which he made by boiling beef to jelly, kneading it with flour, and baking it to a cake that would keep for months; David Dick's antifriction punch press; and William C. Bond's astronomical clock.

Goodyear's award was particularly noteworthy because England and America had long competed to produce what Goodyear termed "metallic rubber." Unvulcanized rubber was soft in heat and brittle in cold. Goodyear's process, patented in 1844, dissolved rubber in turpentine and mixed in about twenty percent ground sulfur and white lead. He learned earlier of sulfur's vulcanizing properties by trying to dissolve rubber in sulfuric acid and instead producing a vulcanized surface. But he apparently discovered heat's virtues by trying to rid the compound of its noxious smell. Goodyear heated the melange on his stove to drive off the vapors and found that heat between 212 and 350 degrees Fahrenheit fixed the entire batch. Goodyear's achievement so neatly symbolized the American nation that no less an eminence than Daniel Webster, then Secretary of State and a candidate for the

Whig party nomination for president, represented Goodyear in a British patent infringement case the next year.

America's international performance enabled its citizens to establish European distribution centers for American goods. The country's Exhibition showing reaffirmed that the nation had become, at least with respect to manufacturing, a full-fledged member of the world of civilizations. Its success encouraged a similar industrial contest in New York City in 1853, and the country to be party to several other international industrial competitions: Paris, 1855; London, 1862; Paris, 1867; and Vienna, 1873. America's Crystal Palace prominence also led the British to establish in 1853 a special commission to investigate American arms manufacture. Committee members coined the term "the American System" to describe high armory practice, and suggested that those manufacturing techniques generally characterized American industry. Indeed, to the British, the American System of manufacturing came to define the distinctly American civilization, even though only a handful of American firms practiced it.

Transoceanic Telegraphy

Acknowledgment that America operated in a world economy placed a premium on up-to-date international information. Prior to the mid-1860s, transoceanic crossings by ship were the sole source of this intelligence, and in light of the new economic realities, they seemed much too slow. International intelligence was paramount: information about world market conditions would reduce speculation and hoarding, permit merchants to carry reduced inventories, and allow them to tap territories most advantageously.

Several Americans in the early 1850s proposed laying underwater telegraph cables insulated with gutta percha to transmit information instantaneously between continents, but Cyrus W. Field deserves the most credit. A retired New York wholesale paper merchant, Field gained Samuel Morse's support and put together a consortium of Anglo-American investors to run a cable on the ocean floor from Newfoundland to Ireland. The consortium consulted with Robert Stephenson, Michael Faraday, and others, and contracted with a British firm to manufacture the cable. William Thomson, later Lord Kelvin, directed that company. It produced a cable about five-eighths of an inch in diameter. Seven copper strands formed its conduction core, and were packed in three thin gutta percha layers. A tarred hemp sheath and eighteen strands of iron wire further protected this cable.

Consortium-owned steamers attempted to lay the cable in summer 1857, but it snapped 380 miles offshore. A similar misfortune occurred in June 1858. A foray a month later initially seemed successful.

On August 4, telegraph service between Europe and America began, but less than a month later the signal failed. August's joyful celebrations devolved into September's recriminations; subsequent investigations suggested that inappropriate testing and faulty storage techniques had damaged the cable's insulation. The 1858 failures and the American Civil War gave supporters pause, but the consortium resumed activities in 1865. It now faced a substantial competitor. Western Union also sought to connect continents, but from Russia's Asiatic coast. Running a line from Western Europe across Russia, underneath the Bering Strait and down through Russian America (Alaska), the Western Union venture would join existing lines at San Francisco. This threat animated the consortium; it employed a group of British electricians, including Thomson, to design the new cable and award the contract. The new cable was one-and-one-tenth inch in diameter, contained three times more copper than the earlier version, and had three times the tensile strength. Nine layers of gutta percha-based insulation bound the core, and ten stout soft-steel wires protected it. Pitch-treated hemp sheathed the steel.

Despite the new cable and extra precautions, the 1865 expedition failed. New cable was made for 1866, identical except that zinc-galvanized steel rendered the hemp sheath unnecessary. This voyage proved successful, and on July 27 the telegraph linked the continents. The consortium's crews also managed to grapple and hoist the previous year's cable, splice it to additional material, and run it beneath the ocean. The second line opened on September 1.

THE CIVIL WAR: A MASS EXPERIENCE

War conditions place strains on a nation's industrial and agricultural capacity, but they also demand redistribution of resources and encourage adoption of improved production techniques, which may improve the nation's production capacity. America's Civil War was striking in how little permanent change it made in northern industry and agriculture. The sole exception may have been Lincoln's 1862 initiative to ensure that Western railroads as yet unbuilt would adopt similar track gauges to those already running in the Northeast so as to further cement the West to the Union. The case was somewhat different in the South, however. That section expanded production but it rarely innovated; it merely applied established northern practices. During the Civil War the South built armories and powder mills to manufacture weapons, erected textile factories to make uniforms, laid railroad tracks to facilitate transportation, employed horse-drawn agricultural implements to increase food production, and started to tap Alabama's abundant iron ore and coal assets to produce iron. Although most attempts proved rather disappointing, Southern industry and agriculture during the war more nearly approximated the North's than it had for several decades.

The Civil War's aftermath intensified Southern industrialization. Northern and English capital fueled expansion, but the war itself provided a homogenizing experience. Northern soldiers wore similar uniforms, used similar weapons, and slept in similar facilities. They also ate similar foods. Borden's condensed milk, made by boiling off water in a vacuum pan to keep out impurities and sealed airtight, as well as his raspberry juice, made the same way proved immensely popular. A California-based canned fruit industry, an offshoot of the Gold Rush of 1849 and subsequent support of Western mining, provided copious quantities of fruit to the Union Armies. California canners even sought to increase their product's appeal by subjecting fruit to higher sterilization temperatures for shorter periods in hope of producing tastier canned fruit.

Southern soldiers also shared among themselves similar material experiences. Civilian populations were likewise affected. Northerners suffered the same shortages and dislocations. Southerners, too, felt roughly the same deprivations. Both reviewed the war through Mathew Brady's photographs. The most significant technological effect of the war was the commonality it reinforced. It was the archetypal mass experience in an era distinguished by attempts to provide common experience.

FOR FURTHER READING

Albion, Robert G. *The Rise of New York Port, 1815–1860* (1939).

Aldrich, Darragh. *The Story of John Deere: A Saga of American Industry* (1942).

Ardrey, Robert L. *American Agricultural Implements* (1972).

Brandon, Ruth. A *Capitalist Romance: Singer and the Sewing Machine* (1977).

Broehl, Wayne G., Jr. *John Deere's Company* (1984).

Chandler, Alfred D., Jr. *The Visible Hand: The Managerial Revolution in American Business* (1977).

Cooper, Grace R. *The Sewing Machine: Its Invention and Development* (1976).

Dibner, Bern. *The Atlantic Cable* (1959).

Gates, Paul W. *The Illinois Central Railroad and Its Colonization Work* (1934).

Gernsheim, Helmut and Alison. *L. J. M. Daguerre: The History of the Diorama and the Daguerreotype* (1968).

Gibbs-Smith, C. H. *The Great Exhibition of 1851* (1950).

Gilchrist, David T. and W. David Lewis, eds. *Economic Change in the Civil War Era* (1965).

Goldman, Joanne A. *Building New York's Sewers: Developing Mechanisms of Urban Management* (1997).

Hounshell, David A. *From the American System to Mass Production 1800–1932. The Development of Manufacturing Technology in the United States* (1984).

Hurt, R. Douglas. *American Farm Tools: From Hand-Power to Steam-Power* (1982).

Hutchinson, William T. *Cyrus Hall McCormick*, 2 vols. (1930).

Jenkins, Reese V. *Images and Enterprise: Technology and the American Photographic Industry, 1839–1925* (1975).

Kutler, Stanley. *Privilege and Creative Destruction: The Charles River Bridge Case* (1971).

Lewis, W. David. *Iron and Steel in America* (1976).

Mabee, Carleton. *The American Leonardo: A Life of Samuel F. B. Morse* (1944).

Marcus, Alan I. *Plague of Strangers. Social Groups and the Origins of City Services in Cincinnati* (1991).

McKelvey, Blake D. *Rochester: The Water-Power City, 1812–1854* (1945).

Nye, David E. *American Technological Sublime* (1994).

Ogle, Maureen. *All the Modern Conveniences. American Household Plumbing, 1840–1890* (1996).

Persons, Stow. *The Decline of American Gentility* (1973).

Reid, James D. *The Telegraph In America* (1879).

Rolt, L. T. C. *A Short History of Machine Tools* (1965).

Ross, Earle D. *Democracy's College: The Land-Grant Movement in the Formative Stage* (1942).

Schisgall, Oscar. *Eyes On Tomorrow: The Evolution of Procter and Gamble* (1981).

Smith, Merritt Roe. *Harpers Ferry Armory and the New Technology* (1977).

Taft, Robert. *Photography and the American Scene: A Social History, 1839–1889 (1938).*

Temin, Peter. *Iron and Steel in Nineteenth-Century America: An Economic Inquiry* (1964).

Thompson, Robert Luther. *Wiring A Continent: The History of the Telegraphic Industry in the United States, 1832–1866* (1947).

Trachtenberg, Alan. *Reading American Photographs: Images as History* (1989).

Wallace, Anthony F. C. *Rockdale* (1978).

Walsh, Margaret. *The Rise of the Midwestern Meat Packing Industry* (1982).

Ward, James A. *Railroads and the Character of America, 1820–1887* (1986).

White, John H., Jr. *American Locomotives: An Engineering History, 1830–1880* (1968).

Communications and the Power to Communicate

THE GREAT CENTENNIAL EXHIBITION: LATE–NINETEENTH-CENTURY AMERICAN NOTIONS IN MINIATURE

In the early 1870s, America prepared to celebrate the hundredth anniversary of the Declaration of Independence. The commemoration was to focus on an international industrial exhibition in Philadelphia, and Congress characteristically chartered a corporation to handle finances. Design of the Centennial Corporation's gaudy 24- by 20-inch stock certificates provided an inkling that Americans had abandoned their mid-nineteenth-century quest for uniformity. The certificates celebrated diversity, while carefully joining relics of American civil religion—the nation's political heritage—with the country's technological productions. A woman personifying America formed the apex of a pyramid at certificate center; female representations of Fame and Art sat at her feet. Independence Hall and the National Capitol were in the background. Fitch and Fulton with steamboat models stood in front of Independence Hall, while Franklin and Morse with electrical and telegraphic instruments assumed a similar posture near the Capitol. Elias Howe and a shipwright also were depicted, offering America a sewing machine and clipper ship respectively. A freedman, a soldier, and a mechanic stood to the pyramid's right; a farmer, a planter, a miner, a trapper, and an Indian were at its left. John Trumbull's painting, "The Declaration of Independence," was placed at the center of the pyramid's base. At its right was a busy manufacturing city, contrasted with a neglected windmill to exemplify progress; at its left was a locomotive, telegraph, steamship, and reaper, contrasted with a Conestoga wagon, pony express rider, and sickle-wielding farmer to connote civilization's development.

The Centennial Exhibition took place between May 10 and November 10, 1876, and attracted more than eight million visitors (more than one-sixth of the nation's population). The exhibition itself was as precisely arranged as the stock certificate but far differently than the Crystal Palace exhibition of twenty-five years earlier. Separate buildings demarcated governmental and conceptual boundaries. Each foreign nation had its own promotional pavilion, as did every American state government. There was a women's pavilion. Various private enterprises, either singularly or collectively, erected their own; the Singer Sewing Machine Company, Pacific Guano Company, and consortiums of shoe manufacturers, brewers, and casket-makers each set up pavilions. But the exhibition's real business took place in just three buildings: the Main Building housed displays of mining, metallurgy, manufacturing, and educational techniques; Machinery Hall showed machines in motion; and Agricultural Hall stocked farm implements and food-preservation processes. Products were organized within these three buildings by nation and type; diversity was therefore accentuated. For example, Machinery Hall's American exhibit included a discrete machine-tool section. The British display in Agricultural Hall situated that nation's steam plows together. The world's industrialists competed at these three venues.

The Centennial Exhibition's judge selection criteria and award procedures also distinguished it from predecessors. Its commissioners dispensed with apportioning judgeships by nation and replaced that practice by choosing men "individually for their high qualifications," no matter what nationality; expertise in technological processes of manufacture became the *sine qua non*. These experts did not issue medals across production categories, or discriminate between the best and second best within categories, but instead separated the outstanding from the mundane and rewarded only excellence. They considered each entry's "inherent and comparative merits" and used these "properties and qualities" as the basis for granting the exhibition's sole award, the Centennial Medal. Judges remained free to grant as many or as few medals as their judgment dictated. As important, judges produced written reports explaining their selections, including dispassionate analyses of award-winners' particulars. Among those American productions cited were Goodyear rubber products; Yale locks; Edison's automatic telegraph; Midvale Steel's axles and shafts; Sharps

At the 1876 Centennial Exhibition, the huge Corliss engine drove all the machinery in Machinery Hall.

rifles; Westinghouse's air brake; Roebling's steel suspension-bridge cables; machine tools produced by Pratt and Whitney and William Sellers and Company; Otis elevators; Gatling guns; Fitts road steam-engines; Brown and Sharpe universal milling and grinding machines; and Pullman sleeper cars. Alexander Graham Bell's telephone was also displayed, as were arc lights and several typewriters.

Neither the qualitative distinctions among products nor the Exhibition's meticulous differentiation by nation and product type undercut its essential coherence. The exhibition's highlight, a gigantic Corliss engine—actually two double-acting vertical high-pressure steam engines working in tandem—symbolized the Exhibition's cohesiveness by powering all apparatuses in Machinery Hall; it bound together all the disparate parts. Contemporaries repeatedly likened the engine to an animal heart, systematically pumping life blood through metallic arteries and leather capillaries to the Hall's other machines. Produced by Rhode Island's George Corliss, the engine stood nearly 40 feet tall, weighed 680 tons, was driven by 20 boilers, and had cylinders 44 inches in diameter with 10-foot strokes. Load dictated engine speed, a characteristic of Corliss-developed engines; rotary valves automatically governed the quantity and rapidity of cylinder-injected steam to enable the engine to adjust itself to power demands. A huge flywheel stored motion, making 36 revolutions per minute (rpm) and weighing 56 tons. Thirty feet in diameter and 2 feet thick, the flywheel's cogs matched cogs on a pinion and turned a primary underground line, which was geared to eight secondary underground shafts. Pulleys and belts connected the secondary shafts to eight principal lineshafts located near the ceiling and traversing the building's length. The Hall's machines ran from belts attached to these 650-foot-long above-ground shafts. One line turned at 140 rpm, while the others rotated at 120 rpm. Each line could transmit 180 horsepower. Machines requiring the greatest amount of power were situated closest to the beginnings of lines.

THE IDEA OF SYSTEM: THE PERVASIVE LATE–NINETEENTH-CENTURY AMERICAN NOTION

The Centennial Exhibition's emphasis on differentiation, while simultaneously championing coherence, was a microcosm of late nineteenth-century America generally. Many internecine tensions buffeted the country in the half-century after 1870, which belied the national spirit that had been evinced by the mid-century population. Rather than continuing to seek nationwide homogeneity and uniformity, late–nineteenth-century Americans waged innumerable struggles with each other. The gap between the richest and the poorest Americans grew precipitously. Businessmen ruthlessly attacked and swallowed up competitors. Industrialists pumped unprecedented moneys into production machinery to replace skilled workers as they battled the laborers those machines replaced. Industrial giants fought among themselves. By 1909, fewer than 1 percent of American firms produced 44 percent of the nation's manufactured goods. In the West and Southwest, ranchers fought with farmers over barbed wire. Ethical and racial confrontations also flared incessantly. The clergy, politicians, businessmen, and professionals called for social, economic, and political reforms while they competed with each other for power. City, state, and federal governments aggressively entered these frays, resulting in a series of jurisdictional quarrels.

Americans in the years between the 1870s and the 1920s proved far more discriminating than their predecessors. They divided all types of people, things, and ideas into groups. This phenomenon was reflected in the Centennial Exhibition's complex layout as well as in its judge selection criteria. Americans constantly made spatial and functional distinctions, and rigorously differentiated among various types of enterprises, peoples, and tasks. For example, at one time or another, they divided the nation's population into groups according to intelligence, socioeconomic status, geographical location, religion, national origin, body type, special knowledge, training, abilities, and the like. Apparently obsessed with identifying diversity, Americans treated these categories as real, crucial, and limiting. Criteria for each category were fixed, and all its elements were treated as if they were representative of that type. Each categorization defined and bounded a specific set of cohorts.

But late–nineteenth-century Americans also recognized that their categories did not stand alone. Although each category was discrete (its unique features could be isolated and studied), and each had its particular merits and liabilities, people of this period conceived of processes, activities, and social structures as composed of sets of these individual components, like machines built from many parts. What made the various processes, activities, and social structures what they were was the relations of components to each other. And because each component varied in capacity and quality, each had to be assigned its proper function or position in the "machine"; relationships had to be *systematized* in a hierarchical fashion. Only in that way could processes, activities, and society operate smoothly and at peak efficiency. In this view, the country's processes, activities, and social structures were *systems* of discrete, fixed, hierarchically arranged parts.

This notion of system placed a premium on uncovering the principles that organized and ordered the many different parts. In the case of the Centennial Exhibition, the new judge selection criteria and its enormous Corliss engine organized the award process and Machinery Hall, respectively. Rarely, however, was consensus easily achieved on actual systematizing principles. Desire for systemization ruled the day, but disputes raged about particulars, especially in social, political, and economic matters. Identification of categories of peoples, position of categories within systems, and even the loci of systems (city, state, or nation in the political sphere) proved sticking points. Most groups sought to serve as the system's guiding spirit, the indispensable decision-makers. Few remained content resting at the hierarchy's base. These leadership contests spawned the period's recurring battles.

Hierarchies were most clearly delineated within industrial enterprises, where ownership granted entrepreneurs great latitude to impose systems of their choosing. Division of labor, specialization of function, standardization of technique, and rationalization of operations became industrial production's touchstones, as did distinctions among managerial elements. System's efficacy also encouraged powerful industrialists to organize entire industries; vertical and horizontal integration of companies, mergers, pools, trusts, and holding companies became commonplace.

The system mania translated into increased industrial output and a flurry of capital expenditures. Industrialists took the machine as their metaphor and passionately exploited the nation's natural abundance. Their efforts were profitable. The value of American production multiplied twelve times in the half-century after 1865. As early as 1890 the value of the country's manufactured goods nearly equaled the total of its three closest competitors. Pig-iron production increased eightfold between 1876 and 1901, and Americans smelted more than seven million tons of steel in 1897. Patents soared from about two thousand yearly in the 1850s to more than twenty-one thousand a year in the two decades before 1900. Between 1880 and 1890, American capital investment in machinery more than doubled. It doubled again in the decade after 1900, while the value of the nation's industrial products rose 76 percent. Americans added seventy-three thousand miles of railroad track in the 1880s and another thirty thousand in the 1890s. They laid electrical and telephone lines and completed water-delivery and waste-removal systems.

Reverence for systems likewise held important intellectual implications. It manifested itself in efforts to rationalize the inventive process—prompting the establishment of research laboratories or, as Thomas Edison termed them, idea factories—and served as a guideline of how to invent. Inventors faced a crucial conceptual choice. They either designed components for existing or anticipated systems, or created new systems to fit their inventions.

THE ELECTRIFICATION OF AMERICA

America in 1920 was dramatically different from the nation a half-century earlier. By the 1920s, virtually every American municipality had been electrified. Central power stations generated alternating current and distributed it throughout cities to light streets, homes, and offices, and to power streetcars and factories. Few Americans had foreseen electricity's potential in 1870 and fewer had anticipated central generation and distribution systems.

How the nation came to adopt electricity is an apt place to begin consideration of technology in late–nineteenth- and early–twentieth-century America. Electricity's significance was considerable, and its partisans were quite explicit about how to electrify the nation. It all started with centrally generated electricity.

The first practical, cost-efficient electric generators—dynamos—were produced in the 1870s by European builders who incorporated principles that other Europeans had uncovered earlier in the century. The dynamos of Z. T. Gramme of Belgium and Hefner Alteneck of Germany were most celebrated. These dynamos neither drove machines nor provided light; situated in factories, they generally replaced batteries and furnished electricity for electroplating.

The Advent of Electric Lighting

Arc Lights These working dynamos held out prospects for developing new commercial uses for the comparatively inexpensive electricity. Charles F. Brush was one of the first Americans to investigate these possibilities. In the mid-1870s, he designed independently circuited two- and four-light, single-dynamo arc lamps.

Brush had not discovered the phenomenon of arc lighting. England's Humphry Davy had passed current across a gap between two pieces of carbon as early as 1808 and generated bright, blinding light. By the 1860s, several lighthouses had installed arc lights, run off either batteries or inefficient dynamos; preventing shipwrecks, saving lives, and protecting property justified high electricity costs.

Nor was Brush alone in adapting dynamos to arc lighting. A few private residences' exteriors and a handful of commercial establishments' interiors were arc lighted in the 1870s. But Brush quickly realized that the arc lights' brilliance made them unsuitable for a substantial home or business market; arc lighting's future would be outdoors. He looked to it to replace gas streetlamps. Sixteen-candle gas lamps had lit American municipal thoroughfares since the early nineteenth century, and more than four hundred gaslight companies existed in 1875. Brush recognized that arc lights must be cheaper and better to displace the established gas streetlights. Independently circuited lights requiring numerous dynamos and extensive quantities of wire would be prohibitively expensive. He therefore focused on designing an entire system based on centrally generated and transmitted electricity. Each of his system's components had to be economical and compatible. Brush faced a host of technical problems in developing his new system: producing long-lasting, regularly burning carbons to reduce carbon replacement costs; manufacturing dynamos powerful enough to light numerous arc lights connected in series (jumping each gap decreased voltage about fifty volts, while wire's high cost prohibited use of separate circuits); designing a means to adjust gaps as carbons burned away; and devising methods to perpetuate series circuits when individual lights failed. Brush proved equal to the challenge. He invented high-voltage dynamos; automatic regulators to keep current constant, not load-dependent; an automatic feeding mechanism to maintain gap distance; and automatic short circuits to circumvent burned-out lights. He made better, less-expensive carbons from petroleum coke rather than gas coke, binding them with coal tar-pitch rather than tar. He also rounded his arc carbons, tapered their tips to promote longer life, copperplated their bases to cut resistance between carbon and carbon holder (which further slowed carbon consumption), and developed a double-carbon arc lamp (essentially two lamps in one) with an automatic switch to reduce the need for maintenance.

Brush took these system elements and in summer 1879 erected the nation's first central electric station to power twenty-two electric arc lamps in San Francisco. Within a year he had stations in New York, Philadelphia, and Boston. Brush's initial success in manipulating dynamos, circuits, and arc lamps to form outdoor electric lighting systems engendered competition and yielded improvements. Before 1882, Elihu Thomson, then of the American Electrical Company and later of Thomson-Houston Electric Company, had devised smaller, more efficient dynamos, superior current regulators, air-blast insulation to promote high-voltage commutation, and lightning arresters. Edward Weston, then of Weston Electric Light Company and later of the United States Electric Lighting Company, increased dynamo efficiency by using laminated armatures. These advances translated into larger lighting systems. A dynamo that would light 40 lamps first appeared in 1882 and was followed by 65-lamp varieties in 1884, 80 in 1890, and 125 in 1894. Early electric-arc-lighting firms competed against each other and gas lighting, but not all companies were equally adept at promoting their goods. Nor were all systems equal. By 1888, Thomson-Houston had emerged as the leader and began to buy controlling interests in its competitors. That process enabled Thomson-Houston to eliminate rivals and gain patents, talented employees, and manufacturing plants. By 1890, it controlled more than two-thirds of the nation's arc lighting systems.

Incandescent Lights Incandescent lighting paralleled arc lighting's development. Much credit for devising and manufacturing an incandescent lighting system must go to Thomas Edison, who had acquired a reputation as an inventor par excellence before ever producing an incandescent lamp. He had contributed to the "printing telegraph" (stock ticker), "speaking telegraph" (telephone), and "talking telegraph recorder" (phonograph). Edison parlayed the backing of telegraph investors and his prominence to assemble an impressive staff of technical associates and to stock extensive facilities. But Edison was not the first to investigate incandescent lighting. Several Europeans and Americans attempted in the two decades after 1840 to develop incandescent bulbs. Using electric batteries as power sources, these men sought to produce long-lasting filaments and vacuums strong enough to prevent combustion.

The inability to evacuate cylinders adequately doomed early efforts. Only after 1875 was an improved mercury air pump, developed a decade earlier by the German Herman Sprengel, employed in incandescent lighting work. Joseph Swan, a British pharmacist long active in the lighting quest, first adapted the Sprengel pump, and he was soon joined by Americans Hiram Maxim, Moses Farmer, and others.

These investigators were Edison's competition, but he pursued incandescence from a different angle, one more nearly akin to the electrical efforts of Brush, Weston, and Thomson. Edison did not explore incandescence; he did not begin by developing a lamp. He simply assumed that incandescence was possible and moved to the twin issues of marketability and practicality. Success depended on incandescence's ability to supplant gas lights, but unlike Brush, Edison focused indoors. He sought to create a DC (direct current) incandescent system that would offer as much illumination (about sixteen-candle power) as gas lights, at a lower or equivalent price. Edison first analyzed indoor gas lighting's costs. This single most important calculation would guide his attempt to produce an incandescent lighting system.

Edison decided to pursue incandescent lighting seriously in fall 1878. A public relations blitz accompanied that decision; Edison asserted in newspapers his priority in the field—in fact, he had done virtually nothing—while offering assurances that results soon would be forthcoming. Edison excelled at this type of campaign; it preempted other investors' claims, garnered him additional financial support, and began to accustom his market to the anticipated new technology. Even as he touted his venture, Edison computed that an economically feasible system would require high resistance filament lamps and parallel wiring. The former reduced copper wiring costs substantially, while the latter ensured uninterrupted service. During late 1878 and 1879, Edison and his associates experimented with materials of various compositions and shapes to devise appropriate filaments, always removing gases occluded in filaments by continuing to evacuate bulbs during heating; Edison's team found that filaments often contained oxides, and oxygen liberated during the initial heating caused filaments to burn. They also designed efficient, low-internal-resistance dynamos suitable for parallel lighting. Edison named these devices Jumbo generators after the great elephant brought to America by P. T. Barnum; Edison appreciated Barnum's adroit use of publicity.

Edison's crew devoted itself to developing the system's other components in 1880 and 1881. They devised fuses to prevent fires, and manufactured household lighting fixtures, bulbs, and sockets. Edison himself envisioned a feeder-main distribution network to cut copper

Huge electricity-generating, central-station-located dynamos were the first requirements for electric light and power systems.

wire costs by about 85 percent; rather than attach large copper mains directly to generators, thin feeder lines would carry current from dynamos to short sections of mains placed at points of dense electrical distribution. Pilot projects were established at Menlo Park and London to demonstrate the system's feasibility and to work out bugs. By late 1881, Edison was ready to construct his first American commercial central station; he placed it at 257 Pearl Street, in the heart of New York City's financial community. Edison men laid underground conduits and insulated the wires with hot asphaltum. They wired households and establishments, and installed meters based on electrolytic deposit of zinc to measure individual electric usage. Jumbo generators drove the DC system. The Pearl Street station began operation on September 4, 1882, and Edison distributed electricity free for the remainder of the year to induce reluctant New Yorkers to sample the system.

To Edison, Pearl Street was merely the first of what he assumed would be hundreds of stations located throughout America. Before Pearl Street opened, Edison had created a system of corporations to control future developments. The Edison Electric Light Company, chartered in 1878, stood at the apex. It owned patent rights to Edison's electric lighting inventions and licensed subsidiary companies. The Edison Electric Illuminating Company of New York (1880) was its first subsidiary. The New York firm built the Pearl Street station, sold its power, and served as the model for expansion in large municipalities. By 1888, Edison Electric Illuminating Companies had been established in Chicago, Brooklyn, Detroit, Boston, New Orleans, St. Paul, and Philadelphia. The Edison Company for Isolated Lighting (1881) installed incandescent lighting equipment in residences and businesses not served by central stations, and built central stations in cities with populations less than 10,000. Other Edison companies held exclusive licenses from the parent company to manufacture components: the Edison Lamp Works (1880) made incandescent lamps; the Edison Machine Works (1881) built Jumbo dynamos; the Edison Electric Tube Company (1881) constructed underground conductors; Bergmann and Company (1881) manufactured a wide range of electric lighting accessories.

No company could seriously challenge the Edison organization's preeminence in DC incandescent lighting; Edison's system was dependable and reasonably priced, and his companies held the important DC patents. But the Edison consortium proved unprepared to deflect competition from another quarter. George Westinghouse's Westinghouse Lighting Company devised in 1886 an alternating current incandescent lighting system. By 1892, more than 1,000 AC central stations were in operation.

Like Edison, Westinghouse was self-educated. When he turned to electric lighting in 1884, Westinghouse's reputation as an inventor almost rivaled that of the Wizard of Menlo Park. He had designed a mechanism to return derailed railroad cars to tracks, his famous air brake, and several automatic switching and signaling devices. Westinghouse first investigated DC lighting systems, but soon focused on the results of a London lighting demonstration. Like several inventors before them, Lucien Gaulard and John Gibbs had attempted to overcome the arc light short-circuiting problem through electromagnetic induction; they generated electricity through primary induction coils joined in series, and established separate secondary coil circuits for each arc lamp. But unlike their predecessors, Gaulard and Gibbs employed high-voltage AC in their primary circuit to reduce long-distance transmission costs (it required thinner wire), and used their secondary coils as step-down transformers to lower voltage for lighting. Westinghouse bought Gaulard-Gibbs transformers in 1885, improved efficiency by replacing iron wire in the core with iron plate, and copper plates in the coils with copper wire, and placed the revamped transformers in parallel. He then tested the system while well-regulated alternators for power generation were built. In fall 1886, the company opened its first commercial central station in Buffalo.

The Growth of Electric Power

The central stations of the early 1880s, as well as the improved dynamos of the preceding decade, inaugurated an era of cheap electricity, and DC electric-light distributors encouraged electric motor development and industrial usage. Three important factors entered into their decision. First, and perhaps most basic, DC distributors saw industrial motor applications as increasing electric consumption and profits. Second, distributors had gained valuable motor design experience from dynamo construction—electric motors were essentially dynamos running in reverse—and hoped to market a new product. Third, they recognized that motor usage would enable them to balance loads somewhat—light by night, industrial power by day—and produce electricity at reduced costs. Edison again led the way. As early as 1880, he employed electric motors to drive some of his lamp factories. By 1887, American industry used nearly ten thousand DC motors, generally for pumping, hoisting, or hauling. Most motors generated less than one horsepower, which made them completely unsuitable for turning ponderous lineshafting. Manufacturers either ran them on current supplied by central stations or operated isolated stations.

The Development of Electric Traction These industrial motors were virtually insignificant in terms of both future developments and the first popular use of electric power—electric traction. Electric traction's proponents capitalized on the increased population and density of cities, and the division of urban space into distinct commercial, industrial, and residential neighborhoods to push their new product. Steam commuter railroads, omnibus lines, and horse-drawn street railways all preceded electric traction, yet each had shortcomings. Omnibuses were slow and required a dozen or more horses, each with only a four or five years' working life. Horse droppings produced constant complaints, and epizootic diseases engendered continual fears. Locomotives threw off soot and sparks. Street railways suffered from many of the same problems as omnibuses. Although they used only a half-dozen horses and were speedier, constant pounding of hooves near rails led to street depressions that disrupted the wooden-wheeled commercial trade. Despite these drawbacks, street railways had become intraurban mass transportation's predominant form. By 1880, more than 100,000 horses pulled nearly 19,000 streetcars on about 3,000 miles of track.

American entrepreneurs had posed alternatives in the 1870s. They devised compressed-steam and compressed-air locomotives and used stationary steam engines and either inclined planes or endless chains to pull streetcars from place to place. After 1880, streetcars powered by electric motors driven by electricity supplied by central stations

Horse-drawn street railways dominated mass
intraurban transit until the late 1880s.

gained support. In conjunction with S. D. Field, Cyrus Field's nephew, Edison developed a three-railed elevated railway. Wire brushes picked up current from the "hot" center rail and carried it to a standard Edison generator, which, hooked up in reverse, served as the motor. The two men demonstrated their contraption at the Chicago Railway Exposition in 1883, but shortly after dissolved their partnership. Edison then abandoned electric traction.

Several technical problems plagued electric traction pioneers. Streetcars started and stopped often, changed speeds frequently, and operated with variable loads. These conditions strained the DC motors then available. Stationary copper brushes touching rotating commutators wore down quickly; arcing, sparking, and fires resulted. Inventors also needed to carry current to motors and then to transmit power from motor to axle. Improved design in one sphere sometimes exacerbated another situation. For example, placing motors under cars simplified power transmission, but complicated brush adjustment and commutator removal for machining.

*New York was among the first cities in the world to
have an elevated railway.*

Electric traction's first generation encountered the aforementioned
difficulties and labored to resolve them. They placed conductors in underground wooden conduits, which were slotted to permit plow-like
devices to gather current; electrified tracks and used the car's wheels
to bring electricity to motors; and strung conductors near rails and employed brass pulleys beneath cars to pick up electricity. They also experimented with overhead conductors and used poles to tap current
as well as overrunning wheeled travelers. They worked on motor
placement and designed various chain drives and double-gearing systems to transmit power to axles.

These early systems each had flaws. Frank J. Sprague developed a
line incorporating their best features and added new ones to make a
truly practical line. Sprague had investigated motor design as he
worked for Edison and left the company the next year to build his own
industrial motors. During the mid-1880s he became the foremost
American supplier of large motors; industry used more than 250
Sprague motors in 1887, some as large as fifteen horsepower. Two
years earlier, Sprague had recognized electric traction's potential demand for his motors, and he experimented on a short section of elevated railway in New York City. Although he failed to interest the city
in electrifying the way, Sprague gained valuable experience and important financial contacts. His acquaintances soon secured a contract
to operate a streetcar line in Richmond, Virginia, and in 1887 they
hired Sprague to design and build it. He quickly decided that an electrified street-level line with single overhead conductor would be most
economical. Sprague's motors were joined to conductors through universally swiveling trolleys running under the conductor and kept in

Americans quickly adopted electric traction. By 1893, more than 60 percent of the nation's street railway mileage had been electrified.

contact by strong springs. He connected motors to car and axle to ensure continuous gear engagement on rough ways. Sprague's Richmond success got him additional contracts and a slew of competitors. Thomson-Houston entered the electric traction business in 1888 and established lines very similar to Sprague's operation. Westinghouse, too, was impressed. It had tried since 1886 to develop AC (alternating current) traction systems but failed to devise suitable motors. In 1889, it turned to DC traction and hired several Sprague engineers to catch up. Edison finally got involved in 1889 and bought out Sprague.

Electric traction proved immensely popular. In 1888, 130 electric streetcars transported American urbanites; four years later, more than 8,000 provided similar service. In 1890, 16 percent of American street-railway mileage was electrified. That percentage nearly quadrupled by 1893. In 1903, it reached 98 percent.

Not everyone championed electric traction as it existed in the early 1890s, of course. Trolley wires and poles were unsightly, and rails disturbed street traffic. Nor did entrepreneurs abandon their quest to improve systems; Westinghouse continued to experiment with AC motors and in 1904 opened the first AC-powered street railway.

The Ascendancy of AC Current Westinghouse's AC motor experiments began in 1888. Lack of a comparable AC motor gave DC companies a competitive edge, which sometimes proved decisive when a city selected its electrical supplier; DC seemingly had more applications, including industrial use. But DC's advantage was more illusory than real. DC motors never gained universal adoption because DC electricity's high transmission costs made steam power cheaper for most tasks. Edison's staff and financiers understood DC's limitations; Edison himself refused to acknowledge the drawbacks, but when his interest and organizational influence waned in the late 1880s, his colleagues explored AC's potential. There they encountered difficulties not unlike those faced by competitors of Edison's DC products in the early 1880s; Westinghouse and Thomson-Houston controlled the relevant patents and employed the top investigators. The Edison combine could withdraw, develop its own AC operation from scratch, or merge with either of the major AC firms. In 1892, it joined with Thomson-Houston to form General Electric.

Westinghouse's quest for an AC motor had led him to Nikola Tesla, a Serbian émigré who announced in 1888 that he had constructed just such a device. Three wires rather than the normal two supplied power to Tesla's motor; the third wire carried a voltage out of phase with the other voltage. The two distinct phases created a rotating magnetic field in the motor's stator windings, which eliminated commutators and brushes. Westinghouse purchased Tesla's patents in July 1888 and brought him to Pittsburgh to perfect the engine.

Westinghouse's commitment to AC power extended to more than Tesla's motor. Adoption of the three-wire motor required designing an entirely new AC system, a polyphase or multiple-phase system. It settled on a two-phase system, which could be treated as two independent AC circuits for lighting, at a frequency of thirty cycles per second to lower long-distance transmission costs further. The company unveiled its polyphase system in 1893. General Electric (GE) did not lag far behind. In 1894, it sold its first polyphase system. Unlike Westinghouse, the GE system had three phases, one at a higher voltage to circumvent the Tesla patents.

The competition between GE and Westinghouse persisted into the twentieth century, but on terms different from previous struggles between electricity suppliers. Earlier customers had been forced to choose the type of electrical system (AC or DC) to employ. By 1900 various devices freed them from that decision: rotary converters could change between AC and DC current; phase converters could change AC phases; motor-generator couplers could run on one type of electricity while supplying another. Customers selected devices best suited to their particular needs; the various electrical systems themselves had been systematized, and customers picked from a wide range of

*Electricity-generating plants relied on water
turbines or coal- or oil-powered steam engines to
produce electricity.*

components. This new situation contributed to the 1896 decision by
Westinghouse and GE to pool patents for fifteen years; competition
now rested on excellence in manufacturing, not ingenuity. Patent-
pooling provided GE access to Tesla's patents, and the company replaced unbalanced AC with balanced, three-phase AC, which was
vastly superior for induction motor operation and quickly became the
industry standard. The sixty-cycle frequency introduced by Westinghouse in the early 1890s as a compromise between lighting and power
requirements served by 1920 as the standard electric frequency.

Electrical suppliers' drive to effect economies of scale joined great
areas and large populations, and the resulting reductions in cost both
reflected and encouraged increased electricity consumption. Westinghouse's Niagara Falls project, completed in 1896, stood as the first
practical demonstration of large-scale power generation. Steam engines gave way to water and steam turbogenerators—turbines—as
transmission voltages reached 40,000 volts in 1897; 60,000 volts in

1900; and about 150,000 volts by 1910. Larger, more economical stations utilized water power to supply low-cost electricity for hundreds of miles.

THE DEVELOPMENT OF TELEPHONES

As with electric lighting, American telephony graphically demonstrates both the centrality of systems in late–nineteenth-century thought and practice, and the debt that many late-century inventors and entrepreneurs owed telegraphy. Alexander Graham Bell himself proposed telephonic central stations, and had labored to redesign telegraphic devices, while much of the telephone's early funding came from telegraph investors. But unlike electric lighting, the telephone system directly competed with the telegraph and ultimately led to its demise.

Bell certainly did not set out to destroy telegraphy. He was passionately involved with speech. Professor of elocution at Boston University, the Scottish-born Bell used "Visible Speech"—mouth and tongue drawings of properly articulated sounds—to teach deaf children to talk. Bell hoped to supplement his meager income through inventing. With no electrical training, Bell tackled the thorny problem of sending many signals over a single telegraph wire. His speech and sound waves work led him to contemplate in 1872 a harmonic telegraph, one that used tuning forks to send and respond to precisely oscillated currents. In 1874 he paused to develop a phonoautograph, a device to convert sounds into written markings that employed an actual human ear. Although the phonoautograph had few practical applications, the vibration of the tiny eardrum and bones intrigued Bell, and he wondered if electric impulses could vibrate a membrane to reconstitute speech. That speculation was the germ of Bell's telephone labors, and he explored it as he continued his harmonic telegraph studies.

Bell's breakthrough came in June 1875. Working on his harmonic telegraph with Thomas A. Watson, a mechanic, in Charles Williams's electrical supply shop, Bell distinctly heard a spring twang on his circuit; his telegraph's make–break circuit had apparently fused, and a magnetized steel spring vibrated over a magnet, which varied the intensity of electricity produced and sent sound over the wire. During the next several months, Watson and Bell attempted to refine the elements of this discovery. They ultimately settled on iron-plate diaphragms. Sound waves vibrated the diaphragms, established electromagnetic currents in copper induction coils located at ends of permanent magnets, and transmitted current through wires. These electromagnetic impulses were received by other diaphragms, which vibrated to emit sound waves.

Bell submitted a patent application on February 14, 1876. His application included a battery-powered telephonic device. A diaphragm in a battery circuit was connected to a wire resting in acidified water. Sound waves vibrated the diaphragm, which varied wire depth and resistance, producing variable current. The receiver was similar to Bell's electromagnetic telephone. Bell's last-second addition of the battery telephone—he scribbled its particulars in the margin—proved propitious. That afternoon Elisha Gray, who also had been investigating a harmonic telegraph, attempted to file a *caveat* with the patent office to construct a similar instrument.

Bell's patent was approved in March. His public lectures trumpeted the invention as he concentrated on improving it. Only 230 telephones were in use in July 1877; competition from telegraphy and the electromagnetic telephone's poor voice quality delayed initial acceptance. But when some Western Union customers replaced telegraphs with telephones, that giant company immediately recognized telephones as a threat to its business, and it challenged the Bell patent, maintaining that Gray had priority. It also employed Edison to improve the battery telephone's transmitter (in Edison's version, vibrations of the diaphragm changed pressure between fine carbon granules, which varied circuit resistance), and converted its subsidiary, Western Electric, the nation's largest electrical supplier, into a telephone manufacturer. Bell countered by filing a patent-infringement suit, purchasing Francis Blake's battery-transmitter patent (a voice-activated diaphragm varied pressure on a connection between a hard carbon block mounted on a strong spring and a platinum bead mounted on a weak spring, which changed circuit resistance), and abandoning the inadequate electromagnetic telephone.

Western Union's interest in telephony guaranteed the device's future. The number of phones in service increased markedly as the dispute moved through the courts. By the time the two parties reached accord in late 1879, and Western Union withdrew from the telephone business and sold its phones to Bell, the telegraph company's telephones numbered nearly 56,000. Six hundred other groups contested the Bell patent, but it stood until the early 1890s.

Western Union's agreement to exit telephony was shortsighted. At least a year earlier Bell had conceived of telephones in a new way—as linked to central exchange systems. "It is possible to connect every man's house, office or factory with a central station, so as to give him direct communication with his neighbors," he wrote in 1878. Bell envisioned for each locality a system of branch wires running from dwellings and shops attached to subordinate cables buried underground and paralleling thoroughfares. These cables would be connected to an underground main cable, leading to a central office. Each call would go to the central office and be channeled to the appropriate party. All telephone lines were above ground when Bell made his

Contemporaries feared that a maze of telephone wires would plague cities. Central exchanges reduced that threat.

statements, and only a handful of rudimentary exchanges existed. Most telephone lines ran from place to place, and contemporaries feared that expansion would result in a Byzantine maze of wires. Invention of the switchbox and, a bit later, adaptation of telegraph switchboards to telephony enabled those connected to a particular exchange to converse with each other, but those mechanisms accommodated few subscribers. Indeed, switchboard development was a crucial gain for Bell Telephone in its acquisition of Western Electric in the Western Union settlement. Western Electric gave Bell control of important switchboard patents, as well as the capacity to produce an almost inexhaustible supply of phones to lease.

Demand quickly exceeded even Western Electric's switchboard capabilities. Bell purchased individual inventors' patents, and Bell exchanges (local companies ceded their stock and often control to Bell Telephone for rights to lease Bell equipment) experimented with modified switchboard designs. Peg switchboards and jackknife switches fueled further exchange expansion. Introduction of multiple switchboards in the mid-1880s allowed exchanges to handle 10,000 phones and paved the way for mature interexchange telephony.

Replacement in the mid-1890s of individual telephone batteries with large common batteries situated in central exchanges completed

From the start, Bell Telephone selected women as operators.

the transformation from individual phones to central stations. There female operators—the first appeared in the late 1880s—responded to signals transmitted in underground cables that lit their switchboard lights, and then manually connected the parties. The powerful common battery both facilitated voice transmission and activated individual telephone bells.

Central exchanges tied telephones into a system, but each system was limited to the locality. Telephony's initial reliance on grounded, single iron-wire circuits made long-distance transmission almost impossible. Interference affected even relatively short calls. Substitution of copper for iron wire, addition of a second circuit-completing wire, and insulation of wires with enamel reduced static markedly. Telephone connections were established between Boston and New York in 1884, and Washington, D.C., and Chicago in 1893. The latter represented the maximum effective long-distance telephone communication prior to 1900.

Long-distance service was vital to Bell Telephone's fortunes after expiration of Bell's patents, when it faced competition from numerous independent phone companies. By 1900, 6,000 independent phone companies had placed 600,000 phones in operation, while the Bell company had only 800,000. Bell lowered prices and improved service to counter independents, but its long-distance capabilities attracted consumers. Competitors generally lacked the capital, rights of way, and organization necessary to establish competing long-distance lines. As a result of Bell's virtual long-distance monopoly, businesses and households often bought service from both Bell and an independent; independents gained an impressive share of local traffic, but only Bell subscribers received long-distance service. Bell's introduction of loading coils in the early twentieth century expanded possible long-distance transmission to about 1,500 miles and reduced signal attenuation.

As the sole competent long-distance company, Bell was indispensable. New product models would not secure it a larger market share, so Bell sought instead to generate economy by standardizing equipment—by minimizing supplies and parts needed for repair. It aggressively bought out independents, maintaining that in telephony the nation deserved "one policy, one system, universal service." Bell favored government telephone regulation after 1906 to preserve its entrenched position and guarantee its investors a dependable, substantial return; Bell became America's telephone company.

Telephone and Radio

In 1907, Lee De Forest formed a company to contest Bell Telephone's long-distance supremacy. Unlike earlier competitors, De Forest planned to send messages through the air, not wires; radio was intended to rival the telephone. De Forest's initiative built on the preceding quarter-century's labors. Heinrich Hertz's 1888 demonstration that electromagnetic radiation produced waves of specific frequencies that resonated with similarly tuned apparatus was soon followed by Oliver Lodge's and Guglielmo Marconi's longer transmissions. England's John Ambrose Fleming opened the electronic era in 1904. He produced a diode (a two-element vacuum tube), which received and rectified radio signals, an application of Edison's earlier observation that a weak current passed in one direction through a vacuum between a light-bulb filament and metal plate. Two years later, De Forest placed a zigzag grid between the two elements, set a small voltage on the grid, and found that it created much greater plate voltage; his three-element vacuum tube, the triode, amplified radio signals. That discovery, and Reginald Fessenden's invention of a dependable transmitter (a high-frequency alternator) the same year, gave De Forest impetus to challenge Bell.

Bell Telephone initially discounted the radio threat and concentrated on developing coast-to-coast service. It devised several electromagnetic repeaters, but they proved too slow and distorted the voice. Its lack of a workable continental system, coupled with the continuing efforts of companies such as De Forest's, led Bell after 1909 to launch a massive search for a suitable repeater. It turned to triodes in 1912, but found De Forest's tubes inadequate for power loads necessary for telephone transmission, and too short-lived. Rather than reject triodes, Bell personnel sought to improve them. Fortifying the vacuum was perhaps their most important contribution. It yielded an effective repeater, and on January 25, 1915, Bell inaugurated its first transcontinental line.

Bell's telephonic interest in triodes also introduced the company to radio. Its 1913 acquisition of De Forest's triode patent seemed to give Bell a commanding position, but both General Electric and British Marconi contested the patent. In addition, GE had helped develop Fessenden's transmitter, and had secured patent control. World War I brought another combatant: the federal government removed patent restrictions on radio and drafted Westinghouse along with GE and Bell to establish wartime communications. After the war, British Marconi sold to GE control of its American subsidiary, which was renamed the Radio Corporation of America (RCA), and GE authorized RCA to sell and distribute GE radio products.

These disputed claims stymied the various parties. No single organization had the critical radio-transmitter and receiver patents. Instead of waiting for the courts, rivals entered into a patent cross-licensing agreement in 1920 and 1921. Peace did not reign long; creation of radio stations, with their potentially enormous market for radio receivers, produced discord. Although Westinghouse established the first station in 1920, Bell's entrance into the fray in 1922 increased tensions. Bell conceived of a nationwide network of Bell-controlled stations dominating American radio, and it refused to allow competitors to use long-distance lines for their feeds. RCA, GE, and Westinghouse took the question to arbitration. The arbitrator's decision became moot in 1925 when the U.S. Court of Appeals ruled that GE was entitled to patent protection for high-vacuum electron-tube use; Bell lost its claim to any fundamental radio patent. Bell left the radio business after its defeat and granted its former competitors telephone-line access for network radio transmission in return for monopolies on ship-to-shore and transoceanic radio telephony.

SYSTEMATIZING THE TECHNOLOGISTS

Individuals demonstrating special skills or technical expertise have always abounded in America and have performed vital functions. The nation's military academies, especially West Point, long had trained men in the building arts, and masters had transmitted their special knowledge to apprentices. By the mid-nineteenth century, broad technical experience had been recognized as apt preparation for business administration, and men engaged in technical occupations had occasionally formed organizations for camaraderie and to discuss objects of mutual concern.

Engineering Organizations

Not until about 1870, however, was the nation's first exclusive engineering organization, the American Society of Civil Engineers (ASCE), established to organize America's engineers. The ASCE soon proved unwieldy. Creation of more specialized organizations followed it: the American Institute of Mining Engineers (1871); American Society of Mechanical Engineers (1880); American Institute of Electrical Engineers (1884); American Institute of Chemical Engineers (1908); and Institute of Radio Engineers (1912). Each society catered to a particular constituency within the larger engineering profession.

Formation of the ASCE and other engineering organizations signaled the emergence of American engineering self-consciousness. This emergence stood as part of the more general late–nineteenth-century division of American society in which expertise replaced character as the *sine qua non* for evaluating competence. Engineers identified themselves as a group fundamentally different from other people. They considered themselves technically advanced planners, designers, facilitators, and administrators, not merely producers or artisans. They argued that special knowledge and skill—expertise—characterized each engineering division and made it distinctive, and mastery of that expertise entitled those engineers to special authority. Each of these societies would systematically seek a superior social role for its constituents.

Although self-identification was a critical step for engineers, gaining public sanction for their authority was paramount; without it they could never have jurisdiction in areas where they claimed entitlement. These societies sought public sanction from their inception, but they did not gain it until the twentieth century. They explored political participation, but the societies preferred to attack the matter internally; they gradually added rules and mechanisms to guarantee that their membership would have the expertise congruent with the social responsibility they proclaimed, and to guarantee that future members possessed such expertise as well. The societies had various membership categories and requirements. They held regular meetings and published periodicals subject to peer review. They established standards of practice and codes of ethics to govern professional and private behavior. All these systematically worked to standardize each division's membership. The societies also sponsored or recommended engineering school curricula, thereby systematizing professional entrance. These varied devices helped convince an often skeptical public that engineers met their self-announced criteria, and therefore deserved the authority that they sought.

The ASCE In the 1870s and early 1880s, engineers had few precedents to follow. Self-definition was the motivation behind building professional institutions, but that placed a premium on harmony, often at the expense of substance. As the nation's first engineering society, the ASCE pioneered molding individuals into an effective national entity. Founded in New York in 1867, the initial membership came almost exclusively from the New York metropolitan area; of its 106 members in 1870, seventy-three resided within fifty miles of Manhattan. By 1880, the society's membership had grown sixfold, and only 114 members lived near the nation's greatest metropolis. The society aggressively pursued a national agenda by forming numerous committees to investigate national standards of practice and standardized methods. But the nascent society's efforts rarely resulted in nationwide changes in engineering practice. In almost all instances, its committees either failed to articulate policy, or the society refused its endorsement.

ASCE lacked clout, not conviction. Public vituperative displays would soil the society's public image as well as its professional credibility. Refusing to decide potentially divisive questions stopped the society from alienating the public or segments of its still-fragile constituency; concern for organizational homogeneity—and survival—was greater than concern for erecting standards. That committee formation to investigate professional problems and concerns marked the end rather than the beginning of ASCE deliberations was less important than the fact that American civil engineers had a single national entity in which to voice their propositions.

The ASCE's committee on college engineering curricula exemplified this thrust. Established in 1874 to chart a standard set of college engineering courses, the committee issued its report later that year and was then excused; it offered no recommendations. It only congratulated colleges for having "done more to elevate the standard of the engineering profession than any other single agency." The committee also noted that an engineer's real worth was judged by his working-world performance. Only "long and varied experience" in conjunction "with a body of practical engineers"—the ASCE—made a master.

The college committee dealt with an emotionally charged issue. Gauging river and stream flow (1875), establishing a single masonry nomenclature (1876), deciding the best rail manufacturing and testing methods (1876), creating standardized railroad signals (1875), and urging federal adoption of the metric system (1874 and 1877) seemed less menacing, yet the ASCE likewise did not advocate a clear position on any of these questions. After considering each subject, the committees either offered no report or articulated a statement that the society summarily dismissed. Any hint of controversy during the 1870s resulted in the society's tabling a matter.

The ASCE proved more willing to embrace conflict in the 1880s. A desire for harmony, crucial during the previous decade, dissipated as the society gained members. The ASCE marked its turf and risked offending some. One mid-1880s incident signaled the organization's new pugnacity.

The ASCE officers' 1884 decision to require members to wear emblems—a bubble level—at meetings and in public produced an unprecedented ruckus. Roughly a hundred members complained that engineers designed and managed projects. Assistants surveyed and used levels; the badge therefore denigrated engineers. The officers refused to budge, however, and the emblem remained the organization's official symbol until 1894.

The ASCE flourished despite conflict. It had 878 members in 1885 and more than a thousand in 1890. The organization confidently had moved beyond cementing a constituency to shaping the profession. It continued that effort during the next several decades. The society adopted a code of ethics (1914), created technical divisions to establish engineering standards (1912), started student ASCE chapters at engineering colleges (1919), and advocated the licensing of engineers by boards of examination (1911). In 1916, the ASCE had nearly eight thousand members.

Systematizing Technical Education

ASCE and other engineering societies increasingly turned their attention to the next generation of engineering professionals. Shaping the collective future—defining and standardizing future engineers, and delineating their rights and responsibilities—would enhance and cement engineering's public standing. A formal collegiate engineering education would become *de rigueur* by 1910, and nearly all engineers accepting their first position after that date would hold engineering degrees. The nation's 126 engineering-degree-granting institutions would award more than 17,000 engineering degrees between 1911 and 1915.

Though engineering societies concentrated on engineering college students from the 1880s, several engineers had examined engineering education earlier. What these purveyors of expertise uncovered no doubt shocked and disappointed them. Only about one in twenty practicing engineers in 1871 had received a collegiate engineering degree. Most had been trained on the job. In fact, only about 800 engineering degrees had been granted prior to 1870 at American military academies, land-grant colleges, polytechnic institutes, and scientific schools. Nor had these early engineers been prepared for collegiate training. Few high schools existed in 1870 and no established curriculum readied college students. Age was usually the most critical college admission criterion, with sixteen years of age often the minimum. These young men generally were so woefully unprepared that several institutions awarding engineering degrees felt compelled to create special preparatory departments to provide prospective engineers the rudiments necessary for collegiate studies.

The essence of creating a college-educated engineering profession was determining what engineering colleges would teach. Questions of curricula were closely intertwined with emergence of engineering self-consciousness. Formation of the Mechanical Engineering Teachers Association (1892), Society for the Promotion of Engineering Education (1893), and the Joint Committee of Engineering Education of the National Engineering Societies (1907) manifested concern. The last group invited the Carnegie Foundation for the Advancement of Teaching and the General Education Board to its deliberations. Individual colleges also experimented and produced initiatives. On one facet all agreed: The reliance on mathematical and physical science methods and determinations should form the backbone of engineering school curricula. These sciences made engineers distinctive and discriminated them from mere workers; professions required scientific bases. But although engineering schools offered students heavy doses of mathematical and physical sciences, and then moved into engineering theory and theoretical design, concerned engineers reached no similar consensus about the curriculum's other aspects. Practice, and its relationship to theory and engineering education, proved particularly troublesome.

Theory versus Practice Before the mid-1870s, engineering educators held especially disparate views about practice. To some, knowledge of science and theory marked professionals; practice was outside engineers' province or was to be learned on the job. For this group, laboratory apparatus to reinforce scientific or theoretical principles served as the extent of collegiate hands-on experience. Another camp stressed practice, and considered creation of masterpieces critical. Masterpieces were engineering benchmarks; their skillful manufacture enabled engineers to rationalize industrial processes.

Both sides modified their positions somewhat in the mid-1870s and after. Mechanical engineering education reflected those shifts. For example, in 1876 Massachusetts Institute of Technology's John D. Runkle adapted Russian technical-school methods to American engineering education. He argued that machine manufacture could be reduced into a number of typical operations and that those operations could be organized into groups, each depending on a distinctive machine tool. He required students to become expert in a tool and the group of operations employing that tool before permitting them to advance to the next tool. Runkle rejected the manufacture of finished products as vocational in nature, but affirmed that engineers needed competence in both theoretical design and practical manipulation to achieve their proper station.

Cornell University's Robert Thurston chose not to follow Runkle's lead. A founder of the American Society of Mechanical Engineers (ASME), he de-emphasized practice at Cornell in the late 1880s and substituted specialized courses such as steam engineering design. Thurston accentuated movement into new areas, not mastery of established techniques, but he also fostered an engineer–industry nexus by inviting industrialists to address students and faculty about manufacturing questions. These noted men provided the engineering curriculum's practical aspects. So too did frequent tours of Northeastern manufacturing facilities.

In 1906, University of Cincinnati's Herman Schneider went further. He divorced theory and practice completely by restricting college teaching to the former. But his cooperative system made practice a full engineering education partner; students attended classes half the school year and worked in industry during the remainder. Schneider claimed that his approach constituted "real practical work" because students' industrial training progressed from the least skillful tasks to purely engineering activities; they gained a feel for the full spectrum of duties.

Schneider's cooperative education was the last major attempt before 1910 to harmonize theory and practice. Other issues also plagued engineering educators. They expressed dissatisfaction over the number of engineering school dropouts (nearly 60 percent), inflexible curricula, and lack of standardized engineering curricula, both across the nation and within individual schools' engineering divisions. This ferment led the joint Committee of Engineering Education of the National Engineering Societies to ask the Carnegie Foundation to investigate American engineering education; it selected Charles R. Mann, a University of Chicago physicist, to compile a report. Issued in 1918, the Mann report attributed engineering school deficiencies to a "lack of coordination," especially an overemphasis on specialization. Mann urged colleges to limit enrollment by drafting a standardized admission test to determine engineering aptitude, and suggested that schools require entering students to take standardized general-engineering orientation courses. Under the present system, he complained, students usually took only science and drafting classes during their first two years. Their initial taste of engineering came in third-year specialized courses, a situation that undermined professional unity. Nor was Mann satisfied with the nature of specialized courses. He argued for the case study method, sometimes known as the laboratory method of teaching. He wanted engineering students to analyze machines and structures for their fundamental operating and structural principles; he insisted that students deduce from applications the principles themselves.

Systematizing Technical Research

The engineering self-consciousness of the last third of the nineteenth century also spawned questions about the relationship between engineers and research, and between engineering research and industry. To be sure, American technologists always had tried to improve established processes or uncover new ones, and had a long, profitable marriage with American industry. But these efforts were primarily ad hoc problem-solving inquiries, which differed in emphasis and usually in method from late–nineteenth- and early–twentieth-century research. After about 1870, research was inextricably linked to a kind of expertise, one characterized by knowledge not only of a particular subject but, especially, of the techniques of systematic, rational inquiry. Investigations rationally conceived and vigorously pursued seemed to produce unambiguous, indisputable, nonpartisan results; they yielded new knowledge.

These investigations were based on precision and verification, which encouraged design of physically discrete, adequately equipped, and hierarchically governed areas (laboratories) to eliminate variability and variables. Investigators in these rigorously controlled laboratory environments measured, weighed, and counted to test and formulate their hypotheses. A few laboratories appeared in mid-nineteenth-century America, but early facilities were primarily pedagogical devices to demonstrate established principles to students or to teach technical competency—not to manufacture new knowledge. Not until the late 1870s did a substantial number of American colleges and universities adopt the research-laboratory idea, and provide permanent institutional homes for laboratories. Johns Hopkins University was perhaps the most influential.

The well-endowed Johns Hopkins University was established in the mid-1870s as an experiment in higher education. Freedom from past practice permitted its president, Daniel C. Gilman, to emphasize original research. The university paid its faculty salaries higher than comparable institutions to attract the most promising people, and reduced teaching responsibilities to allow research time. Its laboratories were "adapted for exact measurement of physical quantities rather than for . . . qualitative illustration." Laboratory apparatus was "for investigation," not "for amusing children." Those on fellowships worked in the professors' laboratories, as did graduate students preparing for research careers. The university supported several research journals and created a press to publish research monographs. Johns Hopkins University's prominence stimulated others to implement the research-laboratory idea. By the 1880s, research laboratories could be found in universities as diverse as Wisconsin, Cornell, Stanford, Michigan, Harvard, and California.

Definition of research as a particular kind of expertise placed the engineering profession in a perplexing situation during the several decades after 1870. Clearly, the vast majority of practicing American engineers had no research training (or even a collegiate education), nor would terms of their employment permit them to engage in research activities. Yet laboratory research was increasingly being seen as the wellspring of technological innovation; it seemed that technological change often was the consequence of laboratory-generated knowledge and that systematically pursued laboratory investigation, though not immediately directed at practical applications, would nonetheless frequently yield major practical applications. This dilemma rarely found explicit extensive articulation within engineering societies because its formal consideration would surely have created an unwelcome, potentially divisive conflagration. Identification of research as an integral part of the engineering profession would grant engineers undertaking research greater status—and economic advantages—than those shunning it, while if the profession disassociated itself from research it would suffer a considerable loss of public esteem.

Engineering leaders attempted to smooth over the anticipated schism by treating it *en passant* as a legitimate professional activity, distinct from engineering practice proper, and justifying regular apportioning of funding, time, and respect. Engineering-society publications and honors reflected that approach. So, too, did engineering colleges, which began after 1900 to define research as a vital professional function, to select faculty with demonstrated proficiencies in research techniques manifested by research degrees—Ph.D.s—and to prepare the most promising students for academic life. Division between engineering researchers and practitioners also held predictable consequences. Equating research with a passionate search for truth engendered concern that those not thus engaged were serfs of industrial interests, which fostered cleavage between engineers, and between the profession and industry. Identification of research as the cradle of innovation, coupled with the profession's failure to go on record embracing research as its own, reduced practical engineering's overall public status. It suggested that the professional groups that had claimed systematic laboratory investigation as their fundamental activity—the scientists—stood preeminent, and that practicing engineers simply applied what scientists had uncovered; engineers seemed mere technicians. Scientists preached, and engineers then practiced what was preached.

Industrial Research Laboratories A dropoff in public acclaim and simmering tensions between business and the profession did not prevent industries from employing engineers. The industry–technical

nexus remained as it always had been, immediately directed at productivity. Not until around the turn of the century did industry establish a new use for corporate-employed engineers. They were to work
in industrial research laboratories, a new type of institution but clearly
derivative of academia. Industrial research laboratories were not responsible to production facilities. Companies generally located laboratories away from manufacturing sites to insulate them from businesses' most pressing demands; laboratory scientists and engineers
were encouraged to investigate natural phenomena, not merely to improve production.

Profitability, not altruism, led industrialists to form corporate research laboratories. They were convinced that systematic investigation
was a critical determinant of technological innovation, and sought to
systematize and privatize research. Original research should inevitably translate into new products, techniques, or processes. Corporate ownership of research institutes would speed and shape development and restrict access to discoveries until they were patented and
implemented. Only the economics of industrial research laboratories
gave pause, because they demanded steep initial investment in equipment and personnel and promised slow returns.

By 1900, many corporations, especially chemical and electrical
concerns, had had nearly three decades of experience with laboratory-
based technology and had a firmer sense of its economic prospects. Indeed, as early as the 1870s, American industries had looked to the nation's colleges and universities to provide private research and
researchers. Companies had consulted with professors who used university facilities, and had employed academics and their students.
During the twentieth century's first decades, several large firms with
sufficient capital to undertake the venture and withstand the temporary lack of earnings decided that corporate-owned laboratories made
sound economic sense. As Willis Whitney, director of GE's pioneering
research laboratory put it, "Our research laboratory [is] a development
of the idea that large industrial organizations have both an opportunity and a responsibility for their own life insurance. New discoveries
can provide it." GE's laboratory was quickly followed by Du Pont
(1902), Goodyear (1908), AT&T (1911), General Motors (1911), Eastman Kodak (1912), and American Cyanamid (1912). By 1931, 1,600
companies reportedly established industrial research laboratories, employing nearly 33,000 people.

Industrial research laboratories stood as only one example of a
much larger cultural phenomenon. Late–nineteenth- and early–twentieth-century Americans in all walks of life acted as if their world was
composed of systems, and worked to design or arrange these systems'
diverse components so as to achieve peak efficiency. Such was the case
in technical education and organization, but in the case of corporations,

peak efficiency meant larger profits; communications technologies and electric lighting and power are clear examples of this. These spheres of activity, however, by no means exhausted the possibilities. Although Americans frequently disputed the elements or order of systems, the notion of system itself pervaded virtually every aspect of American life in the half-century after 1870. In sum, the country's inhabitants reinvented and remanufactured their nation.

FOR FURTHER READING

Aitken, Hugh G. J. *Syntony and Spark: The Origins of Radio* (1976).

Bruce, Robert V. *Alexander Graham Bell and the Conquest of Solitude* (1973).

Calvert, Monte A. *The Mechanical Engineer in America, 1830–1910* (1967).

Cheney, Margaret. *Tesla: Man Out of Time* (1981).

Clark, Ronald W. *Edison: The Man Who Made the Future* (1977).

Fischer, Claude S. *America Calling: A Social History of the Telephone to 1940* (1992).

Friedel, Robert, and Paul Israel. *Edison's Electric Light: Biography of an Invention* (1986).

Garnet, Robert W. *The Telephone Enterprise* (1985).

Grayson, Lawrence P. *The Making of an Engineer: An Illustrated History of Engineering Education in the United States and Canada* (1993).

Hawkins, Hugh. *Pioneer: A History of the Johns Hopkins University* (1960).

Hughes, Thomas P. *Networks of Power* (1983).

Josephson, Matthew. *Edison: A Biography* (1959).

Kevles, Daniel J. *The Physicists* (1978).

Layton, Edwin T., Jr. *The Revolt of the Engineers* (1971).

Leupp, Francis E. *George Westinghouse: His Life and Achievements* (1919).

McKay, John P. *Tramways and Trolleys* (1976).

Mann, Charles Riborg. *A Study of Engineering Education* (1918).

Noble, David F. *America By Design* (1977).

Nye, David E. *Electrifying America: Social Meanings of a New Technology, 1880–1940* (1990).

Passer, Harold C. *The Electrical Manufacturers, 1875–1900* (1953).

Reich, Leonard S. *The Making of American Industrial Research* (1985).

Reynolds, Terry S. *75 Years of Progress: A History of the American Institute of Chemical Engineers* (1983).

Rose, Mark H. *Cities of Light and Heat: Domesticating Gas and Electricity in Urban America* (1995).

Sandhurst, Phillip T. *The Great Centennial Exhibition* (1876).

Sinclair, Bruce. *A Centennial History of the American Society of Mechanical Engineers, 1880–1980* (1980).

Smith, George David. *The Anatomy of a Business Strategy: Bell, Western Electric and the Origins of the American Telephone Industry* (1985).

Wasserman, Neil H. *From Invention to Innovation: Long-Distance Telephone Transmission at the Turn of the Century* (1985).

Wise, George. *Willis R. Whitney and the Origins of U.S. Industrial Research* (1985).

Systematizing the Fabric of American Life: the 1870s to the 1920s

In the late nineteenth and early twentieth centuries, Americans systematically transformed the face of their land. Whereas telegraph lines had merely paralleled existing railroads, and ran only from station to station, electric power and telephone wires and cables proved massive (yet indispensable) intrusions into the landscape as they connected generating plants, central stations, homes, and factories. The nation's inhabitants cut down forests, extracted ores and coal, and built roads at unprecedented rates and in unprecedented numbers. Steam- and then gasoline-powered farm machinery gradually changed the nature of American agriculture. Cities and city structures achieved great size and prominence, and spawned persistent suburbanization.

But the systematic transformation was not limited to the physical environs or the tapping of the country's natural resources. It extended to the social sphere as well. Late–nineteenth-century men and women identified society as a cauldron of diverse peoples, then acted as if that assessment were fact. Educators, other professionals, and businessmen studied the groups they had already defined; reaffirmed that each

143

group had particularistic capacities, capabilities, merits, and deficiencies; and then labored to have their reaffirmations serve as foundations of social and economic policy. The nation seemed complex and diverse, but these observers considered it a single entity, a notion that underscored the importance of uncovering the principles that systematized relations by arranging the many different parts. Those sentiments produced diverse social agendas. Americans agreed that the nation was like a hierarchically arranged organism but disagreed about what segments of the population were its vital organs.

Not all Americans were consumed by disputes over who should hold power. Many were drawn to the less explicitly political question of leisure, itself a product of rigid categorization and compartmentalization, and therefore a fit object of social concern. Those concerned often combined physical and social elements to create leisure institutions of two major types; some were established to cater to a particular segment of society and were tacit acknowledgments of society's divisions, while others sought to appeal across group boundaries and to help organize the nation's fractious social groups. Americans generally found new technologies or technical processes instrumental in achieving either aim.

SYSTEMATIZING THE PHYSICAL ENVIRONMENT

The New City

The urban landscape was redesigned in the late nineteenth and early twentieth centuries. Horse-drawn street railways and then electric traction facilitated urban expansion and population growth, and frequent annexations kept much of this population within city boundaries. This rapid growth seemed to require the sorting out of peoples and activities; as great numbers of immigrants and rural Americans descended on cities, the correlation of a social type with a specific part of the city became an important urban feature.

Residential neighborhoods became characterized by their inhabitants' class, religion, nationality, race, and occupation. The remaining city area also was differentiated, but by activity or function. Mercantile transactions were the central business district's focus, while heavy industry resided in other city sections. Like residential neighborhoods, both commercial and industrial districts seemed congregations of subdistricts, each exhibiting more precise specialization. Service, pleasure, and entertainment districts abounded as few cities failed to develop thriving tenderloin and tavern areas, or parks and parkways.

New Building Materials Both the nature and increasing size of the new city created a persistent call for massive new construction. Brick, cut stone, plain concrete, cast and wrought iron, and wood were standard building materials through the 1870s. Only in that decade did Americans begin to use iron and steel supports; introduction of fireproof tiles lessened fear that fire would buckle and collapse ferrous members. Builders placed iron and steel in tile envelopes, which permitted entrapped air to dissipate heat, but even then generally employed ferrous materials only to brace floors. Solid masonry, brick, or stone exterior walls bore building weight. These load-bearing walls stood on stone or concrete pyramid footings and absorbed downward and lateral thrusts. Their thicknesses were directly proportional to building height, a factor that limited buildings to about ten stories, diminished interior light, and reduced interior space.

Concrete played a relatively insignificant role in these early buildings. American concrete had traditionally depended on natural quicklime cements to bind together their constituent elements—sand, water, and aggregate. Formed by heating broken limestone to drive off carbon dioxide, these cements had worked adequately for concrete bridge footings from the 1810s, but they lacked the durability and binding power necessary for larger structures common to the new city. Americans looked to Europe for assistance and found that English builders long had used portland cement in public works. Identified in 1824, portland cement manufacturers combined precise measures of chalk and clay, heated the mass to a temperature much hotter than other cements to fuse it, and ground the fused material into fine powder. Americans imported some in the 1860s, but large-scale American adoption of portland cement concrete occurred after America began to manufacture it. Lehigh County, Pennsylvania, was the site of the nation's first portland cement works (1871); others were erected near South Bend, San Antonio, and Kalamazoo by the mid-1880s. Portland cement's superiority continually won it adherents, and manufacturers scrambled to satisfy demand. In 1888, the nation produced about 100 million pounds of portland cement, but still imported nearly eight times as much. Introduction of rotary kilns to heat and grind the cement in the late 1890s permitted domestic manufacturers to produce about 1,500 million pounds by 1898, and to multiply that output nearly sevenfold five years later. By 1913, the nation made 36,800 million pounds of portland cement and imported only a negligible amount.

Rapid adoption of portland cement in the 1870s and early 1880s did not, however, signal a sudden rise in concrete-based urban buildings. Portland cement was commonly poured or cast in blocks and used for piers, seawalls, and dams in the late 1870s and 1880s, but its lack of tensile strength rendered it unsuitable for structural elements subjected to forces other than compression. American builders had recognized that iron and steel withstood shearing and tensile forces, and had occasionally fortified masonry arches with iron bars to prevent

Skyscrapers with curtain walls dominated the urban skyline.

cracking. Even more to the point, French and German architects had begun to use concrete reinforced with steel bars in the 1860s and 1870s. Not until the 1880s did American builders begin to experiment with reinforced concrete, and another decade passed before the combination became a primary building material.

The Skyscraper A new municipal building form, the skyscraper, accompanied introduction of reinforced concrete in the mid-1880s, but was not dependent solely on that building material. Symbols of corporate wealth and success, and de facto expressions of urban diversity—architects divided the structures into three distinct sections: entryway, working space, and attic—skyscrapers quickly transformed the city skyline. These concentrated administrative centers dominated central business districts and testified to the large corporations' urban prominence.

The first two structures that broke with the load-bearing wall tradition and might be considered nascent skyscrapers—George B. Post's Produce Exchange in New York City and William Le Baron Jenney's Home Insurance Building in Chicago—were iron-framed. Interior iron skeletons or cages supported almost all the building's weight, exterior walls acted primarily as weatherproofing, and reinforced concrete rafts comprised the foundation.

These techniques were refined and extended over the next several decades to yield what historians have called "true skyscrapers." Steel T-beams and I-beams replaced iron in these new structures, and rivets supplanted bolts and were in turn supplanted by electric arc welding in the 1920s. Masonry yielded to reinforced concrete as walls that once bore building weight evolved into mere curtains. Shelves extending from the steel skeletons bore curtain-wall weight, while reinforced concrete subflooring became standard.

These modifications produced sturdier, lighter, and taller buildings. Steel possessed greater tension and compression strength than iron or masonry, and greater resistance to fatigue, while weighing less than half as much as masonry or stone. The thin steel interior skeletons occupied less interior space, and curtain walls enabled architects to incorporate large glass windows.

Political Control of the Cities

Newly identified groups fought to demarcate significant roles for themselves in cities in the 1880s and 1890s; each aimed to serve as the urban heart or brains. Bosses generally relied on the endless flow of immigrants for political support, often fortified by bribes and payoffs from influence-seeking electric-traction and electric-power magnates. Ministers, small businessmen, and professionals frequently were the most contentious. Engineers staked claim to power on their technical abilities and experience with public works, while doctors maintained that public health was the preeminent municipal issue, construed it to involve virtually all facets of urban social and economic life, and asserted that medical expertise entitled them to urban leadership. Clergymen cited their moral authority, businessmen based their argument on their fiscal management skills, and lawyers cited their legal acumen.

City Planning Others concentrated directly on the cityscape. Some architects and landscape gardeners called for humane, uncongested cities in which civic architecture was interspersed with parks and other nature settings. Others agitated for a functional or efficient city, arranged to encourage the flow of business and human services. These proposals hinged on similar propositions: rational development of the new city required expert wisdom to plan it, and no single group possessed the necessary expertise alone. "City planning," wrote Cleveland's Frederick C. Howe in 1913, "treats the city as a unit. It anticipates the future ... so as to secure orderly, harmonious and symmetrical development." It "means a city built by experts in architecture, landscape gardening, in engineering and in housing; by students of health, transportation, sanitation, water, gas, and electricity."

Urban planning required concerted action. Each expert group needed to bring its particular expertise to bear on a designated part of the urban environment; each had to share authority and responsibility. Dividing the city into a series of discrete functions, the planning for each dependent on different experts, helped resolve tensions among competing interest groups. But it also produced demand for two new kinds of experts, both of whom specialized in administration and in coordinating the various experts' efforts: commission governments, and then professional city managers, to manage the present; city planning commissions, and ultimately a city-planning profession, to direct preparations for the future.

Formal city planning blossomed after 1900. In 1907, the Russell Sage Foundation sponsored the first citywide survey in America, the Pittsburgh Survey. That initiative was followed in 1909 by three landmark events: Burnham's Chicago Plan, the nation's first comprehensive city plan; the first National Conference on City Planning, held in Washington, D.C.; and Harvard's establishment of a city-planning course to train prospective planners, the first such course offered at an American university. Bureaus of municipal research—consortiums of experts to investigate municipal questions and formulate policy—zoning commissions to control development, and comprehensive city plans became common during the next decade as Americans systematically planned the urban future.

The New Agriculture

Late–nineteenth- and early–twentieth-century American agriculture offers a compelling parallel to the rise of the new city. Around 1870, as city newspapers fretted about municipal chaos and inefficiency, agricultural newspapers and societies complained about farmers' isolation, the drudgery of farm work, and farmers' lack of financial rewards and social standing. These indictments, like those in cities, engendered a wide variety of political, social, and economic campaigns, including formation of farmers' clubs, the Grange, the Populist Party, and the Good Roads movement. Each movement sought to overcome obstacles or to add what was missing or defective in agricultural life—to remove, add, or repair systemic elements—so that farmers could assume their rightful places in the modern American social system.

The Railroads and Agriculture Railroads were among the earliest and most sustained objects of farmers' concerns. Farmers, especially those in the South and Great Plains, deplored railroad pooling arrangements, rebate policies, and short-haul discrimination; maintained that these practices eroded farm profits and constituted gouging; and organized politically for redress.

Railroads had helped foster agriculture's westward march by selling land obtained from land grants to prospective farmers and speculators. Agricultural output west of the Mississippi was negligible as late as 1860, but by 1900 North Dakota and Minnesota had become the nation's largest wheat producers; Iowa, Kansas, and Nebraska (and Illinois, which is east of the Mississippi) its largest corn growers; and Texas its largest cotton producer. These states (Illinois excepted) had more than 42,000 railroad miles in 1900, a dramatic forty-five-fold increase in forty years.

Despite the vehement criticism, a railroad–agriculture nexus persisted, often to agriculture's advantage. Although railroad combination and consolidation, particularly in the two decades after 1890, did permit seven groups to control more than two-thirds of the nation's nearly 250,000 railroad miles, railroads reduced rates for agricultural products and enhanced service during that period. Technical factors and industry-wide administrative decisions enabled railroads to furnish cheaper, faster, and safer travel. Swifter, heavier, more powerful locomotives with greater traction moved longer trains and heavier cars, while adoption of the Janney automatic coupler, widespread air-brake employment, and use of iron and steel as universal materials in railroad-bridge construction speeded operations and reduced accidents. Mechanical refrigerator cars and special animal cars with feed bins and watering troughs ensured that farm products reached their market in excellent shape. An industry-wide standard railroad time (1883) facilitated transport, and a similarly derived standard American railroad gauge (1890s) did away with superfluous reloading costs. Spurs were connected to feeders, and feeders to trunk lines, in America's truly integrated nationwide railroad system.

Systematizing the Farm   A reproach to contemporary farm practice paralleled railroad criticism. Farm practice's critics, many of whom were themselves farmers, contended that "guesswork, random efforts [and] 'cut and try' methods" constituted prevailing agricultural practice. These procedures were outdated, and critics urged farmers to renounce antiquated practices, to let brains guide hands and machines, and to farm with "system." They defined system as "a collection of rules and principles" in which each individual activity had "a proper classification and a proper assignment." System was "a place for everything and everything in its proper place," where everything was "done at the proper time and in the proper manner."

These systematic agriculturists assumed that farming was composed of numerous discrete operations and that success was the consequence of rationally conceived and pursued methods. No activity seemed unimportant, and each required scrutiny and rationalization. Organization of farm space was a critical concomitant. The shape and location of farm buildings, utilization of tools and machinery, location of fields, and position of fences were predicated on their ability to enhance farm practice. For example, octagonal and circular barns increasingly replaced traditional rectangular buildings after 1870. Although more complicated and expensive to construct, the new barn designs used space more efficiently and promised to speed farm work. Their self-supporting domes or rounded roofs required no space-consuming posts or support beams, and hay forks could operate unobstructed in their larger lofts. The two designs further reduced wasted space and facilitated farm labor by minimizing or doing away with corners; aisles were circular, not linear, and animal stalls were arranged around aisles, which lessened the number of steps farmers needed to take. Although these innovations seemed minor, advocates hailed them as powerful examples of systematic farming's virtues and as demonstrative of the potential of efficient organization.

The unusual shape of these octagonal and circular barns dominated the rural skyline, testified to their owners' prominence, and served as the central farm focus. Steam-traction engines played a similar symbolic role on the Great Plains, as well as a more practical one. Mounted on steel frames, these monstrous twenty-five-ton vehicles were powered by heavy steel high-pressure engines, which turned tracks or steel wheels with protruding lugs or rivet heads for better traction. Visible from miles away, their popularity stemmed from the plains' peculiar

*Early internal-combustion-engine tractors, such as
this 1908 Caterpillar model, made inroads on the
Great Plains but remained a rarity on farms
elsewhere.*

topography and climate: its firm, level, dry soil supported their great
weight, while the lack of rainfall and need for irrigation made dry farming the only conceivably profitable agricultural form.

Based on the retention of capillary moisture, dry farming required
deep plowing immediately after every rainfall—finely divided soil
holds water nearer the surface where roots can tap it—as well as har-
rowing to create a dust cap to slow evaporation. Speed was essential
because untrapped water would percolate through and compact soils
or evaporate quickly. Russian wheat was one of the few crops that
grew satisfactorily under dry-farming conditions. It converted the
plains into the nation's breadbasket.

Dry farming made steam-traction engines feasible. Pulling draw-
bar-attached steel disk plows and disk harrows, these engines provided the power necessary for frequent deep plowing, and the speed
crucial for utilization of cropland moisture. The largest machine towed
thirty plows and tilled one hundred acres a day. Their belt pulleys,
which could be operated effectively only when engines were stationary, ran threshers. No other type of agriculture offered this potent
combination of uses or this scale of activity.

Nor did the introduction of internal-combustion traction engines—true tractors—spark a nationwide tractor boom. First manufactured in the mid-1890s, tractors were lighter, less dangerous, and more powerful than steam traction, but no more useful. Although these factors enabled tractors eventually to supplant steam-traction engines—frameless, unit-driven tricycle tractors weighed less than five tons and developed more than twice the horsepower of large steam-traction engines—they remained practical only on the Great Plains.

Establishing rational agricultural plans depended on more than fancy machinery and buildings. It required knowing the facts, the costs of farming. A complete farm accounting system—detailed double-entry bookkeeping—enabled agriculturists to learn each act's cost/benefit ratio. Informal time/motion studies—comparisons of time taken to complete various tasks—also served as a technology to systematize farming. Agricultural societies and newspapers were conduits for announcements of investigative results, and they satisfied the farmers' obligation to report findings to their peers for review, verification, and criticism. Collegial sanction often led others to adopt the practices, which tended to standardize farm operations. Implement manufacturers also participated. Hart-Parr, the largest gas-tractor company, created in 1911 the Hart-Parr School of Traction Farming and Traction Engineering. Farmers were quizzed on how to operate, farm with, and fix equipment. They even received lessons in the importance of studying: "study systematically and carefully . . . do it with system . . . do not let pleasure or other work interfere with your study hours if you can possibly avoid it."

The Challenge of Agricultural Colleges The nation's agricultural college professors sympathized with the farmers' plight but generally opposed the systematic farmers' methods to resolve it. They favored systematizing farm activities, but maintained that agriculturists or their allies were incapable of developing rational farming plans. To these academics, the systematic farmer approach was superficial and arbitrary; profit-and-loss statements and time/motion studies were inexact reflections of plant and animal growth principles. Their agenda emphasized uncovering these not-yet-completely understood principles, a task that lay beyond farmers. Only experts schooled in investigative methods—rigorous systematization—commanded the ability to decipher agricultural principles; agricultural college professors usually identified themselves as possessors of that expertise. Successful farm systematization demanded expert-derived knowledge expertly applied; farmers were to practice what agricultural scientists preached.

Rural road quality also systematized relations between farmers and agricultural college personnel. Rural roads were closed by winter snows, and turned by spring and autumn rains into impassable mud rivers, which kept farmers from their markets and increased isolation. Likening a complete country road system to "the arteries and veins in the human system, through which the blood circulates," farmers established state Good Roads conventions in the late 1880s and a national Good Roads convention in 1893. The national convention was funded by A. A. Pope, a leading bicycle manufacturer, and joined rural dissatisfaction over roads with bicycle-hype enthusiasm.

These conventions often offered rural road construction plans. But it was the land-grant college engineers, especially in the Midwest, who capitalized on good-roads sentiment to assert their primacy in road construction and design. They maintained that public works required experts to study, plan, and execute them, and that rural road quality depended on their talents. Iowa State Agricultural College's Anson Marston took the lead and was rewarded in 1903 when the state established a state highway advisory commission. Staffed by Marston's associates and students, the commission tested various construction materials and drainage techniques, and built experimental ways. The state bestowed additional sanction in 1912 by empowering the commission to oversee all state road construction and to specify materials and techniques. The Iowa commission quickly became the training school for other states' engineers, which helped standardize rural road construction nationwide. Establishment of the U. S. Bureau of Public Roads in the USDA in 1919, and appointment of Thomas MacDonald, Marston's prize student and Iowa State Highway Engineer since 1912, as the bureau's first chief, completed the standardization drive.

Systematizing Nature

Americans expressed an abiding love of and reverence for nature, even though they increasingly inhabited cities. The new ten-cent magazines repeatedly sung its praises, municipalities established park systems to preserve it, and urbanites moved to suburbs to celebrate it. A nature-study movement flourished, summer camps became "the customary thing," and Boy and Girl Scouts as well as Campfire Girls enrolled thousands as the nation's citizens hurried to imbue their children with nature's virtues. Adults watched birds, mourned the passenger pigeon's passing, and photographed natural settings.

These acts commemorated nature, but not pure wilderness. Few urged the preservation of land in its pristine wild state, and fewer asked contemporaries to forsake the present to return to the past. Most sought instead to combine nature with the industrial urban present to civilize the future. The wilderness was not inviolable, but nature was; nature was a cornerstone of the future.

Nature Photography Broad agreement about nature's importance inspired a wide spectrum of technological and technologically related activities. For instance, the desire to capture and preserve nature helped fuel an era of recreational photography. The well-to-do began in increasing numbers to photograph natural settings in the late 1870s, and by the mid-1880s most major American cities had one or more recreational photographic clubs.

Introduction of factory-sensitized, gelatin-coated dry glass plates in the late 1870s, and production of gelatinized paper for positive prints a few years later, enabled persons not directly schooled in photographic techniques to take pictures. But photography still demanded skill, money, and care. Glass plates were awkward and easily broken, while developing negatives and printing positives necessitated special equipment and facilities. George Eastman removed some of these obstacles in the half-decade after 1883. Conceiving of film on continuous rolls, not plates, Eastman and associates devised machines to produce flexible, gelatin-coated roll film, holders to advance and keep film in focus, and processes to diminish effects of temperature and humidity changes. He also manufactured inexpensive, simple-to-operate cameras. But Eastman's solution to the developing and printing problem was most novel; his professional staff, not individual camera operators, would process exposed film sent to his Rochester, New York, plant. Experts there would develop negatives, print positives (Eastman also had built machines that coated positive paper), enlarge them if desired, reload cameras, and ship prints and cameras back to photographers.

Eastman further refined procedures during the next decade. Removable film cartridges soon eliminated camera shipment, while adoption of celluloid as the film base improved photographic quality. Eastman poured celluloid, a nitrocellulose compound dissolved in camphor, amyl acetate, and other organic liquors, and allowed the solvents to evaporate; a transparent, tough flexible film, impervious to photochemicals, remained. A coating of silver salt in gelatin emulsion provided the dry photographic surface. The result was an inexpensive, easy-to-use photographic system accessible to virtually anyone.

Mining As the source of raw materials necessary for modern American life, nature was cherished for the bounty it furnished. The commercial mining and logging industries were among the most self-conscious natural-resource-based operations; they repeatedly increased productivity and profits by systematizing procedures and operating on economies of scale. Refiners dominated the mining industry and sought to control prices by gobbling up ore- and coal-bearing properties to eliminate middlemen and restrict competition. Construction of refinery-owned railroads and purchase of ships by refineries joined together mines, refineries, and markets, further lessening dependence on outside parties. Mining sites themselves exemplified centralization of authority and control of expenditures. Located away from major population centers, mining towns resembled colonial iron-making sites. Company employees provided support services, while miners lived in company-owned dwellings and bought articles in company stores.

Late–nineteenth- and early–twentieth-century copper mining efficiently and systematically extracted as much ore as economically feasible, and squeezed every ounce of metal from that ore. From the 1840s until the 1920s (when Southwestern mines assumed importance), the nation's major copper mining occurred on Michigan's upper peninsula near Houghton. By 1870, the process was fairly well articulated. Miners sank narrow shafts that followed often-crooked veins, and bolstered them with timbers. They worked by candlelight, dug with picks and shovels, and placed ore in pushcarts running on underground iron rails. Iron ropes and steam-powered hoists lifted material from the shallow shafts (less than eight hundred feet deep), and steam-powered stamps crushed it. The ore was separated by hand-washing it, and smelting was usually done at mine sites to reduce shipping costs. The crushed, washed ore was placed in small reverberatory furnaces and melted. Miners retracted the furnace top and raked off slag. The metal was heated again and splashed into the air to oxidize impurities. Hardwood charcoal combined with the excess oxygen to form carbon dioxide, and the nearly pure copper was poured in molds to form ingots.

Smelting remained virtually the same during the next half-century, although the other elements changed radically. Nitroglycerin and dynamite enabled miners to reach depths of more than 3,000 feet in the 1880s, and nearly 6,000 feet by 1900. Air pumps provided ventilation. Shafts became wider and straighter as miners dug tunnels into meandering veins. Steam and later electric pumps raised standing water from mine pits. First arc lights and then incandescent bulbs did away with candles. Miners in the 1880s used large, heavy, steam-driven, compressed-air drills rather than picks and shovels. These cumbersome tools gave way by 1910 to one-man diamond-headed air drills.

Nor was that all; mining engineers explored every option and endeavored to rationalize each operation. They further straightened and widened shafts to facilitate conversion to compressed-air (later electric) hoists. Small compressed-air and electric locomotives carried ore on tramways. Larger efficient steam-driven stamps more thoroughly pulverized ores, while concentrators and regrinders replaced hand-washing. After 1900, even the steam from stamps was conserved to run a low-pressure steam turbine, which powered an improved regrinder to agitate incompletely separated material.

Systematizing Iron and Steel Iron mining underwent a similar transformation. American iron mining had moved from the East to the Midwest in the mid-nineteenth century, and late-century miners worked the major deposits of upper Michigan, northern Wisconsin, and northeastern Minnesota. They opened the westernmost deposit, Minnesota's Mesabi, last, although it proved the largest, richest, and most easily extracted. These earlier iron fields required deep shafts to tap high-grade ore, but the Mesabi's deposits lay on and near the surface. Steam shovels easily lifted the ore directly and dumped it into railroad cars. But unlike copper smelting, iron smelting rarely occurred at the mine site. Iron smelting required three times as much coal as ore by weight, and producers reduced transportation costs by locating blast furnaces adjacent to coal fields rather than mines.

The steel industry's integration began at the iron mine. Although iron-ore extraction techniques were similar to those employed for copper—except at the Mesabi—iron mine operators needed to transport the material to far-off blast furnaces; Pittsburgh, the Lehigh Valley, Chicago, and Birmingham, Alabama, reigned as iron-smelting centers. Special thirty-ton hopper-bottomed railroad cars conveyed ore to the Great Lakes, where it was then lifted by electric hoist and dumped into ship holds. Steam-powered bumper beams distributed the load evenly. These 500-foot-long ships carried as much as 8,000 tons of ore to northern Ohio cities. Company employees unloaded ships with steam and electric cranes and placed ore in railroad cars. At the refineries the cars were hoisted and their contents dumped directly into furnaces.

The American iron industry rejected anthracite coal in the systematic drive to boost production. Anthracite burned too slowly for maximum efficiency, and coked bituminous coal became the way to improve smelting speed and generate additional production economy. During the coking process, the coal was baked for two days in open-topped beehive ovens, but iron manufacturers in the late 1880s substituted closed "by-product" ovens to trap vaporized coal tar and coal gas, which they sold as industrial chemicals.

Coked coal was joined with iron ore for smelting in huge, highly mechanized blast furnaces. These furnaces were charged by conveyor-carried hoppers, and used recycled combustion-generated gases to heat blasts. Mud guns efficiently closed furnace tap holes, and conveyors facilitated pouring iron into molds and transporting the cooled metal.

Relatively little pig iron was made into wrought iron. Difficulties in mechanizing that process, coupled with steel's superior hardness, rendered wrought iron economically noncompetitive. Steel became the preferred end product. Americans manufactured at least half their steel by the Bessemer process until 1908, when they adopted the continental

regenerative or open-hearth furnace. Air was channeled over a network of superheated bricks (reverberatory furnaces were much cooler)
before it came to bear on the metal. Experiments demonstrated that this
open-hearth technique worked especially well on charges containing
pig iron and scrap steel. Although it proved slower than the Bessemer
process, steelworkers could extract samples periodically from the
hearth, test them, and, if necessary, adjust the charge's composition.
Ability to control and standardize steel contributed to the open hearth's
popularity. Open-hearth refining dominated American steel in the
1910s and after. Well before that time, manufacturers had further
mechanized steel making. Electric cranes lifted containers of molten
steel from regenerative furnaces and poured it directly into railroad
car-mounted molds for shipment to highly mechanized rolling mills.

Logging Late–nineteenth- and early–twentieth-century loggers also
modernized to exploit nature more fully. Water transport and power
requirements had limited the pre-1870 American lumber industry.
Lumberjacks cut trees only near waterways and floated logs to small
mills where waterwheels moved saws. Unfinished lumber was rafted
down rivers to wholesalers in St. Louis and Chicago for finishing and
commercial distribution. Mill owners' attempts to consolidate forest-
to-market activities and to benefit from economies of scale guided the
industry's post-1870 growth. A massive shift to steam power and railroad expansion enabled them to effect these changes. Railroads themselves consumed lumber for road beds, bridges, piles, and depots.
New railroad spurs into dense woodlands far from watercourses permitted lumberjacks, often under contract to mill owners, to open new
timberlands. Mill owners situated mills close to new logging sites—cut
boards were cheaper to ship than corresponding tree trunks—and sent
millwork directly to retail yards to eliminate wholesalers. A nationwide lumber-grading system developed as mills finished lumber.
Steam-edgers, shingle, lath, and slab saws, and planing, flooring,
matching, and molding machines became standard mill equipment.
So, too, did artificial drying kilns. There fans passed air over steam-
filled pipes in enclosed chambers to cure green lumber, which decreased warping, killed insects, and lessened lumber weight and railroad freight costs.

Innovation marked the new late-century lumber mills. Logs transported to mills by horse-drawn sledge or railroad were deposited in
hot ponds. Heated with steam exhausted by the mills' engines, these
ponds kept timbers from freezing to permit year-round sawing. Electric lights made night milling possible. Each log was attached in turn
to a steamjacker, which hauled it from the water and carried it up
a slide to the second floor of the mill proper. A mechanized log-stop
disconnected the jacker and rolled the log down a slight incline, from

Steam engines powered the lumber industry.

which a steam-powered device lifted it and positioned it on the carriage. Two iron levers held the log in place. The steam-powered, cylinder-run carriage brought the log to head saws, which removed bark, and to a band saw, which cut it into boards. The band saw had replaced the circular saws popular at mid-century because it made a much thinner, less wasteful cut. By steam-propelled live rolls, the boards went first to an edger, who squared the boards' edges and made them standard width; then to the trimmer, who trimmed the ends and cut boards into standard lengths; and finally to graders, who sorted lumber into grades. Automatic loaders placed lumber in carts to be taken to kilns. Steam cranes loaded kiln-dried boards onto railroad cars.

Even mill wastes did not escape scrutiny. Farmers purchased some sawdust for mulch and fertilizer, but mills also used mechanized carriers to collect sawdust and transport it immediately to steam-engine fireboxes. Imperfect boards also became fuel, and a few mills converted defective logs into charcoal and other substances.

Political Control of Nature Federal administrators employed in the West in the 1870s argued that nature was public property requiring national regulation. In the 1880s and 1890s, proponents of that agenda identified themselves as a group defined by their special knowledge and maintained explicitly that their conclusions were nonpartisan and that their methods were scientific—the products of careful study, rational thought, and verifiable techniques. They also asserted that the public interest dictated that they set forest policy. It remained until about 1900, however, for this new group to establish schools to produce forestry-management professionals. Their contention rested on the notion that America needed rational planning to promote systematic, orderly development that would yield raw materials for contemporary life yet protect nature for posterity, that only they could effectively plan that program, and that implementation required national legislation. And they frequently portrayed mining and lumber concerns as systematically ravaging nature and as operating out of selfishness without regard to the future; they cited corporate irresponsibility as demonstration of the imminent need for federal law.

Gifford Pinchot parlayed his experience managing timber at a private North Carolina estate with his political connections to emerge as the most prominent spokesperson for federal regulation of natural resources. In the two decades after 1890, Pinchot and his followers convinced Congress to establish them as the nation's forest-management bureaucracy and to designate vast woodland tracts as national forests. Using their bureaucratic skills to shape national policy, these men stressed sustained-yield forest management, which meant the systematic utilization and replenishment of national forests. A trained forestry force tackled disease problems, fought fires, and supervised cutting and sale of timber and planting of seedlings. Mining was also permitted and regulated in national forestland. Both mining and lumber interests generally favored national-forest management policy. It guaranteed them future raw materials and profits, while expenses incurred by compliance could be passed on to consumers.

SYSTEMATIZING LEISURE

In the late nineteenth century, Americans made a rigid distinction between work and leisure. The ideas that citizens ought to have leisure and pursue leisure activities were new to the period, as was the notion that work and leisure constituted radically different but essential elements of mankind's developmental system. Leisure activities were very seldom pursued to enhance working performance or tied directly to it, although not all leisure pursuits lacked purpose or were simply for relaxation. Zoos, parks, and the more general attempts to involve one's self with nature were considered "rational amusements," activities in which systematic observation actually improved observers. Sports were often linked to physical improvement, a necessary concomitant of mental development. Nor did each form of leisure appeal, nor was it established to appeal, to every American social group, although a few activities did cut across social divisions. On one aspect Americans agreed: systematization and rationalization of leisure endeavors would yield the most efficient, and therefore most satisfactory, leisure. In that sense, the precepts surrounding leisure were virtually indistinguishable from those of work.

Baseball became a popular form of late–nineteenth-century leisure. Crowds as large as that shown above often attended games at New York's Polo Grounds.

Sports and the Growth of the Middle Class

America's upper crust interested itself in horse racing quite early, but the middle class was most responsible for the late–nineteenth-century boom in participant sports. Taking advantage of the new inexpensive summer resorts established precisely for their leisure activities, the middle class lustily pursued archery, lawn tennis, track and field, croquet, and golf. This enthusiasm was soon channeled into creation of national associations to codify rules and regulations, prescribe appropriate garb and equipment, sponsor national competitions, and adjudicate disputes. The United States Lawn Tennis Association (formed 1881), Amateur Athletic Union (1888), and the United States Golf Association (1894) functioned in these capacities. Other participant sports took place indoors, generally in the winter months. The college, YMCA, and private-gymnasium building rush of the 1880s and 1890s provided facilities for gymnastics, handball, basketball, and volleyball.

Rise of spectator sports paralleled that of participant sports. Construction of special-purpose stadia or fields generally required supporters to commit significant funds and urban space. Implicit in the commitment and enthusiastic public response was that performances offered were worth watching; these athletes were expert practitioners. Organized baseball, which acquired the sobriquet the "national pastime," and intercollegiate football, commonly known as "king football," reigned as the most popular spectator sports in the late nineteenth and early twentieth centuries.

Organized baseball quickly capitalized on the middle-class willingness to pay for leisure, and was from the National League's creation in 1876 a for-profit enterprise. Sound late–nineteenth-century business principles marked the incorporation. The league instituted among its members uniform ticket prices, predetermined schedules, and a single set of rules. It stipulated minimum city size for a franchise, demanded financially stable ownership, and penalized violators of league precepts. The league expelled teams for failure to complete schedules, or players for gambling. It adopted a reserve clause in 1882 making salaried players the exclusive property of the club they played for; players were unable to change teams unless sold, traded, or released. A leaguewide salary ceiling kept costs down and profits substantial. Using negotiations, agreements, mergers, threats, and more aggressive tactics, the league beat back challengers and oversaw the organization of subsidiary, or minor, leagues. The National League's monopoly was overturned in 1900 by the Western League (later renamed the American League), whose well-heeled owners raided National League rosters and offered players then exorbitant salaries. Both leagues bore the brunt of unrestrained competition poorly, and in 1903 affiliated. The accord, which also produced the World Series, enabled owners to control salaries and to prevent others from forming competing leagues.

"King football" also owed its popularity to the middle class. As expertise replaced character and a college education became essential for entry into the professions and business, children of those Americans wealthy enough to afford college attended in unprecedented and constantly increasing numbers. Graduates and their parents developed an identification with these schools, which spread to the gridiron. That these sporting events had so little competition from other spectator sports certainly contributed to their success. Princeton and Rutgers played the first intercollegiate football game in 1869, and this student-controlled effort almost immediately led to college-administered contests and salaried coaches. By 1881 football had gained its first national organizational entity, the Intercollegiate Foot Ball Association, which established a system of football rules for games among member institutions. Football conferences quickly formed within the association, rivalries intensified, All-American teams were selected, and crowds in excess of fifty thousand were not uncommon. Nor were the consequences unpredictable; colleges sometimes paid their coaches more than their presidents, while emphasis on victory replaced sportsmanship and led to increasingly violent incidents. Commentators noted unethical, dangerous play from the early 1890s, but the association refused to make major changes in a popular game. Several colleges discontinued football around 1900. President Theodore Roosevelt, an enthusiastic sports advocate, was among those appalled by the carnage. He called representatives of Harvard, Princeton, and Yale (then football powerhouses) to the White House in 1905 and threatened to ban football unless colleges took dramatic action. Eighteen college players died on the gridiron within two months of the White House meeting. Finally, in December 1905, representatives of sixty-two colleges and universities gathered to form the Intercollegiate Athletic Association of the United States (IAAUS, renamed the National Collegiate Athletic Association in 1910) to clean up the game. Dominated by college administrators, not coaches, the IAAUS radically changed football. It created a neutral zone between teams, legalized the forward pass to spread out players, and raised first-down yardage from five to ten yards to encourage passing. The organization also mandated chalk lines on the field to assist referees, and later forbade locking arms and the flying-wedge formation.

A Market for Sporting Goods   Rise of spectator and participant sports created a corresponding demand for sports equipment. Albert G. Spalding parlayed careers as a star baseball player in Boston and Chicago, as promoter of the Chicago White Stockings, and as a founder of the National League to achieve a position in the sports-equipment industry comparable to that of Eastman in photography. His firm, A. G. Spalding and Brothers, was created in the same year as organized baseball. Among its first assignments were publication of the official league rule book, and exclusive manufacture of the official league ball. Spalding doggedly publicized himself and his business, claimed falsely that its products were the result of interchangeable manufacture, and maintained that standardized sports equipment was essential "to insure uniformity and guard against fraud." His company retained its exclusive agreement with major-league baseball into the twentieth century. It also produced the various minor leagues' official balls.

A. G. Spalding and Brothers' National League ties earned it enough money by 1880 to develop a three-acre industrial site, and to erect separate factories for production of baseball bats, croquet implements, ice skates, hunting and fishing gear, roller skates, and sundry other sports apparatus. In 1887, it turned out more than a million

Spalding's advertising prowess enabled the company to capture the lion's share of the sporting-goods market.

baseball bats. Spalding also made baseball uniforms; exclusive supplier of apparel for the National League, the company initially attempted to designate field position by jersey color. It abandoned that effort after a year, but continued as the league's sole uniform supplier, and gradually added the minors. Spalding further expanded operations in the 1880s and early 1890s. By 1895, it was the nation's leading manufacturer of golf clubs, tennis racquets, bathing suits, footballs and football apparel, basketballs, catchers' masks and chest protectors, uniform bags, baseball gloves, and ball-and-strike indicators, which umpires used. Its Chicopee, Massachusetts, plant produced bicycles. Spalding was awarded an exclusive contract to provide all the equipment and uniforms for the 1900 and 1904 Olympic games.

Spalding's connections and genius for publicity, coupled with the firm's deserved reputation for quality, enabled it to dominate the sports market. Its owners pumped profits back into the organization to secure new, better machines, modernize facilities, and explore new production lines. Spalding also relentlessly purchased patents and competitors. The company deflected antimonopolistic sentiments by

The introduction of the chain-driven safety bicycle after about 1890 sparked a middle-class cycling boom.

selling sporting goods under labels of secretly acquired firms. This equipment was often produced at the same plants as regular Spalding apparatus and was in every way identical except for the manufacturer's name. Spalding had the appearance of competition without its liabilities.

Bicycles

Spalding pioneered in sports equipment, but he became a bicycle manufacturer only after dozens had preceded him. The Centennial Exhibition first had brought bicycles to America's attention. These expensive English imports with large front and small rear wheels were popular only with the upper class; A. A. Pope manufactured an American version for the market in the late 1870s. To protect their interests in bicycle racing as sport, upper-class bicycle enthusiasts formed an organization, the League of American Wheelmen. Created in 1880, the league sanctioned races and generally opposed efforts to restrict cycling. This upper-class monopoly was broken by the introduction of cheaper, chain-driven safety bicycles about a decade later. It touched off a middle-class boom, and adoption of rubber pneumatic tires a few years later continued it. Only then did Spalding manufacture bicycles. A slew of cycling academies rose to teach riding, more than eighty-five periodicals regularly followed the craze, and hundreds of cycling clubs opened their doors. Bicycle manufacturers sponsored annual New York City trade shows, while entrepreneurs operated rental establishments. An estimated four million Americans owned cycles in 1895, and several million more rented them.

Ironically, the bicycle boom burst two years later. Before 1900, the league had abandoned bicycles, concentrated on improving roads, and adopted a new name, American Road Makers. The nation had discovered automobiles.

Automobiles

The automobile was a European invention. It quickly became the darling of French high society, which sponsored several competitions in the mid-1890s among the three major engine types—steam, electric, or internal-combustion. Each had advocates. Steam vehicles accelerated smoothly but started slowly and required copious amounts of water and fuel. Electric cars operated simply and quietly, but their huge batteries limited range and utility. Internal-combustion-engine automobiles started immediately and carried large power reserves, but proved noisy and difficult to repair. These contests testified to the superiority of internal-combustion-engine vehicles—their speed and dependability usually translated into victories—and publicized automobiles internationally. An attentive American public followed these races. By 1895, the U.S. patent office had received more than five hundred automotive applications, almost all of which had been filed within the previous two years.

New England bicycle men, Central Michigan carriage-makers, and Lake Erie marine-engine machinists led the American drive to produce automobiles. Their previous involvement with transportation, familiarity with large-scale production, and ownership of machine tools eased the transition. Wealthy Americans constituted their market. Early manufacturers built fast, large, luxurious, and dependable cars, and merchandised their products accordingly. They entered endurance, dirt-track, and cross-country races, attempted to set land speed records, and secured testimonials from famous political and cultural figures.

Hundreds of Americans produced steam-, electric-, and gasoline-powered automobiles by the early twentieth century, and some began to dabble in the middle-class market. Ransom E. Olds was probably most successful in tapping the middle class. The nation's largest automobile producer, Olds manufactured several thousand vehicles a year as early as 1902. Henry Ford's yearly sales did not surpass Olds's until Ford permanently left the luxury-car field some years later.

The middle class's entrance into motoring produced a change in automotive institutions. Those established after the turn of the century generally welcomed a heterogeneous clientele and aggressively boosted motoring; they sponsored state and city legislation and pushed for good roads. One extant organization, the Automobile Club of America, took a slightly different route. Formed in 1899, the New York City club had national aspirations, and although it initially admitted only the well-to-do, it accepted a broader constituency after 1901. In 1902 it unveiled its program to create a system of national motoring organizations. It expected city-based automobile clubs to become its local affiliates, but these bodies balked at ceding autonomy to the New York group. Negotiations continued and a new organization, the American Automobile Association (AAA), was born to sit at the apex of a pyramid of state and local automobile societies. Open only to clubs, not individuals, the AAA championed laws protecting and regulating motoring as well as good roads. A competitor, the American Motor League, tried to recruit unaffiliated individuals, but the AAA's organizational base enabled it to withstand the challenge. Run by leaders of the now-defunct League of American Wheelmen, the league lost all influence after 1904 as the AAA expanded its membership to include individuals.

The AAA benefited from earlier state and local agitation as it attempted to encourage responsible motor-vehicle ownership and operation nationwide. No measure proved as controversial as vehicle registration. New York enacted a registration law in 1901; by 1905, twenty-five other states had followed suit. Many cities and some rural counties previously had required motorists to register vehicles and display identification tags, or license plates. These laws enabled governments to identify vehicle owners and ensure that property taxes and damage claims were promptly paid. But problems resulted when motorists journeyed from one jurisdictional unit to another. Vehicles had to be registered in each place, a factor that slowed interstate travel and cost motorists money. As early as 1902, automobile clubs lobbied the U.S. Congress to establish a single standardized national registration, and in 1905 an AAA-inspired bill was introduced on the floor. Fearing national intervention and a loss of revenue, state legislatures opposed the move and took action. Starting in 1905, they reined in localities, passed single statewide vehicle-registration statutes, and recognized other states' registration policies. By 1912, nationwide reciprocity had obviated the need for national law.

Operator licensing proceeded more slowly. Chicago instituted an eighteen-question test in 1900, the first such move. Administered orally by an examination board, the annual test covered automobile servicing—owners repaired their own cars—motorists' responsibilities, and operators' past driving records. Other localities soon followed, and a situation similar to that surrounding registration ensued. Auto clubs disliked the confusion, but supported registration to keep unprepared drivers off streets. Their involvement led to two pioneering state-licensing laws, both of which superseded local arrangements. The 1906 New Jersey statute required operators to sign affidavits testifying to their driving experience, physical condition, and knowledge of state motor-vehicle laws. Massachusetts enacted more comprehensive legislation a year later. Motorists needed to pass both written exams and driving tests. By 1909, ten states had adopted licensure laws combining affidavits and testing and had entered into reciprocal agreements.

Laws systematized nationwide the leisure activity of motoring. A similar sorting out of automobile and automotive parts manufacturers occurred at roughly the same time. Automobile owners or operators did not inspire this rationalization, nor was it accomplished through legislation. The automobile industry's relatively small sales and its many poorly capitalized manufacturers encouraged speculators to bank on its vast potential late in the new century's first decade, and to attempt to seize control through combination. The result was that by the 1910s a relatively few large firms dominated the industry.

The escapades of William Crapo Durant and Benjamin Briscoe are especially enlightening and demonstrate how comparatively simple it was to form a large early–twentieth-century automotive corporation. In 1908 Durant established by New Jersey charter a holding company and traded the firm's stock for automotive-company titles. Durant's holding company had only $2,000 capital. Yet desperate automotive manufacturers willingly exchanged corporate control for a chance to share in anticipated marketplace domination. Buick, which Durant already owned, and Olds, which had fallen on hard times, quickly capitulated.

Durant gave out $60 million in unsecured stock within a year and acquired more than one hundred small firms. He also gained patent rights to numerous devices to forestall future competition. Many were designed for steam or electric cars and went undeveloped. Others were inferior to those already in use. Two potential acquisitions demanded cash: Durant satisfied Cadillac's terms, but Ford offered stiffer resistance. Henry Ford requested $8 million immediately. Durant countered with a proposal of $2 million right away, a similar amount a year later, and the balance the following year. Ford turned down Durant's firm, General Motors Company.

Briscoe, who had participated with Durant on two earlier ventures, was much less successful on his own. His initiative nonetheless helped order the industry. He set up a holding company, the United States Motor Company, in 1910 and started to trade paper stock for corporate titles. One hundred and thirty companies were "purchased" for $42.5 million in stock within a year. Briscoe soon found that with the exception of his own car company, Maxwell-Briscoe, none of the U.S. Motor Company's acquisitions was profitable. He subsequently ran short of operating money and sought bank loans, which were granted with the stipulation that he hire Walter Flanders to streamline the holding company. Flanders closed virtually all 130 acquisitions, keeping alive only those firms directly related to the production of U.S. Motor's one moneymaker, the Maxwell-Briscoe.

Briscoe's failure, like Durant's then-modest success, nevertheless had the effect of eliminating well over one hundred automobile companies. Although the industry never was unified under a single corporate banner, its streamlining placed a comparatively few large corporations active nationwide in control of production of a leisure commodity. By the mid-1910s, a generous handful of firms made the overwhelming majority of the nation's for-pleasure motor vehicles.

Motion Pictures

The motion-picture industry also was rationalized in the early twentieth century; several large combines came to dominate picture production and distribution. This predominantly urban leisure form was accessible to all social classes, but its origins rested in nature photography and among the upper-class horse-racing set. To settle a wager in 1877, Eadweard Muybridge, an English émigré and photographer of nature settings, brought photographs to motion; twenty-four wet-plate cameras lined up side by side captured a galloping horse. Muybridge used bright light, a white background, and fast shutter speeds to record the horse's movements. He printed these photos on a glass wheel which, when rotated, passed them sequentially in front of a strong light and projected them on a distant surface. Earlier European work alerted Muybridge that continuous projection did not yield the illusion of motion, so he placed a shutter on his projector's lens to stimulate a strobe effect. This produced arrested motion, which human eyes translated into "true" movement. Muybridge's "zooprax-iscope" was within a few years projecting 200-photograph sequences.

Nature study, not motion pictures, fascinated Muybridge, and he did not commercialize his device. But his demonstrations, lectures, trips to Europe, and subsequent examinations of aviary and human movement publicized his techniques. Others investigated cinematography's possibilities, adopting gelatin emulsion film in the early 1880s, roll film and roll holders by 1887, and celluloid in the early 1890s.

*Eadweard Muybridge prepares his cameras to
determine whether all four hooves of a horse leave the
ground when the horse is galloping.*

Thomas Edison was the most commercially successful pioneer. Inspired by hearing Muybridge lecture, Edison's familiarity with contin-
uous-roll processes—telegraphic printers and sound-cylinder phono-
graphs—prepared him to appreciate cinematography's mechanical
elements. Edison initially hoped to join phonographic and photographic cylinders for individual viewers, but he failed to develop adequate coordination mechanisms. He abandoned the modified glass-
wheel principle but remained committed to individual viewing even
as his group patented in 1889 the essentials of the modern motion-
picture projector: reel-to-reel perforated film, sprocket wheels, revolving shutter, and constant light source. Nonprojecting kinetoscopes
were Edison's first commercial cinemagraphic triumph. Announced in
1891, electric-motor-powered kinetoscopes pulled film loops forty to
fifty feet long past electric lights at forty-six frames per second; shut-
ters positioned between film and viewer produced arrested motion.

Edison licensed kinetoscopes to commercial establishments in
1894. Individuals apparently enjoyed peering into oculars, and kinetoscope parlors, like phonographic parlors a few years earlier, became
common urban institutions nationwide. The kinetoscope's popularity
stimulated interest in projection cinematography, and several projectors competed for the late 1890s market. The Biograph projector, designed by William K. L. Dickson, a former Edison associate, debuted
in a Pittsburgh auditorium in September 1896 and quickly spread
across America. Before the century's close, others had improved projection techniques by synchronizing shutter and film motion, and by
positioning a slack loop in the film to reduce tearing. A new recreational institution, movie houses, followed in the projectors' wake.
Americans supported five thousand in 1907 and twice as many three
years later.

*Muybridge's zoopraxiscope projected his horse
photographs and was a progenitor of the modern
motion-picture projector.*

Movie houses required a constant supply of material to present, as
Edison anticipated before he leased his first kinetoscope. In 1892, he
established a motion-picture studio at his West Orange site. Other
manufacturers followed Edison's example; about a dozen New York
or Chicago producers of projection equipment were America's primary early filmmakers and dominated in the years immediately after
1900. Movie houses formed exchanges to distribute films among member theaters.

Competition among producers of equipment and films enabled
exchanges to play producers against one another, while similarity of
projection devices raised the specter of patent-infringement suits and
other costly litigation. Major producers organized themselves into the
Motion Pictures Patents Company (MPPC) in 1908 to surmount both
difficulties. The MPPC cross-licensed patents among member producers and gained an agreement from Eastman, by far the largest celluloid
supplier, not to sell the nitrocellulose-based product to unaffiliated
firms. Distribution exchanges and individual exhibitors had to fall in
line, for without access to films, they would go out of business. The
MPPC formalized this hierarchical relationship in 1910 by organizing
exchanges and exhibitors into the General Film Company, which was
restricted to handling MPPC products.

A few independent picture-producers survived the MPPC. Buying celluloid from Europe and a handful of small American firms,
they managed to generate motion pictures. Independents also attempted to ensure a market for their product by binding together unaffiliated exhibitors in 1910 to create the Motion Picture Distribution
and Sales Company. Their success in lining up exhibitors led Eastman
to reconsider his MPPC agreement, and he began to sell celluloid to

New York and Chicago were the initial homes of the motion-picture industry, but feature filmmakers soon gravitated to sunny Southern California.

independents in 1911. Easy access to film buoyed independents, and in 1912 they established a new consortium, the Universal Film Manufacturing Company, to challenge the MPPC.

Independents' tactics differed from the MPPC. They tried to shape demand rather than explicitly control outlets. Independents emphasized product and hoped to attract audiences through recognition of their performers' and directors' names and efforts. Their success in creating a star system produced a scramble for celebrities in the late 1910s and paved the way for additional competition. Fox, Loew, Paramount, and Warner Brothers each was formed by the early 1920s.

The early motion-picture industry profited through establishment of a technologically based leisure activity designed to attract diverse social groups. In that sense, it differed from automobiles, bicycles, and spectator sports, which achieved profitability by serving more circumscribed markets. But the manner in which these several leisure forms were shaped and shaped themselves—why they were successful inventions of the late nineteenth and early twentieth centuries—was fundamentally the same. Productions, technologies, institutions, and industries that seemed sensible did so because those who viewed them recognized them each as constituting an element in a system of discrete yet interdependent, hierarchically arranged parts, or as the system itself. Nor was the nation's physical environment immune from this conceptual onslaught. The revamped urban and agricultural environs were tangible products of these ideas, as was the infatuation with nature. Work would prove no exception.

FOR FURTHER READING

Ackerman, Carl W. *George Eastman* (1930).

Boyer, M. Christine. *Dreaming the Rational City* (1983).

Condit, Carl W. *American Building* (1968).

Dulles, Foster Rhea. *A History of Recreation* (1965).

Flink, James J. *America Adopts the Automobile, 1895–1910* (1970).

Friedel, Robert. *Pioneer Plastic* (1983).

Fries, Robert F. *Empire in Pine* (1951).

Gates, William B., Jr. *Michigan Copper and Boston Dollars* (1951).

Glaab, Charles N., and Lawrence H. Larsen. *Factories in the Valley* (1969).

Gray, R. B. *The Agricultural Tractor: 1855–1950* (1954).

Hays, Samuel P. *Conservation and the Gospel of Efficiency* (1959).

Hoogenboom, Ari and Olive. *A History of the ICC* (1976).

Jenkins, Reese V. *Images and Enterprise* (1975).

Kolko, Gabriel. *Railroads and Regulation, 1877–1916* (1965).

Larson, Agnes M. *History of the White Pine Industry in Minnesota* (1949).

Lesley, Robert W. *History of the Portland Cement Industry in the United States* (1924).

Levine, Peter. *A. G. Spalding and the Rise of Baseball* (1985).

Lewis, W. David. *Iron and Steel in America* (1976).

MacGowan, Kenneth. *Behind the Screen* (1965).

Marcus, Alan I. *Agricultural Science and the Quest for Legitimacy* (1985).

Maxim, Hiram P. *Horseless Carriage Days* (1937).

Parsons, A. B., ed. *Seventy-Five Years of Progress in the Mineral Industry, 1871–1946* (1947).

Pound, Arthur. *The Turning Wheel* (1934).

Rader, Benjamin G. *American Sports* (1983).

Rae, John B. *The American Automobile* (1965).

Schmitt, Peter J. *Back to Nature* (1969).

Scott, Mel. *American City Planning Since 1890* (1969).

Scott, Roy V. *The Reluctant Farmer: The Rise of Agricultural Extension to 1914* (1971).

Segal, Howard P. *Technological Utopianism in American Culture* (1985).

Smith, Duane A. *Mining America* (1987).

Smith, Robert A. *A Social History of the Bicycle* (1972).

Stover, John F. *American Railroads* (1961).

Webb, Walter Prescott. *The Great Plains* (1931).

Systematizing Workers and the Workplace

THE SYSTEM IN THE HOME

Catharine Beecher's *Treatise on Domestic Economy* (1841) outlined a set of manners, morals, and obligations that Beecher identified as characteristically American, as defining an American homemaker. In that sense, Beecher's volume paralleled Emerson's American Scholar address. Both authors announced a new type of person, one typified by a behavior unlike that of citizens of other nations. Only the locus of concern varied. Emerson called for a distinctly American scholar, Beecher for a distinctly American woman.

Beecher's 1869 effort, *The American Woman's Home*, expressed a radically different perspective. Co-authored by her sister, Harriet Beecher Stowe, the book described in great detail an efficient home's organization and operation. No item seemed too small or insignificant to analysis. The authors scrutinized the kitchen, enumerated its constituents, and explained their proper alignment in terms of the requirements of kitchen work. Food preparation, cleanup, and storage were kitchen work's designated subsets. Flour bins, sinks, dishes, and strainers each received the Beechers' attention as they attempted to reduce kitchen form and activity to specific rules. Nor was their treatment of the kitchen and its elements unusual. To the Beechers, efficient housekeeping was the product of rationally conceived designs, plans, and procedures, the consequence of study. Systematized households and household work resulted from study.

In the years after the Beechers' book, Americans redesigned their living spaces. The new sanitary kitchen and bathroom depended on electric light rather than gas to free them of soot. White walls and fixtures suggested cleanliness. Wood or coal-burning stoves gave way to oil or gas ranges, often with thermostats, after about 1890. Linoleum replaced wood because of its ease of cleaning. Tubs and toilets were positioned to facilitate easy cleaning. The second floor characteristically housed only bedrooms, with built-in closets and laundry chutes to the basement to organize their use.

The idealized first floor was likewise systematized. A front porch, not a front hall, welcomed visitors. In addition to the newly reconfigured kitchen, a new creation, the living room, graced the main floor and performed several distinct functions. Replacing the front and rear halls, parlor, and library of an earlier era, it held bookcases, inglenooks, and a fireplace. Families used it to entertain guests and for family amusement. The dining room also held several discrete capabilities. Families often ate all but breakfast there, which usually was served in a kitchen nook. The dining room's built-in buffets provided storage space for the family's fine china and a piano often graced a wall. A window box was ideal for reading. A walkway, generally circular, stressed directional flow and joined and organized the three rooms.

The desire to rationalize home design and home activities appeared repeatedly after 1870. A new profession, interior decorating, emerged to outfit the homes of the well-to-do, who had enough money to purchase someone's expert taste. But establishment of domestic science, domestic economy, or home-economics courses, usually at land-grant colleges, was perhaps the most obvious manifestation of the home systematizing mania. College kitchens, dining rooms, and laundries supplemented lectures and served as laboratories in which students experimented in and learned housekeeping science. Division of home economics into subunits quickly followed. Foods, household administration, textiles and clothing, and the like emerged as distinct fields of inquiry within the broad rubric of home economics. The identification of domestic economy as an area of study—one composed of discrete and differentiable subdisciplines—and of its investigators/teachers as a specific group, led to annual conferences, beginning in 1899, at Lake Placid, New York (it was no coincidence that Melvil Dewey, creator of the famous Dewey decimal system to systematize libraries and the progenitor of the discipline of library science, hosted the inaugural event) and to creation of the American

Home Economics Association in 1909. It also produced a definite periodical literature. (Dewey in his system placed home economics between political economy and law.) The *Journal of Home Economics* (1908) catered to researchers; it was preceded by general-circulation magazines such as *Good Housekeeping* (1885), *American Kitchen Magazine* (1894), and *Sanitary Home* (1899).

New Household Machinery

Women were certainly not overlooked in the late–nineteenth- and early–twentieth-century reconceptualization of American society. The household, especially the kitchen, became their factory, while they served as production experts and, if unable to afford servants, laborers. Indeed, the home required rationalization as much as the factory. Brains were to guide hands to systematize households and housework. Reduction of drudgery and speeding of operations were the goals; the amount of work, whether great or small, was less important than how that work was pursued. Working patterns derived from study were cherished, as were machines that enabled women to accomplish household tasks more quickly and more scientifically. Machines had an intrinsic virtue; they were consequences of rational, systematic thought put into practice. That they were composed of physically discrete mechanical parts precisely arranged for a particular purpose clearly resonated with the notions of late–nineteenth- and early–twentieth-century Americans.

All machines were not equal. Machinery had to enhance or at least not detract markedly from human performance. But consonance between machines and post-1870 organizational ideas surely eased their introduction into all facets of American society, and fostered their incredible proliferation. Machinery was a metaphor for society that held true no matter what the locus; it was as accurate for the household as it was for large-scale production.

Patents for various household machines were issued regularly from the 1850s, but the American public generally accepted these household contraptions only after 1870. By the 1890s, the market for these machines was sufficiently great to support enough manufacturers to finance trade papers such as *House Furnishing Review,* while a decade later a manufacturer-sponsored Home Furnishing Goods Exhibition was held at New York's Madison Square Garden to join retailers with consumers and manufacturers.

The Washing Machine Washing machines and vacuum cleaners led the mechanical incursion into the household. The earliest washing aids mimicked the time-honored practice of rubbing fabrics over ribbed washboards; clothes were hand-cranked through roller beds turning

American women embraced electrical machinery in their zeal to reduce housekeeping to a science. This 1911 electric kitchen epitomized that effort.

in opposite directions. Not until 1851 did a washing-machine patent employ different principles. James T. King patented a device that exploited the natural circulation of steam and boiling water. Two concentric half-full cylinders constituted the machine's working parts. A fire was set beneath the outer cylinder, while soap and clothes were placed within the inner, mobile cylinder. Steam and boiling water caused the inner cylinder to move, and stirring the outer cylinder's water by hand-crank reinforced the movement. Agitator-type machines, devised about 1870, were similar but included a crank-activated plunger operating in the vertical plane.

Washing machines proved immensely popular from the 1870s, but few families bought their own. Commercial laundries served urban areas while cooperative laundries (several families purchasing a single machine together) made inroads in rural regions. Rinsing generally occurred in separate vessels at these locations. Clothes were then wrung either by hand or between hand-powered rollers. The persistence of hand-rinsing and wringing until the twentieth century resulted from the lack of a cheap mechanical prime-mover. Wringing by centrifugal force became feasible only with the advent of small variable-speed electric motors.

Competition was brisk as vacuum-cleaner manufacturers sought to capitalize on an untapped market.

The Vacuum Cleaner The history of vacuum cleaners in America followed a somewhat similar course. People washed or beat rugs and carpets by hand throughout the nineteenth century. Although two mechanical-cleaner patents were awarded around 1860, neither proved commercially practicable. Both devices were essentially the same process; as people rolled the mechanisms over carpets, the revolving wheels turned fan blades, which created suction, lifted dust, and deposited it inside the apparatus. One machine also employed contact brushes to stir up carpet dirt and promote deeper cleaning. Both worked poorly; they lacked the suction necessary for the task. Electric cleaners promised to solve the suction problem, but the early electric motors' great size and weight restricted machine movement. Designers of electric vacuums either situated the motor in a central place, such as the basement, and moved tubes and hoses from place to place, or built a large truck on which to roll the cumbersome cleaning unit. Not until the 1910s did all-in-a-piece portable vacuum cleaners with small motors come on the market. By 1920 they had become standard household equipment among the wealthy.

Food Preparation and Diet

The household rationalization drive did not ignore food. An outpouring of cookbooks marked the late nineteenth century. Newspapers and magazines had cooking columns, and cooking schools opened to spread "scientific cookery." Food preparers learned that a meal itself was a system. It included food values, systematic measurement of ingredients, and recipes. Scientific meal planning took into account digestion, appearance (garnishing), and the best way to serve food and remove dirty dishes. Diets were constructed according to occupation, sex, nationality, and age. Measuring cups and measuring spoons had become by the 1880s the equipment of scientific cooks.

Systematizing Food

Presentation and Composition President Woodrow Wilson's inaugural dinner consisted of cream of celery soup followed by cod with white sauce. Roast capon, mashed potatoes, and cauliflower preceded a whipped cream-topped clear gelatin desert. Custard concluded the meal. Wilson's choice of an all-white meal conveyed its artificiality. It was not natural but human-made, the product of rational determinations. As important was its rather bland character. It epitomized the new American cuisine that surfaced during those years. It marked a sharp contrast to typical immigrant food: pork, brown bread, thick soups, and heavy pies. Adoption of an American cuisine marked persons as modern, as fully integrated into the American socioeconomic and political system.

Food was clearly something manufactured. Smoothness, unvarying texture, and evenness of quality all were indications of expert manipulation. In this context, Crisco was the model foodstuff. Heralded as "an absolutely new product" and as "a scientific discovery which will affect every kitchen in America," this patently synthetic food improved upon nature's lard and butter. Unlike lard and butter, which turned rancid after time and changed their taste depending on the season, Crisco never varied. It was pristine; no human hands ever touched it. Chefs and home economics teachers tested the white, pure, creamy material experimentally. Procter & Gamble sponsored Crisco cookbooks to demonstrate to homemakers this miracle food's virtues. Its recommended uses included as a frying agent, an ingredient in baking, a sandwich spread, a base for a white sauce, and a glaze.

All scientific foods were not necessarily cooked at home. In some cases, persons contracted with experts to create this fare in large central kitchens and deliver it daily to their home. New York was the initial site of these services, which also depended on the Aladdin system to ensure dinners were delivered warm. Essentially a series of domed containers stored in refrigerator-like boxes and placed in wheeled carts, the patented Aladdin system quickly spread to institutions, such as hospitals, where it met considerable success.

Nor were all scientific foods aimed at a middle-class market. Alphonse Biardot, a gourmet French chef, came to America in 1887 and established a soup company to compound ox tail, green turtle, and printanier soups. His company, Franco-American, moved to Jersey City, New Jersey, in 1890 and branched out to include plum pudding and spaghetti a la milanaise. Biardot merchandised his own products by appearing in cooking stores and selling directly to retailers. He was so proud of his scientific cooking techniques that he gave tours of his industrial kitchen.

Other over-the-counter scientific foods depended directly on scientific input. John Dorrance received his Ph.D. in chemistry in Germany and returned to his father's preserve company infused with the knowledge that soup at its best was a scientifically metered, well-balanced meal and that it ought to play a central part in the American diet. Dorrance attempted to reduce soup manufacturing to a nutritional and manufacturing science. Dorrance also decided to reduce shipping costs, so he tried to rid soup of its water. His condensed soups—he boiled off the water—proved quite popular. As Dorrance assumed control of his father's Campbell Preserve Company, his younger brother Arthur received a chemical engineering degree from MIT and got an assistant chef's job at the Hotel Ritz in New York. There Arthur learned about the Franco-American Company and invested heavily in it. He also combined his engineering and culinary talents to work with the New Jersey Agricultural Experiment station to create a new tomato, the Rutgers tomato, that would be the basis for Franco-American tomato-based soups. The Rutgers tomato was highly resistant to various funguses and ripened from the inside out, which reduced packing and shipping damage. By the mid-1910s John had become majority owner of Franco-American, which during World War I became a wholly owned Campbell subsidiary.

Delivery The attention placed on creating a healthy, scientifically determined standardized American food depended on the availability of foodstuffs. Foods needed to be available in good numbers year-round. Chicago, then Omaha and Kansas City emerged as America's beef production centers. Adapting disassembly techniques first practiced for pork, packers added friction hoists, overhead conveyors, chutes, and moving benches as they worked to increase production while reducing manual labor and laborers. Like producers of fresh fruits and vegetables, they relied on railroads to provide transportation, but they refused to wait for these companies to deliver refrigerator cars. As early as the late 1860s, packers and fruit growers were insulating boxcars with sawdust and packing them with block ice to carry meat, which discolored quickly. Gustavus Swift's forced-air-circulation refrigerator cars placed ice blocks at the top—much as with home refrigerators—to dominate the industry after about 1880. Carl Linde, a Swift employee, developed the mechanical refrigerator car at about that time. These expensive devices, cooled by the natural expansion of compressed air, could maintain temperatures indefinitely.

Canning

Meat packing received considerable attention, especially after Upton Sinclair's *The Jungle*, but canning was more significant. Virtually anything was canned; Americans had access year-round to fruits and vegetables. Canning technology modifications concentrated on the bath to kill microorganisms without destroying taste or food quality; the storage vessel—the can; and the means to seal it. From the 1870s, superheated steam—steam under high pressure to raise its temperature—became the preferred sterilization method but doubts remained as to the duration of exposure. Cans themselves were made first by heating and rolling iron bars into thin sheets and then coating them with tin. By the 1880s, however, William R. Jones, an employee of steel magnate Andrew Carnegie, converted the process to steel. Thin sheets were cleansed in acidic baths and reheated and annealed to make them pliable. The sheets then went to a cauldron of molten tin, covered by a palm oil layer. The oil coated the steel as it was dipped into the tin and enhanced the tin coat. After cooling, the sheets were scrubbed with bran and were ready to be cut for cans.

After mills slit and rolled the sheets into cylinders and after tops and bottoms were cut and bent by foot-controlled circular dies—accurate to thousandths of an inch—cans were ready for soldering. Precision machines replaced hand-soldering and solder baths supplanted soldering irons. In both instances, canners reduced the quantity of solder needed. In 1896, tops and bottoms were crimped by machine to further reduce soldering—a rubber-based compound helped form the seal. Carried farther on conveyors, they were dipped into water to check for leaks. These cans, now called sanitary cans, were never touched by human hands.

Preparing Foods for the Can Two sites dominated early canning activity—California and the East Coast from Baltimore to New Jersey. The California industry began to serve the forty-niners gold rush market with fruits and vegetables, and when that market receded, it tapped Nevada silver miners. Explosive growth followed in the decades after the Civil War. California's then-small population convinced canners to use machinery at every turn. Grading machines, essentially vibrating conveyors with different-sized holes, separated produce by size, but other tasks provided greater challenges. Each fruit or vegetable required different care. Turnips needed to be scrubbed, strawberries required delicate handling, and spinach brought sand and grit to the cannery. Loosening the tough, fuzzy skin of peaches proved especially difficult. Stemming, coring, slicing, blanching, peeling, or pitting machines all were different. Each machine could accomplish one and only one task for one type of produce; each was a single-purpose, special-purpose machine.

California canning was a continuous feed process. Machines delivered the precise amount of brine or heavy syrup. Exhausters heated material for specified periods at specified temperatures. When the fluids expanded to their maximum size, machines crimped and sealed the cans, which shrank to provide a characteristic hissing sound when the vacuum was broken upon opening.

East Coast manufacturers also created special-purpose, single-purpose machines to cut corn off cobs, shell peas, and trim fish, but human workers fought virtually every new device as a threat to their livelihood. Impetus for trade associations—Association of American Food Processors in 1882, the National Association of Canned Food Packers in 1890 and a National Canners Association in 1907—came from a desire to systematize relations within and across the nation's canning establishments, which employed over 50,000 persons by 1900. Canners had not been inactive but had rigorously vertically integrated their industry.

H. J. Heinz has been singled out for purchasing whole crops of vegetables before they were planted to ensure a ready supply of materials for pickles, sauerkraut, macaroni, and horseradish, but others went much further. Louis McMurray, scion of a Baltimore canning clan, provided a more representative portrait. Capitalizing on his family position, he quickly bought agricultural lands to raise the products he would can. Heavy syrup came from McMurray-owned corn stalks. He grew his mushrooms using the manure that his cattle produced and was concentrated in his fertilizer mill. These cattle were fattened on McMurray-produced corn husks and cobs. McMurray ran a box-making factory to ship his cans and a can-making factory to make the genuine articles. His foundry and machine, blacksmiths', and carpenters' shops produced the raw materials for these ventures and other products as well. McMurray invested in potential canning technologies. In the early 1880s, he backed Welcom Sprague, whose continuous chain-fed machines would cut sugar corn off cobs for virtually the entire industry.

SYSTEMATIZING FACTORY WORK

Americans accorded production machinery new prominence in the half-century after 1870, but the nature of the workplace, the factory, engendered the earliest concern. Correspondents to and essayists in technical periodicals complained that these structures were poorly designed, disorganized, or not organized to best advantage. They discussed whether hollow square, L-, or H-shaped factories best facilitated work, contemplated one-story versus multifloored buildings, and debated locations for foundries, drafting rooms, and foremen's offices. Commentators also maintained that factory administration was outmoded, chaotic, or wasteful, and therefore a detriment to productivity.

Suggestions, debates, and complaints intensified after 1900. By 1920, few factories resembled their 1870 predecessors. Factories and factory work had been reconceptualized and rearranged. Mass-production techniques and scientific management methods were products of that reconceptualization.

Building Systematic Factories

The Predecessor to the Systematic Factory Factories in 1870 looked and functioned very much like their mid-century counterparts. Line shafts and countershafts traversed rectangular multistoried buildings and transmitted power from waterwheels or steam engines to pulleys and belts to drive machinery. Machines requiring the most power were placed closest to prime-movers. Work processes generally moved from the top floor down. Raw materials or disassembled pieces emerged as finished products on the ground floor; gravity helped reduce handling. Individuals who had demonstrated mastery in many factory tasks—foremen—doled out work (often contracting with employees for a specific number of items by a specified date) and supervised its completion. A building boom in the 1870s and 1880s inspired by fire insurance companies did little to change the traditional physical layout; substitution of tile-protected iron for timber merely reduced fire hazards. Nor did introduction of electricity result in changed factory organization. Factory electric lighting began to replace gas in the 1880s, and was common a decade later. And although electric companies championed electricity's other industrial applications, electric motor use was rare in the 1880s, employed only to operate stationary cranes or as replacements for steam engines or waterwheels to turn line shafts.

Systematizing Factory Administration

Attempts to coordinate factory activities, not modify factory hardware, had a more telling impact before the century's end. Cries for "systematic management" culminated in unit cost analyses for specific products. These detailed factory cost-accounting systems yielded production and inventory control plans, as well as wage plans, to stimulate production and lower costs. Rationalization of factory endeavors stemmed from the proposition that each factory operation contributed to the system's efficiency, as measured by profitability. It required experts to develop central factorywide, cost accounting-based plans. Job cards and time clocks produced the requisite data. Establishing central offices staffed by clerical forces was among the fruits of rationalization, as were centralized purchasing and standardized materials. Storing supplies in designated areas and permitting only foremen to requisition materials also checked waste and promoted control. Premiums granted to workers who exceeded production quotas and piecework rates aimed to spur production and productivity. Foremen in these facilities were reduced to head-worker status—responsible for supervising their departments, gangs, crews, or shops, but not for routing materials or instituting procedures. Their job was to implement central policy, not conceive or tamper with it.

The Central Office The central office stood at the new factory system's apex. Before the central office, manufacturing establishments had consigned paperwork to small "cages" on factory floors. Industrialists' offices had resembled mid-century parlors, not places of work; people were greeted and deals were negotiated there. Clerks had been more nearly apprentice businessmen (virtually all were men) than office help. They had copied contracts, delivered missives, and written letters to learn about business in expectation of owning their own. The term "secretary" had referred to either rolltop desks with pigeonholes, or to managers of entire businesses. Letterpresses and simple ledgers had constituted recordkeepings' mainstays.

After 1870, offices became businesses' brains, the sites at which material was gathered, examined, and analyzed to derive future business needs and strategies. Spatial arrangements reflected their significance. Post-1870 offices grew larger, more populous, and (in the case of manufacturing) physically distinct. Although every office operation dealt with record generation, collection, maintenance, or retrieval, each required its own specialist; filing, shipping, and billing clerks had different tasks, as did typists and stenographers. Each specialist, many of whom were women, standardized the appropriate record forms and established precise record-keeping systems. Routinization, argued one commentator, "is the machinery of progress." It is like "oil, which if properly applied, will make the machine run smoothly."

Office equipment and specific office procedures emerged from that milieu. Desks, filing cabinets of standard dimensions, standard ledgers, standard-sized paper and envelopes, carbon paper, and typewriters (which spawned an entire class of office equipment including addressographs, mimeographs, adding machines, and check-makers) were the implements that rationalized the office.

The Case of the Hospital

Record-keeping proved at least as compelling in medicine. From about 1880, hospitals and public health agencies adopted double-entry bookkeeping and systematized and standardized patient records. They divided the hospital by department, then color-, shape-, or size-coded each to denote the types of treatments provided. By the mid-1880s, some had adopted a new machine invented by Herman Hollerith in 1884. Hollerith had been a census clerk, who left government service to teach mechanical engineering at MIT. His tabulating machine was essentially a system in itself. It included a key punch, verifier, sorter, and tabulator. Operators key-punched in data on cards that the machine could read if holes were punched out at particular spaces. Several different parameters could be identified by this technique, which hospitals used to identify mortality patterns. The U.S. Census adopted the Hollerith machines in 1890, saving the service an estimated $5 million in labor costs. Railroads adopted it in the 1890s, initially to process railroad freight bills and then for other purposes. Hollerith organized the Tabulating Machine Company in New York City to push his machines. The company ultimately became International Business Machines (IBM).

Design of Systematic Factories Factories designed and erected after about 1900 were usually significantly larger than earlier manufactories. Most were several buildings, not single massive structures, and suburban locations often replaced more expensive city sites. Structural steel and reinforced concrete were predominant construction materials, which encouraged new factory forms, larger windows, and flexibility of design. Using information gathered by systematic-management crusaders, architects tailored facilities to the type of industrial manufacture to be performed there, and by the 1910s buildings were designed to enhance work flow between departments. So, too, were factory offices. Managers restructured them to make

*Laying out factories to facilitate flow and reduce
handling were two goals of late–nineteenth-century
managers.*

paperwork proceed efficiently and to enable office workers to focus
exclusively on their jobs. Flow charts simulating paper routes became
the basis for locating desks, which also were positioned to discourage
conversation and peering out of windows.

New Use of Electric Power Electric power did not play a significant
role in turn-of-the-century factory design. To be sure, from the late
1880s, trade associations pushed electric power as cheaper, cleaner,
quieter, and more adaptable. But electric power accounted for only
about 5 percent of mechanical drive capacity in 1900, and only about
25 percent in 1909. Not until 1920 did electric motive power surpass
steam and water. By 1929, 78 percent of industrial power was electric.
The ways in which factories utilized electric drive power are telling:
until about 1905 most facilities employing electric motors used them
merely to turn factory lineshaft/belt systems; a large electric motor
simply replaced a waterwheel or steam engine as the plant's prime-
mover.

Electric group drive superseded single large-motor arrangements and remained the predominant electrical form through World
War I. Introduced in the early 1890s at a few facilities, group drive
did not free industry of lineshafting. A group-drive factory housed
several shorter, separate lineshafts—generally from 30 to 150 feet
long—each powered by its own motor. These electric engines acted
independently; each turned its line at a different speed and enabled

manufacturers to match machine and line speed. In practice, similar machines (grinding, stamping, milling, or the like) ran on the same line. Group drive's shorter shafts led to innovative factory design, simplified expansion, and operating economies. Only lines in use, not whole factory lineshaft systems, required power. Malfunctions idled only single lines, not complete enterprises.

Unit drive did not become popular until about 1920, although several leading industrialists had introduced it nearly a decade earlier. The union of motor and machine in a single device permitted factory owners to remove all shafting, belts, and pulleys, leaving overhead space for traveling cranes. Motor failure disabled only a single tool. Machines became truly portable, and factory design and expansion knew no restraints. Most manufacturers chose to minimize handling and emphasize production flow; they organized factories by the natural sequence of manufacturing operations.

Systematization of Large-Scale Production

Efficiency and standardization worked to reduce the human variable in production's equation. Men and women were inconsistent, wasteful, and fallible. Machines more closely approached perfection, and manufacturers revamped production systems to stress precision and exactness. Substitution of special-purpose machines for filers, and establishment of rational jig/fixture and model-based gauge systems, objectified fitting. High armory practice and interchangeable parts became tests of expert production and badges of technological sophistication.

Mechanical engineers justified these practices on other grounds. Machines speeded production and, because they increased volume and capacity, lowered unit and labor costs—factors that compensated for their steep capital investment and higher operating expenses. Demand existed for additional production units. Standardized production granted benefits of economies of scale. Utilization of special-purpose machine tools imposed order on manufacturing plants by emphasizing sequential flow.

Whether these claims of systematization's industrial benefits had economic bases, or were merely rationales to encourage manufacturers to recognize the legitimacy of production specialists, may be debated. It can be argued, for example, that sequential flow was virtually impossible in late–nineteenth-century lineshafted or group-driven factories without extensive product handling and movement, which would raise costs astronomically. Similarly, several industries would have been better served by adding personnel to satisfy temporary demand, thereby keeping capital costs down. Also, economies of scale depended on markets: demand must be and remain high.

Adoption of Systematic Techniques Northeastern machine-tool- and bicycle-makers successfully adopted these techniques. Several factors worked to machine-tool and bicycle manufacturers' advantage. Both capitalized on heightened demand. The equation of precision with efficiency sparked a special-purpose machine-tool boom, and the bicycle craze of the late 1880s and 1890s opened a strong market for a new consumer good. Both industries required comparatively little new capital investment because they owned many of the requisite machines. From mid-century, machine-tool manufacturers had had a slow, steady market for their product. Northeastern bicycle-makers came from the ranks of firearm, sewing-machine, or agricultural-implement producers, or contracted for parts from these firms; they merely adapted their special-purpose machine tools to a new product. Their success also stemmed from refining established techniques and instituting strict quality-control systems. Bicycle-makers, most notably A. A. Pope, modified drop-forging to reduce machining, and created inspection and testing departments. Gauged several times before sale, Pope bicycles gained a reputation among professionals for expert manufacture.

High armory practice—a system of jigs and fixtures and special-purpose machine tools to manufacture interchangeable parts—reigned preeminent among the Northeast's technologically advanced. But not all manufacture of interchangeable parts depended on special-purpose machine tools. Western carriage- and wagon-makers competed for the national bicycle market from about 1890, but did not adopt high armory practice. Their skilled English- and German-born mechanics replaced drop-forging with sheet steel stamping or pressing, which produced interchangeable parts and minimized machining; the more precise stamping and pressing employed special-purpose dies that eliminated the need for most special-purpose machine-tooling. Machinists sat fixed at presses while runners carried material from station to station.

Stamping and high armory practice yielded interchangeable parts, but neither achieved the pinnacle of efficiency. Both were constrained by lineshafting or group drive's apparent physical limitations. Left unmodified, these power transmission systems would never permit optimal sequential flow. As important, however, neither practice addressed efficient assembly. Indeed, there was no reason to do so. Without the speed of production generated by sequential flow, no assembly bottleneck existed. Henry Ford created a facility that maximized flow. Only at that time did he confront the need for rapid assembly.

Henry Ford's Systematic Techniques Ford prepared for high-volume automobile manufacture as early as 1906. His advisers included several gifted machinists and mechanics steeped in European production techniques, plus Walter Flanders, a machine-tool salesman who, as a Vermont machinist apprentice, had become well acquainted with high armory practice. Together these men emphasized interchangeable parts, special-purpose machine tools, and rational jigs, fixtures, and gauges, and impressed upon Ford the importance of sequential machine-tool arrangement. Lineshaft requirements hampered introduction of sequencing, however, and Flanders left in 1908, just after Ford announced the Model T, the car for the masses. Ford's crew outlined the Model T production process before situating machinery or beginning manufacture. Their central plan called for use of pressed steel rather than cast or drop-forged parts whenever possible to reduce machining, as well as renewing efforts to place machines sequentially to facilitate flow.

Demand soon exceeded production capacity, and in 1910 Ford opened a new plant in Highland Park, Michigan. The extensively planned facility would make only a single standard product, the Model T. Ford's staff designed and employed machine tools especially suited to Model T manufacture within the new factory setting rather than adapt tools from earlier sites; Ford's new special-purpose machine tools were also generally single-purpose machine tools. Freedom to create new machines that were fitted precisely to both the task and environment enabled Ford to overcome the problem of power transmission, and by 1913 to organize machinery according to true sequential flow.

Highland Park machinery was group-driven. But Ford's mechanics capitalized on the rigidity implicit in single-purpose machine tools and in a single standard product to make the plant's lineshafting/belting systems simulate unit drive. Indeed, each production machine filled one and only one place on one and only one line. Relationships to neighboring machines were static. Sequential positions were fixed. These assumptions encouraged Ford operatives to customize lineshaft-to-machine power transmission. A specialized system of pulleys and especially of gears for each machine delivered the proper power from lineshaft to machine, which ensured correct cutting-tool speed. Customized gearing and pulley arrangement mediated machine- and shaft-speed differences. This power transmission revolution led to a corresponding revolution in the organization of production, which drew plaudits as early as 1913. One commentator marveled that "so thoroughly is the sequence of operations followed that we not only find drilling machines sandwiched in between heavy millers and even punch presses, but also carbonizing furnaces and babbitting equipment in the midst of the machines. This reduces handling to a minimum."

Ford's ability to arrange the new facility to better advantage speeded production but created assembly bottlenecks. The company initially moved subassembly tables from their traditional position against walls to the middle of floors and placed parts bins at table centers; parts were accessible to workers on both sides. Final assembly was prosecuted by a series of assembly gangs. Each gang was responsible for a particular assembly aspect and each member had a small, specified task. Automobile chassis were mounted on sawhorses in rows; the gangs moved sequentially down the rows, and runners distributed parts just prior to use.

These procedures quickened assembly but failed to match production's pace. Assemblers worked at their own speeds and lost time traveling from station to station. Introduction of moving assembly lines, first used in 1913 for flywheel magneto subassembly, increased speed, eliminated human variability, and reduced waste. Pulled by endless chains at set rates, moving assembly lines required workers to remain stationary and to repeat a single straightforward operation. By July 1914, Ford used gravity-slide and conveyor-fed assembly lines for all sub- and final assembly. Production assistants persistently adjusted lines, seeking to determine points of best advantage. As with other facets of Ford's operation, the company publicized its assembly-line methods. Its aggressive publicity encouraged other industries to attempt to reproduce its techniques.

SYSTEMATIZING THE HUMAN ELEMENT
Scientific Management

Scientific management fervor swept America during the new century's first two decades. Its promise to promote industrial harmony and efficiency by impartially systematizing employer–employee relations and production was appealing. Its partisans claimed its method was scientific and its determinations therefore beyond reproach. Application of scientific management techniques required experts steeped in its precepts, and its proponents (generally American Society of Mechanical Engineers members, until about 1910) offered themselves to industries as consultants.

Scientific management summarized those themes fundamental to America in the half-century after 1870. The term originated with Frederick W. Taylor, its foremost proponent and publicist. Taylor and his apostles took the systematic management crusade as their starting point and sought to objectify it. Rather than base wage plans on an individual's or a group's past productivity, Taylorites wanted to use detailed job analyses, and time and motion studies of the work involved, to determine "scientifically" the standard time and output required. Those standards would establish differential piece rates. Workers not meeting these standards received lower rates, while those exceeding

Moving assembly lines became the archetypical
expression of Ford's methods.

them were paid more per piece. Taylorites boosted establishment of central planning departments in factories to administer these practices, schedule work, and coordinate purchasing. Eight "functional foremen"—each with different specialized responsibilities—implemented and helped shape planning-department policy.

Despite excitement about scientific management's potential, and Taylor's success in publicizing his principles, few industrialists adopted the master's system exactly as he outlined it. Labor often chafed under scientific management methods, and managers guarded against usurpation of their authority. Owners complained about the lengthy stay of consultants and frequently found their suggestions impractical. As important, Taylor and his disciples sometimes disagreed. For example, Frank Gilbreath incurred Taylor's disfavor in 1911 by rejecting stopwatch-determined and recorded-time studies as imprecise. Gilbreath instead advocated "micromotion." According to Gilbreath, micromotion—filming workers and dividing each minute into 100 equal units—was the correct method for "standardizing performance of labor" because it eliminated "all error due to the human element or to differences in mental reaction times"; it was scientific, while stop-watches were subjective. Several big-city hospitals used Gilbreath's micromotion techniques to try to increase the efficiency of surgical procedures. Finally, Taylorism did not suit mass-production facilities. A shop-based management system was superfluous in plants in which work tasks were separated into constituent elements, and where moving assembly lines guaranteed regularized execution. Taylorism proved short-lived, but a general desire to systematize factories and factory operations scientifically was more enduring.

Industrial Social Welfare and Social Science

Large industrial concerns established libraries, choral groups, and clubhouses for laborers after about 1870. They hired counselors, instituted wage incentive plans, and improved work environments. These initiatives aimed to harmonize employer–employee relationships, to reduce turnover and soldiering (pretending to work while actually loafing), and to quash unionization and job actions. Manufacturers recognized that labor would continue as a vital aspect of the industrial system, and that efficient production depended on its efficient performance, even as they endeavored to reconstitute or replace it with machinery. Creation among laborers of positive, predictable behavior would forge them into a reliable and productive cohort. Many industrialists understood that economics was only one facet of the labor question; proper job performance was coterminous with and a product of proper living. As one commentator noted, "family quarrels have an almost immediate effect on the output of lathes and drill presses."

Ford's Approach to Industrial Sociology Although Henry Ford came to that realization rather late, he quickly moved to the vanguard of those trying to systematize employee–employer relations. In 1914, he launched a landmark three-pronged program to increase labor efficiency: the Five Dollar Day, the Ford Sociological Department, and the Ford English School. These efforts attracted almost as much notice as the moving assembly line.

The Industrial Workers of the World's militant unionism, a daily absentee rate at the Highland Park plant in excess of 10 percent, and a 370 percent yearly turnover rate (requiring Ford to spend nearly $2 million to train new workers in 1913) were the immediate impetus for his novel decision. He paid $5 a day to every "qualified" Ford worker, "even the lowliest laborer and the man who merely sweeps the floors." This "profit-sharing plan" more than doubled the average

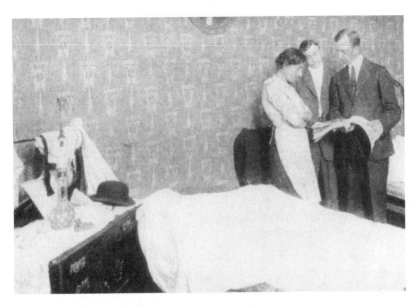

*Ford Sociological Department operatives inspected
the homes of workers and offered practical advice.*

Ford factory worker's pay. Rather than increasing expenditures, however, the $5 day constituted "efficiency engineering," Ford main-
tained, and would stand as "one of the finest cost-cutting moves we
ever made."

Statistics backed up Ford's contention. Turnover fell to 16 percent
in 1915, and absenteeism dropped to 0.5 percent. The Ford Sociological
Department determined who qualified for this wage. Its operatives,
some 250 by 1920, visited homes, interviewed families, neighbors, and
clergy, and sought to corroborate workers' statements. Using a Henry
Ford-inspired code of conduct stressing family, community, thrift, and
character, they checked and rechecked whether employees met the
profit-sharing template. Unmarried men under age twenty-two, married men living by themselves or involved in divorces, new employees
with less than six months' seniority, and any worker "living un-
worthily as a profit sharer" were deemed unsuitable. Later the list included those taking in male boarders, frittering away evenings un-
wisely, sending funds to Europe, spending money foolishly, using
alcohol, and speaking a language other than English. A full 40 percent
of the Ford force failed to qualify.

The Sociological Department revised its determinations every six
months. Those not initially qualified were to reorient their lives in the
intervening period, but continued "unworthiness" led to dismissal.
Yet the Sociological Department did more than investigate; it also

provided Ford employees and their families with information useful for daily existence. Department employees discussed such rudimentary activities as family budgets and savings accounts; gave elementary lessons in home management and hygiene; taught how to shop to best advantage; and showed how to distinguish among cuts of meat.

The Ford English School followed a similar educational premise. While teaching English, the school also instructed Ford's non-English-speaking employees in thrift, industry, and economy and mandatory courses in domestic, community, and industrial relations. The school aimed, like the Sociological Department, to weld systematically the diverse groups comprising Ford's labor force into a standardized, dependable cohort. Its commencement exercises, held in the city's largest hall, reflected that thrust:

> On the stage was represented an immigrant ship. In front of it was a huge melting pot. Down the gang plank came the members of the class dressed in their national garbs and carrying luggage such as they carried when they landed in this country. Down they poured into the Ford melting pot and disappeared. Then the teachers began to stir the contents of the pot with long ladles. Presently the pot began to boil over and out came the men dressed in their best American clothes and waving American flags.

Systematizing Hiring Others tried to systematize the employment process. From about 1900, a few corporations established departments to investigate job applicants. Rather than try to mold disparate individuals into a cohort, these industrial concerns instituted policies "of questioning, of research, of careful investigation . . . of seeking exact knowledge and then shaping action on discovered facts." These deliberations presumably produced a more homogeneous labor force, selected for its likely dependability and productivity. But systematic examination, despite its pretenses, lacked science's rigor.

An emerging group of psychologists stepped into the void. In 1912, Harvard's Hugo Munsterberg maintained that psychology would revolutionize industry by detecting "those personalities which by their mental qualities are especially fit for a particular kind of economic work." Several businesses attracted by the idea of a precise, nonpartisan, indisputable approach to worker selection, and the promise of lower turnover, freedom from labor unrest, and enhanced efficiency, used industrial psychologists' tests. By 1914, American companies had by test selected traveling salesmen, motormen, conductors, telegraphers, typists, stenographers, and telephone operators. Industrial psychologists invaded factories in 1915 when Northwestern University's

*These workers' homes near Pittsburgh steel mills
would never have passed muster with Ford's
Sociological Department.*

Walter Dill Scott devised intelligence, dexterity, and general-ability tests for industrial workers. The federal government's support of psychological testing of soldiers and workers in selected industries during World War I further bolstered industrial psychology's credibility and prestige. Scott and others capitalized on this increased familiarity and formed industrial-psychology consulting firms. Scott's company alone had more than sixty business clients in 1923.

New Relations between Labor and Owners

By hiring industrial psychologists, scientific and systematic managers, and others to expertly and systematically select, train, and keep a labor force, industrialists acknowledged the existence of a "labor problem." Labor required fitting; it had to be shaped to pursue dependably its specific task within the general production system. Certainly there was no longer any role for skilled artisans; mechanization and extreme division of labor had rendered them obsolete. But labor/employer problems were not products of new or revamped means of production. Instead, they emerged from the same premise from which those new and revamped means of production blossomed: namely, that systems, including social systems, were composed of diverse fixed (and limited) elements hierarchically arranged.

This notion led to a radical disjunction among capital, managerial, and labor elements, a fact which labor recognized and institutionalized in the new trade unionism of the late nineteenth and early twentieth century. Prior to the 1870s, Americans had formed unions sporadically, usually for ad hoc local situations. Most had served as social clubs or self-insurance agencies. Those few organizations involved in more worldly pursuits had usually attacked the status quo and sought a return to an idyllic past. The majority of those activists had considered the nation as composed of two groups: workers and monopolists. Mid-nineteenth-century unionists defined employers, managers, and virtually everyone else as workers, and identified their interests as coterminous with those of the overwhelming majority of Americans; America was a social unit, not a social system, and should rid itself of those structures and individuals not acting uniformly. These unions attracted suffragettes, as well as prison, land, currency, and utopian reformers, because they had detected similar problems and advocated similar goals.

A different perspective emerged in the 1870s and predominated by the late 1880s. Labor as a class became self-conscious; it ceased to identify its interests as identical with employers. Owners and management were its natural antagonists, yet it recognized that its relationship to these classes dictated its members' well-being. Labor proved willing to accept loss of status and social mobility in return for better working conditions and more money. This view led to repeated confrontations, generated state and national legislation, and produced new organizations.

The American Federation of Labor Formation of the American Federation of Labor (AFL) in 1886 and its rise during subsequent decades resulted from labor's new self-consciousness. Its president, Samuel Gompers, argued that the AFL was a product of the realization by "wage-workers of this continent" that they constitute "a distinct and practically permanent class of modern society; and consequently have distinct and permanent interests." Only "true" workers—hand laborers—could join the organization, which emphasized labor's economic power to counterbalance organized capital. Deeming work stoppages of primary importance, the AFL entered politics only to defend labor's economic position, and backed, for example, immigration-restriction legislation to limit the labor supply and protect wages. Begun as a consortium of unions organized by trade, the AFL gradually became the head of a system of local, district, and state affiliates. It stood as labor's spokesperson and defender, but also as an acknowledgment that labor was neither the brains nor the heart of the socioindustrial system, only its hands and feet.

The Growth of Industrial Education In its role as working people's protector, organized labor often butted heads with industrial leaders. Such was the case with the question of vocational education after 1900. The vocational-education movement dated its formal start to 1880, when C. M. Woodward established St. Louis's Manual Training School, which prepared high-school-aged students to become machinists or woodworkers. Similar high schools were opened before 1886 in Chicago, Baltimore, Philadelphia, Toledo, Cincinnati, and St. Paul.

These early industrial schools had been formed under the auspices of church missions and private philanthropic agencies to solve the social problems of poverty and pauperism. Alarmed by the high dropout rate and the apparent inadequate supply of industrial workers, reformers rejected traditional schooling for poor children, and trained them systematically to become useful, productive citizens able to fill a niche and participate in the American socioeconomic and political system. City and state governments eventually adopted and funded these programs. At their heart were two assumptions: identification of a segment of the American population (designated by their heritage and their lack of wealth) as inherently incapable of developing beyond a specific point; and the propriety of selecting and planning the direction of a class of people to a particular life's work, not necessarily with their consent. The poor could become neither managers nor employers, only laborers. Vocational guidance, coupled with specialized education, would ensure that they achieved their highest possible station. Democracy's meaning had changed from freedom of individual opportunity to freedom for groups to assume their appropriate place within American life and sample its fruits.

State laws mandating that children attend public school or its equivalent until age sixteen helped shape industrial education, as did the various post-1905 state commissions seeking its most prudent form. Laws usually caused manufacturers to release young employees for a few hours daily to attend general-purpose trade schools, while the commissions frequently resulted in creation of more specialized industrial courses and additional public funding. Wisconsin enacted the most daring measure in 1911. It required places with populations in excess of 5,000 to erect industrial schools. Local boards of industrial education, composed of employers and laborers in equal number, levied taxes and framed instruction. Passage of the Smith-Hughes Act in 1917 nationalized vocational education by providing

Vocational and technical high schools trained
future generations of laborers to work
machinery essential to American industry.

matching federal money for precollegiate industrial education, but required states to gain project approval from a national vocational education board.

WORLD WAR I: A SYSTEM OF THOUGHT'S LAST BATTLE

The United States entered World War I at about the time of the Smith-Hughes Act's passage, and the war effort dwarfed other concerns as the nation faced a situation it had never before encountered. It needed to raise, equip, and send an army across the ocean, and to provide support as well as furnish matériel for its beleaguered allies. That America remained undaunted by these prospects stemmed from nearly a half-century of experience rationalizing and systematizing virtually every facet of life. Participation in World War I placed new demands on the country, but not fundamentally inconsistent or unfamiliar ones. Only the scale would be different; Americans treated the war as the culmination of previous efforts, not the inauguration of a new agenda. The nation would manufacture what it needed; it would become like a factory to prepare and fight "a war to end all wars." Systematization of industrial organization, management, and production, as well as transportation and communication, and scientific and technological efforts, would "keep the world safe for democracy."

Marshaling Resources for War

The nation began preparations for mobilization after the *Lusitania's* sinking in 1915. The Naval Consulting Board (NCB), created by the naval secretary and composed of Edison and other industrial leaders, solicited nominations from the national engineering societies for state industrial preparedness committees, which compiled preliminary resource inventories. The National Research Council (NRC) was formed a year later to coordinate scientific research. Its mission included inventories of scientific personnel, equipment, and research; integration of government, university, industrial, and foundation science and scientists; and communication among investigators. The Council of National Defense (CND), also established in 1916, had a broader mandate. Its six officials, all cabinet members, coordinated the entire premobilization campaign.

The CND increased its authority after Congress declared war on April 6, 1917. The declaration empowered President Woodrow Wilson to commandeer essential industries and mines, seize and operate all transportation and communication systems, and control distribution and fix prices of war-related commodities. Wilson delegated these powers to several boards and placed them under the CND's supervision. The CND completed the NCB's inventory and assigned the naval board the task of screening inventors' suggestions and devices for their military potential. The NRC was designated the CND's research arm, and was directed to coordinate war-related scientific research and resources. Antisubmarine weapons, precision rangefinders, and dependable gas masks resulted, as did psychological tests used both to determine potential officers and to weed out unacceptable draftees.

The War Industries Board, headed by Bernard Baruch, controlled industrial production. It regulated all extant industries that manufactured war matériel; developed new industries, plants, and supply sources; established prices; and determined production and delivery priorities. Some 30,000 different articles fell under its purview. Baruch ruthlessly slashed product variety to free resources. Little escaped his axe. For example, he reduced the number of typewriter-ribbon colors from 150 to five, mandated a lower maximum length of shoe uppers, and regulated the quantity of steel in corset manufacture. The last initiative saved an estimated 8,000 tons of steel annually. Baruch's systematic frugality, coupled with reallocation of resources and production capability (he had, for instance, fifty munitions factories built in the war's first few months), enabled Americans during the war to produce 2.5 million rifles, 181,000 machine guns, 3,000 artillery pieces, 3.5 billion rounds of small-arms ammunition, 5 million gas masks, and 8,000 training planes. CND-sponsored fuel, food, and transportation boards received similar authority and worked comparable miracles.

New War Technology on Land

American manufacture of machine guns was a response to the changed nature of land warfare. These killing machines made traditional military advances foolhardy, and impossible without massive loss of life. Rifles, bayonets, and hand-to-hand combat no longer carried the day, and horse cavalry was relegated to history's scrapheap; warfare ceased to be considered glorious and became impersonal.

Machine guns came of age in World War I, but their invention dated to the late nineteenth century. Hiram S. Maxim, an expatriate American who had lost the incandescent-light race to Edison, devised the first fully automatic machine gun in 1884 and demonstrated it in 1887. The force of recoil from Maxim's gun operated the ejection, loading, and firing mechanisms. Maxim also developed a smokeless powder when he found that black powder residue clogged his new gun's barrel. Military men marveled at Maxim's display, but failed to grasp the machine gun's revolutionary killing potential. Most continued as late as 1914 to regard machine guns as nothing more than adjuncts to conventional weaponry, even after arms manufacturers such as Colt produced lighter, improved versions. This misapprehension had vanished before America entered the war, and the nation's soldiers quickly familiarized themselves with the weapon.

Industry also contributed new armament designs. Machine-gun-supported, barbed-wire-fortified trench warfare dominated the European theater, while thick metal fragmentary hand grenades further bolstered defenses and gas masks warded off poisonous phosgene. Assaults on these congealed lines proved difficult. Artillery was one manner of attack. Trench mortars lobbed bombs, and glycerin recoil artillery, sometimes mounted on mobile railroad cars, fired streamlined tracer, incendiary, and armor-piercing shells. Internal-combustion-engine vehicles spearheaded the other primary land assault mode. Caterpillar tractors, and armored tanks mounted with machine guns and equipped with pneumatic tires, attempted to burst through lines and drive the enemy from trenches.

New War Technology at Sea

Torpedo-armed German submarines transformed traditional sea warfare practices as drastically as the machine gun changed land war. Rather than engage in conventional naval bombardments, submarines killed quietly, and battleships, even the awesome *Dreadnaught*, quaked at the thought of these underwater death merchants. Submarines also disrupted war matériel shipments and blockaded ports, both of which were impediments to conducting a transatlantic war.

Americans led in developing antisubmarine measures. Its subchasers were small wooden craft with radio listening devices to detect a submarine's presence. They carried depth charges, which detonated upon reaching a certain depth to force submarines to surface, and guns to finish them off. Subchasers sank more than 200 submarines. American destroyers were sleeker and swifter than their European counterparts. Their five-inch guns and torpedoes proved potent anti-sub weapons. New electrically detonated deep-water mines prevented submarines from moving through mined areas.

Convoys were the most effective antisubmarine measures. Systematic assemblages of subchasers, destroyers, cruisers, and other ships, convoys tied up many ships and were expensive but protected transports and merchantmen. Submarines attempting to penetrate the convoy's shell were detected by subchasers and attacked by numerous vessels. Convoys negated submarines so completely that by war's end Germans refrained from assaulting them. Allied shipping losses had become minimal.

New War Technology in the Air

World War I was the first major conflict to see a new dimension, the air, added to warfare. The American military was especially unprepared for this type of fighting; it possessed a scant 109 airplanes, mostly trainers, and had only eighty-three pilots when Congress declared war. European combatants operated far larger air forces and had highly refined the art of aerial warfare. Scouts, machine-gun-fitted fighters, and multi-engine bombers filled the Western European sky as air duels, strafing, and bombing runs, as well as aerial reconnaissance and photography, were commonplace. That air power would assume such prominence was surprising; the first manned flight of a powered, heavier-than-air craft had occurred a mere thirteen and one-half years earlier. That Americans would lag so far behind Europeans was equally surprising; airplanes were an American invention.

The Advent of Powered Flight Orville and Wilbur Wright made the first successful airplane flight on December 17, 1903, at Kitty Hawk, North Carolina. Others had flown earlier. The French had pioneered hot-air balloon flight in the late eighteenth century, and gas and hot-air balloons had been popular nineteenth-century entertainment. Hiram P. Maxim's (Hiram S. Maxim's son) railbound, steam-engine-powered vehicle and Otto Lilienthal's gliders had attracted considerable attention in the 1890s. Samuel Pierpont Langley, the Smithsonian Institution's head, had helped galvanize American interest in flight. He parlayed his scientific reputation (and Theodore Roosevelt's support) to land, in 1898, a $50,000 governmental grant to build and fly a heavier-than-air-powered craft. Relying on design studies that he had begun in 1886, Langley constructed the gasoline-engine-driven *Aerodrome*. Several attempts to launch the plane proved fruitless, the last occurring nine days before the Wrights' flight.

A comparison of Langley's and the Wrights' notions of the problem of flight indicates that Langley lagged far behind. He sought to "urge a system of rigid planes through the air at great velocity." To Langley, flight was similar to running a knife through butter. Propeller and wing shape were crucial, as were centers of gravity; proper angles of incidence would enable the system of rigid planes to slice through or "deform" air, which was to Langley a homogeneous elastic substance—almost identical, perfectly elastic cubes. Langley's design of his inclined-plane launch mechanism stemmed from that consideration. The Wrights held a more sophisticated view, perhaps because of their bicycle-racing and bicycle-making experience, which also familiarized them with strong lightweight materials and wood- and metal-working tools. They regarded propeller and wing shape as important, but conducted their own wind-tunnel tests and emphasized the air's fluid nature. Flight could never be reduced to a system of rigid planes; continual coordinated compensation to the various forces acting on the aircraft was essential. The Wrights created aerial stability through constant adjustability born of flexibility. Their conception of control was three-dimensional, and its most telling features were their plane's roll and yaw stabilizing devices. A mechanism that, through a series of lines and struts, provided immediate compensating helical twists across the entire wing reflected their commitment to fluid dynamics, as did their decision to link the rudder to this wing-warping apparatus. Coupled with a hand-operated forward elevator, their control system suggested a much more complex idea of the requirements of flight.

The Development of American Aviation Neither the Wrights' Kitty Hawk success, nor their repeated flights near Dayton, Ohio, during the next few years, triggered an American aviation boom. The first company specifically formed to manufacture airplanes did not produce one until 1908, and the U.S. military purchased its first aircraft a year later. It had only six in 1914. Stunt-flying appealed to the American public after 1910, and in the early teens a few entrepreneurs established commercial air service between nearby but hard-to-reach places.

America trailed Europe in airplane design, but its infatuation with automobiles and industrial rationalization helped it pull ahead in airplane engine construction. In 1916, Packard Motor Car's J. G. Vincent and Hall-Scott Motor Car's E. J. Hall created the Liberty engine for airplanes, and developed techniques for its mass production.

This powerful, dependable internal-combustion engine came in eight- and twelve-cylinder models and became the American staple. Many were shipped overseas and fitted in English and French aircraft during the war, but the premobilization engine blitz did not extend to planes themselves. In the year prior to Congress's declaration of war, the American aviation industry produced a mere 411 aircraft. The slim total did not dissuade the nation from planning to make more than 8,000 training planes and 12,400 fighters and transports by spring 1918. It managed to produce only half that number, almost all trainers. Fighters were purchased in Europe. Despite this drawback, America amassed an air force on Old World soil of more than 5,500 planes by Armistice Day. Its pilots had shot down an estimated 850 enemy aircraft.

Production of Munitions During the War

The nation was almost as inadequately prepared to produce munitions as airplanes. The American chemical industry long had relied on Germany and, to a much lesser extent, other European powers for the bulk of its organic chemicals, generally coal-tar derivatives. German government/chemical industry connections had undercut American domestic prices, discouraged production, and enabled Germany to establish a virtual international monopoly. With the war, however, Germany refused to ship coal-tar derivatives (such as benzene, phenol, toluene, xylene, and naphthalene), and its submarines prevented other nations from taking up the slack. Acetone and glycerin were also in short supply.

These several chemicals had many industrial uses. All were essential to production of explosives. Nitroglycerin and dynamite required glycerin. Some smokeless powder used acetone as a solvent. Benzene and phenol were picric acid intermediates. Toluene was TNT's basic component. Other modern explosives employed xylene and naphthalene. The German boycott did not sting only America; England and France were acutely affected. When America entered the war, its allies increasingly looked to the New World for munitions.

America quickly mobilized its resources. The steel industry rapidly completed conversion from beehive to by-product ovens, and chemists distilled the resulting coal tar and separated it into its components. Others cracked long petroleum chains for the shorter toluene and other products, or attempted to synthesize these materials. In 1915, America produced only 2.5 million gallons of benzene, 623,000 gallons of toluene, and 196,000 pounds of naphthalene. In 1918, it manufactured eighteen times more benzene, nearly eleven times more toluene, and more than thirty-two times more naphthalene. Commercial glycerin came from recovered and purified soap and candle industrial refuse.

Destructive distillation of seaweed and timber yielded acetone. Government money built the massive new ordnance plants, Nitro and Old Hickory. Dynamite production was four times as great in 1917 as it had been in 1913, and black and smokeless powder manufacture skyrocketed during the same period—from 866,569 pounds to more than 438 million pounds. American picric acid and TNT production was valued at $651,000 in 1913 but reached $394 million four years later.

The End of a System of Thought

America's ability to mobilize its material and human resources contributed to the allied victory. Armistice Day received an enthusiastic welcome, but the nation did not return to the way of life it had previously known; there was no return to "normalcy." Several social, demographic, and economic changes had accompanied the war effort. Unions had gained affiliates and strength. Rural southern blacks who had made the pilgrimage North to work in war plants frequently stayed in northern cities. Women had logged long hours replacing men in factories. The nation's essential industries had become familiarized with mass-production techniques, the war had awakened American entrepreneurs to the potential of new industries, and the public anticipated new goods and services. The aviation industry began its takeoff; air mail and passenger service, crop dusting, and express delivery of parts and perishable commodities were postwar products. The American organic-chemical industry also came of age; governmental confiscation and sale of German patents and property protected wartime investment, while stiff tariffs shielded the nascent industry from postwar foreign competition. American sources of supply, tapped during the war for munitions, continued to produce essential chemicals, which were transformed into plastics, solvents, gasoline additives, dyes, and medicines. These new sectors of industry became increasingly important in the postwar world.

But America also seemed changed in a different way. Its pursuit of the war had been conducted according to an organizational idea that had begun to be implemented some five decades earlier. Land, air, and sea warfare were separate and separable types of combat. Mobilization, production of ordnance, and manufacture of aircraft were distinct activities, united in their war effort contribution, and given priorities according to their importance. This notion of systems as composed of discrete circumscribed elements hierarchically ordered connoted more than assignment of position or place, of course. It defined processes and procedures, as well as relationships among components. As important, it assumed that these elements were virtually

Airmail took off after World War I. Here two Americans deliver mail from Canada.

inviolable, and that each possessed an almost intrinsic property, quality, or ability; identification of each element was without reference to others. In that sense, World War I marked the culmination of that mode of thought. The portrayal of components as rigid and encapsulated gave way in the 1920s and with it went the post-1870 view of the nature of systems. The technologies of the 1920s and after would be built upon or explained according to different premises.

FOR FURTHER READING

Allen, Edith. *Mechanical Devices in the Home* (1922).

Armstrong, David A. *Bullets and Bureaucrats* (1982).

Baldwin, Keturah E. *The American Home Economics Association Saga* (1949).

Bennett, Charles A. *History of Manual and Industrial Education, 1870 to 1917* (1937).

B'evier, Isabel, and Susannah Usher. *The Home Economics Movement* (1918).

Bilstein, Roger E. *Flight in America* (1984).

Bliven, Bruce, Jr. *The Wonderful Writing Machine* (1954).

Boorstin, Daniel J. *The Americans: The Democratic Experience* (1973).

Chandler, Alfred D., Jr. *The Visible Hand* (1977).

Cowan, Ruth Schwartz. *More Work for Mother* (1983).

Current, Richard N. *The Typewriter and the Men Who Made It* (1954).

Davies, Margery W. *Woman's Place Is at the Typewriter* (1982).

Ellis, John. *The Social History of the Machine Gun* (1975).

Eppright, Ercel Sherman, and Elizabeth Storm Ferguson. *A Century of Home Economics at Iowa State University* (1971).

Frederick, Christine. *The New Housekeeping* (1912).

Freudenthal, Elsbeth E. *Flight into History* (1949).

Grob, Gerald N. *Workers and Utopia* (1960).

Haber, Samuel. *Efficiency and Uplift* (1964).

Hallion, Richard P. *Rise of the Fighter Aircraft, 1914–1918* (1984).

Haynes, Williams. *The American Chemical Industry*, vol. 3 (1945).

Kanigel, Robert. *The One Best Way: Frederick Winslow Taylor and the Enigma of Efficiency* (1997).

Lifshey, Earl. *The Housewares Story* (1973).

Macksey, Kenneth and John H. Batchelor. *Tank* (1970).

May, Earl Chapin. *The Canning Clan* (1937).

Mayr, Otto, and Robert C. Post, eds. *Yankee Enterprise* (1981).

Montgomery, David. *The Fall of the House of Labor: The Workplace, the State, and American Labor Activism, 1865–1925* (1987).

Nelson, Daniel. *Workers and Managers* (1975).

Nevins, Allan. *Ford, the Times, the Man, the Company* (1954).

Rodgers, Daniel T. *The Work Ethic in Industrial America, 1850–1920* (1978).

Taylor, Frederick Winslow. *Scientific Management* (1947).

Turck, J. A. V. *Origin of Modern Calculating Machines* (1921).

PART THREE

From Industrial America to Postindustrial America

THE 1920S TO THE PRESENT

The notion of system, such a crucial aspect of late–nineteenth- and early–twentieth-century thought, underwent drastic revision in the decade after about 1920. Whereas systems in the earlier period were static entities, composed of diverse, fixed, and limited parts hierarchically arranged—the system equaled the sum of its different parts—the new systems of the 1920s and after were dynamic, predicated on a much more complex relationship among the parts. Each part seemed to acquire a share of its definition from its interrelationships with the other parts in the system; the parts seemed to reflect on one another. Flexibility, adjustment, and compensation characterized these modern integrated systems, which were greater than or different from the sum of their parts.

This idea of systems as complicated dynamic processes opened new technological possibilities. It produced a reconsideration and reorientation of technological processes and the acknowledgment that previously unforeseen factors might affect technological decisions. But it also made it conceivable to seek technological solutions to virtually every problem, including social problems. The introduction of new technologies into a system would vary the dynamics or increase integration and shift equilibrium to a more favorable spot. From this perspective came efforts as diverse as introducing electricity into rural regions to conquer poverty and isolation, automobiles into cities to reduce urban crowding, and agricultural and industrial technologies into Third World countries to combat communism.

This unabashedly optimistic assessment of technology's critical influence continued into the 1950s and early 1960s. But now technology seemed a way to convert American plenty into individual empowerment and freedom. In effect, terms of analysis had changed. Americans focused not on the whole—on the system—but began to concentrate on the parts of systems, whether individual persons, single companies, or particular social groups. The shift from overall system to individual component did not undercut American faith in technology and technological solutions. Accentuating or liberating the individual "part," generally in hopes of expanding its options, choices, and opportunities, emerged as the central concern of this new formulation. New technologies and technological solutions seemed to foster individual autonomy and control.

The idea of technology as an overwhelmingly positive means to enhance individual flexibility and authority waned in the later 1960s and continued to dwindle during the next several decades. American society remained fixated on the individual but that previously benign condition was transformed into a potential menace by a new perception that the resources of the nation (and the world) were limited. This sense of limits appeared to circumscribe individual options, restrict choices, and undercut opportunities. It pitted individuals, companies, and groups in direct and potent competition with each other; what one company, individual, or group received seemed to come only at the expense of reducing the "pie" available to all others. A new immediacy resulted; if individuals passionately competed for diminished, nonrenewable resources, the future could well not be better or even as good as the present or past.

These fearsome prospects contributed to a disillusionment with traditional decision-making apparatus in the late 1960s and after. A critique of professionalism as elitist, not objective, and expertise as the product of privilege and bias emerged. Technology as the production of so-called "objective" experts became a subject of immense concern. Most Americans conceded that technology was a powerful force. But now disputes raged about its introduction and implementation as it seemed to produce positive benefits for some and negative consequences for others. Technology after the mid-1960s was increasingly seen as both a cause of and cure for social problems; it was a social question. But in an era shorn of the aura of expertise, the means to decide the relative merits of a particular technology were not clear. Each technological initiative was subjected to individual scrutiny. Like beauty, the impact of a technology seemed to be in the eye of the beholder. And each beholder increasingly maintained that only his or her perspective mattered.

Technologies long established, such as the space program, nuclear power, and the like were particularly vulnerable to this thrust. Yet those technologies, new or identified as new, such as personal computers or videocassette recorders, generally avoided being labeled social questions. The reason for this was clear. Proponents of the new technologies announced their discoveries in such a way as to personalize them. Through their personal behavior and by how they publicly explained their new technologies, these men and women abandoned or rejected any pretense of society, a social order, or even social groups themselves. Rather than present technologies as questions of society, then, they marketed these new devices, processes, and techniques as questions of persons. There were little or no social implications, only personal ones, questions simply for independent, rigidly isolated individuals to decide for and about themselves. This lesson was not lost on others. Many established technologies and practices would recognize and adapt to this new milieu and redefine themselves to be publicly palatable. By the mid-1990s, the transformation was virtually complete. Technology had to a large degree ceased to be a social question.

Technology as a Social Solution: the 1920s to the 1950s

EMERGENCE OF A NEW NOTION OF SYSTEMS
The Hawthorne Experiments

In 1924, the National Research Council selected Western Electric's Hawthorne Works, a facility of nearly 30,000 workers located on Chicago's west side, to investigate labor productivity and factory illumination. Carried out by Massachusetts Institute of Technology (MIT) electrical engineers, this rather modest old-fashioned study identified two groups of workers, then subjected one to various lighting conditions and left the other constant. Much to the engineers' surprise, productivity of both groups increased no matter what their lighting conditions. Researchers concluded that lighting was at best only a minor worker performance factor, and that they needed to control numerous other variables before estimating its precise importance.

The understandably curious Western Electric sponsored additional tests in April 1927. Rather than seek a simple correlation between lighting or any other single feature and productivity, these and later tests aimed to understand work environment dynamics. The tests continued for nearly a decade, cost more than $1 million and tens of thousands of worker hours, and ultimately produced new methods to bolster worker productivity. They became the basis of a new managerial workplace technology.

An interdisciplinary team of MIT researchers conducted these new experiments. They isolated six female relay assemblers in a small room located at the corner of the regular relay assembly room to investigate relationships among working conditions, monotony, and fatigue. The team observed the women under normal conditions to achieve a base line, then acclimated them to their new surroundings. Researchers next exposed the women to several working situations, recorded their conversations, and noted productivity changes. Observers found that productivity increased in the new environment. New wage systems were instituted and output again moved ahead. Productivity increases also followed introduction of rest pauses, variations in the length of the working day and week, and provision of free nutritionally balanced lunches. Only when all perks (except the new wage system) were withdrawn did productivity level off. It moved upward again as each perk was reinstituted. These findings puzzled researchers. Each factor in the working environment seemed "so dependent on its relations to other factors that it was impossible to consider it a thing in itself having an independent effect on the individual." They also recognized that the women had formed a social network among themselves, and had developed a sense of participation in critical determinations.

Social networks provided the next test focus. Management wanted to know the implications of social networks. The Harvard Business School's Elton Mayo supervised the research team's investigations of Hawthorne's fourteen male bank-wiring operators. Mayo's staff reported that worker networks were very intricate social organizations that erected their own rules. Identification with a network prevented deviant behavior—behavior outside the network's norm—and protected the network from outside interference or control. Worker social networks often adopted perspectives different from management's— they disputed, for example, management's conception of a fair day's labor, and repeatedly produced at lower network norms. Researchers then concluded that network standards determined individual productivity. The traditional nexus between ability and performance (measured by Walter Dill Scott's industrial psychology firm and others) was of only peripheral significance.

Western Electric's management pondered methods to stop soldiering, while Mayo compared results of the assembly and bank-wiring room tests. He argued that the women's productivity had accelerated in each instance because they had an *active* role in the experiment, and therefore wanted it to "succeed." The women considered themselves taken into management's confidence, as partners in the enterprise, not antagonists. Another test was then occurring that confirmed Mayo's assessment; Western Electric interviewed its employees about management programs but found it impossible to keep them on the topic because workers wanted to discuss what interested them. Researchers altered the interview process, made it nondirective, and permitted laborers to talk about whatever they wished. During follow-up contacts sometime later, workers often mentioned improved factory working conditions, and a few even applauded the new wage system. But their impressions were fallacious; the company had changed neither working conditions nor wages. Employees gained from their interviews feelings of belonging and recognition. By listening to their thoughts, management seemed to value their opinions; that attitude appeared to hold important implications for worker well-being and, ultimately, productivity. Put more boldly, worker grievances often lacked integrity, and were instead manifestations of a sense of alienation from management, a posture readily modified.

The company at last had an answer it could apply. It established "personnel counseling" in 1936, and staffed these posts with long-term, well-liked Western Electric employees. It instructed them to deal "with attitudes towards problems, not the problems themselves"; counselors only listened. Worker productivity blossomed under this arrangement as workers felt accepted by management and placed the company's interests within their social networks. So, too, did the number of counselors grow. Western Electric's five counselors in 1936 soon expanded to ten in 1938, twenty-nine in 1941, and sixty-four in 1954.

Personnel counseling quickly spread outside Western Electric. A generation of human relations experts invaded American factories and succeeded the scientific managers of an earlier day. Questions of fatigue, working conditions, lighting, monotony, and the like receded as attitudinal adjustment of workers emerged. Worker productivity became a state of mind, not a result of physical situations, but it still could be engineered.

The New Notion of Systems

The Hawthorne studies were at odds with late–nineteenth- and early–twentieth-century American industrial experiments. Earlier investigators had added performance incentives or penalties, selected or trained a workforce appropriate to the tasks at hand, refashioned the physical environment, or reshaped the assigned job. They had based these programs on a particular understanding of the nature of work, workers, and the workplace that stemmed from the notion of system as a static entity composed of discrete, fixed, and limited parts that were hierarchically ordered. The Hawthorne experiment proceeded from very different assumptions, which marked the mid-twentieth century as fundamentally dissimilar from the late nineteenth and early twentieth centuries. "Interdependence of relationship" identified the more modern system. Its parts appeared "so closely integrated as a whole that no change can occur in any of its phases without affecting other phases in some measure."

Much more complex than the earlier representation, the post-1920 system accentuated relationships among things previously considered only peripherally related, and suggested interconnections where none had been established formerly. Parts within these new systems had little integrity of their own, and lost whatever intrinsic character they had possessed when examined outside the system. Each part received a portion of its definition from its relationships to other parts; its definition was relative or indeterminate because parts interacted with each other. Introduction of new stimuli upset the precise balance and resulted in adjustment and compensation throughout the entire system, a factor rendering ideas of permanent or natural hierarchical order meaningless.

A new vocabulary accompanied this transition, as did new definitions of old terms. Businesses began to tell employees that their jobs required "utmost cooperation and teamwork" and often used analogies to a symphony orchestra or a surgical team to make their point. *Ecology, multipurpose, interdisciplinary, populations, decentralized, culture, networks, dynamics, pluralism, federal, interdependence, communities, region, and dynamic equilibrium* were words used to describe and explain the new post-1920 system and its elements. Before 1920 very few Americans had conceived of systems in roughly the same manner. The Wright brothers' conceptions about flight is perhaps the most prominent example, but these scattered individuals never extended their analyses' terms. As articulated by post-1920 Americans, these ideas blurred distinctions between technology and other endeavors and made it conceivable to seek technological solutions to social questions. They also produced reexamination and reconceptualization of established technologies. Scrutiny was applied to devices, processes, and activities that had served for half a century. Technical design likewise underwent revision: machines designed in the art deco style were conscious attempts to merge aesthetic and technological interests. Technology implicitly became an art form, among its many newly perceived interactions.

THE GOVERNMENT AND SOCIAL ENGINEERING

Government involvement in technological activities rose exponentially as Americans increasingly looked to technologies to resolve social questions or to ameliorate social situations. Its participation in this social engineering movement was characteristically managerial. Particularly in the 1920s and early 1930s, government served as coordinator, gathering together a diverse but appropriate team of experts to consider a multifaceted problem and to design a technological solution that took into account numerous social, cultural, economic, and political factors. Governmental authority in these instances was informal; it held legal power only to form and convene teams, and relied on its power of persuasion to implement recommendations.

Businesses and industries certainly captured the spirit. Industrial exhibitions in the 1920s and 1930s stressed "A Century of Progress" or "the World of Tomorrow." Exhibitors portrayed "a happier way of American living through the interdependence of man and the building of a better world of tomorrow with the tools of today." Industry did more than talk. It gave equipment and contracts to the nation's leading technological universities to devise technological solutions to present problems. Industry no doubt expected profitable products to emerge. Nonetheless, it seemed as if "the scientific men of the country may be brought together to make an intelligent and coordinated attack on the great problems which are facing the nation."

Hoover and National Planning

Herbert Hoover favored this governmental role. His 1928 election to the presidency epitomized America's burgeoning social-engineering love affair. Trained as a mining engineer, Hoover had directed the World War I food relief effort and later served as commerce secretary. He remained convinced of modern life's complexities, and he viewed their resolution as an engineering task. Unlike engineers of earlier decades, Hoover regularly recognized that technical solutions had profound social and cultural implications. To Hoover, planning, especially national planning, required close cooperation among leaders of business, labor, agriculture, the professions, and other segments of society. These men and women would confer, analyze demographic trends, and formulate consensual, multidimensional, nonpartisan strategies to guide pluralistic America's future.

These views guided Hoover's attempts to regulate key emerging industries such as aviation, radio, electric power, and highway construction. Cooperation between public and private economic sectors, not direct governmental intervention, was his touchstone. Hoover wished to remove the executive branch from politics (an arena despised by most engineers as corrupt and imprecise), and limit it to evaluating and implementing policies and programs formulated by consortiums of private sector leaders. Efficient private regulation, in effect, was his ideal, with heavy reliance on technical expertise and cooperative associations.

Roosevelt and the New Deal

The Great Depression undermined Hoover's approach to government involvement in social engineering. But while Franklin D. Roosevelt and his "brain trust" dismissed Hoover's noninterventionist stance, they remained committed to social engineering's prospects. Acting during crisis and backed by congressional support, Roosevelt's administration employed federal funds and authority to relieve short-term economic distress and to work for future prosperity. Roosevelt's concept of a "New Deal" demanded the engineering of a planned, well-managed economy.

Roosevelt's New Deal exemplified a second type of government and social engineering nexus. Like Hoover's approach, it was managerial, relied on the wisdom of specialists (many in governmental posts) operating in tandem, and depended on government-inspired coordination. But most crucial, Roosevelt made government an active participant, balancing against and compensating for various disruptive forces; one often targeted was the greed of the private sector. Only government possessed the all-encompassing perspective necessary for effective policy, and its legal authority could compel uncooperative populations to comply with its programs.

Critics of the New Deal—The Technocrats Critics attacked Roosevelt's New Deal vision, but not the idea of government as a social-engineering agent. Hooverians found the New Deal too radical, while radicals (such as Upton Sinclair, Father Coughlin, and Huey Long) argued that it failed to go far enough. The Technocrats, a group of engineers seeking to replace politics and politicians in government and to reduce its decisions to purely technical grounds, fell into the latter category.

Technocracy's leaders were apparently inspired by their association between 1919 and 1921 with the iconoclastic critic Thorstein Veblen. Veblen had advocated the voluntary abdication of all absentee and greedy owners of big business; their replacement by diligent, reform-minded technicians and workers; creation of a national directorate to supervise the reallocation of all goods and services; and elimination of the artificial price system based on the equally artificial monetary system. These changes, Veblen contended, would increase America's industrial output by 300 to 1,200 percent.

With a few optimistic modifications, the Technocrats, led by Howard Scott, an enigmatic New Yorker with a mysterious past, adopted the Veblerian platform as its own. Technology would provide universal abundance in a system in which relative values of commodities would be determined by amounts of energy necessary to create them, and in which all citizens would receive "energy certificates." But Technocracy's appeal was limited; at its peak in the mid-1930s, the Technocratic movement had enrolled only a few thousand members.

Scott and his associates grew increasingly embittered and threatening as they failed to gain widespread approval. Their militaristic demeanor and structure, special insignia and salute, and gray uniforms and fleet of gray automobiles scared away many technical professionals, who otherwise were attracted to the pitch. It became, then, another fringe group of the Great Depression, and the term "technocracy" has become one of derision.

The Administration of New Deal Technologies

Criticism by the Technocrats and others did not measurably alter Roosevelt's New Deal. Removing people from relief rolls was its immediate objective and economic revitalization its long-range goal; social engineering would accomplish both. In New Deal thought, American pluralism was a strength rather than a detriment; New Dealers attempted to incorporate different social segments and specializations whenever they initiated projects. Its unprecedented support for the social sciences, arts, and humanities stemmed from a belief that modern life was constructed of more than new buildings, dams, and other structures. America's diverse peoples would interact and change one another and yield a society greater and healthier than the sum of its constituent social elements.

Carried to its logical conclusion, this argument proved contradictory. Successful efforts to merge the same dissimilar elements in every project according to New Deal premises would produce an America of almost inconceivable homogeneity, destroying the country's pluralistic vigor. This irony was particularly clear in programs to modify the nation's physical landscape. Defining cities as blighted and rural areas as backward, New Dealers hoped to create new environments "fit for life and the living." These environments would merge the best of the urban and the rural; ideally, they would yield a homogenized, nationwide, quasi-suburban existence (except suburbs surrounded central cities) in which America and Americans would achieve free and full expression. Two relatively new technologies were to aid this transformation: electric power and automobiles. The former would offer benefits available in cities, while the latter would facilitate the decentralization of population.

The Army Corps of Engineers This prescription for America's ills sparked public-works engineering projects of unprecedented scale and complexity. Numerous federal bureaus such as the Forest Service, Geological Survey, National Weather Service, Wildlife Service, and Bureau of Reclamation lent their expertise to these endeavors. Among the most frequently involved was the Army Corps of Engineers. Until the New Deal, the Corps had been restricted to improving only one aspect of river utilization—navigation—but it was authorized to plan other river

The Army Corps of Engineers participated in many multipurpose projects in the 1930s. The Bonneville Dam was among the largest.

uses. By the late 1920s, the Corps was empowered to devise flood-control plans as a regular adjunct to projects it had undertaken, to establish a hydraulics laboratory to study flood prevention, to survey America's 200 major river basins, and to consider the hydroelectric power-generation potential of navigation projects. Hoover turned this information over to private enterprise for action. Only after Roosevelt's election did Congress grant the Corps power to engage in river development other than navigation. In fact, it mandated that each new Corps project have multiple purposes. Congress, in effect, gave the Corps primary responsibility for flood control along all American rivers and the ability to construct major hydroelectric plants. The huge Bonneville Dam on the Columbia River near Portland, Oregon, begun in 1933 and completed five years later, was its first significant effort. Within a decade, the Corps' dams were producing billions of kilowatt-hours of electricity.

Rural Development—The Tennessee Valley Authority and Rural Electrification The Tennessee Valley Authority (TVA), established in 1933, was a conscious attempt to use government power and funds to make over a poor, predominantly rural seven-state region traversed by the Tennessee River. Technology— introduction of cheap, plentiful electricity—was to generate new government-regulated industries and thereby to improve the lives of the region's inhabitants. It was most definitely "an experiment in social reconstruction." According to its leading proponent, Arthur E. Morgan, a prominent civil engineer and president of Antioch College, the TVA's purpose was to create "an integrated social and economic order" in the valley; "the improvement of that total well being, in physical, social and economic condition, is the total aim." Morgan envisioned a comprehensive, detailed regional plan that overlooked no aspect of life in the region. It would even encourage residents to stop smoking and drinking.

The TVA failed to fulfill Morgan's social objectives. Dissension among supporters, as well as opposition from other sectors, doomed its cooperative communitarianism. But the TVA did produce numerous technical and economic achievements: dam construction, flood control, navigation, land reclamation, crop diversification, and above all, cheap electric power generation. Establishment of employee hiring and training programs, homes, schools, libraries, small local cooperative industries, recreational areas, and the model town of Norris, Tennessee, enabled the TVA to effect some social change.

The TVA model was popular among New Dealers, who exported it to other regions. To be sure, electricity was in some demand in rural environs. In 1930, only 13.4 percent of farms were electrified; the Midwest and South trailed far behind New England and the West. Electrification seemed to urbane New Dealers a potent cure for the "disease" of ruralness. Electricity appeared likely to foster new economic growth; reduce rural health problems, loneliness, and cultural deprivations; and enable rural inhabitants to employ modern electrical conveniences. But efforts to create elsewhere public regional agencies similar to TVA—especially in the Missouri Valley and the Pacific Northwest—failed. So, too, did ambitious plans for Pennsylvania and the Northeast. The reasons behind these failures were rarely technical. Private utility companies objected to government intervention and formed holding companies to pool profits and power. Even those power engineers backing government involvement often disagreed on the precise mechanism for cheap electricity generation. Some favored outright public ownership, others supported public regulatory commissions, and still others preferred limited public ownership with "yardsticks" for measuring private utility performance.

Inability to create new TVAs did not stymie New Dealers. Power engineers gained crucial federal assistance in implementing their various proposals in 1935. Roosevelt's Rural Electrification Administration (REA—headed by the mechanical engineer Morris Cooke, a former disciple of Hoover and Frederick W. Taylor), renewal of the Federal Power Commission, and enactment of the Public Utility Holding Company Act to regulate and reduce electric holding-company power spearheaded the campaign. REA assistance helped farmers form cooperative power pools and build electric lines themselves. A quarter of the cooperatives purchased TVA power, but the overwhelming majority bought power wholesale from private suppliers at higher rates. Federal agencies and regulations, as well as court challenges, ultimately forced private concerns to lower electric rates and to contribute actively to rural electrification.

By World War II this hodgepodge network was virtually complete, and nearly all rural dwellings received electricity. With electric power came good lighting, running water, indoor plumbing, refrigeration, electric irons, washing machines, and radios, as well as electrified farm tools and machines from grinding wheels to wood saws.

New Urban Landscapes New Dealers were less successful in redesigning urban America. They did, however, create numerous model communities across the nation to demonstrate what city life in America could become. Their "garden cities" program hoped to dot America with comprehensively planned communities of approximately thirty thousand people, with balanced industrial and agricultural economies, that would be circumscribed by fields and forests, or greenbelts. Modern technologies—automobiles and electricity—would enable residents from decaying industrial cities to relocate there and thus eliminate urban overcrowding and poverty. Rapid-transit systems and superhighways would link the economically, religiously, and racially diverse populations of these new cities to nearby garden cities, and join them in turn to regional centers with populations of some sixty thousand apiece.

The Roosevelt administration managed to construct only three garden cities: Greenbelt, Maryland (1937); Greenhills, Ohio (1938); and Greendale, Wisconsin (1938). None proved popular. Each lacked an industrial base to complement their greenbelts and pastoral settings. All eventually lost government sponsorship and became purely commercial and largely residential private enterprises.

A wave of suburbanization, which began about 1920, helped kill the garden cities. Ironically, modern technologies, especially automobiles and buses, had provided a potent alternative to inner-city congestion for urbanites of even modest means. Formerly, suburbanization had congregated along streetcar and rail lines, but automobiles enabled urbanites to flee inner cities and settle wherever there were roads. Suburbanization yielded an unprecedented roadway-building commitment and new public expenditures to make cities suitable for cars: from new traffic arrangements and equipment such as one-way streets, automatic traffic signals, and garages, to suburban spin-offs such as freeways and parkways. These freeways offered fast, safe driving conditions, thanks to controlled-access roads, wide median strips, strong divider fences, and cloverleaf intersections.

Urban mass transit became a casualty as its emphasis on standardized travel (mass-transit vehicles generated economies of scale by carrying numerous passengers on regular routes at scheduled times) conflicted with the rise of suburban sentiment. In 1929, Detroit's voters rejected a $280 million proposal for a new subway system plus additional streetcars, while four years earlier Los Angeles residents were not even given an opportunity to vote on a proposed subway and elevated track system. Local transit companies themselves sometimes opposed major new mass-transit initiatives, for decreased ridership in the wake of automobiles made them fearful that increased fares to pay for bonding measures would further reduce the number of passengers.

General Motors (GM) also apparently assisted the decline of urban mass transit. For, as alleged in a 1974 Senate antitrust hearing, between 1932 and 1956 that automobile company had helped destroy 100 street-railway systems in forty-five American cities. GM, Standard Oil of California, and Firestone Tire and Rubber, three industrial giants who directly benefited from a motor vehicle increase, had formed a holding company, National City Lines, which in turn bought street-railway companies in sixteen states. National City then converted the companies to operating small, more flexible GM buses, which played to the suburban trend. Operators who promised to purchase only GM equipment finally purchased the companies.

It was the frustrated garden-city vision, rather than the suburban-based accentuation of automobiles, that gave what became the interstate highway system its early inspiration. Commentators had boosted the economic value of a nationwide system of interconnected paved roads from the 1920s, but regional and national planners both inside and outside the Roosevelt administration openly pressed in the 1930s for construction of a government-financed national network of highways as much for its human as economic benefits. To New Dealers, these superbly designed roads would run through sparsely populated areas and replicate a phenomenon produced by other forms of transportation a century earlier: communities would spring up along these roadways, and urbanites appalled by big-city living would flock to these places. The result would be urban deconcentration and the rise of presumably balanced, integrated small cities, which joined diverse peoples harmoniously with nature.

Revitalizing the American Home

Electricity was the wave of the present and future and incorporated whenever possible. Gas-dependent technologies were passé, a symbol of an earlier, dirtier time. Synthetics and plastics replaced metals and woods, a rational, not natural, solution to humanity's ability to engineer progress. Engineering the American dream began for Roosevelt's New Dealers with the single family home. From the 1920s, plywood, latex glues, composition-board, drywall, and weather-resistant exteriors signalled progress in house building. Of no less importance was the interior. Electric appliances marked owners as progressive.

The wooden-encased Kelvinator, the first electric refrigerator, was marketed in 1918. Within a decade, the electric refrigerator had become a self-contained appliance, composed of a compressor, condenser, evaporator, and motor in a single, hermetically sealed steel compartment. Its thermostat and automatic controls impressed housewives and subsequent modifications further enhanced the machine's luster. Nontoxic and nonflammable Freon, developed by GM chemists in 1930, provided more efficient cooling while placing the coils at the unit's bottom, and also raised the food compartment and lessened bending. Two-temperature refrigerators, first sold in 1939, worked through cooling coils in walls. This machine made ice cubes, and, more important, its wall-cooling mechanism caused little condensation and required no manual defrosting. Prices plummeted as demand enabled manufacturers to work on economies of scale.

Electromechanical thermostats made electric stoves possible by 1930, and also fostered electric toasters, hot water heaters, clothes dryers, and dishwashers. Automatic washing machines spun dry as well as agitated clothes. Thermostats allowed oil-burning furnaces to replace wood or coal burners.

Stocking the American Home

Increasingly in the 1930s, American homemakers did their food shopping outside the home. Home delivery was a casualty of the depression as owners could ill afford to pay extra hands. As women did their own shopping they found it convenient to stop at a single new institution, the supermarket. This place integrated a grocery, butcher shop, bakery, and other former specialty stores under one roof. The speed at which supermarkets proliferated was truly amazing. In 1936, there existed only 600 American supermarkets; the largest chain had 20 outlets, compared to over 14,000 traditional groceries. By 1941, only 4,000 groceries remained. There were 8,000 supermarkets nationwide and A & P had 1,646 stores.

Frozen Foods

Frozen foods paralleled the supermarket's rise. Introduced in 1923 by Clarence Birdseye, who noted on a Labrador trip that fish caught at 50 degrees below zero tasted much better than cold-stored fish, his process quick-froze the product in dressed, ready-to-cook form. It transferred heat away from the product—from room temperature to freezing in 90 minutes—by direct contact between the thing to be frozen and a metal surface chilled to minus-40 degrees. Postum Company, which later became General Foods, purchased Birdseye's patents in 1929 and marketed quick-frozen vegetables and fruits in 1930. It concentrated on large population centers as it tried to create demand for the new product. As late as 1933, only 516 outlets sold frozen foods. General Foods contracted with supermarkets in the mid- and late 1930s to include frozen-food cases in stores and with farms to freeze their as yet unplanted harvest. By 1940, frozen foods were nearly a quarter-billion-dollar industry.

REVITALIZING RURAL AMERICA
Balancing Agriculture and Industry

Not all attempts to revitalize American life came from the government, or depended on extensive governmental involvement. Privately undertaken and financed efforts to change America both pre- and postdated New Deal programs, and originated in a number of sectors, including industry. Most of these would-be reformers concentrated on rural revitalization.

Rural regions demanded immediate attention, while the lack of a rigid rural bureaucracy compared to cities made social-engineering prospects more promising. As important, reformers recognized that rural and urban America were inextricably intertwined, and that a program aimed at one necessarily modified the other. New industrial technologies or processes always served as the agents of change, and manipulators generally established small pilot projects to show the utility of their vision. They presumed in each instance that their demonstration of the virtue of a new balance between agriculture and industry would inevitably attract a significant popular following and even government support.

Ford's Village Industries Using his great wealth, Henry Ford concocted about 1920 perhaps the most novel rural revitalization scheme. He planned to improve rural America through industrialization, but sought to keep that industrialization in balance with agriculture. During the next quarter-century, he opened nineteen small plants at picturesque rural settings to manufacture Ford components. One rustic factory employed only nineteen persons. Located in tiny river communities within sixty miles of Dearborn, Michigan, these village industries were each initially outfitted to match the area's hydroelectric capacity. Rather than build new facilities, Ford converted existing

*Henry Ford's nineteen village industries produced
small parts for Ford vehicles and enabled farmers
and other rural Americans to supplement their
incomes while maintaining their traditional
occupations, residences, and values.*

structures into small factories whenever practical (gristmills proved
particularly attractive), stocking them with the latest tools and machines. Conveyor belts and assembly lines reigned supreme within
these small industrial sites. Raw materials were trucked to these plants
each morning. Every evening finished products were collected and
shipped to Ford's huge Highland Park and River Rouge complexes.

These rural communities were explicitly not company towns. The
plants were the only Ford presence. Ford always selected his labor
force from within the community and often tried to reflect the local
population demographics; he even reserved comparable percentages
for the elderly, handicapped, and other disadvantaged persons. His
notorious Sociological Department had no village industry jurisdiction. Ford's sole stipulation was that employees of his rural facilities
also farm. They were asked to purchase plots of land and to grow
crops during their spare time. That generally meant before and after
work and on weekends, but Ford initially permitted his rural laborers

to absent themselves from factories for months for harvesting and other sundry agricultural chores. Those employees unable to acquire farmland were strongly encouraged to take up gardening.

As with almost everything done by Ford, his village industries attracted attention. Roosevelt's Farm Security Administration even attempted to establish a variant of the program. It established the village of Jersey Homesteads in 1933 in the midst of 1,200 acres of woodlands, hired unemployed New York City garment workers to run a garment factory there nine months a year, and had them work on a government-owned farm during three spring and fall months. Jersey Homesteads quickly failed, apparently because the garment workers strenuously objected to farming. So, too, did Ford's village industries prove an economic catastrophe; estimates suggest that only Ford's millions sustained the project. When Ford died in 1947, the company swiftly sold off most village-industry plants.

The Chemurgy Movement Ford also was involved with the chemurgic movement, which probably came closest to securing the place its founders thought it deserved. William J. Hale (chairman of the National Research Council's Division of Chemistry and Chemical Technology, and Dow Chemical founder Herbert Dow's son-in-law) coined the term *chemurgy* in 1934 from the Greek *chemi*, the art of transforming materials, and *ergon*, work. Its proponents sought to blur traditional distinctions between agriculture and industry and to establish instead an industrial–agricultural continuum; agriculture would become the predominant source of industrial chemicals.

Although the word chemurgy entered the American lexicon in 1934, and a national organization was formed the following year, its practitioners had begun chemurgic labors more than a decade earlier. They derived chemicals and made products from soybeans, barley, flax, wheat, rice, oats, bananas, beets, tobacco, pecans, peanuts, cotton, pineapples, artichokes, peat, sorghum, and even chicken feathers. But corn was their favorite raw material. Chemurgists destructively distilled, pulverized, chemically digested, and fermented corn cobs to produce furfural; charcoal; acetic, formic, butyric, and oxalic acids; methanol; calcium acetate; xylose; pentosans; and ethanol. They treated cornstalks with pressurized steam, pulverized them, or had them chemically digested to yield lignin, glue, nitrocellulose, rayon, paper, and boards of varying densities, from a cork substitute to a replacement for steel in automobile bodies or Pullman cars. From cornstalk processing, chemurgists recovered liquid natural gas, flotation oils, polyhydroxyl alcohols, and adhesives.

As Hale articulated it, agriculture would provide industrial stability. Defining "an agriculturist simply as an organic chemical manufacturer . . . nothing else," he incorporated agriculture as an integral part of his new industrial order; agriculture would become the cheap, dependable source of chemicals necessary for the American industrial machine. These precepts led Hale to propose a revolutionary new agricultural system. Corporate-owned "agricultural supply centers," not privately owned farms, constituted its essence. Hale envisioned each "agricenter" as encompassing several thousand square miles and each operating under "a real industrial leader." Working in conjunction with lawyers, bankers, scientists, and other industrialists, each agricenter's leader would negotiate contracts with chemical manufacturers to set next year's production goals.

Hale's agricenters would be scientifically managed, and efficiency experts would review and modify farm practices. Superintendents would implement policy and ensure that laborers, who would be paid hourly wages, followed it. Agricenter corporations would supply seeds, fertilizers, machines, and other necessary items as agricenter scientists and engineers worked to improve agricultural machinery and yields. Processing plants would be established nearby to transform agricultural products into industrial chemicals.

Hale's vision resulted in formation of the National Farm Chemurgic Council. The organization got its start in 1935 when Hale and Carl B. Fritsche, a Detroit industrial engineer, prevailed on Henry Ford to sponsor a "Conference of Agriculture, Industry, and Science" to discuss chemurgy's prospects. Held in Ford's company headquarters at Dearborn, Michigan, the meeting attracted 300 participants. Most represented large industrial concerns, or were academics with close industrial ties. Physicist Robert Millikan of California Institute of Technology and Karl T. Compton, president of Massachusetts Institute of Technology, were the organization's most noted academic partisans.

Ford provided the council invaluable national publicity and legitimacy. He also was no stranger to chemurgy. Ford's automobiles had employed soybean-derived plastics for upholstery, body finishes, horn buttons, and distributor covers. The Ford Motor Company had also made extensive use of products based on corn, cotton, flax, sugar cane, and wood in automotive manufacture. Ford's chemurgic interests had resulted in the "Industrialized American Barn" display at the 1933–1934 Chicago World's Fair. This exhibit described how entrepreneurs could utilize empty or deteriorating barns to process crops for industrial uses. Sitting in the midst of a soybean patch, Ford's barn was filled, not with hay, but with various soybean-processing tools and machines.

Neither the council nor chemurgy generally gained the massive public support that its proponents had anticipated. Farmers certainly disliked Hale's vision and were concerned about more immediate forms of relief. Most processes to transform crops into industrial raw materials proved more costly than alternate means. Political factors also complicated the issue; the movement's predominantly corporate, Republican leadership continually criticized New Deal programs, especially those taking land out of production or catering to small farmers. "In the midst of the chemical revolution we are chemically disorganized; in the depths of depression we are chemurgically incapacitated," complained Hale. Unable to effect the changes necessary to implement its new agricultural–industrial order, the council contented itself with reporting on chemurgic processes, objecting to government policies, and publicizing the chemurgic idea.

Failure of explicit social-engineering attempts, such as chemurgy or the TVA, to produce new settlement types, or to redress the balance between industry and agriculture, or between the urban and the rural, in a fashion consistent with their proponents' objectives did not discredit those objectives or planning. Paradoxically, lack of success reaffirmed to both social engineers and the American public generally the need to design comprehensively planned, integrated environments "fit for life and the living." Failure was attributed to the same phenomenon that made planning so desirable—modern life's complexity. Modern life was such a complicated system of interrelationships that social engineers had failed to grasp all the various relevant factors, or to understand completely how the system's different elements influenced and changed each other. That stance, coupled with the assumption that those difficulties could be ironed out soon, made planning even more compelling, and intensified efforts.

CHANGES IN PRODUCTION TECHNIQUES

The social engineers' inability to foster the precise modifications that they sought did not mean that traditional American modes of production persisted unchanged. The post-1920 notion of system permeated virtually every facet of American life. As Americans considered and pursued their endeavors, they incorporated the idea of system as an interlocking network of mutually interacting parts, although not necessarily such an idea's potential social and cultural ramifications. In some cases, that incorporation simply resulted in a reconceptualization of established practice without physical change, while in others processes or activities were altered. It was from this intellectual context that mid-century technologies—and economic and business principles—were conceived and applied. Redefinition of salient points led to identification of new relationships, which created new understandings, desires, and needs. These in turn translated into investigation into new areas, development of new human productions, and formulation of new marketing strategies. In essence, virtually no enterprise remained unchanged.

Changes in Agriculture after 1920

Food production and each of its constituent activities were scrutinized and redesigned by agriculturists and others in the post-1920 period. The upshot was creation of a more highly integrated agriculture, and a much tighter agricultural–industrial connection.

The Multipurpose Tractor No single aspect of farming was more indicative of this shift than the tractor boom of the mid-1920s and after. Tractor demand had temporarily risen during World War I as farmers employed them in the Midwest and West to combat labor shortages. But post-Armistice sales dropped to prewar levels. The explanation was simple: tractor utility was physically circumscribed by intellectual constraints. It was in conception a single-purpose machine developed to capitalize on the unique Great Plains agriculture. Tractors could draw implements but not power them (tractors towed, for example, gasoline-engine-powered combines as well as plows), or could power mechanisms, such as threshers, while stationary. But tractors could not pull and power machinery simultaneously.

Only with a new understanding of the interrelatedness of farm endeavors did manufacturers seek to redesign tractors. Development of "power takeoffs" in the 1920s transformed and popularized the tractor. Essentially splined drive-shafts extending from tractor rears that could be mated to correspondingly shaped implement fittings to deliver power at any time, power takeoffs created what advocates termed "general purpose tractors." Possibilities seemed endless, and sales skyrocketed after 1923 when manufacturers perfected power-takeoff tractors suitable for row-crop cultivation. The industry quickly recognized the chaos generated by each manufacturer's policy of producing power takeoffs and compatible implements to its own specifications, and agreed in 1927 to standardize industry-wide shaft fittings and size, as well as the speed and direction of shaft rotation.

Adoption of general-purpose tractors (and later combines) with power takeoffs was so swift that by about 1950 horses had virtually disappeared from American farms. Farmers weighed the decision to replace horses with machines in favor of tractors and combines, but for these most significant investments, agriculturists needed to balance a variety of factors, some of which were intangible. A manufacturer's reputation, expertise, or price was an insufficient post-1920 determinant. Indeed, the idea of cost itself had become multifaceted. Before choosing a machine, noted a commentator in 1931, farmers must at least take into account "adaptability to local conditions; initial cost; maintenance costs; power costs; design and construction; suitability of construction materials; reliability and size of manufacturer; dealer's service record; ease of operation; ease of adjustment; ease of repair;

appearance of machine; whether it needs protection from the weather; ease of sharpening; availability of replacement parts."

Inventing Crops to Fit the Machines Circumstances surrounding combination corn-pickers/huskers, also products of the 1920s, reveal another aspect of agricultural change. These early devices sold poorly because they performed miserably. They shelled too thoroughly, husked inadequately, had difficulty with stalks of different heights, and failed to strip broken or blown-over stalks. Not until the late 1940s did these machines gain popularity. Their acceptance then did not stem from improved machine design, but from "design" of a machine-compatible corn, bred to meet the machine's needs as well as the limitations of the environment in which it was grown.

This multipurpose hybrid corn could be tailored to fit almost any environmental situation or set of physical parameters. It usually was bred for stronger stalks and roots, easy husking, disease resistance, yield, climatic adaptability, and uniform stands and ear size. Henry A. Wallace was a pioneer hybrid-corn industrialist, but credit for hybrid corn belongs to the Connecticut Agricultural Experiment Station's Donald F. Jones. Between 1918 and 1920, Jones announced a mechanism to make hybrid corn practical.

Americans had bred corn from the 1870s, but had focused on one variable, yield per acre. By the 1890s, corn breeders equated the corn's appearance with vigor and high yield, and chose seed kernels from ears deemed most nearly perfect. This method, like the others before it, rarely produced uniform high-yielding crops. Individual stalks and ears differed dramatically even for seeds planted from the same ear. George Shull, operating at the Carnegie Institution's facility at Cold Spring Harbor, New York, explained in 1908 the diversity. He determined by inbreeding (self-fertilizing) corn plants that common corn varieties were in fact combinations of large numbers of strains; each kernel on an ear might be from a different strain. Only through "selfing" (self-fertilization) for several generations would "pure" corn breeds reveal themselves. And these breeds, most of which were very small, would breed true; their progeny would bear a remarkable resemblance to each other and their parents. Shull also several times crossbred two dissimilar purebred corn plants, sometimes with extraordinary results: favorable crosses would produce plants larger and more prolific than their parents, but these plants would not remain vigorous in succeeding generations.

Shull's experiments proved puzzling, but Jones deciphered them a decade later. To Jones, inbred corn's dwarfishness and lack of vigor stemmed from the transfer of corn's hereditary factors in generally indivisible groups. That precluded the possibility of getting the most favorable characteristics in single plants; traits were inextricably linked, and breeding for a desirable trait most likely would also expose undesirable ones.

Yet Jones recognized inbreeding's utility. It revealed the root stock, the good and bad traits, which were linked. He devised the double cross, "which brings together the greatest number of different factors," as a method to rid plants of inferior characteristics because "favorable growth characters tend to be expressed rather than unfavorable ones, whenever the two are paired"; inferior traits would be suppressed by favorable ones. Jones's double cross used four purebred lines and two generations. If these different lines were each selected with a specific purpose in mind, high-yield hybrids could be created that were adaptable to an extraordinary variety of climatic conditions, were resistant to many common diseases and pests, and produced similar stands and ears.

Double crossing took time, skill, and capital. Hybrid seeds were good for only one generation because hybridization's pluralistic vigor quickly disappeared. These factors dissuaded farmers from producing their own hybrids. The first significant hybrid seed company, Wallace's Hi-Bred Corn Company, was created in the mid-1920s to sell farmers hybrid corn seed. The new seed-corn industry encountered initial resistance from farmers, who balked at paying premium prices for seed when they could grow their own. But shrewd marketing techniques, such as entering corn-yield tests or planting a patch of hybrid corn on farmers' land at company expense, established the superiority of hybrids and converted many farmers before World War II. Hybrid seeds accounted for more than 95 percent of American corn acreage by the mid-1950s. Average yields per acre had quadrupled since the 1920s. And farmers could harvest their crops with mechanical pickers/huskers.

Even before farmers accepted hybrid corn, seed companies, the USDA, experiment stations, and the Rockefeller Foundation were applying hybridization techniques to other crops. They developed hybrid sorghums, rices, and wheats, successes that led an enthusiast to proclaim in 1947 that "the principles and practices first discovered and developed by the hybrid-corn makers are destined . . . to banish hunger and want."

The Genetic Manipulation of Animals A similar reconceptualization of meat- and milk-producing animals, and how they could be adapted to enhance farm profitability, also occurred in the 1920s. As with corn, farmers had long artificially selected and bred animals. Until the 1920s, form and size (the yield per animal) predominated as farmers aspired to breed purebred animals conforming to idealized standards set up for these established breeds at farm shows.

Farmers recognized in the 1920s that strict adherence to purebred criteria did not necessarily make economic sense. A number of tastes and needs characterized pluralistic America, and meeting each of these demands would increase profits. Farmers also realized that purebreds might not be the best-suited animals for particular environs. Some were more susceptible, for instance, to heat, drought, and pests. These considerations led farmers to embrace crossbreeding, and they looked to Europe for new purebreds. Danish hogs and British sheep, for example, were imported and crossbred with American varieties as farmers attempted to expand their markets and to develop "better" animals.

Agricultural scientists, led by Iowa State College's Jay Lush, opened new possibilities. They redefined breeds as those animals most closely approximating statistical norms; breeds became aggregations of hereditary characteristics coalescing around specific points. This population-genetics approach produced new flexibility (animals could be bred around new, more suitable points), and scientists and farmers began to explore the creation of new "breeds." These efforts produced Santa Gertrudis, Beefmaster, Brangus, and McCan "purebred" cattle. A Swine Breeding Laboratory opened at Ames, Iowa, in 1936 to carry on this sort of work, while breeding research intensified at the USDA's Beltsville, Maryland, experiment station.

The introduction of artificial insemination techniques facilitated breeding, and became the technology that enabled these new breeds to become commercially viable. First employed systematically among New Jersey farmers, the technique spread quickly across America; where a bull normally could service thirty to fifty cows yearly, with artificial insemination he could service more than 2,000. From 7,539 cows artificially inseminated in 1939, the number grew to 1,184,000 in 1947, and to 7,500,000 in 1962.

Changes in Industrial Manufacturing after 1920

American industrialists reconceptualized industry, industrial processes and organization, and marketing strategies. Rarely were these new developments trumpeted by individuals directly responsible. The self-aggrandizement of Singer, McCormick, or Ford seemed out of place in this new highly integrated industrial system.

As important, many industrialists failed to grasp the radical nature of the changes they made. But industrial success after 1920 did not require manufacturers consciously to evaluate the differences in perception between themselves and their industrial forebears. It did necessitate, however, that they understand the milieu in which they operated and develop approaches in accordance with that understanding.

The Rise of General Motors The dramatic rise of General Motors (GM) in the mid-1920s and the contrasting decline of the Ford Motor

Company during the same period provides a compelling example of the new industrial system. Ford had conceived of his Model T as the car for the masses. Its single style enabled him to mass-produce cars, and to organize single special-purpose machines and machine tools to facilitate flow and generate economies of scale in his plants. Ford's rigidity stemmed from both his assumption that there existed a correct "American" approach to things and his quest to perfect automobile manufacturing; he conceived of his corporation's role as the producer of "American" cars. But Ford's insistence on a single standardized automobile had become the butt of jokes in post-1920 America.

GM's Alfred P. Sloan, Jr., capitalized on this discontent to effect a revolution in automobile manufacture and sales in the 1920s and after. Arguing that a corporation's primary responsibility was to provide a high return to investors, Sloan rigorously maintained that corporations needed to determine and tap the market's demand rather than merely produce supplies, and that demand itself was plastic: it could be created, modified, or stimulated. What corporations required were concepts, strategies, and implementation. To Sloan, added volume alone spawned profits, and added volume came from carefully planned products superbly marketed. Product superiority and improved manufacturing techniques figured in corporate profits only incidentally, but they, too, could be stimulated. Corporate well-being was simply the consequence of effective management.

Although Sloan downplayed technological superiority as a crucial factor in corporate success, his GM stewardship was marked by a number of technical innovations: high-compression engines fueled by tetraethyl lead to prevent knock in the early 1920s, independent front-wheel suspensions to promote handling in the early 1930s, and automatic transmissions in the late 1930s. But Sloan's "better ideas" were tactical. He reorganized GM according to his precepts and introduced several programs consonant with his notion of demand's relative nature. He conceived of post-1920 automobile purchasers as primarily second-time buyers and contended that as a group their objectives differed from first-time owners. The latter desired transportation, while the former sought "comfort, convenience, power and style."

Sloan helped these second-time buyers achieve their dreams. The General Motors Acceptance Corporation, established about 1920, provided loans at low interest to purchase higher-priced GM cars. Sloan also fostered used-car markets, making it attractive for motorists to sell cars to purchase higher-ticket items. And Sloan was careful to see that GM offered a car "for every purse and purpose." He argued that each "General Motors car should be integral, that each car in the line should properly be conceived in its relationship to the line as a whole." This continuous line of products would tap everyone, from the poorest American able to afford a car to the wealthiest, with no duplication.

Each of the five GM vehicles would be sold in a different price range and highlight different features. This policy was in place by 1922. Chevrolet became GM's lowest-priced car and Cadillac its highest. The other three brands—Oakland, Oldsmobile, and Buick—aimed at various segments of the burgeoning middle class.

Sloan's pricing and product-line strategy was reflected in his reorganization of GM. He rid the company of unnecessary duplication of effort, but recognized that different markets required different approaches. Each of its five automotive divisions needed its own staff (executive, engineering, styling, production, marketing, sales, and the like), but overall GM must have "a system of co-ordination so that each part may strengthen and support each other part." Sloan's reorganization, planned in 1920 and implemented in 1924, gave divisions most of the autonomy associated with independent companies, established interdivisional groups to harmonize activities and smooth out difficulties, and provided the corporation's chief executive with ultimate authority.

Nowhere was the dual "federal" nature of GM's organization structure more apparent than in the implementation of Sloan's greatest car-selling coup, the annual model change. The culmination of the ideas that resulted in continuous-line pricing, credit purchasing, and used-car markets, the annual-model-change concept emerged about 1925. Sloan decreed that there should be a single basic GM style each year, but left it to each division's stylists to modify that form to suit constituencies. Sophisticated planning went into predicting and stimulating consumer tastes; development of an annual model started two years prior to that model year. Divisions also kept close tabs on how each year's models sold. Unlike Ford's static Model T, GM's annual models could not be marketed as new the following year. To prevent unprofitable model-year surpluses, GM's divisions required dealers to complete detailed sales questionnaires every ten days. Divisional inventories, purchases, and production rates were adjusted to approach each reporting period's estimation of demand. That flexibility permitted divisions to keep on hand smaller inventories of manufacturing materials. GM turned over inventories roughly twice yearly before adopting the annual model change; after 1925, the company turned them over an average of twelve times.

Annual models made change the normal state of affairs. This had profound manufacturing implications. Refitting facilities yearly with new special, single-purpose machines would be prohibitively expensive; wholesale adoption of Ford's mass-production techniques was incompatible with annual models. GM overcame that dilemma by introducing flexible mass production. It employed in its plants movable, general-purpose machines. Each had adjustable speeds and was powered by an individual electric motor. Workers resituated and set these machines at each model year's onset to form new lines facilitating product flow and mass production. GM also expedited model-year conversions by eschewing large central facilities for smaller, more specialized, and quickly modified plants.

GM adopted one final manufacturing feature. It strengthened fixtures to increase precision. More precise measurements enabled GM to extend interchangeability outside divisional boundaries. GM reconciled mass production with product variety by using some car parts in more than one division. Pontiac, established as a division in 1926, was perhaps the first beneficiary of this technique. The more expensive Pontiac used many of the parts used in the high-volume Chevrolet. Higher-priced vehicles benefited from volume economies generated by lower-priced cars, and mass-production benefits spread throughout the entire GM product line.

GM's initiatives captured for the company the largest share of the American automobile market. Ford abandoned his beloved Model T in 1927 and replaced it with the sportier but almost as static Model A. Ford's conversion to Model A production required him to shut down operations for six full months. In contrast, Chevrolet could gear up for a new model in a mere three weeks. But the Model A did not seize the post-1920 public imagination. By 1933, Ford had stopped selling the Model A, adopted the annual model change, switched to flexible mass production, and embraced the concept of a product line aimed at a wide spectrum of buyers.

The Development of Plastics Newer, less well-developed industrial sectors also were changed, but often more subtly than the automobile industry. In the case of plastics, for instance, the crucial conceptual shift revolved around product definition. Pre-1920 plastic manufacturers presumed that plastics ought to be single-purpose substances that would replace a particular material in a certain set of related uses. This was true for celluloid and for Bakelite, the first useful noncellulose plastic. Compounded by Leo Baekeland, who had produced high-quality photographic paper for Eastman, Bakelite's ivorylike hardness made it suitable for billiard balls.

Announcement of Bakelite was greeted enthusiastically and added fuel to the search for special-purpose plastics. Researchers attempted to create a plastic for every specific function, or to find a precise function for every plastic substance created. Design from the 1920s onward demanded flow and movement; molded plastic seemed the perfect material for consumer goods. Casein, furfural, acetate, and pentosan plastics emerged from those efforts. So, too, did rayon, which resulted from the textile industry's effort to produce artificial silk. Composed of acidified cellulose—generally wood pulp—treated with caustic soda and carbon disulfide, rayon was drawn and spun

Bakelite, the first useful non-cellulose-based
plastic, was manufactured in ovens like this
one from 1909. Bakelite and other plastics
gave way to general-purpose plastics, such as
nylon, in the 1930s and after.

into threads, and then woven. Eight million pounds of rayon were produced in America during 1919, and the output increased more than sixteenfold a decade later. In 1939, America produced more than 328 million pounds of rayon.

The chemical industry's significant interest in and experience with plastics led to studies of polymers and polymerization, which culminated in the development of polymerized fibers. Nylon, developed by the Du Pont Company, and the most important of these new plastics, was the first material marketed as a new, completely synthetic substance, designed not to replace one compound for one activity but many compounds for many activities; nylon was a general-purpose plastic. Its introduction followed from a carefully orchestrated Du Pont campaign. The company hired in 1928 Wallace Carothers, then instructor in organic chemistry at Harvard University, to head its well-funded organic-chemistry research group. Aware that certain polyesters and polyamides could be changed by cold stretching from random molecular arrangements into long, linear ones (like those found in natural silk and stretch-spun rayons), Carothers decided to study the synthesis of these high-molecular-weight polymers in hope of developing a multipurpose plastic. By 1934, Carothers' group had produced nearly one hundred "superpolymers." The one labeled "66" seemed to hold the most commercial promise. Du Pont technicians investigated this polymer (hexamethylene diamine-adipic acid) for forty-four months and worked out its economical manufacture. The company announced its creation as Nylon in 1939. Nylon proved stronger than silk and much more adaptable. It replaced that natural fiber in women's stockings. As a consequence of the company's aggressive wide-ranging marketing, nylon had by 1941 replaced natural bristles in scores of household and industrial products: catgut in sports racquets, surgery, and musical instruments; gutta percha in wire insulation; some natural cements; steel machinery bearings; metal as a machine housing substance; and leather. Umbrellas, shower curtains, and parachutes were among nylon's other early uses.

NEW MARKETING AND DELIVERY TECHNOLOGIES
Using Radio to Reach a National Market

Advertising played a prominent part in Du Pont's nylon marketing efforts, and the company took advantage of several intricate nationwide webs of radio stations to promote its product. This strategy did not, however, mark the chemical company as unique. Radio had been a prime advertising medium for manufactured consumer products for more than fifteen years.

Before the mid-1920s, entrepreneurs conducted large-scale advertising only through the mail or in local newspapers. The earliest radio stations (which were owned by manufacturers) did not even accept advertising, but offered instead only public-service programming, which served radio manufacturers by establishing markets for radio receivers. Reduced prices for receivers had led to mass purchase of radios, which indirectly proved the medium's advertising potential. As early as 1922, WEAF in New York City (owned by Bell Telephone) allowed manufacturers to purchase air time to advertise products; advertising quickly became the principal revenue source of radio stations. This thrust occurred despite opposition from then Commerce Secretary Hoover, who, as head of the federal agency regulating radio, claimed that advertising undermined radio's public-service capabilities.

The new multipurpose radio received a boost in 1926 when Bell rented to stations long-distance wire connections. In that year, David

Sarnoff, head of RCA, created the National Broadcasting Company (NBC) as an RCA subsidiary. A year later there were three major national networks: both the Blue and Red networks of NBC, and the rival Columbia Broadcasting System (CBS). Advertising could then be national as well as local, and more than $10 million was spent on it by 1928. No federal regulation existed of either the content or the frequency of ads, which increasingly accompanied programs ranging from entertainment to sports to news.

Congress made halfhearted efforts to oversee radio's development by enacting the 1927 Radio Act, which established the Federal Radio Commission, and the 1934 Communications Act, which replaced that agency with the Federal Communications Commission. Both bodies presumed public ownership of radio's frequencies, which were allocated to private groups for short-term licenses renewable for proper operation and public service. In practice, few licenses were ever revoked, and most were therefore *de facto* long-term ones. In effect, regulation was primarily concerned with assigning frequencies, setting power-output limits, and controlling geographical access to radio facilities.

By 1941, on the eve of World War II, there were 660 American radio stations, 160 affiliated with NBC and 107 with CBS. Together these network stations comprised 86 percent of the licensed, and lucrative, nighttime broadcasting, and were invariably in key markets. In that year the federal government, under Supreme Court directive, forced RCA to dispose of one of its two networks, the Blue, which soon became the American Broadcasting Company (ABC) and a new competitor for advertising dollars. But networks and independent stations, while remaining relatively free of government regulation, were never without public scrutiny. Their advertising rates were directly proportional to the numbers of listeners they attracted, and those numbers were a function of their entertainment and public-service broadcasts. Networks and independent stations faced something of a dilemma; their profitability depended on determining before the fact what type of programming would draw the largest audience. In that sense at least, expected demand dictated actual supply. Mid-century radio programmers found it safer to copy a competitor's success (a practice that produced particular genres simultaneously on virtually all radio stations) than to initiate a new potentially risky form of programming.

The Railroads after 1920

In the 1920s railroads retained their traditional position as the nation's preeminent long-haul freight carriers, but they already faced increasing competition from newer modes of transportation and would ultimately be supplanted. The railroad decline, however, was not a result of refusing to adopt new technologies. In fact, they quickly embraced them. Yet railroads were complicit in their own demise. The technologies railroads incorporated were inconsistent with mid-twentieth-century desires, and so laid the seeds of their destruction; railroads made themselves anachronistic and eventually almost obsolete.

Railroads after about 1920 concentrated on becoming bigger, faster, and more efficient. Rails were repeatedly strengthened to absorb heavier loads, signals and traffic-control systems were made almost automatic, and air brakes were vastly improved to function under even the greatest burdens. Steam locomotives attained a weight of more than 600 tons and could travel at 70 mph. They began to be replaced in the 1940s by faster, lighter diesel locomotives, which were more powerful and capable of transporting larger loads. Where many different companies produced steam locomotives, only a handful manufactured diesels, thereby allowing greater standardization of models and fewer total locomotives.

These technical factors enhanced railroad operation on high-volume, long-distance, point-to-point runs, but they severely hampered other forms of delivery. Mid-century railroads lacked the flexibility demanded by an America consciously attempting to decentralize manufacturing facilities and markets; they were in effect single-purpose carriers. Aside from the question of exceedingly high capital costs, huge locomotives maximized economies only when pulling a very large number of cars or very heavy cargo over considerable distance. That they were unable to offer a competitive price and to achieve a return justifying their great expense under other circumstances left a substantial void to be filled by other types of carriers.

New Delivery Technologies—Trucks and Buses

Trucks and buses capitalized on this opportunity, and also conveyed goods to areas inaccessible to railroads. Crude trucks and buses were built as early as 1900. But World War I demonstrated their utility both at home and abroad. Pneumatic tires, developed by the Goodyear Tire and Rubber Company in 1916, prevented these heavy vehicles from destroying roadways, cargo, and themselves through constant pounding. But pneumatic tires were not the only technological innovation that helped trucks and buses corner an increasingly impressive share of haulage. In 1927, the Fageol brothers of Kent, Ohio, introduced the twin-coach bus; its engines were placed underneath the passenger compartment to make the vehicle's whole body suitable for heavier loads, as opposed to earlier bus bodies that were simply placed on truck chassis. In the 1930s Charles Kettering and others at GM improved existing diesel engines to make them more reliable and powerful for buses and trucks alike.

*Buses offered a flexibility unavailable from railroads.
Numerous small lines capitalized on this advantage
by merging to form the Greyhound system.*

Larger trucks later separated their power unit from the cargo units, which became detachable semi-trailers.

Several railroad companies belatedly recognized trucking's potential, as well as their failure to form a flexible railroad network, and ironically established their own trucking subsidiaries to combat independent trucking firms. Numerous small bus companies sprinkled throughout the nation offered railroads a more direct challenge. They consolidated themselves into the Greyhound system, which from 1929 became America's largest bus line, delivering products and passengers nationwide. The foothold gained by these early trucking and busing haulers testified to railroad shortsightedness. These smaller, flexible carriers captured a profitable share of the freight and passenger trade in an era of poor roadways and no interstate highway system (which was not inaugurated until 1956).

The Growth of Commercial Aviation

A more vigilant railroad industry probably could not have prevented development of yet another carrier, commercial airlines. It specialized in longer-distance haulage than many truck and bus concerns, and offered competition to railroads in that sector. Like railroads, the speedier airlines had huge capital costs.

Commercial aviation's roots go back to early airmail service that began in 1918 when the U.S. Post Office used army aircraft and young World War I veterans for the initial New York–Philadelphia–Washington route. Despite considerable loss of life, the Post Office had by 1924 established regular transcontinental mail flights. A year later, however, the federal government transferred mail service to commercial airlines, which were invariably eager for the contracts, given their generally precarious financial conditions.

Those airmail routes eventually became parts of the first major airlines, including American, Delta, and United. These airline "families" emerged in the 1920s and 1930s. In that latter decade, flimsy cloth-covered biplanes gave way to all-metal craft, beginning with the Ford Trimotor. The Douglas Commercial, or DC-3, inaugurated in 1935, promptly became the principal civilian airliner (the American military also used it in World War II). Thousands were eventually built, and hundreds still operated as late as the 1970s. Its principal competitor, the Boeing 247, came from the company founded by Seattle lumberman Bill Boeing who, having secured an early airmail contract for Chicago–San Francisco service, then began building planes to fulfill it.

Two events in the 1920s helped solidify the aviation industry's legitimacy. Charles Lindbergh's solo transatlantic flight in 1927 drew attention to the airplane's potential. The establishment of the Daniel Guggenheim Fund for the Promotion of Aeronautics in 1926 fostered aviation achievement. The fund enabled eight universities to form aeronautical engineering programs to train students and undertake research. Offshoots of Guggenheim-sponsored research included instrument-only flight, short-takeoff-and-landing aircraft, and weather reporting services.

In the next decade other technological advances followed. Planes powered by air-cooled, internal-combustion engines operated at unheard-of speeds. Consequent emphasis on increased altitude, size, and sturdiness engendered other mechanical modifications: stronger airframes; cockpit controls and instrument panels; electric, hydraulic, and de-icing systems; power plants; and pressurized cabins. Commercial implications were readily evident, and not just in America: in 1929, for example, 105 million passenger-miles were flown worldwide, while in 1939 airplanes logged more than 1,250 million passenger-miles. As air traffic increased, so did support facilities; navigation and communications equipment; and airport controllers, ground crews, and other technical personnel.

As competition for mail, freight, and passenger contracts intensified, and as charges of favoritism and even fraud surfaced, the federal government became more intimately involved. The 1930 Air Mail Act had tried but failed to establish large airline systems instead of small piecemeal carriers. Four years later, President Roosevelt ordered the army to resume airmail service. By now ill-equipped for the task, its Air Service quickly lost pilots and planes, temporarily increasing postal rates. The 1934 Air Mail Act simultaneously restored airmail service to private operators while separating commercial airlines from their manufacturers, thereby dissolving several aviation conglomerates. The 1938 Civil Aeronautics Act established a Civil Aeronautics Board (CAB), which in turn set up regular passenger and freight routes and continued subsidized mail service, thus virtually guaranteeing the industry profitable enterprises. Meanwhile the New Deal's Works Progress Administration provided funds for building and enlarging terminals and runways.

To be sure, extensive mail subsidies kept the industry aloft, and government regulation and assistance were crucial. But even these factors were insufficient to sustain commercial airlines in their competition with railroads. What fortified early commercial aviation and what entitled it to this unusual level of governmental support was its new modern character. A "winged gospel" permeated America as the new technology's exciting, liberating potential captured public imagination. Airplanes would eliminate urban congestion, poverty, industrial competition, and even war. Aviation was to be a panacea; it would resolve most social questions. In that sense, aviation, with electricity and automobiles, would pave the way for a new America "fit for life and the living."

FOR FURTHER READING

(See the end of Chapter 8)

Technology as a Social Solution: World War II and the Aftermath

THE DESKTOP COMPUTER?

In the later 1930s, a physicist at Iowa State College, John V. Atanasoff, and his graduate student, Clifford Berry, began to build a revolutionary machine. Atanasoff taught mathematics at Iowa State and found himself frustrated at the time it took to solve large, integrated systems of linear algebraic equations. After considering his options, he decided that electronic machine power constituted "the only practical means" of solving them, and he set about to make a machine that fulfilled his modest objectives. Over the several years it took to complete this project, Atanasoff was able to cobble together about $7,500 to support his efforts. The prototype he developed was about the size of a small desk and used vacuum tubes, not electromagnetic relays, and was digital (binary), not decimal. Capacitors mounted on two rotating drums constituted its memory unit. Positive charges at the condensers' ends corresponded to zero and negative charges to one. Each drum stored thirty binary numbers, each fifty characters long. Atanasoff added to this relatively small memory capacity by storing additional material in binary form on cards. Machine-generated electric sparks marked the cards, which were formatted like the drums. His machine read the cards by applying a voltage to them; the carbonized spots left by sparks would be interpreted as ones, and the uncarbonized spots as zeros.

Atanasoff found that in about one case in 100,000 the sparker failed to leave a carbonized spot. And because some of his equations required millions of sparks, the occasional omission constituted a significant problem. In late 1940, before he could remedy this difficulty, the federal government asked Atanasoff to undertake classified military research. A later call to Washington, D.C., for more extensive war-related research forced him to put aside his machine.

Atanasoff had not been shy talking about his machine or its potential applications. He saw it as a functional device, useful and well-integrated in a number of businesses and daily activities. A market existed, he believed, for thousands, if not millions, of these small manipulators.

About a year and a half before Atanasoff left for Washington, he met John Mauchly, then a Ursinus (Pennsylvania) College professor of physics, who was using old-fashioned analog calculators to analyze weather statistics. Atanasoff discussed his machine with Mauchly, maintained that when perfected his device could outdo the most powerful computing device then built, the Bush calculator, and invited him to see it. Mauchly traveled to Ames, Iowa, in June 1941, and moved from Ursinus to the University of Pennsylvania's Moore School of Electrical Engineering later that month. In September 1941, he wrote Atanasoff to ask if there was "any objection, from your point of view, to my building some sort of computer which incorporates some of the features of your machine." Mauchly also wanted to know whether, if he got the Moore School interested, the way was "open for us to build an 'Atanasoff Calculator' (a la Bush Analyzer) here?" Atanasoff requested that Mauchly not develop Atanasoff's ideas until a patent application was filed. Atanasoff never filed that application.

In August 1942, Mauchly wrote his superiors at the Moore School, who were then also engaged in World War II research—firing-table calculations— that "a great gain in speed of the calculation can be obtained if the devices which are used employ electronic means." He urged that they consider the merits of "the use of electronic circuits which are interconnected . . . for solution of difference equations." His formal proposal secured a Mauchly- and J. Presper Eckert-headed interdisciplinary research team to construct what became the ENIAC (Electronic Numerical Integrator and Computer).

The ENIAC's support from the University of Pennsylvania was but a pittance when compared to the amount of money government threw at the problem. By now a war raged. Any technological solution that could help end it merited support. Ironically, the ENIAC did not go into operation until 1946, well after the war ended. As large as one boxcar, weighing thirty tons, and costing many millions of dollars, its

*The ENIAC required operators to trip thousands of
switches to program the machine for even
rudimentary calculations.*

18,000 vacuum tubes worked 1,000 times as quickly as electromagnetic
relays. Its nearly one million parts required over 600 miles of wire. The
ENIAC was programmed by plugging cables from one of its parts to
another, much like telephone switchboards. IBM punch cards carried
data. Its initial project, a simulation for the then-untested hydrogen
bomb, used a million cards.

The Pennsylvania group then joined with Princeton mathemati-
cian John Von Neumann to build in 1950 the first stored-program
computer, the Electronic Discrete Variable Automatic Computer
(EDVAC). This second government-financed computer had a memory
much larger than ENIAC and did not require manual programming.
The Sperry-Rand Company's Universal Automatic Computer (UNI-
VAC) was private enterprise's initial computer. Designed by Eckert
and Mauchly, the UNIVAC was about the same size as the EDVAC
and had many of the same features.

The ENIAC has been generally hailed as the first electronic, digital,
integrated, multipurpose system that harmoniously combined work
done by several elements within a single device. In short, its proponents claimed it to be the first computer. But its technological difference
from Atanasoff's pioneering device was much less than met the eye.

How one stored numbers was a most significant variation. Atanasoff stored them on drums and on cards, although his spark residue detector remained imperfect. The ENIAC used over a thousand vacuum tubes, hundreds of miles of wire, and two twenty-horsepower cooling fans to store much less data, which it did dependably. What separated the two devices was vision, perhaps, but more importantly, money. Atanasoff was an inventor. He devised all sorts of mechanical contraptions in his garage, patented many, and sold quite a few. Practical and market concerns dominated his thinking. Mauchly and Eckert operated in a situation that until that time had been far from normal. They were fortunate to work in the shadow of World War II, a time of virtually limitless funding. Their resolution to Atanasoff's storage problem worked but was patently impractical and changed the face of what was to come. Their computer—and for several decades thereafter, all computers—were expensive, monstrous devices that broke easily. Only the military could afford these ponderous machines. Availability of huge sums of money increased some options but foreclosed others.

At War's Eve Prior to the eve of World War II, New Deal efforts circumscribed government involvement in technological enterprises. Already existing technology—automobiles, electricity and airplanes—was applied. Research and development came from large foundations, such as the Carnegie or Rockefeller Foundations, or from the corporate sector, often funneled through the nation's colleges and universities. For example, the electric infrastructure for the Berkeley Radiation Lab and for California Institute of Technology was built with equipment donated and manufactured by GE and Westinghouse. It was used to work out the parameters of high-voltage electric transmission from remote mountain stations to West Coast cities. Sperry Gyroscope had a contract to fund applied microwave research at Stanford. Although agricultural experiment stations had long mastered contract research, government as late as 1940 spent more on agricultural research than military research. That all changed with World War II.

TECHNOLOGY IN WORLD WAR II: SOLVING THE PROBLEM OF TOTALITARIANISM

World War II shattered the peace that had reigned since 1918 and placed dramatic new strains on the nation, but the country responded in a characteristically mid-century way. This way was "total war"—"everybody's war"—and the country's technological capabilities promised to win battles at home and abroad. Increased production and belt-tightening within the United States, coupled with new sophisticated weaponry, would enable America and its allies to defeat totalitarianism's forces. These heady sentiments about engineering a

*Total war was everybody's war as women assumed
factory jobs formerly reserved for men.*

social and technical, as well as military, victory translated into new institutions and policies, many backed by unlimited resources. Withholding or conserving assets was nonsensical; anything less than total
victory would be a complete catastrophe. Development of new
weapons figured prominently, and Roosevelt appointed a National
Defense Research Committee in 1940 to prepare for war. Composed of
representatives from private foundations, universities, government,
and industry, the committee established a contract system to encourage the nation's foremost scientists and engineers, regardless of geographic location, professional affiliation, or occupation, to undertake
weapons research. Its functions were subsumed the next year by the
Office of Scientific Research and Development (OSRD), which received the greater charge of overseeing and coordinating all wartime
research and development.

   In every case, the OSRD turned to interdisciplinary research
teams. Gathering specialists from many different disciplines and stak-
ing them to work on a related problem fit precisely with the model
used by first Hoover and then Roosevelt to solve the nation's social
ills. Its adaptation to military and defense matters came with limitless
funds and wartime powers. The OSRD tried two different approaches.
One resulted in the atomic bomb, the other in radar.

America's production capabilities helped to combat the totalitarian menace. This plant was converted to manufacturing airplanes.

Creation of the Atomic Bomb

The OSRD stimulated and funded production and development of numerous new armaments, but most significantly it sponsored research on what would become the atomic bomb. Several significant investigations predated the OSRD's formation, especially in Nazi Germany. Two radiochemists, Otto Hahn and Fritz Strassman, announced in 1938 that they had successfully bombarded uranium with neutrons to yield several lighter elements; the uranium's absorption of neutrons caused its nucleus to split, a process called fission, which released enormous amounts of energy (200 million electron volts versus the one or two per atom released by the most powerful conventional chemical reaction) with a corresponding decrease in matter. Their work reaffirmed contemporary atomic theory, which hypothesized that matter and energy were continuous, interchangeable states ($E = mc^2$); that all elements were composed of identical units (protons, neutrons, and electrons); and that elemental physical properties and characteristics were simply a consequence of the number of protons in the nucleus. These last two postulates held out prospects for transmuting elements and for creating new ones with particular properties—an important part of bomb research—but it was Hahn and Strassman's demonstration of conversion of matter into energy that initially excited scientists. Fission reactions could release other neutrons, and they contemplated self-sustaining reactions—chain reactions—whenever fissionable material achieved *critical mass* (the mass necessary for a statistical guarantee that sufficient free neutrons would strike other atoms). Neutrons could be slowed to yield controllable chain reactions or left unimpeded to produce violent explosions. But only one uranium isotope (U-235) was suited to fission because whenever a neutron entered its nucleus, it released one or more neutrons.

These considerations, and Nazi Germany's documented efforts to develop nuclear power, led Albert Einstein and other prominent scientists in 1939 to implore Roosevelt to establish a nuclear research program. Roosevelt's National Defense Research Committee, and later the OSRD, authorized contracts for uranium-isotope-separation research, a crucial first step, because although U-235 is the only fissionable uranium isotope, it comprises only 1/140th of the world's uranium supply. Successful chain reactions require its separation from other uranium isotopes—especially the prevalent U-238—and its concentration. Gaseous diffusion was among the funded separation methods; investigators diffused the highly corrosive gas uranium hexafluoride through a permeable membrane and, because lighter molecules pass more quickly, separate U-235 from U-238. Small molecular weight differences, coupled with gas-handling difficulties, rendered this separation technique problematical.

Two years later, OSRD-supported University of California physicists used a particle accelerator to bombard the relatively plentiful U-238 and transmute it into a new manmade fissionable element, plutonium-239. This nuclear material manufacturing process proved promising, a fact verified the following year when the OSRD notified Roosevelt that a nuclear bomb could be developed in twenty-four months. Further support for this assessment occurred in December 1942. Enrico Fermi, an OSRD-backed émigré from fascist Italy, achieved the first successful controlled release of nuclear energy. Located under the University of Chicago's football stadium, Fermi's nuclear pile employed graphite lattices and strips of cadmium and boron steel to slow and absorb neutrons.

Fermi's demonstration and the OSRD's strong recommendation helped convince Roosevelt of the bomb's immediacy. He authorized the Manhattan Project to keep bomb research secret, and charged it with building an atomic device within three years. General Leslie Groves headed the huge, secretive project, which in effect was a gigantic interdisciplinary research team composed of scientists from numerous disciplines and the Army Corps of Engineers. Project members left their normal projects and environs for secretly constructed plutonium-generating reactors at Hanford, Washington; a gaseous-diffusion facility at Oak Ridge, Tennessee; and a physics research laboratory at Los Alamos, New Mexico. Under its director, Berkeley physicist J. Robert Oppenheimer, Los Alamos scientists and engineers designed and built bombs from the materials produced at Hanford and Oak Ridge.

The Development of Radar

The Manhattan Project effectively removed the OSRD from atomic research, and it then devoted all its efforts to conventional weaponry. The nexus between the OSRD and universities became especially pronounced as several interdisciplinary research centers were established on selected campuses to focus on particular types of weapons development. Investigators from across the nation, for example, were brought to the MIT Radiation Laboratory for radar research. Harvard spearheaded antiradar measures, and Johns Hopkins University's Applied Physics Laboratory became America's proximity fuse center. In most cases, the OSRD supported research that had been underway prior to the war and followed up preliminary work done by the Army, the Navy, or foreign powers.

Such was the case with radar (*radio detection and ranging*), which was as much a British as American invention and predated World War II. In 1935, Robert Watson-Watt, radio department superintendent of Britain's National Physical Laboratory, successfully transmitted radio waves at a moving aircraft and received their reflection or echo, which he timed to determine the plane's location. By 1939, round-the-clock radar stations twenty-five miles apart blanketed Britain's coast. During the Battle of Britain, they enabled the Royal Air Force to meet incoming Nazi fighters; radar provided the number, range, direction, and altitude of enemy planes, day and night alike.

Prewar American developments were as extensive. The Naval Research Laboratory (NRL) produced the duplexer (a waveguide switch allowing single radar antennas to both transmit and receive) in 1936 and the XAF (a sea radar with a fifty-mile range), which it installed on two battleships in 1938. The Army Signal Corps contributed in 1937 the SCR-268, the first precision radar, which directed antiaircraft batteries. It also offered the SCR-270 model, and positioned it at Pearl Harbor, but the system was unfortunately deactivated as the Japanese attacked. The NRL also developed in 1941 the first airborne radar, the ASB, with homing, bombing, and search capabilities. Bendix, RCA, and Westinghouse shared the task of manufacturing more than 26,000 ASB units during the war, which were installed in night fighters and torpedo bombers.

Modern radar began in 1940 when the British developed the high-power, multicavity magnetron, which was the first vacuum tube capable of producing enough power to make radar feasible at wavelengths of less then fifty centimeters (microwaves). It alone produced a strong pulse at superhigh microwave frequencies, which performed better than existing radar using long or medium (one- to two-meter) wavelengths. Indeed, all of the 150 distinct radar systems developed in America in World War II—ground, ship, and air varieties—operated on microwaves. Microwave radar required smaller antennas, distinguished more clearly two targets close together, and found especially low-flying aircraft more accurately.

Researchers at MIT's Radiation Laboratory developed a more powerful version of the British magnetron, the SCR-584, used for the first automatic tracking and gunfire-control radar. They certainly were liberally funded. The federal government spent more on radar research than it would on the Manhattan Project. More than 3,800 people, including more than 1,000 scientists and social scientists, participated in the project, which fixed MIT as a major research institution. Other radar advances enabled pilots to drop payloads during poor visibility; to determine vessels' range and bearing; to obtain accurate fixes without emitting position-revealing signals; and to see territory ahead. Besides radar advances, radar countermeasures were actively developed and implemented. Frederick Terman, a Stanford electrical-engineering professor on loan to Harvard, headed the American effort. Mechanical reflectors, electronic jammers, and other means saved countless Allied soldiers and their equipment.

The Development of Sonar

The origins of sonar (*so*und *n*avigation *a*nd *r*anging) were also found before World War II, but unlike radar, sonar was a predominantly American invention. American researchers had before 1920 transmitted sound underwater at higher-than-audible frequencies and obtained ranges of distant objects by timing the echoes. Devices that detected submarine propeller sounds or received echoes from hulls were developed in the following decades, but they worked well only under laboratory conditions. Wave motions, varying water temperatures, false echoes, or search ships rolling and pitching disrupted them. Not until World War II were practical instruments developed. These included sound-range charts, underwater flares, underwater sound recorders, bathythermographs to measure water temperature variations, improved depth charges and torpedoes, and sono-radio buoys to transmit underwater sounds to nearby ships and planes. These sonar-based devices cut losses of ships and men and enabled the Allies to detect, track, and destroy German and Japanese submarines with unprecedented accuracy.

The Development of Proximity Fuses

Proximity fuses were an exception to the OSRD's practice of supporting preexisting weaponry. Ideally, fuses should detonate projectiles at points where maximum numbers of lethal fragments will pass through targets. Conventional fuses, however, especially timed ones, often exploded prematurely, belatedly, or inadequately. Proximity fuses were small, rugged radar sets placed in artillery shells, designed to detonate them at set distances from their targets. These proximity fuses made battlefield weaponry more effective. Industry, particularly Bell Laboratories, Crosley, Eastman Kodak, Raytheon, and Sylvania, worked with Johns Hopkins to surmount problems of firing shocks, temperature variations, and assembling complex small weapons with minimal errors and maximum safety. Acoustic and electrostatic proximity fuses also were tried but failed to impress. Photoelectric and especially radio fuses worked much better, and the Army and the Navy adopted both. By the war's close, a quarter of America's electronics industry was devoted to producing them.

Proximity fuses were useful in almost every encounter. They shot down dive bombers, Japanese *kamikazes,* and German flying bombs, and were shot at enemy soldiers on attack or in foxholes with remarkable accuracy. The German V-1 flying bombs, or buzz-bombs, which traveled at 350 mph or more, posed the greatest challenge; only the most determined Allied effort, using SCR-584 radar as well as advanced radio proximity fuses, prevented a catastrophe.

The Role of Aviation in World War II

Airplanes played a far larger role in World War II than in the previous conflagration, and were integral parts of most military operations. Air reconnaissance and bombing missions were essential features of modern warfare. The B-17 "Flying Fortress," B-24 "Liberator," and B-29 "Superfortress" bombers had been designed before America entered the war, but wartime production and performance needs prompted repeated modifications, from leakproof fuel tanks to aluminum airframes (which increased speed, capacity, range, reliability, and stability). In total, the nation produced more than 296,000 aircraft during the war.

Superior airpower and conventional weaponry as well as America's material resources helped decide the war, but the atomic bomb marked its formal conclusion. The first atomic weapon was tested at

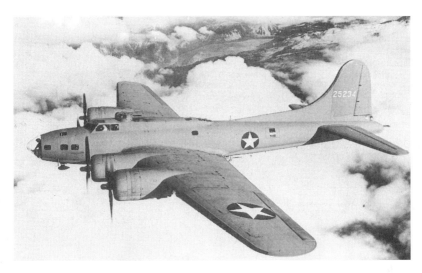

The B-17 "Flying Fortress" practices for a bombing
run as it flies above the clouds.

Alamogordo, New Mexico, on July 16, 1945. Conventional high explosives surrounding the subcritical volume of plutonium-239 in its core were detonated, compressing the fissionable material into a smaller volume that exceeded the critical mass. Buoyed by the test's success, President Harry Truman issued Japan—the war with Germany had ended—an unconditional-surrender ultimatum that hinted at a new aerial weapon of unprecedented power. Japan's silence led to the dropping of "Little Boy" (an enriched U-235 bomb triggered by firing one subcritical mass into another) on Hiroshima on August 6, 1945. The blast killed 80,000 persons and destroyed or heavily damaged 96 percent of the city's buildings. Japan's continued silence produced the Nagasaki bombing (using "Fatman," which was similar in design to the Alamogordo bomb), which took 39,000 lives and leveled 40 percent of the city's structures. Each bomb contained more explosive power than 20,000 tons of TNT. Japan surrendered on August 15.

Other Government Support Not all government money went to funding armaments. Generous government backing led to Samuel Ruben's mercury cell battery, which packed more capacity in less space and proved durable enough for wartime conditions. Government support converted the shipbuilding industry from rivet-based construction to welding. To save steel from rivets and to train draftees in the shipbuilding arts more swiftly, the Navy established welding schools and mass production platforms to build the vessels it needed to fight the war and survive enemy submarines. Medical equipment also received

The atom bomb called "Little Boy" was detonated
over Hiroshima, Japan. It was 29 inches in diameter
and 120 inches long. The force of its explosion was
comparable to that of 20,000 tons of TNT.

a boost. Military exigencies produced numerous new, refined X-ray machines, suitable for diagnosing chest wounds and tuberculosis.

Synthetic materials also found lavish government support. An artificial rubber industry, dominated by the Big Four rubber manufacturers—Goodyear, Goodrich, Firestone, and U.S. Rubber—had existed in America since the 1920s. But with the Asian source of natural rubber cut off, the government pumped funds into research institutions—Bell Labs, Cornell, Chicago, and Minnesota universities—to establish techniques and parameters to create a standardized, multipurpose product, useful for many military applications. In the case of polyethylene, the government went further. It actually built a factory for Du Pont to make the material during the war. Polyethylene found use for radar coverings, as Plexiglas, waterproofing, and as plastic bags and bowls.

The case of sulfa drugs and antibiotics was somewhat different. Sulfa-drug development was a free-market activity since the 1920s, as was penicillin in the 1930s. Only the war changed matters. America and England embarked upon crash programs to produce and purify the wonder drugs on an industrial scale. Creation of streptomycin benefited from the war, but not through direct government funding. Before the war, its creator, Selman A. Waksman, had parlayed moneys from an agricultural experiment station, the National Research Council, and Merck Chemical Company to use his Rutgers laboratory to investigate interactions and antagonisms of soil microorganisms. He coined the term "antibiosis" to explain these antagonisms, which he assumed were chemical substances. Waksman further felt that if he could isolate these substances, he could produce them in large quantities and use them to rid the human body of pathogenic microorganisms—disease germs. In 1938, backed by Merck money, he began his investigations into possible antibiotics. Waksman's laboratory did not secure new government contracts, but his personnel remained in his laboratory during the war. By 1943, it had identified and purified streptomycin, which attacked virtually all bacteria immune to penicillin.

AMERICAN TECHNOLOGY IN THE POSTWAR WORLD

World War II reaffirmed America's technological strength, but the nation faced many challenges soon after its conclusion. Rapid demobilization strained the country's economy, while veterans' programs placed pressure on colleges and the housing industry. Communists would control China and the Korean War would soon ignite. Yet an unabashed optimism gripped America. Victory over the Nazis and Imperial Japanese indicated that American enterprise could forge a new and better future. Ralph Flanders, president of the Federal Reserve Bank of Boston and a former U.S. senator, acted for a generation when he founded in 1946 an American venture capital corporation just to fund the many industries that would spin off from World War II-era research and development.

Solving Problems at Home

On the home front, the GI bill enabled an entire generation to attend college or technical school with a twofold benefit. Returning veterans would enter the workforce gradually after they completed their studies, and they would be much better educated than their predecessors. Other veterans, perhaps older, settled down and started families. Several entrepreneurs capitalized on this demographic glut and the inexpensive mortgage rates provided in the GI bill to offer the American dream, a single family home. William Levitt was the most noted.

Levittown

Levitt wanted his Levittown to be a total living space, "a complete, integrated, harmonious community." Village greens would be interspersed with shops, meeting halls, and restaurants. Bowling alleys, baseball diamonds, swimming pools, and playgrounds also would be fully integrated. Landscaped lots would feature staggered setbacks to provide visual interest and serpentine roadways restricted traffic flow. In those senses, Levittown reflected the pre-war TVA or the efforts of the Resettlement Administration. To make this dream (and product) available to almost everyone, Levitt had to slash costs. He accomplished that task by restricting choices and working on economies of scale.

Levitt's houses all had an identical Cape Cod design. For $7,900, homeowners got a 12- by 16-foot living room with a built-in eight-inch television, a tiled bath, a kitchen with a Bendix clothes washer, and two bedrooms. Growing families could convert the unfinished upstairs into two more bedrooms. A picture window and fireplace graced the living room and radiant floor heating warmed the house, which had no basement. For an additional $1,261, owners could get color-coordinated living-room furnishings.

Levitt's construction practices kept prices down. He bought his appliances from a single manufacturer, who offered him the best deal. He then divided construction into twenty-six separate tasks. At the central warehouse, workmen precut lumber to size, assembled plumbing fixtures, prefabricated staircases, and built kitchen cabinets. Concrete foundations provided the house's base. A series of specialty teams then went from house to house in designated order to work on preassigned tasks. Wall specialists preceded kitchen specialists who preceded bathroom tiling specialists. In this fashion, Levitt's teams could finish a house with 800 square feet of living space every 15 minutes.

Levitt benefited from techniques applied to build barracks and other dwellings during World War II. Levitt, along with the Andersen Window Company, adapted special high-speed cutting and spray-painting machines to create standard-sized, tightly sealing prefabricated windows that replaced the cumbersome weight-and-pulley systems.

Goods and Services

Levittowners and others who served in the war expected to continue to receive many of the same services they had become familiar with while in the military. By 1950, for example, virtually every American hospital with more than fifty beds owned an X-ray machine. Well over 75 percent of hospitals with fewer than 50 beds also purchased these devices. Doctors issued prescriptions for antibiotics as if they were candy and farmers added them to feed to protect their animals.

Military men and women also became acquainted with frozen foods and apparently enjoyed them, but with a different outcome. The frozen-food industry had been such a vital part of the war effort that it was excused from having to meet steel conservation requirements. An initial boom followed the war. Gourmet restaurants offered their specialties as frozen entrees while Birdseye and other manufacturers targeted housewives, offering entrees such as chicken a la king or fried chicken. But by late 1947, frozen-food sales had plummeted. Two factors contributed to the collapse. Frozen foods required special, heavily insulated railroad cars or trucks to keep temperatures at zero degrees Fahrenheit or below, which forced frozen-food prices higher. Second, relatively few homes had either refrigerator freezers or upright freezers before the 1950s. Frozen food remained a limited commodity.

Solving the Problem of Communism

Even in wake of the Soviet Union's aggressive postwar stance and the Communist Chinese assault of the mainland, America's technological superiority, national character, and continued vigilance appeared to offer protection from the "Red Menace." The Research and Development Board, formed in 1947, awarded contracts to universities for Defense Department research. Six years later Congress created two additional assistant defense secretaries—one for research and the other for development—to replace the Board and to extend the contract system.

Success in attracting huge government contracts and grants—normalcy during the war—had changed some universities in its aftermath. Rather than return to the status quo, they worked to retain the supply of federal dollars that had become a way of life for several years. In most cases, they capitalized on research that had been funded during the war. Stanford, for example, had been the site of significant microwave research during the war and under the direction of Frederick Terman, an electrical-engineering professor and administrator, the university turned its attention to securing first related military research and, later, any military research. It even set up the innovative Stanford Research Institute in 1946 to help attract federal money.

Nor was private enterprise immune from the lure of government largess. The boost given artificial rubber research continued after the war's conclusion as the Soviet Union replaced Germany and Japan as a threat to America's natural rubber supplies. Government funded much of this research, which resulted in commercial products such as thermoplastics, polyester and acrylic fibers, polyurethane foams and plastics, linear polyethylene and polypropylene, as well as superior forms of artificial rubber.

America's technological might also held out hope of nonmilitary solutions to communism's spread; it would engage in a Cold War against communism. The nation's industrial prowess could inaugurate a worldwide era of plenty; it could stop and isolate communism by re-making the world in the United States' image. The Marshall Plan, resurrection and modification of Japan, foreign aid, and establishment of the United Nations were attempts by the United States to engineer a new world order. Americans conceptualized the world as an evolving whole (undeveloped, underdeveloped, developing, and developed countries constituted this evolutionary framework's vocabulary), and depended on desire for material goods to carry that vision to fruition. Democracy would mean the right to vote for the candidate of your choice *and* the right to material prosperity. More specifically, Truman attempted to halt communism abroad by "making the benefits of our scientific advances and industrial progress available for the improvement and growth of underdeveloped areas." Technical missionaries undertook irrigation and hydroelectric-power projects, programs to increase agricultural productivity, and disease-eradication campaigns in thirty-three nations during the early 1950s. America devoted its "full energy to help these countries grow and flourish in freedom"; technical development became a cornerstone of foreign policy, much as it had formed a basis of New Deal domestic policy.

The nation, however, did not neglect military might. Turbojet engines and jet planes became Air Force staples; the F-80 fighter found extensive use in the Korean War. Huge defense contracts established Douglas, Boeing, and other airline manufacturers as integral parts of the military–industrial complex.

Rocketry was another outgrowth of the war. Clark University physicist Robert Goddard had achieved the first successful flight of a liquid-fuel rocket at Auburn, Massachusetts, on March 16, 1926. Goddard received little acclaim for his 184-foot flight, and died barely noticed in 1945. The German V-2 rockets (which were 5 1/2-ton bomb-carrying missiles) acquainted the American military with liquid-fuel rockets during World War II, and both America and the Soviet Union utilized captured V-2 rockets in postwar years. In 1946 the Army created the Atmospheric Research Panel to conduct V-2 research, but as the V-2 supply ran out, new rockets were developed: the Aerobee from Johns Hopkins University's Applied Physics Laboratory, and the Viking from the Naval Research Laboratory. These probed the upper atmosphere, or "near space," to altitudes of 150 miles, and made feasible earth satellites and space probes requiring greater rocket thrusts.

Atomic power grew in prominence after the Soviet Union exploded an atomic bomb in September 1949. Truman ordered a crash program to develop the hydrogen bomb, the dreaded next stage in nuclear weaponry. Several physicists active in the Manhattan Project, including Fermi and Oppenheimer, opposed Truman's initiative. The devastation of Hiroshima and Nagasaki concerned them, as did the vast destructive potential of thermonuclear weapons. Their advice was rejected, particularly once Edward Teller and others devised practical means to control fusion reactions. (Hydrogen bombs require nuclear reactions different from Fermi's fission reactions: not splitting heavy atomic nuclei, but, rather, fusing together the nuclei of light elements at extremely high temperatures to convert mass into energy.) The first American H-bomb was tested in 1954. Possessing the explosive power of fifteen million tons of TNT, it was more than 750 times as powerful as the A-bomb. A year later, the Soviet Union exploded a less powerful but similar device.

Spin-offs: Audio Tape

The story of the creation of a successful audio tape recorder matches expectations about how things should occur. War places persons in unusual positions and they are changed by what they see and do. When they return to their normal environment, they bring those changes with them. Some of them become technological artifacts. Yet rarely is it so simple. Human beings are not simply amoebas, changed by their experiences. They begin, instead, complete—a total sum of ideas, conceptions, and preconceptions that color, restrict, and guide what they see and how they respond to it. In that sense, nothing truly changes them so much as they that take that experience and interpret it in a meaningful way. Often they act on that interpretation.

Such was the case with audio tape. The Germans long had pioneered in this area. Their huge chemical combines had coated plastic tape with microscopically small bits of magnetic material from the 1920s, and by the war they were quite proficient. Others in Germany developed techniques for magnetizing and reading the tape; as with the telephone, sound waves were converted into electrical impulses. Those electrical impulses magnetized the tape, which was read and reconverted back into sound.

The German government had quite early recognized the propaganda value of recording speeches and situations and playing them at a later time. In fact, this technology seemed so lifelike that it was virtually indistinguishable from live recordings. Reality became, in effect, a continuum of possibilities; editing—changing reality—was conceivable and time as a prescribed measure ceased to matter. After Germany's surrender and the American occupation began, John Mullin, a member of the technical unit of the U. S. Army Signal Corps with a degree in electrical engineering, heard a delayed broadcast of an orchestra, which he took for the real thing. He inquired how this was done and was given one of these German devices, a magnetophon. He took it apart, sent the artifact and information about the artifact to his superiors and the Department of Commerce, and retired from the Army.

Mullin took his magnetophon knowledge with him and got a job in 1946 with a friend at a small motion-picture studio. There he built his own device and gave a demonstration at the annual meeting of the Institute of Radio Engineers in 1946. Ampex Electric, a small magnetic-motor company that had had government contracts during the war but now needed a new revenue source, hired Mullin and funded his quest to produce a broadcast quality machine.

Until that time, radio broadcasts in America, if they were delayed, were prerecorded on vinyl disks, which sounded quite distorted. Bing Crosby, one of the biggest radio stars, found the quality of vinyl intolerable. As a consequence, he rarely gave anything but a live performance, often to the consternation of everyone around him. But Mullin was not alone in his desire to create an audio tape recorder. The government technical reports on German industries—Mullin had done one on the magnetophon—were open to the public and a way to wealth and innovation after the war was to secure these reports and use them as the basis for a new product. Several looked into audio recording.

Ampex acted first. It took its machine to ABC—Crosby's boss—and won a test to show what the machine could do. By 1947, Ampex had won a contract from the radio network to produce these tape machines for broadcast use. The next year it developed a far superior playback head and delivered its first tape recorder, the Ampex 200. Crosby found himself so impressed with the device that he loaned the company $50,000 and then invested in it. Bing Crosby Enterprises became the sole distributor of Ampex products on the West Coast. By 1948, the government turned to Ampex and used it much as the Germans had: to broadcast material on Radio Free Europe and on the Voice of America. The tape recorder became a weapon in the Cold War.

Spin-offs: Mid-Century High Tech

The war proved a goad to technology. It provided money and opportunity but not ideas. Much of what was cutting-edge emerged from ideas earlier in the century. To be sure, the technologies identified by contemporaries as modern—airplanes, electricity, and automobiles—were dated: heavier-than-air powered flight had been accomplished as early as 1903, and automobiles and electricity were products of the previous century. The newest technologies remained virtually unknown to the public. Only in the later twentieth century would these technologies gain substantial industrial or public constituencies. Yet these truly high-tech endeavors were as much a part of mid-century America as the TVA. And they received a significant boost from the war. These new technologies were characteristically conceived from mid-century notions about the nature of systems and of parts within those systems. What was different about them, however, and what separated them from something like the TVA project, was the locus of technological concern. Generally developed by physicists or electrical engineers laboring in universities or industry, these technologies concentrated not on system–part relationships in society, but on how they were manifested in the contemporary physics of indeterminacy, quantum mechanics, or electronics; the area of inquiry was often atomic or subatomic. Other technologists focused on the macroatomic level and strove to integrate several functions within single machines, taking care, of course, to establish compensatory mechanisms to balance interactions among elements. From these mid-century undertakings came television, transistors, a new class of servomechanisms, and computers.

The Development of Transistors

Transistors were the product of a quest beginning in the 1930s to find adequate substitutes for amplifying-triode vacuum tubes (which were bulky, fragile, short-lived, and consumed large amounts of energy). Even as the triode search was beginning, however, researchers produced solid-state replacements for another vacuum tube, the rectifying diode. Indeed, World War II radar receivers employed small, very durable silicon–tungsten, copper–copper-oxide, and copper–selenium rectifiers. Materials for these rectifiers required extensive purification, thus acquainting investigators with the properties of these substances in pristine and slightly altered states. Invention of these rectifiers—and ultimately solid-state amplifying triodes—depended on understanding the nature of subatomic systems formulated in the previous decades. It included solid-state and surface physics, Einstein's photoelectric effect, and quantum mechanics. Of particular importance was the notion that electrons occupied and were restricted to energy levels in solids called *bands,* that voids that could not be occupied by electrons stood between the bands, and that electrons could jump bands (without going through the voids) under certain conditions. This notion overthrew traditional conductor–insulator distinctions and established a continuum between them. From these assumptions came the concept of semiconductors, which made the idea of amplifying transistors appear logical and their development seem possible.

Bell Laboratories was among the earliest proponents of solid-state amplification. Long-distance telephony used huge numbers of vacuum-tube amplifying triodes, which were expensive, burnt out quickly, demanded large amounts of power, and disrupted service frequently. In the mid-1930s, Bell hired scientists and engineers explicitly to form a special interdisciplinary solid-state research team. As early as 1939, Bell researchers Walter Brattain and William Shockley installed a grid-like device within a semiconductor in an attempt to replicate a vacuum-tube triode, but it failed to amplify current. The war interrupted the research, but Brattain and John Bardeen returned to test Bardeen's theory that surface states immobilized current and made grid formation impossible. During their explorations of semiconductor surfaces they found that with two closely spaced electrode wires, a positive charge on one electrode would greatly enhance the semiconductor's capacity to carry current and lead to a 100-fold amplification in the second. Brattain demonstrated this amplifying effect on a germanium crystal to appropriate Bell staff on December 23, 1947.

Creation of the point-contact transistor in miniscule impure germanium—impurities doped the crystal and gave the semiconductors positive or negative charges—resulted in Nobel Prizes for the three Bell employees. Shockley's subsequent sandwiching of minuscule impure semiconductors yielded the junction transistor in 1951. It would prove more useful than the point-contact transistor because on the subatomic level (and in practice) it more nearly resembled Lee De Forest's amplifying gate-like grid. But both were limited in their applicability, were temperamental (easily damaged and not reliable), and were expensive to produce. Manufacturing semiconductor material of sufficient purity required time and money; vacuum tubes remained dominant for the time being.

FOR FURTHER READING

Aitken, Hugh G. *The Continuous Wave* (1985).

Akin, William E. *Technocracy and the American Dream* (1977).

Arnold, Joseph L. *The New Deal in the Suburbs: A History of the Greenbelt Town Program, 1935–1954* (1971).

Baxter, James Phinney, III. *Scientists Against Time* (1947).

Bilstein, Roger E. *Flight in America, 1900–1983* (1984).

Borth, Christy. *Pioneers of Plenty: The Story of Chemurgy*, rev. ed. (1942).

Boyce, Joseph C. *New Weapons for Air Warfare* (1947).

Boyer, Paul. *By the Bomb's Early Light* (1985).

Braun, Ernest, and Stuart MacDonald. *Revolution in Miniature*, rev. ed. (1982).

Burks, Alice R. and Arthur W. *The First Electronic Computer* (1988).

Cohen, Lizabeth. *Making of a New Deal: Industrial Workers in Chicago, 1919–1939* (1990).

Conkin, Paul K. *Tomorrow a New World: The New Deal Community Program* (1959).

Corn, Joseph J. *The Winged Gospel* (1983).

Crump, Irving. *Our Army Engineers* (1954).

Douglas, Susan J. *Inventing American Broadcasting* (1989).

Foster, Mark S. *From Streetcar to Superhighway* (1981).

Gillispie, Richard. *Manufacturing Knowledge: A History of the Hawthorne Experiments* (1991).

Graham, Otis L., Jr. *Toward a Planned Society: From Roosevelt to Nixon* (1976).

Hallion, Richard P. *Legacy of Flight* (1977).

Hamilton, David E. *From New Day to New Deal: American Farm Policy From Hoover to Roosevelt, 1928–1933* (1991).

Hawley, Ellis W., ed. *Herbert Hoover as Secretary of Commerce: Studies in New Era Thought and Practice* (1981).

Johnson, Charles W., and Charles O. Jackson. *City Behind a Fence: Oak Ridge, Tennessee, 1942–1946* (1981).

Kuhn, Arthur J. *GM Passes Ford, 1918–1938: Designing the General Motors Performance-Control System* (1986).

Lewis, W. David, and Wesley Phillips Newton. *Delta: The History of an Airline* (1979).

Lowitt, Richard. *The New Deal in the West* (1984).

Lubove, Roy. *Community Planning in the 1920s* (1963).

Lush, Jay L. *Animal Breeding Plans*, 3rd. ed. (1945).

McCraw, Thomas K., ed. *Regulation in Perspective: Historical Essays* (1981).

Meikle, Jeffrey L. *Twentieth Century Limited. Industrial Design in America, 1925–1939* (1979).

Morgan, Arthur E. *The Making of the TVA* (1974).

Schlebecker, John T. *Whereby We Thrive: A History of American Farming, 1607–1972* (1975).

Scott, Howard. *Science versus Chaos* (1933).

Simonds, William Adams. *Henry Ford and Greenfield Village* (1938).

Smith, Terry. *Making the Modern: Industry, Art, and Design in America* (1993).

Soule, George. *A Planned Society* (1932).

Stewart, Irving. *Organizing Scientific Research for War: The Administrative History of the Office of Scientific Research and Development* (1948).

Tichi, Cecelia. *Shifting Gears: Technology, Literature, Culture in Modernist America* (1987).

Williams, Robert C. *Fordson, Farmall and Poppin' Johnny* (1987).

Expressing the Self: Individualism in an Era of Plenty, From about 1950 to the late 1960s

In 1956, William H. Whyte, Jr., published *The Organization Man*. Assistant managing editor of *Fortune,* Whyte criticized unthinking, uncritical worship of corporate organizations and pilloried the gospel of scientism, the notion that expert determinations were always nonpartisan and not subject to error or debate. He railed against any organization's use of the concepts of belonging and togetherness to manipulate members and objectives, and called on his contemporaries to challenge the status quo. Whyte conceded that the organization was here to stay, and he did not advocate nonconformity. Rather, he urged men and women to examine the premises they took for granted, to vent their individual proclivities, and to redirect their various organizations. Individualism tempered by critical thought would awaken America from its blissful organization-inspired ignorance and produce a better tomorrow.

Whyte's book drew plaudits from many corners, became an immediate best-seller, and remained popular for some two decades. Its cry for intraorganizational individualism struck a chord with its readers, as did its attacks on professional, technical expertise as the sole criterion for making decisions. Americans acted out their interpretations of Whyte's book in the decade following its publication, although not always in the same ways, or even ways that Whyte might have appreciated. Tensions repeatedly erupted between the post-1920 organizational idea's implicit holism and post-1950 individualism; the previous period's systematic notions appeared increasingly less important than freeing each individual part—person, company, or group—to pursue its unique destiny in the United States. Opportunity served as the watchword as individuals began to assert their interests and proclivities in search of a more fulfilling existence. Technology remained a means to give flight to individual expression, which often had material components. Technology would indeed give each American the opportunity to "keep up with the Joneses," the 1950s idealized personification of unfettered opportunity.

The attack on corporatism was not restricted to material goods but permeated American society. For example, Jack Kerouac, Allen Ginsberg, and the other "beatniks" railed against the collective status quo and sought instead what they recognized as individual artistic expression. Authors as different as Sloan Wilson, in his *Man in the Gray Flannel Suit* (1955), and Ayn Rand, in her *Atlas Shrugged* (1957), romanticized the emotional benefits of individual liberation from collectivism. Movies, such as *High Noon* (1950), *Bridge Over the River Kwai* (1958), and *West Side Story* (1962), warned of dangers to the individual of unchallenged organization. Musicals, such as *Damn Yankees* (1955), had protagonists uttering such personalized heresy as "there are some things more important than being a hero"; personal happiness took precedent over group aims. Social scientists, such as sociologist David Riesman in *The Lonely Crowd* (1950) and psychologist Leon Festinger in *Theory of Cognitive Dissonance* (1962), explored the social pathology of organizational living and thinking.

The anti-corporate message resonated with the young, who labored through their day-to-day activities to express opposition to conventional mores. The term "juvenile delinquency" became a common part of the lexicon and the Senate formed a special committee in 1956 to investigate the epidemic of drag racing and youthful disobedience sweeping America. The actor James Dean emerged as a potent symbol of this rejection of orthodoxy, as did a new form of music, rock and roll. Its driving rhythms and beat aimed directly at the young. Although a succession of individuals became stars and heroes, none duplicated the success of Elvis Presley. Presley's public persona embodied individual liberation. He dressed as far from customary as possible.

Elvis chose loud colors, wore jackets without collars, pants way too tight, and pointed shoes with heels; he grew his hair long and slicked back, and growled rather than sang his songs. His gyrations

*Elvis Presley's seemingly conscious attempts to flout
social convention made him a hero to a generation
seeking individual liberation.*

while playing guitar truly gained him the moniker Elvis the Pelvis. In
short, Presley lacked taste, the very essence of collective propriety.

THE CONSUMER REVOLUTION

Although parents certainly objected to Elvis and rock and roll generally, the individuation of American society occurred relatively pain-
lessly. Opportunity for individual expression, especially material expression, proved far more extensive than ever in the nation's history.
Groups formerly deprived of their civil rights began to agitate and receive a portion of those rights. Freedom of religion became more than
a concept as Catholics, Jews, and others gained not simply the freedom to believe as they chose but not to have to sacrifice greatly for
their religious decisions. America truly seemed a place of plenty. The
material opportunity of the 1950s and early 1960s affected virtually
everyone, although by no means equally. Nonetheless, almost all
Americans had more choices by the mid-1960s than they had had
twenty years earlier. In this heady world, technology was a benison
that could convert plenty into possibilities.

No group gained more choices than homemakers and their families. Food was re-engineered to increase choice, variety, speed, and convenience. Housing was reconfigured to enhance comfort, individuality, and privacy. Consumer electronics granted individuals regular access to entertainment and information, no matter where they were, while new photographic techniques transformed reality into almost-instant memories. Pregnancy no longer was a matter of chance as technology converted fertility into a matter of individual control.

Food Production

Meat Increasing the supply of a previously limited commodity while reducing price or keeping it relatively stable stood as one way to augment individual options. It gave many persons new opportunity to gain access to that market. Such was the case with meat. New technologies enabled manufacturers to expand production and keep costs low. Between about 1950–1969, beef production nearly doubled. Pork production rose about 25 percent. The number of chickens produced increased eightfold.

Food engineering began at the farm. Artificial insemination of cattle and the creation of new breeds of beef cows guaranteed a strong supply of yearlings. From about 1960, freezing embryos for implantation later and inducement of estrous were added to the artificial breeding arsenal. But the greatest technological strides came in feeding. By the mid-1950s, agricultural scientists had convinced farmers to feed antibiotics to swine to enable those animals to metabolize their feed more efficiently, vitamin B-12 to increase feed utilization in chickens and hogs, and rations of urea-corncobs-molasses plus a growth supplement to beef cattle to ensure maximum weight gain per unit cost. Diethylstilbestrol (DES), an artificial female sex hormone, was a particularly important chemical substance. In small doses, DES as a cattle-feed additive reduced the quantity of feed necessary for an animal to reach market weight without lessening the grade of the beef, a savings to the livestock producer and a potential savings to the consumer. In large doses, it chemically caponized male chickens, rendering their meat as soft and juicy as that of hens.

Use of these chemicals reflected a more general shift from range to commercial feeding. Farmers found that commercial feeds permitted them to design their animals to best economic advantage. An entire scientific feeding industry rose to foster and serve that demand. Industry technologists compounded and tested feeds to provide farmers with the exact ratios that their businesses required.

Nor were these feeding companies alone. Several giant chemical companies saw profits in supplying feed-additive chemicals and moved aggressively there. Du Pont pioneered research in urea, which it manufactured in great quantities, as a protein source for artificial feeds, and Eli Lilly Company established an entire agricultural subsidiary, Elanco, to produce and market DES as a cattle-growth promotant.

These diverse feeding and chemical companies created industry-wide consortiums to facilitate cattle feeding. Feed producers, chemical companies, and agricultural and veterinary scientists employed at land-grant colleges and experiment stations regularly gathered together, exchanged information, and tried to direct the industry's future to meet anticipated consumer demand. Editors and reporters of trade publications often joined these forums, as did USDA officials, who discussed national priorities and policies as well as research done under its auspices.

Consumer appetites helped propel the new feeding industry. Homemakers demanded the best for their families and the most tasty beef—succulent, tender, well-marbled beef; beef graded choice or prime—was difficult to produce on grass-fed, range cattle. Formerly the province of the wealthy and exclusive restaurants, mass production of choice and prime meat required feeding animals special diets and dietary supplements and confining them somewhat to develop the level of marbling necessary to grade high. A vice president for the supermarket chain Safeway was among the first to recognize and act on this potent demand. He resigned his vice presidency to build a feedlot in Bakersfield, California. By 1953, he produced more than 50,000 well-marbled cattle yearly. Others, including the actor John Wayne, invested heavily in the new feedlot industry.

Prior to the 1950s, beef-cattle production had been a predominantly Midwestern industry. It moved west in the next decade and a half. Texas emerged as a leading feedlot state. One of the earliest Texas feedlots began in 1955. Durward Lewter, a county agent, and Clint Murchison, a Dallas investor and soon to be owner of the new National Football League Dallas Cowboys, established a lot that held 34,000 cattle at all times. This 125-acre facility had its own nutritionists and veterinarians and used computers to keep track of the animals. By the early 1960s, similar huge feedlots dominated animal agriculture in Southern California, Arizona, Colorado, Oklahoma, Nebraska, and Kansas. By 1963, feeder cattle accounted for more than 70 percent of the nation's slaughtered beef.

Crops Crop production also underwent drastic change as agrochemical became a production standard. Farmers added anhydrous ammonia, stored as a liquid under pressure, to the soil to unleash precise quantities of fertilizer as they became necessary. Herbicides regularly protected crops from weeds, which competed with crops for space, sunlight, and nutrients, and which reduced crop quality, increased production costs, and decreased profits. These early herbicides were

Agricultural chemicals have become increasingly common on farms. This mound of chemicals constitutes the average amount used annually on this gentleman's 78-acre farm in the early 1950s.

synthetic plant growth hormones called auxins and worked by causing the naturally faster-growing weeds to grow at uncontrolled rates and ironically, to starve to death. Substances, such as 2,4-D and 2,4,5-T, were developed and used during World War II but found extensive agricultural use only in the 1950s and 1960s. The chemical 2,4-D seemed especially promising. It killed most broad-leafed plants, which included most weeds, and appeared harmless to plants useful to mankind, as well as to persons exposed to it through airplane spraying, dusting, or aerosols. Even though producers learned to reduce their per acre use of 2,4-D from about three pounds to less than a half of a pound, American farmers expanded their application of the chemical from less than 10 million pounds in 1953, to 36 million pounds in 1960, to an amazing 79 million pounds in 1968.

Insecticides and other pesticides followed close behind. The insecticide DDT (dichloro-diphenyl-trichloro-ethane) offered what seemed the most potential. Discovered in 1939 by a Swiss scientist, Paul Muller, it became available in America three years later. DDT quickly gained fame when the U.S. Army used it in occupied Italy to combat lice, and then in the Pacific to combat malaria. By the 1950s, it became the insecticide of choice as Americans employed it against virtually every parasite. Like herbicides, DDT appeared to increase productivity without harming desirable plants, animals, or humans. It spawned an entire generation of related insecticides: chlorodane, toxaphene, gamma BHC, dieldrin, and aldrin, which also were applied extensively.

Changes in techniques and tools accompanied the new chemical agriculture. Five- and seven-bottom plows became common, tractors capable of pulling such a prodigious load replaced their lighter, less efficient predecessors; six- and eight-row seed drills followed. Each drill incorporated a shield that kept furrows open for the deep deposit of seed while reducing drag. The self-propelled combine began to replace the power-takeoff tractor for harvesting. The new device's large cutter bars could be adjusted for height or speed of cut and could cover a far greater area in less time than earlier machinery. They also increased farmer comfort. Padded seats, radios, and even air conditioning became staples as self-propelled combines captured about a quarter of the farming market by 1960.

In the case of some crops, the ability to design technologies to mechanize particularly onerous farm tasks led to crop redesign. If quality became a casualty of the process, then some other consumer-oriented factors were required for compensation. Without this trade-off, mechanization would not prove profitable. The rubbery-tasting hard tomato was the product of such a compromise. Two staff members at the University of California-Davis, Jack Hanna and Coby Lorenzen, marketed in 1961 a mechanical tomato harvester and a strain of tomato plant that would bear its fruit within a limited period, ripen simultaneously, hold on the vine for thirty days without deteriorating, survive mechanical harvesting, and withstand shipment. But such a tomato was necessarily hard and tasteless. Nonetheless, it was available nearly year-round, rarely became bruised or rotten quickly, and cost much less then the more difficult-to-ship product. Its rapid saturation of the market testified to its popularity with homemakers. For the first time, homemakers in cooler climates could afford to serve their families tomatoes year-round.

Food Processing

In the 1950s, food processors sought to improve on nature's bounty to provide American homemakers with additional options for virtually every meal. Processors adopted chemical emulsifiers to give food an improved texture; flavor enhancers to improve taste; vitamins to raise nutritional content; and spoilage retardants to prolong food shelf life. Each new technology enabled homemakers to go to market less frequently than in the past and yet offer their families a wider variety of foods than ever before.

Kraft Foods was particularly adept at improving on nature in service of individual opportunity. In the decade and a half after 1950, Kraft created Minute Rice, which dramatically speeded rice cooking time and so granted homemakers additional options while reducing their starch preparation time; Kraft Deluxe Process Cheese Slices, the first commercial-packaged, sliced, processed cheese food product made by moisturizing, homogenizing, and pasteurizing natural cheese and by cutting it into individual portions; Cheez Whiz, a pasteurized processed cheese spread that could be smeared directly on crackers or bread to make a speedy, healthy, and tasty snack; Tang, a dehydrated powder that when mixed with water replaced and improved upon (both in taste through the addition of table sugar and in nutrition through the addition of vitamins) the time-consuming, labor-intensive, freshly squeezed orange juice; Shake 'N Bake, a seasoned coating mix to replace toasted crumb or flour breading for frying and baking; and Cool Whip, a whipped cream enhancement that was neither whipped nor cream but a ready-made, always available, colored nondairy topping.

Freezing

Frozen food came of age in the 1950s as homemakers selected frozen items for their convenience. Increased demand and volume enabled processors to expand, mechanize, and diversify their product line. In 1952, Swanson Foods introduced TV dinners in fifty principal cities. Its success encouraged the company to market the product nationally a year later.

These individual frozen items each replicated a home-cooked dinner for a single person—each included an entree, starch, vegetable, and usually a dessert—but eliminated home preparation and cooking time. Each TV dinner was presized and precooked; it only needed heating in its own individual aluminum package. Thermoplastic trays began to replace the aluminum tin in 1964, and a five- and six-compartment device was employed by the Green Giant Company a year later. A much more exotic cuisine accompanied these changes. Mexican, Chinese, Italian, and other foods became TV-dinner staples. So too did a Weightwatchers' menu as that diet company marketed in 1965 a line of its own dinners.

The diversification of TV-dinner options testified to the product's huge success. Increasingly, homemakers purchased these dinners

Nearly a half-century ago, TV dinners liberated homemakers from the daily grind of preparing supper.

from supermarket chains. Although created in the 1930s, national supermarket chains did not dominate American food until the 1950s and 1960s. As late as 1955, they accounted for only about 15 percent of American food purchases. Fourteen years later, that total reached nearly 55 percent. Availability of frozen foods, first truly popularized by TV dinners, accompanied the rise of supermarket chains.

Frozen-food processors recognized the burgeoning frozen-food markets and outlets. They turned to automation, with its high initial costs but with the promise of drastically reduced labor costs in the future, to meet the demand. In the later 1950s, frozen-food processors introduced automatic tray loaders, pneumatic pea cleaners, electronic weight checkers, metal detectors, and automated warehousing with IBM punch cards. They even designed harvesting equipment to prepare products in the field for immediate processing and therefore increased taste and freshness. A porter-way harvester for peas, spinach, lima beans, and broccoli was the most successful. A flexible cutter bar that cut close to the soil removed the plant from the stalk, while a complex shaker system agitated the plant to leave the worthless leaves, hearts, and other matter on the ground. The harvester then loaded the desired product on the trucks. In the early 1960s, a snap-bean harvester for green beans and an electronically controlled asparagus cutter joined the porter. The asparagus-cutting machine was a self-propelled, four-wheeled device. An electric eye set six inches off the ground guided the cut. When a stalk broke the beam, the machine deployed a piano-wire projection to detach the upper portion of the asparagus plant.

Processors had developed new freezing techniques and products by the 1960s. Polybags, three-layer plastic bags that retarded spoilage, had an immediate impact. Each polybag layer was composed of a different kind of plastic. The center layer served as an oxygen barrier, preventing oxygen from entering the food area and hastening decomposition. The inner and outer layers provided strength and durability. Polybags could protect produce from freezer damage and that enabled processors to switch to liquid nitrogen as a convenient way to generate extremely cold temperatures. Carrots were frozen in fourteen seconds, for example. In 1961, Green Giant carried this technology to its next level by introducing boil-in bags. Vegetables in polybags were frozen with butter. Homemakers simply placed the bags in boiling water to heat them for consumption. Freeze-drying technology for coffee and soups also gained some currency. Freeze-drying did little to change volume but did reduce weight. It found little use because of the expense of vapor-proof packing. Fluidized belt freezing proved more popular. Operating in a quite cold atmosphere, the twin-belt assembly rolled and pressed the product during freezing, ensuring even freezing and mixing.

Beef Packing

Feedlots produced sufficient supplies of prime or choice beef. New heavily mechanized plants slaughtered the animals and distributed the meat. Iowa Beef Packers, founded in 1960, became one of the largest of the new breed. Mechanical stunners knocked cows senseless and mechanical knives cut their jugular veins. Carcasses then were stored in a refrigerator overnight to reduce temperature and to stop dehydration. Automated hide-skinners were followed by chainsaw-wielding butchers and then electronic slicing and weighing machines as the various parts of the animal moved on conveyors. Rarely was beef shipped on the carcass. Carcasses were wasteful and more expensive to ship as they included bone and fat with meat. As important, sides of beef did not fit into neat packages. Sections of beef—loins, chucks, rounds, and the like—were placed in polybags, which were then evacuated, heated to force the bags to shrink snugly around the meat, and sealed off. The bagged meat was then refrigerated. Meat packed this way would remain unspoiled for extended periods, often as much as a month, and could be shipped to stores throughout America.

Housing: Levittown Revisited

By the early 1950s, the dream that had been Levittown was dead. Commentators dismissed the idea of an integrated community as detrimental to the public weal. Lewis Mumford attacked this style of living as a travesty, as nothing more than "a multitude of uniform, unidentifiable houses, lined up inflexibly, at uniform distances, on uniform roads, in a treeless communal waste, inhabited by people of the same class, the same income, the same age group, . . . conforming in every outward and inward respect to a common mold." Mumford's critique was misplaced. The Levittowners had already moved beyond regimentation to individuality. By 1954, the Levittown community concentrated on individualizing the basic house. Area lumber yards and interior decoration experienced an unprecedented boom as Levittowners passionately remodeled. As early as 1957, the *New York Times* contended that no Levittown home remained unaltered. Each had been to some degree personalized. Walls had been taken down, inner space reallocated, and additions added on. Levittowners transformed carports into garages, finished attics, moved windows, expanded kitchens, and constructed recreation rooms.

More Work for Father? Exterior space also underwent change. The grass lawn became the symbol of personal responsibility and individual success. Its care generally devolved to the primary breadwinner in the family, who tended the lawn during time off from work. It became the duty of each to demonstrate personal skill and commitment by manicuring and keeping the lawn as sculpted as possible. Lawn grass needed to be weed- and pest-free, and to that end property owners dumped considerable amounts of pesticides and herbicides on lawns. Regular applications of fertilizers ensured the availability of proper nutrients year-round, while frequent watering guaranteed a lush green carpet. A slew of technological implements—spreaders, shovels, hoes, and irrigation devices borrowed from agriculture—aided upkeep. Electric and gasoline-powered, self-propelled mowers, clippers, pruners, trimmers, and edgers each contributed to making the lawn immaculate. There could be no mistake about where a person's lawn ended. Fences ruled the 1950s and early 1960s.

The fence demarcated individual space. It set ownership as something personal, an expression of individualism. The period's fences— wire but not chain link, western (split rail), and even some picket— had to be erected, maintained, and painted but did not lend themselves to securing property from intruders; fences were not so much to keep people from burglarizing dwellings or trespassing as they were to keep people from walking on the grass. Fences stood to celebrate individual property. They did not attempt to restrict vision from outside the perimeter but were nearly invisible. Celebrating a person's property required that the bounty and its owners remain in plain sight. Neighbors and passersby needed to see the yard and people doing yardwork. They must observe the car and its washing, even the process of grilling outdoors. Outdoor cooking, generally done by the same person who did most of the lawn care, became a particular favorite of the 1950s and 1960s. Electric starters and briquettes first began to supplant charcoal and lighter-fluid technology, and gas grills at the end of the 1950s provided yet another option. The new outdoor responsibilities were onerous, but no less an authority than Levitt came to see Levittown-like creations as a bulwark against communism. "No man who owns his own house and lot can be a communist. He has too much to do," maintained the builder.

The Ranch

Even as the Levittowners were transforming their Cape Cod houses into individual domiciles, a new housing style swept America. The ranch house dominated the 1950s and 1960s, providing "comfort, performance and beauty." It embodied individual options and flexibility. Its relative lack of walls left it up to owners to group the furniture as they chose to express their own living patterns. Imaginative lighting further personalized space. Private bathrooms and bedrooms abounded and separated the family from public areas. High ceilings, L-shaped living room—dining room combinations, and innovative, open kitchen designs, especially the U-shaped kitchen surrounding an island counter, provided considerable room for personalization. Three general zones divided indoor space: housework center, living area, and private rooms. The mandatory picture window and the sliding glass doors opening onto the back porch and connecting the porch either to the kitchen or the living room truly integrated indoor and outdoor space. Both created a "very personal and yet thoroughly adaptable background for good living." The two glass portals made the condition of the lawn and the landscaping of the yard wall decorations. The lawn and yard were a personalized living painting.

The kitchen rested at the center of this new architectural form and served as the house's nerve center. The socially prominent kitchen connected to the living room was a gateway to the private rooms and provided access to the outdoors. In fact, kitchen sinks were always placed under windows so that homemakers could monitor outdoor activity.

The kitchen's location enabled homemakers to care for their families without leaving the room. It was from the kitchen that homemakers could rear their children in accordance with the newest precepts, which supposed that developing individuality, individual options,

Straight-edged appliances provided homemakers the option of placing each piece to best advantage.

and individual proclivities were social benisons. Formulated by the physician Benjamin Spock and others, this child-rearing philosophy—this new social technology—rejected a sense of norms or standards. Parents ought not focus on their duties or obligations but rather on enjoying themselves and their children. Abandonment of any sense of rigidity, including rigid schedules, was paramount. Spock and others called for breastfeeding on demand, downplayed toilet training, dismissed templates or learning curves to measure progress in reading and talking, and urged special efforts to encourage individuality at the expense of discipline.

Ranch house design provided homemakers the environment within which to rear children to express individuality. Ironically, the technology of building ranch houses depended not on uniqueness but on standardization. Widespread single-family home ownership was based on low-cost housing, and large-scale, standardized, or prefabricated construction reduced unit cost. The way that John La Pan, a Hoosick Falls, New York, ranch-house builder, constructed his houses typified the new single-family construction ethos. La Pan had worked as part of several World War II construction teams and was quick to seize on the new individualism of the 1950s. He purchased parcels of

*Individual variation emerged from this seemingly
endless sameness as each family customized its ranch
house to fit personal needs.*

land, subdivided them, and used pre-WW II technologies to fabricate
houses that would permit individual declaration. He erected his houses
on poured concrete slabs, which included small cellar holes for furnaces and water heaters. Precut rafters, standard height ceilings, and
walls in four- by eight-foot modular units enabled La Pan's workmen
to put up an entire home in hours. Cutting drywall to fit non-standard
spaces became a thing of the past, and reduced the number of drywall
seams to tape and plaster. He included many cabinets in his design
(most were painted steel, wall-hung models) to increase individual options but used standardized sizes of cabinets and countertops to speed
construction and reduce unit cost. For example, La Pan's kitchens used
built-in sink-cabinet units, placed linoleum on floors and counters, and
covered kitchen walls with colorfully patterned washable wallpaper.
By the 1960s, La Pan had completed over 10,000 homes.

La Pan's ranches and the houses of other builders differed little
from each other in how they were built or even in their basic floor
plan. Nonetheless, their inhabitants relentlessly worked to personalize
them and make them unique; they focused on differences rather than
similarities. Much of their labor was reflected in home furnishings.

Appliances

Homeowners selected a wide range of "labor-saving" devices and out-fitted houses to suit individual dispositions and goals. Producers catered to these tastes. Americans purchased more than three-quarters of all the appliances manufactured in the world during the 1950s. Kitchens again were a focal point. An important change in the shape of appliances testified to the new flexibility. The streamlined appliances of the 1930s and 1940s gave way to the straight-edged models of the 1950s and after. Streamlined appliances suggested flow and integration, an organic sense. Straight-edged appliances were functional; these boxy devices fit anywhere in the kitchen, which had itself been formalized to match drywall size and other building constraints. Their owners organized, arranged, and positioned stoves, refrigerators, dishwashers, and washers and dryers to achieve best advantage.

Manufacturers continually modified existing products and formulated new options. Electric devices were extremely popular. Maytag offered the first home electric clothes dryer in 1953, while electric can openers, frying pans, four-slice toasters, rotisserie-broilers, and steam irons were commonplace before decade's end. Electric garbage disposals and blenders were popular in the 1960s. Washers, refrigerators, and ovens also underwent change.

Homemakers now operated any of these machines at the push of a button. Washers gained two-speed motors and delicate (cold water wash/rinse) cycles in the 1950s and permanent-press cycles and large capacities in the first part of the 1960s. The General Electric Spacesaver refrigerator did the impossible. First offered in 1956, the Spacesaver seemed all interior; insulation and cooling coils appeared to disappear. Easy-open doors, held shut by magnets rather than the traditional latch, made opening refrigerators a snap. Manufacturers boosted models with freezer compartments anywhere, even on the side or bottom, to increase homemaker efficiency and ease. Double ovens with finger-tip control, built-in ovens, and, in the early 1960s, self-cleaning ovens and combination microwave/conventional electric ovens came only in the color white until the mid-1960s, when avocado and harvest gold took American homes by storm. This splash of color was also found in the built-in and portable dishwashers of the period as well as in the new laminated countertops, vinyl floor coverings, and indoor/outdoor carpeting for kitchens.

Furniture

Choice also dominated furniture. Traditional styles coexisted with the new forms of the 1950s. These new forms took improving upon nature as a theme. Artificial materials, such as Naugahyde, replaced leather, while laminated plastics replaced wood. Chrome-plated steel, especially in kitchen tables and chairs, proved quite popular. Tops were of enamel, plastic, and linoleum for ease of cleaning. In living rooms, boxy furniture, mimicking the design of the new boxy appliances, sat next to molded plastic seats on wire frames. Hardwood seats were contoured or at rigid angles. In all cases, lines were sleek and minimal. Wooden tables either minimized or accentuated grains to demonstrate their difference from something natural or organic. Contemporary furniture based on colonial or other kinds of classic designs always offered enhancements to set these new pieces off from their predecessors. Everything manufactured during the period consciously bore the mark of those who produced it.

Automobiles

Automotive design exhibited a similar conscious eclecticism. That was not entirely surprising because a division of General Motors, the largest automotive producer, was under the trademark "Frigidaire," the largest refrigerator manufacturers. Straighter lines, extensive use of chrome and glass, and garish tail fins characterized the new designs. Each of these elements served to bound the car, to have it stand out, and make it distinct from its environs. Within that context, each consumer particularized his or her own car. Each chose engine, body style, interior and exterior colors, and hubcaps. Each also selected from such options as air conditioning, radio, and heater. Manufacturers recorded selections on punch card-based control systems to keep orders straight. Size and purpose also figured as design factors. Luxury cars, such as the Cadillac and Mark II, demonstrated personal success. The full-sized Impala, Fury, and Fairlane were family cars. The compact Falcon, Valiant, Lark, and Corvair made the perfect second car, suitable for short commutes. The two-seat convertible Thunderbird and Corvette of the early 1950s and the Mustang a decade later suited the sporty crowd, ideal for men on the go, while its opposite, the station wagon, seated up to nine and catered to families in motion. The V-8 1955 Chevy, the first muscle car, aimed at rebels without a cause, as did John DeLorean's GTO some years later.

Automobiles of the 1950s and 1960s were heavier and more powerful than their predecessors. For example, an average mid-sized auto in the 1950s contained an extra forty-four pounds of chrome. Yet extra weight did make operation more physically demanding and thus hamper individual choice. Much of this period's automotive design targeted women, persons generally less physically strong and experienced in car maintenance. These cars required less physical exertion and were markedly safer than earlier vehicles. Power steering and power brakes made control of these behemoths possible and convenient for even the smallest person. Automatic transmissions, found in more than half American cars manufactured after 1954, removed the need to learn to shift. New taillight assemblies, including tail, stop, back-up, and directional lights, reduced accidents. Puncture-proof tubeless tires eliminated any need to know how to change tires or the strength necessary to do so.

Automotive manufacturers moved forcefully to tap the period's affluence by emphasizing individual options and choice. In 1955, for example, GM spent more than $162 million on advertising. A Chevrolet ad from 1956 captured the tone of the era when it suggested that contemporary American life demanded two-car families to ease homemakers' burdens. "Going our separate ways we've never been so close! The family with two cars gets twice as many chores completed, so there's more leisure to enjoy together." The results of these campaigns were dramatic. Some 70,000 automobiles rolled off American assembly lines in 1945. More than 110 times that many were shipped to showrooms by American manufacturers a scant decade later.

Many new cars visited the shopping centers popping up in the 1950s. Accentuating speed, convenience, and choice and situated near major thoroughfares, these centers depended on drivers, not pedestrians. A fully equipped branch of a major department store or a supermarket anchored each; specialty stores, drug stores, and restaurants supported them. A huge parking lot surrounded the center and provided immediate access. By 1955, more than 1,800 shopping centers dotted the American landscape. Contemporary mass marketers K-Mart and Wal-Mart both entered the mix in 1962. They were joined by drive-in movie theaters, drive-in restaurants, and drive-in bank tellers. In 1964, America had more than 4,000 drive-in theaters and more than 30,000 drive-in restaurants.

Electronics: Sound

Choice became the watchword in sound, albeit in two senses. Technologists labored to make sound accessible and convenient no matter the location and to improve the quality of sound in some locations. The term "high fidelity," or more commonly "hi-fi," came into popular parlance in the mid- and late 1950s as consumers demanded more faithful reproduction of original musical performances. Wider frequency response from bass to treble resulted less from technical innovation than from an understanding that a market existed to bear that reproduction's additional cost. Hi-fi became increasingly chic, standard equipment for any enthusiast by the early 1960s.

High-fidelity recordings were increasingly offered in stereo. The first stereo long-playing records (LPs) went to market in 1958 and quickly, two-channel gear—speakers and amplifier—marked the

*Personal transistor radios were the first major piece
of consumer electronics. Americans marveled at
radios no larger than a pack of cigarettes.*

connoisseur. Reel-to-reel tape also conveyed trendiness and Ampex's
1964 player/recorder, which sold for $399, became the first best-seller.
Phillips marketed the first tape cassettes and tape-cassette players that
year but the technology did not become profitable until about 1970.

Portable radios, those not dependent on centrally generated electricity, were cheap enough for almost everyone and became the first
major transistor-based consumer product. Raytheon did manufacture
transistor hearing aids before 1952—Bell Labs waved all patent royal-
ties—but for an extremely limited market.

Patrick Haggerty, president of Texas Instruments, deserves credit
for understanding the transistor radio's potential. He capitalized on
the ascent of youth-oriented, individualistic, rock and roll to establish
a demand for TI's transistors, and persuaded a small company, Re-
gency, to build transistor radios by Christmas 1954 after skeptical
major radio-makers refused Haggerty's initiative. They had good reason to do so. Early transistor circuits were time-consuming, difficult,
and expensive to construct, and were easily broken. The task involved
wiring together by hand thousands of components: transistors, diodes,
resistors, and capacitors. Laborers, usually women, used tweezers to
pick up miniature elements, connected them under magnifying
glasses, and soldered them with toothpick-sized tools.

These new marvels, initially called "personal transistor portable
radios," came with earplugs to permit their use anywhere. IBM's Tom

Watson purchased several of these radios and pronounced himself so impressed that he decreed that IBM would make no new tube-based business machines after June 1, 1958. New battery technologies proved almost as important as transistors in making these audio receivers go. New nickel-cadmium batteries provided these devices extended life, far in excess of the then-standard zinc chloride power packs. Battery use skyrocketed with the new emphasis on choice. Union Carbide, for example, made batteries for hearing aids in the early 1950s and for watches later in the decade. Under its consumer products division, Eveready, the company manufactured the first nine-volt transistor battery for Sony—a later portable radio staple—and developed the first standard alkaline battery. Kodak also drew on batteries. It introduced built-in flash cameras, usable anytime and anywhere but requiring substantial power to trip the flash. Mallory Company made powerful alkaline manganese cells in a new size, AAA, to fit these cameras. Their popularity convinced Mallory to devote itself full-time to making alkaline batteries and in 1964 changed its name to Duracell.

Electronics: Visual

Television granted Americans unprecedented visual access to a wide range of events that they otherwise would have been unable to sample. Cultural events; governmental inquiries, including the McCarthy hearings; and national disasters, such as the assassination of President John F. Kennedy; entered living rooms and enabled Americans to participate in contemporary affairs and culture as never before. Existence of three national networks and, in many places, of several local channels allowed individuals to tailor their choices to their personal tastes. This technology was warmly embraced in early 1950s, for early television seemed a technical marvel. Americans rushed to purchase these huge vacuum-tube-based sets. Small screens, need for frequent repair, poor reception, pictures better described as green and gray rather than black and white, and long warm-up times did not detract from television's initial popularity. Families and others gathered together to view the new medium. Radio and movie audiences plummeted in size. In the later 1950s and early 1960s, solid-state electronics, improved sound and picture quality, and color were added.

Yet by the mid-1950s, several persons were beginning to criticize television programming. Senator Estes Kefauver's congressional committee on juvenile crime in the mid-1950s fingered television as a cause of juvenile delinquency, and Senator Thomas Dodd later chaired a Senate subcommittee in 1961 to investigate television violence. Dodd was especially concerned about syndicated shows, which would be repeated many times and corrupt the nation's youth. FCC Chairman Newton Minow's characterization of the medium in 1961 as "a vast wasteland" typified the then-contemporary critique. Minow complained about the "procession of game shows, violence, audience participation shows, formula comedies about totally unbelievable families, blood and thunder, mayhem, sadism, violence, murder, western bad-men, private eyes, gangsters, more violence and cartoons" broken only by "commercials—many screaming, cajoling and offending." To Minow and others, the medium was not the message; programming was. The problem was not choice itself but that Americans had choices and chose incorrectly; it was not what Americans were offered to watch that was really the problem but rather what they decided and wanted to watch. In that sense, Minow's critique mimicked then contemporary dismissals of new mechanical devices—cars, refrigerators, cameras, and the like—as mere "gadgets." Indeed, *gadget* came to suggest a lack of seriousness, a lack of maturity, on the part of those employing them. To those issuing the critique, Americans had chosen badly. They had not been able or willing to fend off the proliferation of mechanical marvels and debased themselves by accepting these trinkets. Rather than worship the material, Americans should concentrate desire for individual expression and fulfillment on things important to those complaining—the arts, philosophy, and literature. Democracy as an ideal in this Cold War era was frequently raised and Americans generally agreed that democracy meant choice. But while one group saw it as choosing to reject democratic society's material consequences in part because mass-manufactured gadgets implied a "rigidity of taste," an unthinking sameness reminiscent of dogma and communism, another contingent reasoned the opposite. Material plenty and the genius reflected in the design, manufacture, and marketing of these wondrous products was the guts and product of democracy and should be celebrated with pride. As historian David M. Potter noted in 1954, "it is not our ideal of democracy but our export of goods and gadgets, of cheap . . . magic-working machines, which opened new vistas to the human mind and thus made us 'the terrible instigators of social change and revolution.'" Riesman suggested a similar prospect a year later when he called for Americans to replace ideas of a Cold War with a "Nylon War." If Americans dropped consumer goods on Moscow, the act would force the Soviet Union to stop weapon production to manufacture "consumer goods or face mass discontent on an increasing scale."

Videotape Recorders

Early television was limited. Live shows required production crews to broadcast directly from the site. Film provided a noticeable deterioration of quality. Cathode-ray scanning proved different from projection film, and filmed video pictures changed contrast almost by the second. Networks reduced the problem in the early 1950s through kinescope recordings. This technique depended on film—both 35mm and 16mm—but film recorded directly from the face of the cathode-ray tube, not from the actual event. Film then needed to be developed, washed, dried, and projected as negatives. Kinescope technicians recorded sound separately on magnetic audio tape. In less than three hours programs could be broadcast.

This solution pleased few; and several groups, including Bing Crosby Enterprises, RCA—the parent company of NBC—and Ampex, looked to audio recording as a guide to creating a videotape recorder suitable for telecasts. Iron oxide tape remained the only constant between the two mediums. Nascent videotapers needed to devise heads to convert electrical impulses from visual stimulus into magnetic signatures—recording—and then from magnetic signatures to pictures—playback. They had to engineer a drive that would appear to operate at constant speed, even as the tape reels worked at varied speeds, which were measured in inches per second. Techniques to erase tapes—to saturate them for reuse—were essential, as were ways to represent a much greater bandwidth.

Capitalizing on their initial audio success, Crosby Enterprises received the initial contract to deliver video recorders. But its twelve-head recorders soon proved unwieldy. By the mid-1950s, it left the business. RCA had more success. It shunned all attempts to devise a black-and-white machine and went directly to color. But RCA engineers concluded that cathode-ray color—real-life color as a combination of the three primary colors, each from its own cathode ray tube—would require a six- or seven-channel track. Each color required its own channel, as did two for sound and at least one for directions of how to integrate the conglomeration. Even as its engineers worked on these questions, RCA moved on other fronts. It pioneered tension-tape servos to keep speed constant, eddy current brakes to accurately translate current into magnetic markings, luminance/chrominance separation, and synchronization.

Ampex went further. Ray Dolby, a 19-year-old college dropout, joined the firm in 1952 and quickly created the basic videotape circuitry still in use today. In addition to rotary switching, Dolby did away with the mixing problem by using four transverse heads, which scanned and recorded transversely. Two-inch-wide videotape moved past Dolby's heads at either 15 or 7 1/2 inches per second. The heads themselves were mounted on a disk, which rotated rapidly past the tape at right angles to the path of the tape. By 1956, the networks were sold on Dolby's black-and-white machine. Yet Ampex realized that without the ability to tape in color, its dominance would soon end, and in 1957 it signed a cross-licensing agreement with RCA to secure color technology. Ampex then embarked on an aggressive marketing campaign that targeted educational stations. It lent these stations video recorders and encouraged them to tape and broadcast educational activities. But Ampex wanted the stations to lend these tapes to schools, colleges, and the like, all of whom would have to buy machines to show them. RCA competed with a fully transistorized unit in 1960 and another upgrade accentuating ease of operation a year later, but Ampex's domination was secure. In 1962, Ampex sold over a thousand of these $50,000 machines. Two years later its new machine proved the only video recorder to meet the network's enhanced performance standards.

Consumerism: Biochemical

Corresponding to the huge boom in mechanical technologies was a growth of chemical technologies devoted to increasing human options. Pharmaceutical manufacturers concentrated on creating new products to enable individuals to control even the most mundane aspects of human life as well as to free them from the recurring blights of disease. Voluntary associations, government, and others actively assisted in this effort, although all participants understood that it remained the responsibility of the industry to work out the chemical syntheses and industrial manufacturing techniques that would produce the new panaceas. From these labors came entire families of psychotropic drugs to cope in the dizzying, go-go world of the 1950s. Current in the 1950s, the term "coping" replaced more permanent notions of success and control. Coping was a never-ending process; it implied that success and control were temporary states, their maintenance requiring continual adjustment. The initially universally hailed Valium in the early 1960s may well have been the most auspicious of these new site-specific brain drugs. Valium promised to be "mother's little helper," to empower homemakers to overcome those little life nuisances that hampered them from maintaining a smooth existence. But the mind was not the sole locus of the pharmacological industry. Vitamins, sex hormones, and other behavioral modifiers granted individuals the power to design aspects of their lives. For example, the artificial sex hormone DES found extensive and paradoxical use as both a morning-after pill to induce spontaneous abortions in women not wishing to be pregnant and a way to maintain to term problem pregnancies. Jonas Salk's polio vaccine offered temporary immunity to the scourge, and Albert Sabin's permanent vaccine a few years later received the most attention in the war against disease. But the widespread availability of antibiotics, each produced in large industrial fermentation vats, proved a much greater individual health blessing. A host of often-fatal bacterial diseases yielded to these miracle drugs. By 1957, American pharmaceutical companies produced nearly 350 different antibiotic substances.

Reproduction—Personal Choice Pill

Female oral contraceptives convince the body that it is pregnant, prevent ovulation, and therefore prevent pregnancy. Female sex hormones provide the means to mislead the body, but true female animal sex hormones, produced by grinding up ovaries, cost several thousand dollars per ounce, far too expensive for popular usage. Around 1950, another organic source presented itself. Farmers recognized that animals eating certain plants had difficulty bearing young. Investigators postulated that substances in plants acted as female sex hormones to prevent pregnancy—by then researchers had focused on progesterone as the single female hormone that persuaded the animal body of a pregnancy—and they set out to identify these chemicals. These vegetative estrogenic substances were not identical to their animal counterparts; chemists labored to design processes to convert these substances into progesterone or progesterone-like chemicals. For this industrial–organic chemistry synthesis to be successful, chemists had to devise means to change structure and configuration on an industrial scale and to have access to large and plentiful supplies of the plant material. As important, progesterone seemed unstable when taken orally; progesterone required further chemical manipulation to convert it into a substance that was active when swallowed.

By the early 1950s, each of these hurdles had been surmounted. Mexican yams produced an abundant source of the raw material and two pharmaceutical firms, Syntex and Searle, learned to transform the plant material into an orally active human contraceptive. In 1957, an inadvertent contamination led Searle to realize that small amounts of estrogen added to the pill reduced potential side effects and the material became added to the manufacturing process. Searle first introduced the pill as a menstrual regulator, but by 1960 began to offer the drug as an oral contraceptive.

Acceptance of the pill was immediate and dramatic. Many American women opted for the convenience of the pill even before its manufacturers advertised its pregnancy-preventing properties. Over a half-million American women of child-bearing age took the pill regularly in 1959, ostensibly to regulate their menstrual cycles. When the pill finally gained FDA sanction as a contraceptive some years later, it quickly became the contraceptive of choice for many Americans.

Business and Government, Research and Development: Technologies in the Making

Business and industry also shared in the heady atmosphere of the 1950s and 1960s. Both sought to extend options and to open potential markets as investment, progress, and the future all held seemingly infinite promise. Business and industry stressed new ventures, new techniques, and new processes. A vast expansion occurred as new areas of inquiry, new types of business organization and practice, and new business techniques, coupled with venture capital, produced numerous spinoff companies. A strong cultural preference existed for things "new and improved," which signaled relentless progress; the past was to be passed and to remain in the past. Despite the "newness" refrain, many nascent companies in fact depended on older science, particularly the science of the 1920s and 1930s, including solid-state and surface physics. Such was the case with electronic consumer goods. Consumer electronic sales mushroomed from $3.4 billion yearly in 1950 to about $11.5 billion a scant decade later. A corresponding investment in corporate research accompanied this sales boom. Corporations spent $2.6 billion for research and development in 1949, $6.2 billion six years later, and $12.4 billion in 1959. Industrial research laboratories totaled about 5,400 in 1960, nearly doubling in a decade.

Businesses spent freely on research and development because science seemed to offer almost inexhaustible opportunities for profits. Companies needed only to select in which science-heavy areas they opted to specialize or to reorient their previous projects and plans to take advantage of new scientific insights.

The federal government also participated in the research-and-development explosion, but only in part to assist American business and industry. Even though it lacked a personal profit motive, government recognized its obligation to provide a stable, regularized environment for American commerce and manufacturing. Creating such an environment was a twofold task. Government must provide for the public interest in those circumstances where others could not, such as maintaining and even improving the transportation infrastructure. But it also had to ensure that new science, the raw material upon which American business now seemed to depend, was forthcoming at regular intervals. Government investment in research and development, including the creation of the National Science Foundation in 1950, resulted.

A science-centered national economic policy marked a new role for the federal government. There the apparent lessons of World War II proved deterministic. If science did not exactly win the war or even win the then-flourishing Cold War, it nonetheless seemed much too important to ignore. The Department of Defense (DOD) benefited almost immediately. Its budget went from $13 billion in 1949 to $50 billion in 1950. Rarely did it go below $40 billion for the rest of the decade. As impressive was the fact that the research-and-development (R & D) portion of the DOD budget grew faster than the total budget and even faster than business's research-and-development efforts.

To be sure, certain events contributed to the burgeoning defense research and development budget. An intercontinental ballistic missile breakthrough in 1955—the electronically guided missile—the Soviet Union's launch of Sputnik in 1957, and the undeclared war in Vietnam in the mid-1960s led to dramatic increases in defense department R & D. But by the mid- and late 1950s, the federal government had established other ways to funnel funds into scientific research as part of the attack on communism, the ultimate collective, anti-individualistic scheme. Foremost in this new enterprise was enlisting the nation's major private and public colleges and universities. Through fellowships, locating national laboratories at the sites of major research universities, and construction grants, government transferred large sums to these educational institutions. The DOD was hardly alone in this venture. The National Institutes of Health, Atomic Energy Commission, and the USDA each stepped up research funding and channeled ever-increasing amounts to higher education. Federal R & D investment increased an average 14 percent per year in the fifteen years after 1950. Washington created the Advanced Research Projects Agency (ARPA) to coordinate defense-related research with the proviso that such research need not possess immediate applications. The National Defense Education Act (NDEA) of 1958 sealed the government–university compact. It provided extremely low-cost loans, very forgiving cancellation terms, and a lenient repayment schedule to students opting to attend four-year colleges and universities. This act accomplished much more than providing opportunity for a college education. It enabled universities and colleges to raise tuition markedly and to use the extra revenue to support scientific research. Lack of specific earmarks for NDEA money was no accident. Its framers argued that the proper way to pursue science was not to follow one government-mandated path a la the Communists—Lysenko's domination and ruin of Soviet agricultural science served as a model of what not to do—but rather to give rise to individual scientific expression, to let each school's scientific research compete in the marketplace of ideas. As a consequence, the act encouraged each university to design its own individual scientific mission and interests. Yet the situation was not without peril. University embrace of government-funded research occurred so precipitously that President Dwight D. Eisenhower made the centerpiece of his 1961 farewell address the dangers to universities of the massive federal intrusion in their affairs through their dependence on federal science funding.

Controlling Information Flow: Business Machines and Practices

Businesses demanded increased information control. Equally significant, post-1950 businesses included many more individuals in decision-making processes. Scientists and engineers, marketing staffs, advertisers, and designers as well as the more traditional chief operating and financial officers had input in establishing policy, or at least procedures. Each required access to data to make informed choices in this new governance milieu. Speed often was of the essence, and having several copies of important material quickened the process.

Makin' Copies

Prior to about 1950 three ways existed to duplicate documents. Businessmen and women used carbon paper to make a limited number of copies at the same time they made the original or they retyped the document on a ditto master and mimeographed as many copies as they wished. The third means, photostat copies, were no less than photographs. Businesses printed images of documents on photosensitive paper, an expensive and excruciatingly slow process. None of the aforementioned means offered the flexibility necessary for coordinated decision making. With this potential new market in mind, 3M produced the Thermo-Fax office copier around 1952 and Kodak quickly followed with its Verifax. Both used heat-sensitive paper to make photograph-like copies, but neither process proved adequate. After initial exposure, documents continued to darken when exposed to light and quickly became unreadable. Verifax copies had the additional liability of smelling bad as they darkened.

The Haloid Corporation worked at roughly the same time to produce a reliable copying machine according to different principles. Laboring under patents first secured by Chester F. Carlson, an arthritic inventor who found it difficult to copy patent specification by hand, the Rochester, New York-based company experimented with photoconductivity to create what it called electrophotography. Carlson's patents took advantage of the discovery that certain materials—semiconductors—underwent a change in their electrical conductivity when exposed to light. He placed an electrostatic charge on a plate of a semiconductor—selenium was most frequently used—exposed it to light, and then dusted it with powdered ink. The powder adhered to the places charged by exposure to light and the image could be reproduced when touched to paper. The first of these copiers failed to gain a market, not because they did not work but because they were much too complicated, time consuming, and unreliable. Operators had to hoist plates, fiddle with a gravity lever to dispense enough powdered ink to cover the charged plates, crank paper on rolls past the plates, detach the paper from rolls by hand, and perform other similar messy and difficult tasks.

From about 1950, then, the Haloid Corporation, which in 1961 changed its name to Xerox, dealt with engineering, not conceptual, problems, as it strove to make its copying machine virtually automatic. In 1955, an estimated 20 million copies were made worldwide.

A year later, Xerox made more than 20 million copies just testing its machines. Offering devices throughout the 1950s, Xerox became the major business copying tool. Yet it remained until 1960 for Xerox to sweep the market. Its 914 model was truly simple to operate and dependable to use. Its cylindrical selenium-coated drum, which held an electrostatic charge only when dark, replaced the bulky, awkward plates of earlier models. Tractor feeds would position a typed page directly on the drum. A bright, consistent light source shined on the page and the parts of the drum beneath the typed words retained their charge. Oppositely charged powdered toner would be injected over the drum and stick to the charged surface. The drum would then be automatically rotated over a piece of paper and the toner ink would be transferred to the paper. Strong heat would fuse the ink image to the paper and make it permanent as tractor feeds led the paper out of the machine. In 1966, U.S. businesses made over 14 billion Xerox copies.

Manipulating Data and Keeping Track of Stock: Computers

American business likened marshaling data and information to make better business decisions to mobilizing to fight a war. Remington Rand took that model seriously when it hired General Leslie Groves, who had headed the Manhattan Project, to direct its research-and-development efforts. More significant was the company's purchase in 1950 of the patent rights to Mauchly- and Eckert-devised computers. Its UNIVAC became the first significant business computer. The UNIVAC gained incredible publicity for itself and computing generally when, in the first hours after the 1952 presidential election, the machine correctly predicted an Eisenhower landslide. The Korean War provided computers yet another boost. The federal government invested heavily in machines to calculate ballistics and other military-related matters.

By 1955, the newest devices replaced electromechanical relays with vacuum tubes and hard-wired memories with magnetic storage tapes. IBM proved especially adept at marketing these new wonders. They targeted colleges and universities, promising them the most modern computers at deeply discounted prices if the institutions would establish computer courses. This course of action was no accident. Students would learn and train on IBM products, and when they graduated into the business world, would demand that their companies adopt similar products.

IBM's maneuver was so successful that by 1960 American business and government employed more than 5,000 computers. Part of the company's success stemmed from its creation of an "automatic programming" code. As early as 1953 it sought to establish a series of English or algebraic expressions that the computer would automatically convert into binary machine instructions; it would be a formulator–translator as each word or symbol might represent thousands of lines of binary directions. This "vocabulary" could join together a set of activities and therefore decrease or eliminate the need to pay programmers to write each set of instructions from scratch. A computation task that required a programmer's attention for a week or more could be accomplished using a canned vocabulary in a matter of minutes or hours. This new language, FORTRAN (from FORmulator–TRANslator), debuted in April 1957 and quickly became the universal language for scientific computing. The federal government reflected on FORTRAN's immediate success and urged creation of a similar standard language for commercial data processing. Common Business Oriented Language, known as COBOL, was the product. Unlike FORTRAN, COBOL depended on English-like grammar so that business persons could easily see what job was being undertaken. The government insured COBOL's domination when in 1960 it refused to purchase any computer that could not run the language. Dartmouth College furthered compiler-driven computing by creating in 1964 BASIC, a computer language based upon English words and grammar.

In the early 1960s, IBM led the shift from tubes to transistors. Again, a tenfold increase in speed accompanied the transformation. By the middle of the decade, IBM emerged as the world's largest semiconductor manufacturer. The computer giant and other companies developed software to sell their machines. Firms gave away these canned programs for specific tasks, as inducements to adopt their machine. Special payroll, invoicing, stock control, production, and planning programs enhanced machine utility and converted businesses into computer proponents. IBM software proved so popular that Honeywell and GE soon made machines that could run the IBM wares. IBM went a step further, however. In a move that cost over $5 billion in research and development, it established a new unified product line in the early and mid-1960s. Rather than create a series of machines and then write canned programs for each different member of the series, IBM created a series of machines that all used the same software. The same canned programs could run on all of these new machines. The computer had become an indispensable facet of business enterprise.

New Businesses and Business Organizations: The Locus

World War II had proven that electronics had huge commercial and military possibilities. The transistor fortified that position and also drew attention to material science, especially semiconductor research. Several major universities moved expeditiously to capitalize on these new fields. Stanford University was among the most successful. In 1956 it established a new type of institution, the Stanford Industrial

Park. Abutting the university, the park was to attract and provide a haven for embryonic electronics firms by taking advantage of the university and its environs. Stanford professors offered new companies expertise in electrical engineering, while talented students provided a ready-made, highly trained work and design force. Stanford's proximity to various military and naval installations promised new firms lucrative government contracts and its proximity to San Francisco, the West's financial center, made venture capital accessible. The area's pleasant climate and cultural attractions offered further inducement to locate there. The university encouraged graduating students to establish electronics companies in the park or nearby. Such was the case with the park's first tenant, Varian Associates. The Varian brothers developed the pioneering Klystron tube for radar and microwave communications in Stanford's own laboratories a few years earlier.

Spinning Off Again

In 1955 William Shockley left Bell Laboratories to set up Shockley Transistor Company in Palo Alto, near what would become the Stanford Research Park. Shockley's disassociation with Bell Laboratories reflected a situation that would soon become endemic to American business. Creative individuals in scientific or middle-management positions would remain with parent companies for historically short tenures. These men and women routinely left to start up other, often competing firms. As free agents operating in a time of seemingly endless possibilities, they negotiated generous terms with new bosses or became bosses themselves.

Nowhere was the situation more apparent than in semiconductors. In fact, Shockley kept his creative staff together for less than two years before the first group headed off on its own. Led by Robert Noyce, eight Shockley employees negotiated with Fairchild Camera, a small East Coast optics company interested in semiconductor research and development, to establish in 1957 a new, autonomous company, Fairchild Electronics. Fairchild Electronics was not immune to these spinoffs. Persons left to begin their own companies almost from the start. In 1968, for example, Fairchild employees spun off thirteen separate companies.

High Technology: Second-Generation Semiconductors

From the outset of Texas Instruments' transistor radio triumph, various companies had tried to make a better transistor. They attempted to substitute selenium, silicon, boron, and several compounds for germanium and labored to devise means to dope the semiconductors precisely and expeditiously. The extremely plentiful silicon quickly became the semiconductor material of choice, but it required great care in its manufacture. Doping rooms needed to be scrupulously clean and furnaces heated well in excess of 1,000 degrees Centigrade so that the doping substance, generally either boron or arsenic, could vaporize and diffuse into the silicon surface.

But two individuals, Noyce and Jack Kilby, deserve credit for inaugurating the next generation of semiconductor technology. Rather than see transistors as separate pieces of semiconductor material, they envisioned each semiconductor crystal as a potentially complete circuit. Kilby, an original member of the Texas Instruments portable radio team, recognized quite early that silicon could function in ways that mimicked an entire circuit. Everyone knew about the rectifying transistor. But Kilby reasoned that undoped silicon could act as a resistor, while particular n–p junctions could serve as capacitors. If these three types could be included on a single silicon crystal, a complete, speedy, cool, low-voltage circuit could be established. Kilby produced such a circuit in September 1958.

Noyce came to the same conclusion, but from a different angle. His specialty was photolithography, the use of light-sensitive chemicals to etch minuscule structures or prepare them for etching. His initial thought stemmed from the desire to protect doped silicon crystals from contamination. Fairchild regularly coated these crystals with silicon dioxide. Noyce's photoetching techniques enabled him to print copper wires on top of the coating and therefore to make a single-point contact transistor. But Noyce reasoned that if you could establish with printed wires a single-point contact transistor, then you could use printed wires to connect separate transistors on the surface of a single crystal. Only then did Noyce turn his attention to the possibilities of a silicon resistor and capacitor.

Both Noyce and Kilby received patents for ways to place many transistors on a single silicon crystal chip. Their idea of a fully integrated circuit led to exponential increases in speed and flexibility for machine design. Industry quickly adopted this new technology. RCA boasted that its computers operated fully integrated circuits as early as 1964. Kilby remained at TI but Noyce left Fairchild a few years after RCA made its first integrated circuit computer. With fellow employee Gordon Moore, Noyce set up a new company, Intel, in 1968 to manufacture these integrated circuits, called microchips.

Government and the Infrastructure: Transportation for the New Manufacturing

Manufacturers in the post-1950 period increasingly scorned railroads, and that carrier's percentage of the nation's freight haulage dipped well below 30 percent by 1980. It rebounded a bit in the following decade. The much more flexible trucks and buses continually seized a greater share of transportation, and passage of the Federal Highway Construction Act in 1956 was instrumental. Detroit actively lobbied for that act, as did rubber manufacturers, such as Goodrich and Goodyear. The federal government sold off its World War II-era rubber plants to commercial vendors in 1955, and these operators quickly introduced new copolymer and terpolymers, suitable for tires and other uses. The Highway Act specified that funds collected from taxes on gas and tire sales, plus truck use, would go into a new Highway Trust Fund, which would pay for the largest building program in American history: 41,000 miles of interstate highways connecting 90 percent of America's cities with populations of more than 50,000, including 5,000 miles in urban areas, with 90 percent of the cost paid by the federal government, and the states paying the rest. By 1973, 82 percent of the interstate highway system had been completed (although the project's actual costs have far exceeded original estimates) and 16 percent was under construction.

Air

Air transport also contributed to the railroad's demise, becoming the foremost transporter of mail and passengers over long distances even before Boeing introduced the first successful commercial jet, the 707, in 1958. These jet engines added to air's advantages by proving easier to maintain than conventional internal-combustion engines, and by permitting greater passenger and cargo capacity as well as speed.

Government and the Infrastructure: "New and Improved" Environments

Those who did not reach out to redesign and to extend their dominion in the 1950s and 1960s were those who ceased to change, and therefore stagnated. Government aggressively took up the challenge, on both the local and national levels. The Army Corps of Engineers, the nation's largest engineering organization with more than forty thousand employees (most of them civilian), picked up the pace of its long-standing effort to control the Mississippi River. By 1970, the Corps had developed more than twenty-five thousand miles of inland waterways and spent more than $8 billion constructing dams, reservoirs, levees, dikes, floodwalls, and river-channel diversions and enlargements. But state and local efforts, particularly around major metropolitan areas, proved even more striking. The new forms of living in the 1930s, the single-family home, had by the 1950s become a national obsession. Persons fled inner cities for more pleasant suburban environs. Long-standing but unimproved roads linking these places with the cities that spawned them became logistical nightmares. Creation of expressways in metropolitan regions enabled persons to get downtown easily, but they also had the consequence of allowing businesses to relocate on the periphery of cities. There cheaper land, lower taxes, and less congestion prevailed. Metropolitan cities often countered this situation and catered to their citizens by redesigning the urban infrastructure. This urban renewal effort sought to raze those areas deemed troublesome or offensive—slums and tenderloin areas, in particular—to create a state-of-the-art business environment. No one pursued this course more successfully than Robert Moses. Moses redesigned New York City, spending more than $25 billion refurbishing the place as bulldozers razed things deemed old or unprogressive. Moses's up-to-date metropolis was a monument to concrete construction techniques. He built new, more modern housing, business facilities, freeways, bridges, and tunnels to make the city more accessible to daily commuters from Long Island and New Jersey. As important, Moses's activities came to symbolize what was right and possible in mid-century America. His city was the site of options and opportunities.

Government and the Infrastructure: Energy Too Cheap to Meter

The awesome force of nuclear energy also affected peacetime nuclear-power policies. The 1946 Atomic Energy Act, America's first important legislation concerning nuclear technology, established the Atomic Energy Commission (AEC), which monopolized nuclear materials and thus stymied private initiatives even while taking formal control of atomic energy out of the military's hands. The ongoing Cold War made the AEC extraordinarily security-conscious and unwilling to risk civilian efforts. But newly elected President Dwight Eisenhower reversed this trend in 1953 by beginning an "Atoms for Peace" program that encouraged civilian construction of nuclear power plants. The first of these plants, in Shippingport, Pennsylvania, opened in 1957, followed by three others in 1959 and 1960: Rowe, Massachusetts (the Yankee plant); Morris, Illinois (the Dresden); and Indian Point, New York. These and several other early commercial reactors were primarily demonstration models intended to test different reactor designs. Nineteen types were seriously considered, and eleven finally constructed, before light-water varieties were deemed most practical. The nuclear boom continued well into the 1960s, when even the environmentally conscious Sierra Club favored nuclear energy as a clean, environmentally friendly form of power.

*Napalm found extensive use as a defoliant in
Vietnam. At least ten people were killed during this
strike.*

Government and the Nation's Defense

American military might became increasingly technologically dependent. Artificial means seemed to overcome natural limitations. The
Korean conflict made the shortcomings of superior mobilization and
industrial strength apparent. Human-wave assaults overwhelmed superior firepower; when bullets ran out, sheer numbers mattered.
Korea had been fought from precepts similar to those that held during
World War II. The subsequent stalemate demonstrated that any subsequent war depended not upon amassing ground troops for assaults or
even defense but on action at a distance. Electronics, photoptics, and
aerial action had become the basis for conventional war, a fact borne
out in the way that America conducted the Vietnam War. Planes flew
at unprecedented heights, apparently outside the boundaries of radar
detection, although the Soviet Union's downing of the American U-2
spy plane in 1959 would prove otherwise. Electronic gun and bomb
sights permitted precise targeting, while infrared detectors enabled
soldiers to see almost as well by night as by day.

Aerial photography, including use of photosensitive polymers and
precisely measured packets to replenish fouled developing solution,
allowed for almost instantaneous reconnaissance; soldiers could then
target bombs and jungle-clearing defoliants, such as napalm—a Dow
Chemical-produced gasoline gel that proved almost impossible to

remove—white phosphorous, and Agent Orange. Surface-to-air, air-to-air, and air-to-surface missiles became crucial facets of the strike force, as did the ubiquitous helicopter, the ultimate individual fighting weapon.

Lasers

The possibility of creating lasers attracted considerable attention and military money in the 1950s and 1960s because these theoretical devices had remarkable military potential. Lasers could function as weapons, destroying enemy armaments at a distance. Using quantum mechanics, especially the discharge of great amounts of energy when electrons moved to lower quantum states, researchers recognized that production of lasers required them to harness, control, and reinforce that quantum occurrence. (The term laser is an acronym for Light Amplification by Stimulated Emission of Radiation.) By the early 1950s, the components of the problem were clear. Researchers had to devise regenerative circuits to get electrons to feed back radiation on themselves to keep them in perpetual states of excitation. They must keep the emissions at a constant wavelength and have waves of the same length in phase with one another. Finally, investigators needed to channel the energy release at a constant rate to form a continuous beam. The earliest work revolved around finding a substance and shape to enhance coherence and included universities, such as MIT and Columbia, as well as GE, Bell Labs, and IBM. By 1960, this consortium of experimenters had created two types of lasers: ammonia gas and synthetic ruby. Of the two, the synthetic ruby proved more promising. Cylindrical, with its ends polished into mirrored surfaces, the ruby was excited by a flashbulb located near the end and was able to emit brief laser pulses.

Use of the ruby confirmed the virtues of crystalline substances, and in 1962 investigators created the first semiconductor lasers. Years of experience doping silicon and other material enabled researchers to use similar techniques to tune lasers with increasing precision and therefore power. But the military and others also found another use for the laser's intense, directional beam. A coherent light source could transmit an incredible amount of information over distances. Photodiodes could receive and decode this data. By the late 1960s the military introduced lasers to carry information in Vietnam.

Nuclear Weapons

Some conflicts seemed to rely on conventional weaponry, but the United States' Cold War policies depended on its nuclear capabilities. As early as 1957, the nation placed its faith in nuclear-powered submarines carrying nuclear warhead-tipped missiles. These vessels were hard to detect, remained submerged for long periods, and delivered their weapons at a moment's notice. Although nuclear weapons were essential to the nation's defense, disarmament protests began soon after the Soviet Union exploded its hydrogen bomb in 1955, and persisted into the early 1960s. A thriving bomb-shelter industry emerged, and movies, novels, and television offered visions of a world after nuclear war. Nuclear war seemed inevitable, especially in October 1962, when America blockaded Cuba to force out Soviet nuclear weapons. In general, Americans accepted the possibility of a nuclear war fatalistically, as the price to pay to protect democracy, and naively made preparations for life after the event.

Citizens' groups in America reacted more passionately to the disclosure that atmospheric nuclear tests released large quantities of radioactive strontium 90, which found its way into cows' milk, and pressed the government to stop that practice. The Soviet Union and the United States agreed in 1963 to end atmospheric tests, but continued underground testing as both nations sought technological breakthroughs and labored to increase nuclear "throw weight" and accuracy. One-hundred-megaton bombs, each the equivalent of a hundred million tons of TNT, entered arsenals.

SPACEFLIGHT

The history of spaceflight was inextricably bound up with the Cold War. The "Space Age" formally began on October 4, 1957, when the Soviet Union successfully launched the first artificial satellite, *Sputnik I*. This technological achievement by the supposedly backward Soviets shocked Americans, as did the launching a month later of *Sputnik II* (which carried a dog), and the failure another month later of an American satellite launch. Together they spurred an unprecedented American commitment to space exploration. Within a year President Eisenhower established the National Aeronautics and Space Administration (NASA). Its enabling legislation declared that "it is the policy of the United States that activities in space should be devoted to peaceful purposes for the benefit of all mankind." By January 31, 1958, America's first successful satellite, *Explorer I*, had been launched, followed by *Vanguard I* on March 17, 1958.

Yet from the start, the phrase "space race" between America and the Soviet Union was more accurate than "space age." The race was invigorated on April 12, 1961, when cosmonaut Yuri Gagarin in *Vostok I* became the first person to orbit the earth and return safely. On May 25, 1961, President John Kennedy stirred the nation with a pledge to land a man on the moon, before the Soviets, by 1970, a move that increased public interest and federal funding.

Yuri Gagarin, the first human to orbit Earth, again
dons his spacesuit to star in the Soviet documentary,
"First Voyage to the Stars."

The seven original *Mercury* astronauts—described by some as the Cold War equivalent of medieval knights individually battling godless communism—became national heroes as they ventured into space. Their most memorable flights were those of Alan Shepard (on May 5, 1961, aboard *Mercury 3*, the first American in space) and John Glenn (on February 20, 1962, aboard *Mercury 6*, the first American to orbit the earth). Following the Mercury program (1958–1963) came the Gemini program (1962–1966), which included the world's first successful orbital rendezvous and manned flights of record length. It was succeeded by the Apollo moon program (1961–1972), which competed with superior Soviet rocket thrusters by developing more powerful booster rockets and lunar landing vehicles. This program culminated with the *Apollo 11* moon landing of July 20, 1969. As millions around the world watched, Neil Armstrong and Edwin "Buzz" Aldrin conducted experiments on its surface, collected rock and soil samples, and returned safely to earth.

FOR FURTHER READING

Armi, C. Edson. *The Art of American Car Design* (1988).

Barnouw, Erik. *Tube of Plenty: The Evolution of American Television* (1975).

Boyne, Walter J. *Power Behind the Wheel* (1988).

Braun, Ernest, and Stuart MacDonald. *Revolution in Miniature.* rev. ed. (1982).

Bromberg, Joan Lisa. *The Laser in America, 1950–1970* (1991).

Burns, Alan. *The Microchip* (1981).

Clark, Clifford Edward, Jr. *The American Family Home, 1800–1960* (1986).

Cravens, Hamilton. *Before Head Start: The Iowa Station and America's Children* (1993).

Fairbanks, Jonathan L., and Elizabeth Bidwell Bates. *American Furniture: 1620 to the Present* (1981).

Halberstam, David. *The Fifties* (1993).

Hayden, Dolores. *Redesigning the American Dream: The Future of Housing, Work and Family Life* (1984).

Hightower, Jim. *Hard Tomatoes, Hard Times,* rev. ed. (1984).

Hurt, R. Douglas. *American Agriculture: A Brief History* (1994).

Kelly, Barbara M. *Expanding the American Dream: Building and Rebuilding Levittown* (1993).

Leslie, Stuart W. *The Cold War and American Science: The Military-Industrial-Academic Complex at MIT and Stanford* (1993).

MacIntosh, R. W. D. *Frozen Foods: The Growth of an Industry* (1962).

Marling, Karal Ann. *As Seen on TV: The Visual Culture of Everyday Life in the 1950s* (1994).

Morawetz, Herbert. *Polymers: The Origins and Growth of a Science* (1985).

Mossman, S. T. I., and P. J. T. Morris. *The Development of Plastics* (1994).

Nmungwun, Aaron Foisi. *Video Recording Technology* (1989).

Robertson, William H. *An Illustrated History of Contraception* (1990).

Schiffer, Michael Brian. *The Portable Radio in American Life* (1991).

Skaggs, Jimmy M. *Prime Cut. Livestock Raising and Meatpacking in the United States 1607–1983* (1986).

Williams, Edwin William. *Frozen Foods: Biography of an Industry* (1970).

Wilson, John T. *Academic Science, Higher Education, and the Federal Government, 1950–1983* (1983).

Public and Private:
Technology as a Social Question:
The Later 1960s to the 1990s

ESTABLISHED TECHNOLOGIES AND
THE QUALITY OF LIFE, OR NEW TECHNOLOGIES
AND OLD ISSUES

By the later 1960s, the chemically intensive, hybrid seed-dependent agriculture of the postwar period was under considerable scrutiny. Rachel Carson's pioneering critique of DDT had come to symbolize the potential dangers of the "Green Revolution." Although the revolutionary green technologies of the 1950s and 1960s resulted in skyrocketing agricultural yields, they apparently came at a price. In her classic *Silent Spring* (1962), Carson made connections between DDT's use as a pesticide and the upsetting of nature's ecological balance. Many traditional wildlife species, unable to reproduce in sufficiently healthy numbers, died out. She also detected a sudden rise of cancer, leukemia, hypertension, and cirrhosis of the liver rates in persons living in areas of heavy pesticide use or eating foods contaminated by them. Yet Carson, a fish and wildlife biologist, initially lacked support of her peers. Most scientists decried Carson's claims. But other chemical agents were soon identified as biohazards. For example, the herbicide 2,4,5-T was cited as apparently causing birth defects in animals and humans.

Carson's initiative, and protests, lawsuits, and legislation by others, resulted in a virtual DDT ban. The 1979 ban allows only special use of 2,4,5-T. The way American agriculture was conducted, its heavy fertilizer, pesticide, and herbicide application, irrigation systems, and aquifer and ground water pollution all became fit subjects of public debate in the wake of Carson's crusade. Both federal and state laws banned some substances and practices and more tightly regulated others. Other, presumably safer, pesticides and herbicides continue in use. Integrated pest management (which considers the environment as a whole), sometimes without chemicals, has made inroads, as have more traditional solutions, such as introduction of pest predators, lures, and drainage.

But as agricultural producers have reexamined pesticide and herbicide usage and had it reexamined for them, just the opposite has happened in personal lawn care. In 1988, American homeowners placed 67 million pounds of pesticides on their lawns, worth over $700 million. That was roughly ten times as much pesticide use as that of American farmers in the same year. In 1984, American lawns received more fertilizer simply to keep them lush than all of India used to grow crops to feed nearly a half-billion humans.

Infatuation with lawn care had other consequences. Fertilizer manufacture is a highly fossil fuel-dependent industry; it expends a nonrenewable resource and produces massive amounts of carbon dioxide, implicated in global warming scenarios. Ground water pollution also results from chemicalized lawn care. Over 30 percent of the water used on the East Coast and double that on the West Coast goes to lawns, where it picks up pesticides, herbicides, and fertilizers and runs off with those contaminants to underground aquifers, the origin of much of America's drinking water.

Entire industries have risen to provide lawn care. Sales of edgers, fertilizer spreaders, leaf blowers, turf aerators, rider mowers, and the like exceeded $4.5 billion in the United States during 1991.

Sod farming has also flourished. An average sod lawn of 5,000 square feet cost about $1,500 that year. With these new practices came new companies. Over 10 million Americans subscribe to professional lawn care companies, which now number over 6,000.

Grass seeds have been engineered to approach genetic uniformity. A few types, noted for their lushness and deep green color, have been produced as more diverse grass breeds have been allowed to go out of existence and their genetic stock lost.

Little note has been taken of the heavily technologically dependent lawn care revolution. The contrast to American agriculture is revealing. Concern about agricultural hybridization as a biological menace has been a long-standing issue. The hybrids' greater genetic uniformity compared to the native strains they have replaced makes them susceptible to a single plague. A new disease strain or insect pest could wipe out a year's harvest; the 1970 corn-leaf blight killed a fifth

*Keeping up the yard, house, and automobile proved
new chores for first-time homeowners. Riding
lawnmowers and other mechanical contrivances
seemed to ease the workload.*

of the South's corn crop. Other agricultural commentators have worried about irretrievable loss of distinctly different germ plasms as natural varieties are broken down into their constituent pure breeds.
They fear that seemingly nonproductive purebreds will be destroyed,
but that those pure strains might have proved essential in the future;
such plants could have a crucial resistance to a new disease or pest.

An economic critique of the Green Revolution accompanied biological fears. By the 1970s, commentators regularly asserted that
Americans had needlessly created a capital-intensive agriculture
marked by larger and larger farms in fewer hands. Rural areas had
lost people, and the quality of rural life plummeted. Critics also contended that experts at the United States Department of Agriculture
(USDA) and land-grant universities produced this agriculture, which
made it impossible for small family farms to compete. But there remain other perspectives. Consumer groups have maintained that
American agriculture is hopelessly antiquated; its bias towards
smaller, inefficient production units, such as family farms, is simply
emotional and has accomplished little more than driving food prices
up and keeping them high.

The dramatic consequences of the Davis tomato, which to many
has come to symbolize the folly of the Green Revolution, pointed to
the economic fallout of high-tech agricultural mechanization. By 1967,
the hard tomato and mechanical harvester combination was used on

90 percent of California's tomato acreage, easily a majority of the nation's crop. An estimated 32,000 migrant tomato-pickers lost their jobs. Although California tomato acreage actually increased, three-quarters of the state's tomato farmers left the business, selling their land to larger growers. Formerly significant tomato production in the states of New Jersey and Ohio was virtually eliminated. Similar harvester–produce combinations are employed for lettuce, grapes, and other crops, resulting in similar "technological unemployment."

Individuation, Limits, and Society

Why did the Green Revolution engender so much public attention and approbation while the practices of homeowners went virtually unnoticed? What was at the root of this apparent disjunction between what food producers were required to do and what homeowners had chosen to have done?

As it turns out, the Green Revolution/lawn-care dichotomy is merely symptomatic of a larger phenomenon, one that initially emerged from ideas of society and social organization first articulated in the late 1960s. The first received definition as a public matter, a case where a small social group potentially foisted its noxious technology onto virtually everyone, while the second was identified as a private matter, a question of individual rights and happiness.

The relative merits of either stance are not the issue here. Nor is the question of whether one or the other position was right, correct, or true. Crucial is understanding the parameters of the new view, a view that provided the framework for the late 1960s and after. This new social world was rigorously personalized. A compelling sense of material and spiritual limits cast the individualism of the 1950s and 1960s in a new light. For the first time, individuals seemed cast off, bound to no one and unable to rely on anyone else. Yet this new view ought not be confused with total individual isolation, disengagement, or freedom. Instead of complete separation from all else, each individual seemed to rest alone at the vortex of a seemingly endless set of social interactions. Forces external to the individual—persons, institutions, policies (all manner of human interactions)—exerted powers on him or her. These impingements interfered with each person's strivings, and hampering those strivings produced frustration, depression, and anger. Individuals responded to this urgent, apparent sense of socially generated restriction and restraint in the only manner that seemed feasible; they took it as a personal attack. With no one to rely upon, and with their material and spiritual survival depending entirely on their own efforts, they acted on their own behalf. These actions were extraordinary in their scope, ranging from joining coalitions focusing on single issues, to engaging in public protests or violence, to simple grumbling and other

The term "environmentally friendly" became a potent sales pitch in the 1970s, replacing the "new and improved" pitch of an earlier era.

antisocial behavior. Only through action of some kind could they empower themselves, convert themselves from passive creatures—victims—into active participants, and hope to achieve or receive what social distance or respect to which they felt they had been entitled. To remain mute or idle was to guarantee failure and to become complicit in your own downfall.

Put another way, this was a world of limits, itself a potent reminder of the existence of forces external to the individual, where the economic and spiritual pie seemed finite. And whenever any person or group received a piece of the pie, there remained that much less to be divided among others. Even more distressing were those incidents in which persons appeared to receive portions of the pie to which they were not entitled or seized more than a "fair" share. Those situations were not merely disconcerting but downright menacing. With limited resources, gluttony and greed were not questions of conscience but became instead socially destabilizing sins.

But the matter proved far more complicated than simple avarice. Each decision was personalized as individual autonomy was desirable, even prized. Objective measures, measures that huge segments of society agreed upon, did not exist. The individual and each individual's determinations of each particular situation reigned supreme. What the individual felt and, therefore, knew it was missing—not some measurable deviation from a precisely articulated and reasoned-out norm—was critical. Here virtually any personal stance, any individual position or perspective, seemed defensible by the person or persons espousing it.

This period's verbiage reflected this intellectual framework. Psychobabble—with its mantras of "I'm OK, You're OK," "maintaining your own private space," "assertiveness training," "releasing your inner child," and "getting in touch with your feminine (or masculine) side"—sought personal healing. This meant getting "centered"—and, therefore, being empowered. Personal identity, often arrived at after the passionate investigation of one's biological/racial/religious/social/national/ and/or geographic heritage, was treated as if it were indelible and used as explanation for the status quo; like personal psychology, it was a social force with which to be reckoned. As with psychology, personal fulfillment meant personal expression, in this case recovering what was missing or had been forgotten; individuals decided what promises they needed to keep to God, to a spouse, or to a heritage in order to emerge as complete.

In the political sphere, the terms "participation," "sharing," and "dialogue" had lost their long-standing meanings to become nothing less than demands that authority be ceded over a specific segment or social area, which often meant isolating the members of that area from the effects of others and, thus, freeing them from some of the stifling social forces. This discourse was juxtaposed with another, calling for Americans to "get government off our backs," "unleash free enterprise," revive "individual prerogative," and "restore traditional American values." Despite their apparent difference in tone and thrust, each of the aforementioned political agendas took a similar thing for granted: the supremacy of the individual and the fact that others received unfair advantages in a limited world and therefore infringed upon and hampered quest for spiritual and material self-fulfillment, which necessarily had to take place in a social sphere. Everything and everybody was wrong. It simply depended upon which individual was doing the evaluation to determine the culprit in any particular case.

Technology quite naturally received a lion's share of attention. It stood as a far-reaching, multifaceted force. Its effects seemed everywhere. Persons used the term *technology* either to focus on an individual technology, such as television, or as if it constituted a single entity, a monolithic force. In the latter case, it served as a useful substitute for all manner of social impingement. Persons could posit blame for the status quo on technology, the few who "created" it, or "the organization" that sustains it. In all cases, however, type of analysis was similar. Americans demanded to know or understand technology's impact on society. Within that broad context, disagreement raged. To some, technology remained a social blessing, pristine in every way, while to others it was a villain, a destroyer of individual expression or fulfillment. But most post-1970 Americans adopted neither position outright. They saw technology as a force, but not as monolithic, regarding it instead as a social question. Some technologies seemed harmful and others beneficial, but most appeared to combine aspects of the two extremes; technology was both a social solution and progenitor of social problems. Relationships between technology and society became more explicit in the post-1960s decades. What constituted the most crucial relationships in any particular case, however, was the individual's province to decide.

Long-held adjudication mechanisms fell under this individualistic onslaught. Reliance on experts as impartial analysts was one casualty. By the late 1960s, any thought of a coherent expert opinion had become a pipe dream. Debates and disputes took place in public, not within the confines of professional organizations. Antagonists regularly sought—and found—experts to sustain their differing positions. Newspapers frequently served as forums for these often contentious displays. And the way that one argued in a newspaper was considerably different from the dispassionate forms prized in engineering or scientific societies. Swinging public opinion required drama, perhaps even hyperbole. Issues were cast in black and white, either as harmless or as dreadful menace. Only in that way could disputants build a majoritarian opinion in support of their position. But majorities proved ad hoc and temporary, as individuals retained the right to modify their initial assessments as they sought to achieve autonomy. Public debate flourished, but the public interest was not necessarily served.

Much, even most, of the contentiousness revolved around technologies familiar to many Americans. Nuclear power, television, the space race, and similar well-established technologies, developed in the 1950s and earlier, bore the brunt of the technology as social question assault. So, too, did oil spills, radiation from magnetic fields such as power lines or computer screens, and toxic waste disposal. Americans poured out their personal frustrations and fears on the familiar, leaving untouched the unfamiliar, such as technologies in development but not yet introduced on a mass scale or introduced but not recognized as new. And when many of these new technologies were in fact introduced or became well known, those presenting them had learned to be savvy about the public sphere in which these new technologies competed. Unlike established technologies, which already had a reputation and a history before the 1970s, advocates of these new, later technologies marketed them in a way that seemed to reduce or mitigate their threat to individual autonomy. Slogans such as user-friendly or environmentally friendly replaced the "new and improved" of an earlier era. Enthusiasts needed to convince an individuated public of their technologies being beneficial, benign, or unavoidable; new technologies must not intrude upon individual autonomy and perhaps should even assist individuals in isolating themselves from social forces. The method proponents chose was relatively straightforward and in keeping with the period's rigid individuation. They opted to personalize each new technological innovation. Rather than dwell on larger issues, they sculpted it to something manageable, approachable, and seemingly profitable to each person. Instead of casting their efforts toward social units or groups at all, these men and women targeted their crusades squarely at the individual as if each was hermetically sealed from social action or interaction or sought to achieve that goal. And without invoking society or attempting to establish a broad social purpose beyond individual liberation through isolation/autonomy, the question of a technology's impact upon society fell away. It had become meaningless, redefined out of existence, a casualty of the new discourse.

Certainly by the later 1980s, some proponents of established technologies now under attack for nearly two decades understood the radically altered milieu in which they operated and labored to redesign their public face and campaigns to present themselves and their technological products as more palatable, less menacing, perhaps even as technological marvels. As in the case of new technologies, old technologies gained standing when they demonstrated utility in fostering individual autonomy and freedom from social encroachments.

This complicated argument will be considered in two distinct parts. This chapter will discuss old technologies and the public response from the late 1960s to the 1990s, while the next chapter will consider during the same period new technologies and those old technologies made new again in the 1980s and after.

Established Nationwide Technological Programs

The nuclear power industry symbolized the intense public debates over the social costs of technologies as reactors designed in the 1950s came on line in the mid-1960s. These grand complexes were larger in size and capacity than their predecessors and, in theory, lower in cost. Each operated like earlier models. Nuclear fission produced heat. The heat was removed by water, which became steam. This superheated steam

This nuclear plant at Three Mile Island,
Pennsylvania, was the site in 1979 of America's
most serious nuclear accident.

caused a turbine to spin, the shaft of which was connected to an electrical generator. Electricity was then carried out of the facility on power lines and the exhausted steam condensed and pumped back into the reactor. But these newer devices had much more strenuous safeguards than older reactors. Each nuclear pellet—the fission site—remained sheathed in a dense metal tube. Six-inch-thick steel walls encircled the fuel assemblies and constituted the core, which was engulfed in water. A concrete wall was next, generally from four to seven feet thick. Other layers of steel and concrete often surrounded these walls. Alternative water sources for emergency core cooling and use of both human and automatic controllers provided redundancies in case one system failed.

Rising coal and gasoline prices, and growing concerns over environmental pollution from coal-fired plants and over diminished fossil fuels, spurred these projects, as did federal financial assistance. For a time, half of all new power plants were nuclear, and what had been costly individual demonstration units became integrated into a seemingly viable industry. But their construction also engendered public concern.

Throughout the later 1960s and into the 1970s, public protests and demonstrations accompanied each new reactor opening, which totaled sixty by 1979. Protesters sometimes chained themselves to fences at reactor sites or stormed the facility. Yet this concern palled when compared to the 1979 debacle at central Pennsylvania's Three Mile Island (TMI) plant. The TMI reactor nearly suffered a "meltdown," or melting of the reactor core, with consequent uncontrolled release of radioactive material into the atmosphere.

The inability or unwillingness of any technical expert or utility company official on the scene to explain to the public exactly what had happened, and what hazards might exist, proved more damaging than the incident itself. And the TMI incident was considerably less serious than the apparent meltdown in 1986 at Chernobyl in the Soviet Union. But the TMI accident helped sway American public opinion away from support of nuclear power. Especially after TMI, lengthy, costly legal and environmental battles delayed and often halted projects, including many already partially built, or even some that had been completed after expenditures of billions of dollars.

The repeated newspaper, magazine, radio, and television advertisements by the nuclear industry (after TMI and then Chernobyl) stating that at least American nuclear plants are inherently safe, if no longer so inexpensive to operate, have largely fallen on deaf ears. TMI itself is still being decontaminated. Forecasts on the eve of TMI of a rise in the percentage of American electricity produced from nuclear power—from 10 percent in 1978, to 20 percent by 1985, to 50 percent by 2000—have proved false.

In addition, concerns have arisen about earthquakes, airplane crashes, and sabotage destroying nuclear plants; about transportation and storage of hazardous nuclear waste products; and about manufacture of reactors by unfriendly countries. Ironically, greater attention to energy conservation, combined with relatively modest oil and natural gas prices, have meant reduced need for the kind of endless electrical power growth anticipated earlier and used to justify building most nuclear plants. Contributing as well to this change has been renewed interest in alternative energy sources such as water, wind, sunlight, and geothermal sites. Indeed, electricity from newer coal plants has become cheaper than that from newer nuclear plants.

Yet it would be premature to write the nuclear power industry's obituary. Need for ever more electrical power will rise again. Alternative energy sources are insufficient and fossil fuels remain finite. Global warming, a likely consequence of fossil fuel consumption, may lurk over the horizon.

Nuclear power controversies thus epitomize the declining contemporary faith in technical expertise, and the parallel public concern over the potential implications of many technological pursuits. Few technologies, in fact, have been as widely associated as nuclear power with social and economic advance. Prophecies of not just virtually free electricity ("power too cheap to meter") but also the elimination of hunger, disease, normal aging, air pollution, slums, and even war were common after World War II. So, too, were forecasts of "miniature reactors" in every home and factory, "atomic engines" in every family car and truck and in every commercial ship and airliner, and "radioactive fertilizers" for every farm. Some envisioned small nuclear explosions to expedite various navigation and irrigation projects.

Symbolic, perhaps, of the controversies surrounding nuclear power is the ongoing dismantling and eventual burial of the Shippingport nuclear reactor, following its 1982 closing. Robots are dismantling the plant to reduce human exposure to radioactivity, and the radioactive sections then will be barged down the Ohio and Mississippi Rivers, through the Panama Canal, to a burial site in Hanford, Washington, where plutonium was first produced. The ground on which the reactor has stood eventually will be returned to its original contours and sodded—once made free of manmade radioactivity. This process will cost far more than the facility's original construction. Other later, larger reactors and several early nuclear-powered submarines will undergo similar procedures, with their radioactive sections likewise transported to Hanford or to other public or private burial sites. Simple demolition or abandonment of reactors or, with submarines, sea burial, would not contain the radioactivity and would thus pose environmental hazards. Indeed, many reactors due to reach the end of their lives (generally, thirty years) by shortly after the turn of the century instead may be either entombed in concrete or non-reactive glass, or mothballed behind guarded fences for many years until their radioactivity diminishes, and only then be dismantled.

Not surprisingly, the federal government's 1986 announcement that America's first nuclear-waste dump would be built in the West, rather than the East or the Midwest, brought cheers from the latter two regions and sighs and protest from the first—where nuclear power long has been most favored. Meanwhile, as experiments continue in New Mexico on potential burial techniques, the Hanford complex remains off-line because of various safety violations and concerns, thus disrupting plutonium production. Still, two University of Michigan nuclear engineers lament, "We suspect that if nuclear power is to be accepted and implemented, it will [nowadays] be only as a last resort, when the public realizes that all other options . . . have been exhausted or recognized as unsuitable or insufficient."

National Defense and Nuclear Debate

Public clamor intensified in the late 1960s and early 1970s as both the Soviet Union and the United States engaged in another Cold War battle by building larger nuclear stockpiles. Other countries, most notably

China and Israel, also joined the nuclear weapon club. Cold War catch-words proved as chilling. Mutually Assured Destruction (MAD), Multiple Independently Targeted Reentry Vehicles (MIRVs), and "window of vulnerability" became euphemisms for thinking the unthinkable.

Perhaps because of less-than-complete support among their citizens, America and the Soviet Union began Strategic Arms Limitation Talks (SALT), and reached two accords. SALT I (1972) established temporary offensive-weapon limits (subsequent treaties were to make final determinations) and prohibited sea- and space-based anti-ballistic missile development, testing, and deployment. The U.S. Senate never ratified SALT II (1979), although both nations roughly abide by its provisions. It controls the number and type of nuclear weapons and limits new system development and testing. Ultrasensitive electronic monitoring gear, as well as conventional intelligence gathering, guarantee both countries' compliance.

Americans in the mid-1970s carried the nuclear debate to a new level. Led by a disparate collection of technicians and scientists, opponents of nuclear weapons asked whether the nation possessed the technical and scientific capability to undertake certain projects, and whether those projects would fulfill their advocates' expectations. Disputes raged over the potential effectiveness of superhardened silos for intercontinental ballistic missiles (ICBMs), and the desirability of mounting ICBMs on mobile railroad cars. President Ronald Reagan's Strategic Defense Initiative (SDI), or "Star Wars," further focused debate in the 1980s. Many prominent scientists, engineers, and lay persons condemned the plan to destroy enemy nuclear missiles in outer space—a nuclear shield—as unworkable, untestable, and outrageously expensive. SDI's defenders contended that the proposed system of hundreds of lasers, mirrors, and targeting instruments could be coordinated, that it would distinguish between weapons and decoys, and that it merited the expense.

Concerns also had arisen about nuclear war's aftermath. Some scientists maintained that a nuclear exchange would produce enough smoke and atmospheric debris to cause severe cold and darkness across the globe, creating a "nuclear winter" lasting several years. Others predicted only a brief nuclear "autumn." Both relied on computer simulations to prove their points, but data fed into computers varied and, as a consequence, so, too, did conclusions. Similarly, some supported the concept of limited nuclear war (limited in either the number of missiles launched or the geographical areas affected), while others worried about accidental nuclear war produced by the very systems designed to prevent such catastrophes. What had been portrayed as frightening fantasies in such movies as *FailSafe* (1962) and *War Games* (1983) seemed painfully real. Still others disputed America's ability to respond to nuclear attacks and argued that a single warhead could disrupt the nation's power grid, wipe out computer memories, and create political, social, and economic chaos.

In 1993 the General Accounting Office provided declassified summaries of the first comprehensive review in thirty years of the nation's nuclear arsenal. Pentagon officials had deliberately exaggerated both the Soviet nuclear threat and the capabilities of high-tech weapons systems designed to counter it, from the B-1 bomber to the MX missile. By contrast, the huge costs of those systems were intentionally underestimated by billions of dollars.

Doomsday scenarios seem more distant since the collapse of the former Soviet Union. Russia and the United States have agreed to stop targeting each other. Decommissioning a large number of nuclear warheads is scheduled. Yet reduced threats of a global nuclear holocaust have produced new issues, not the least of which is the dismantling of much of America's and Russia's nuclear weapons. Technologies to accomplish this task exist in a rudimentary fashion. Yet debate continues between the two countries about the permanence of the techniques, who needs to pay the huge costs, and where the fissionable material will be stored to protect against environmental contamination or terrorist attacks.

Americans also learned that the Cold War had other costs. President Clinton acknowledged that the federal government in the 1950s had conducted experiments designed to determine what would happen to those surviving a nuclear attack and had subjected citizens in several Rocky Mountain states to large radiation doses. Clinton belatedly apologized for that action.

Decline of Support for the Space Program

Public and congressional support declined sharply after the 1969 moon landing, which seemed a grand climax rather than a stage in ongoing "space-faring" activities. America had won the part of the Cold War that had begun with Sputnik; the nation landed a man on the moon before the Soviet Union and thus demonstrated its mastery. Indeed, public interest in this monumental event was short-lived; five successive moon landings attracted far smaller television audiences. More important, Americans questioned whether the space program was worth the money. What exactly beyond a desire to soar in the heavens did citizens receive from the program? Were there not more compelling social issues here on earth? Not surprisingly, the twenty-fifth anniversary of the moon landing generated far less celebration that the twenty-fifth anniversary of the opening of major bridges and dams. Indeed, environmental concerns over possible future degradation of the moon's surface by further landings, along with anxieties over the growing debris floating in space—roughly 3.5 million pieces of space junk—also diminished the celebratory spirit.

In 1972 NASA began the space-shuttle program to provide practical means for further scientific exploration, future colonization, and commercial activities (especially carrying private communications satellites, including foreign ones, into space). NASA had long been involved in commercial ventures and in 1962 had launched Bell Telephone's *Telstar I* satellite. Constantly orbiting satellites are now routinely used for business communications and weather reports, as well as for military surveillance. The shuttle, however, promised to be more practical than its predecessors: a reusable spacecraft—including its fuel tanks, orbiter, and, not least, booster rockets, which would fall into the ocean once the satellite was in space. The shuttle would save millions of dollars otherwise spent on new vehicles; a key public criticism of NASA was cost. The shuttle would make space transportation routine. It also would service the space stations that NASA deemed its next major project.

The shuttle's appealing multiple uses promised to keep NASA alive following the loss of purpose and support after the Apollo program ended. Getting crucial military support required major design modifications, such as limiting efficiency for high-orbit launches, while obtaining President Nixon's approval necessitated severe funding cutbacks and in turn other design changes, such as reduced payload capacity. These alterations and budget cuts affected the shuttle's overall development and contributed to technical problems and cost overruns that plagued it from the start. Indeed, NASA canceled other, less-expensive projects of potentially more scientific value than the shuttle to compensate for those added expenditures. The shuttle's final cost of $11 billion doubled NASA's original estimate. Meanwhile, the European Space Agency, a cooperative organization started in 1972, developed the largely French-built *Ariane* rocket booster at one-twelfth the shuttle's cost, using older and cheaper components to launch satellites at competitive prices. Its first successful launch was in 1979.

The initial twenty-four shuttle missions, beginning with *Columbia* on April 12, 1981, were generally so successful that renewed public interest in the space program had faded once again by the time of the *Challenger* explosion on January 28, 1986. By then, it was widely assumed, shuttle missions were almost routine spaceflights (it was not accidental that America's first female astronaut, Sally Ride, went into space aboard a shuttle in 1983). That tragedy, however, not only claimed seven lives—among them that of the first "teacher in space," civilian Christa McAuliffe—but also postponed for years further shuttle launches, as well as future NASA projects like space stations.

The aftermath of the *Challenger* tragedy also publicized long-standing tensions between NASA and the military—which has its own ongoing space projects—regarding priorities, planning, oversight, and secrecy; competition between NASA and European cooperative ventures with European-made rockets; tensions within NASA over occupied versus unoccupied vehicles, and over large, expensive, showy projects favored by engineers versus smaller, cheaper, less visible ones favored by scientists; and tensions among NASA's top administrators and lower-ranking technicians over shuttle safety. The inability or refusal of key NASA officials to explain the situation to the public until forced to do so by government investigation, along with their extreme reluctance to take responsibility for their decisions, damaged public confidence in them.

The initial fiasco surrounding the Hubbell telescope may have marked the nadir of the space program. At an unprecedented cost of $3 billion, the shuttle crew undertook a mission that many Americans greeted skeptically. NASA was to position a huge telescope beyond the earth's atmosphere to get clear pictures of the heavens. This dubious mission came to a poor end when once positioned the expensive telescope failed to operate. Apparently at least one mirror was connected improperly and the telescope's performance suffered. Knowing nods greeted this characteristic failure on Earth.

Technologists and Public Criticism

Technologists have responded to public criticism like that leveled on the space program, nuclear power, and nuclear weapons in very different ways. Some have stressed that technical experts do indeed worry about ethics and the quality of life, and have formed such organizations as the Union of Concerned Scientists and Physicians for Social Responsibility to act on them. Others have chosen to meet the challenge head-on. They question not just the competence of the general public to understand what they deem complex technological issues like nuclear power but the very right to decide those issues through local referendums and legislative processes. Thus the two University of Michigan nuclear engineers, asked whether "democracy is a viable form of government in a technological era," imply that it is not.

Criticism of the Army Corps of Engineers: A Case Study

The critique of expertise has stung engineers at every level. Beginning in the late 1960s public support for the Army Corps of Engineers especially weakened. The kinds of projects that had been widely hailed as technological achievements in earlier decades now became sources of contention. Resistance by the Corps to criticism, especially from "non-expert" outsiders, hurt not merely its image but also its operations.

Among the most serious criticisms came those from TVA's first chairman, Arthur Morgan, himself an internationally acclaimed civil engineer who had personally supervised numerous large-scale projects akin to those of the Corps. In a 1971 book entitled *Dams and Other Disasters,* Morgan documented long-term Corps opposition not only to environmentalists, Indians, and other citizens who got in the way of Corps enterprises but also to basic civil engineering practices that likely would have lessened floods and costs alike: reservoirs, jetties at river outlets, cutoffs across river bends, and other alternatives to dams and levees. Moreover, the Corps, Morgan showed, repeatedly claimed that it had supported technical advances that it had actually long rejected. The West Point emphasis on tradition, on avoiding originality, and on applying short-term military solutions to long-term, nonmilitary engineering problems, Morgan concluded, must finally cease.

The initial major confrontation between the Corps and environmentalists took place over a proposed flood-control project along Illinois' Sangamon River. Opponents stopped the project by providing convincing technical evidence of its unsuitability, not on traditional aesthetic and conservation grounds but precisely on economic and health grounds. Later, controversial Corps projects were also sometimes halted, or at least modified, through similar arguments that challenged the Corps' very expertise. In general, moreover, only those controversial projects begun before the late 1960s, or those enjoying strong political support, have escaped modification or termination.

Indeed, the Corps, like other government agencies, has been belatedly involved in water resource development and environmental studies, especially since passage of the 1965 Water Resource Planning Act, the 1968 Wild and Scenic Rivers Act, the 1969 National Environmental Policy Act (requiring environmental impact statements for every proposed Corps project), and the 1972 Federal Water Pollution Control Act. The last law gave the Environmental Protection Agency regulatory powers regarding water quality that deprived the Corps of some of its traditional authority, while simultaneously requiring the Corps to inspect and upgrade its dams in the name of both health and safety. Moreover, the Corps is now actively concerned with quality of life issues and the social, cultural, economic, and demographic effects of its proposed projects, not just the environmental effects. If, on the one hand, the Corps has finally institutionalized comprehensive planning, it has on the other hand rejected its hitherto automatic commitment to undertaking huge, expensive public works projects as the only water resource management measure. Thus the Corps currently provides leisure facilities for more Americans than any recreational or sports agency.

Gentrifying urban neighborhoods forced longtime residents to move to other parts of cities while yuppies claimed their buildings.

Criticism of Urban Planners: A Case Study

Engineers and planners modifying the urban environment also suffered this type of criticism. Beginning in the 1960s, those living in or near razed neighborhoods—these were generally poor people and/or persons of color—publicly objected to destruction of their neighborhoods and formed associations to combat it.

Each organization assumed the mandate of controlling the development or change within that neighborhood; it was the neighborhood's right to decide what constituted quality of life within that neighborhood, not experts serving suburban or corporate interests, a stance that frequently pitted individual associations against city government and its engineers (and even against other associations). These associations got a boost particularly following the 1973 oil embargo, when former suburbanites and young suburban-bred professionals reversed a century-old trend and settled in increasing numbers inside city limits. These new well-to-do urbanites cherished the architectural diversity and potential convenience of inner cities and packed economic clout sufficient to make city engineers and elected officials listen. The result was "gentrified" neighborhoods in which shells of old buildings were restored and preserved, while the insides were refitted for new uses. However, this process was sometimes accompanied by concerted drives to force long-standing "undesirable" residents out of their neighborhoods.

Infatuated with urban life, these "yuppies" (young urban professionals) led a resurgence of inner cities, and demanded urban mass transit to suit their needs. San Francisco, Washington, and Atlanta bowed to the pressure and opened new rail/subway systems in 1972, 1976, and 1979 respectively. Several Western cities are currently reviving or building new modern versions of the electrified street-railways abandoned decades ago for automobiles. And Los Angeles is even building a subway. These initiatives require tearing up some parts of the urban environment and almost always run afoul of the interests of some neighborhood associations—especially those that have not undergone gentrification—which protest and often sue.

Systems Engineering

The social dislocations of the late 1960s and after produced yet another response among technologists, that they could engineer a method to remove social ills. Proponents of this approach found solace in the general systems theory of the 1920s but added a new twist. Rather than examine the dynamics of the system or the system itself, late-twentieth-century systems analysts focused solely on the final or end product. That single focus enabled them to treat any element of the complicated system in a singular fashion: how did it contribute to the output and how could its contribution to the output be enhanced. That question permitted analysts, who generally work in teams, to treat each of the parts of a system as if they were discrete elements, a direct repudiation of the understandings of earlier systems analysts. Means to measure contributions seemed rational and quantifiable, the product of experts and the province of those same persons.

Like the Technocrats of an earlier era, systems analysts see the world as chaotic and in need of the kind of order only they can provide: efficient, honest, nonideological, and apolitical. Like the Technocrats, too, they readily employ jargon, as demonstrated by the words of Simon Ramo, a founder of the giant defense-related corporation TRW: "As the end result, the approach seeks to work out a detailed description of a specified combination of men and machines—with such concomitant assignment of function, designated use of matériel, and patterns of information flow that the whole system represents a compatible, optimum, interconnected ensemble for achieving the performance desired."

But by focusing on output and by assuming that the output is an agreed-upon commodity, systems analysts distort rather than resolve. As social critic Theodore Roszak observed, "the good systems team does not include poets, painters, holy men, or social revolutionaries, who, presumably have nothing to contribute to 'real life' solutions." Critics have complained that systems analysis is not only elitist, self-justifying, self-perpetuating, and narrowly conceived but also inefficient, inadequate, and unscientific. Nor does systems analysis have a particularly stellar record in the field in which it initially was embraced: the military. There, a seemingly endless progression of poorly made weapons and vehicles, and enormous cost overruns, have many Americans equating military expenditures with waste and greed.

The Military–Industrial Complex: The Federal Government

No single clarion call more neatly summed up the technology as a social question than the term "military–industrial complex." By 1970, it had become a stock phrase for what ailed America. An unholy alliance of the military and other parts of the national government, large (often multinational) industrial conglomerates, and research universities had so come to dominate all facets of American life that personal freedoms had been severely diminished. Many thought them all but erased. Most Americans acknowledged the importance of a national defense and perhaps even a national defense establishment. And most understood that defense concerns required considerable investment in and dependence upon technological development and implementation. Yet the concept of a military–industrial complex as employed in the 1970s and after suggested that the tail now wagged the dog: need of the military and industry to sustain themselves had produced a technological juggernaut, whose only purposes were profits and power for those in charge. This insatiable creature craved larger, more expensive weaponry, both conventional and nuclear, and extended its tentacles throughout all facets of government activity, trampling on personal freedoms wherever it went. Critics saw the war in Vietnam as just one symptom of this monster's existence and the phrase from the war "we had to destroy the village to save it" as a chilling reminder of to just what lengths it was willing to go. A bloated defense budget, including $600 toilet seats; President Reagan's attempt to win the Cold War by spending the Soviet Union into submission; repeated revelations of illegal covert operations; a series of defense contractors who never seemed to worry about cost overruns or product quality; and think tanks eager to spin out scenarios for virtually any occasion provided further confirmation. These symptoms spoke of an entrenched technologically dependent oligarchy, impossible to dislodge, sustained and fueled by federal moneys.

For a good portion of the public in the nearly three decades after the late 1960s, any new government-sponsored, defense-related technological initiative was suspect. That questioning emerged less than a decade after the hullabaloo over Sputnik. Congress quickly added in as its members complained of the extravagance of researchers and the lack of oversight other than from their otherwise suspect peers. Senator William Proxmire's monthly Golden Fleece Awards exposed and ridiculed federally funded research he deemed frivolous. Department of Defense and NASA budgets were pruned and demands were made that government fund only relevant work, work of sufficient national importance that it commanded governmental intervention. In the eight years after 1968, federal support to universities declined by more than 10 percent.

Agencies that regulated the consequences of scientific and technological activity typified the kind of relevant work that blossomed in the new suspicious milieu. Each tackled a facet of the larger, more nebulous problem of ensuring the quality of American life from those simply seeking profits and power. Each agency struck at some aspect of the military–industrial complex but, unlike earlier regulatory mechanisms, their mandates were not restricted to specific industries. More than twenty such instrumentalities were formed by Congress in the 1970s alone. The Environmental Protection Agency (1970) and the Occupational Safety and Health Administration (1973) were among the most powerful and active.

Establishing these agencies indicated that technological progress no longer was automatically equated with social progress; the environment, peace, and other quality of life issues seemed to hold at least as much appeal as improvements in hardware. This technology–quality of life union, now always subjected to individual scrutiny and interpretation, was a repudiation of technical expertise as the sole evaluation criterion, and a rejection of engineers and scientists as the most appropriate decision makers. Reports of unsafe automobiles, chemicals, nuclear power plants, and the like reinforced suspicions of a wary public, further tarnished the image of American engineers, and led to calls for the federal and state governments to set the matter right. Technological issues seemed far too important to be left to engineers and scientists. In this milieu public review became an established precedent as such mechanisms as environmental impact statements and sunshine laws spoke to right to know. Creation of the Office of Technology Assessment (1972) to predict the impacts on society of any particular technological act marked the apex of this relevancy campaign.

Government and the Assessment of Technology

The Office of Technology Assessment was especially concerned with unintended, indirect, or delayed effects of technologies. The term technology assessment (TA) had been coined in the late 1960s by Connecticut congressman Emilio Daddario, who was instrumental in the OTA's creation. Its establishment reflected, on the one hand, America's fading faith in technological progress and, on the other hand, its desperate desire to anticipate and so perhaps to prevent or solve problems stemming from new technologies.

TA was ordinarily concerned with present and future phenomena alone. Assessments would cover such technological issues as auto safety, consumer product safety, occupational safety, and nuclear power safety. Some practitioners began including historical perspectives in their public policy considerations. That in turn led to a formalized "retrospective technology assessment" (RTA), a term coined in 1974 by Joseph Coates, then of the National Science Foundation.

RTA was popular in the later 1970s and early 1980s. Some projects drew analogies between past predictions of the impact of technological developments on society and current ones; the railroad, for example, was studied in conjunction with the space program. Others have examined the same general phenomena—pollution, for instance, or telephones—in both earlier and more recent times in hope of utilizing past expectations and policies to illuminate present and future ones, and so to minimize "future shock."

Direct connections among the past, present, and the future are never easy to draw, except superficially, and historians who had engaged in RTA faced dilemmas about not oversimplifying their findings while still making them meaningful. Paradoxically, growing knowledge of technology's rich and varied history made it ever harder for historians to generalize too boldly about what really happened, much less what might yet happen, in any given situation. Paradoxically, too, TA and RTA required assumptions (about events or processes being repetitive or cyclic) that historians normally reject, yet which were necessary for any practical applications. It was, finally, the conservative Republican Congress that abolished the Office of Technology Assessment soon after taking power in 1995, claiming OTA was a relic of big government, of outdated government intervention better left to the private sector.

Carter and the New Accessibility

President Jimmy Carter supported RTA and TA. But his policies redirected what government deemed relevant and ironically weakened assessment's claims on the public purse. Carter's background was as a nuclear engineer. His platform was morality. Carter approached morality as if it were an objective commodity that could always be discerned by rationalist, even scientific, principles. His methods were personal. Face-to-face contact would break down barriers erected by irrational fears. His approach was populist, seeking to enfranchise in the government decision-making process many who felt themselves un- or underrepresented. In the USDA, for example, Carter established a consumer advocate, a radical notion in a bureaucracy dedicated to expanding agricultural production and profitability.

Carter's presidency coincided nicely with a public willingness to testify to and about the problems unscrupulous or uncaring technologically dependent companies caused American citizens. Public disclosures and government action led to closing to fishing Virginia's James River and parts of the Chesapeake Bay because of kepone pollution, a pesticide implicated in human nervous disorders. Polychlorinated biphenyls (PCBs), used in electrical appliance manufacturing, were dumped into the upper Hudson River, which halted commercial fishing there. Times Beach, Missouri, was identified as a dump for dioxin, a chemical by-product in wood preservation, antibacterial soap, and herbicide production. Because of the possible threat to health, the town was abandoned in 1983 and its borders sealed. The situation surrounding Love Canal in Niagara, New York, probably garnered the most attention. Hooker Chemical and Plastics Corporation's years of dumping chemicals in this old canal bed became a critical situation after the land was filled in and a new housing tract and school built on the site. Leakage from the toxic site was reported in home basements in 1978. High incidences of birth defects, miscarriages, liver cancer, and seizures among residents and their children devastated the area. Ultimately more than 1,000 families were relocated. The canal itself was capped and fenced off. The houses in which its victims had resided were razed.

Because of the disclosures about Love Canal and the other environmental catastrophes, Congress embraced new legislation. The Toxic Substances Control Act required manufacturers to inform the EPA of the estimated production volume, uses, and any existing health-related studies for any commercial chemical. The Resource Conservation and Recovery Act enabled the EPA to regulate disposal and disposal sites of noxious substances. The Comprehensive Environmental Response, Compensation, and Liability Act created a superfund of billions of dollars to clean up abandoned toxic waste dumps. Superfund expenses totaled over $8.5 billion by 1990.

But Carter's legacy was not simply to establish other watchdogs and extend already existing ones but rather demand that science be made accessible and translated into technologies. To decrease the power of the military–industrial establishment, Carter and Congress began to adopt measures and procedures to take away their virtual monopoly. Science, which had solely been their province, now was supposed to become available to all who sought it, while technologies, to Carter the products of science and those things that eased the burdens of modern living on each individual, was now one of funding's foremost goals. Only through such a program could the malaise be lifted that Carter felt had infected the nation.

He inaugurated measures to make it so. His transition team established the Office of Science and Technology Policy. There a wide range of industrial and scientific leaders regularly advised the president, forming a de facto business/science nexus. Carter's Executive Order 12044 made all regulatory agencies integrate cost–benefit analyses into regulatory decisions and established a new regulatory analysis and review group within the White House to oversee and coordinate the effort. Carter argued for and won new NSF programs to spark creation of small technology businesses based upon agency science fundings. His alternative fuels program reflected this new thrust toward private sector technological application. Carter fostered a strong overall increase in government science spending in all areas except military research and development. His philosophy was simple. "New technologies can aid in the solution of many of the Nation's problems," Carter argued. "These technologies in turn depend upon a fund of knowledge derived from basic research. The federal government should therefore increase its support both for basic research and, where appropriate, for the application of new technologies." To these ends, he recommended new measures to increase access to science outside the military–industrial establishment: a new patent policy to encourage industrial development of government-sponsored research; expansion of NSF programs to foster university–industry cooperation; expansion of NSF support to small businesses; and further reduction of regulatory costs. Congress acted on some of Carter's proposals. It gave universities, small businesses, and nonprofit organizations the right to patent applications derived from federally funded research and required national laboratories to set up Offices of Research and Technology Applications to facilitate technology transfer from those laboratories to small business.

The Reagan Revolution and After

Ronald Reagan's presidency treated science and technology as the cornerstone of national commercial policy. Reaganites saw technology less as a way to solve America's social and other problems and more as a means to make products and profits. Arguing that a rising tide raised all ships and that profits by manufacturers would "trickle down" to workers, Reagan and his followers labored to make technology profitable. Making America competitive in global markets was one of their aims, and the massive trade deficits and galloping inflation Reagan inherited seemed clear indications that the nation was failing there. They initially sought to decrease regulatory action, which they deemed outrageously expensive. For example, Reagan ordered the FDA to cut back safety protocols of many new drugs and "fast-track" them to the commercial marketplace. He also issued an executive order requiring all regulatory agencies to conduct "regulatory impact analyses" for any new rules. Agencies needed to demonstrate that expected benefits of the new rules outweighed costs and that the course of action set by the new rules was the least expensive way to achieve those ends. As important, Reagan took the decision making out of agency hands, leaving the Office of Management and Budget to make the final decisions.

Reagan also used federal authority to foster technological and scientific growth. Impetus came in part from studies suggesting that more than half of American manufacturing's productivity increases since World War II were the product of new, improved technologies. But Reaganites also looked to Japan, a leading competitor, and attributed its international commercial success to its potent industry–government connection, especially in science and technology. Reagan strove to translate the Japanese model to America. Like the Japanese, Reagan forcefully targeted high technology as the most productive science/government/industry junction. He aimed to stimulate technological innovation and adoption by industries through tax incentives—credits and shelters—and dramatically increased research funding, especially in areas related to the national defense and high tech, such as computers, biotechnology, and materials research. His early policies cemented the university–small business nexus as government funded science done at universities (and national laboratories) was regularly spun off as technologies in startup businesses. Universities signed all sorts of agreements with venture capitalists and others, established institutes and centers for and with industries, and created jointly owned or administered laboratories and research consortiums. By 1983, over $4.5 billion had been invested in small high-tech firms.

In the decade 1976–1986, the percentage of the American labor force devoted to science and technology rose from 2.4 percent to 3.6 percent. Technologically intensive efforts had come to assume a far greater share of the American economy, a realization that led to calls for a cabinet-level Secretary of Science and Technology to plan and guide the nation's efforts. Arguing that "technological innovation—high tech—is key to enhanced competitiveness," advocates urged further government–private enterprise cooperation and transfer of federally funded science for development as technologies in corporate America. Transformation of the National Bureau of Standards into the National Institute of Standards and Technology (NIST) broke new ground. The revamped agency's mandate was to modernize American industry, particularly its

*President Bill Clinton tells corporate CEOs that a
successful American economy is the backbone of a
successful American society.*

manufacturing base; it was to bring high-tech practices and know-how
there. Improved product quality was a goal, as was rapid commercial-
ization of technological innovations. Its staff provided whatever information and skills businesses required, often traveling to sites to encourage manufacturers to employ the newest technologies.

This hands-on approach continued through the Bush presidency
and into the Clinton years. Neither the collapse of the Soviet Union in
1989 nor the Republican revolution's Contract with America to down-
size the federal government in 1994 led to policy change. Defense department funding did not diminish significantly and Republicans have
avoided balancing the budget by downsizing science funding. Instead,
Vice Presidents Quayle and Gore have chaired committees on national
competitiveness, both of which called for a firmer, more extensive
government–business technology connection. Clinton's "it's the economy, stupid" has evolved into "building a bridge to the 21st century."

Federal science and technology funding, especially in high-tech,
environmentally friendly areas, filtered through American business is
to pave the way. Where, however, the Reagan and Bush administra-
tions studiously avoided an avowed industrial policy, fearing conservative critiques of excessive government intervention, the Clinton administration embraced it. In implementing industrial policy, the
Commerce Department enjoyed a prominence not seen since Herbert
Hoover was Secretary of Commerce.

THE NEW AMERICAN MANUFACTURING

The federally driven, headlong rush to modernize American manufacturing and business practices has not been universally hailed. Incorporation of technologies into the workplace and substitution of new technologies for older ones have engendered considerable concern, especially among those workers who found themselves displaced. Periodically, the issue of retraining workers to fill the jobs of the "new" economy surfaces, but few programs have been initiated.

Robotics

The National Institute for Occupational Safety and Health reported sadly that on July 21, 1984, a 34-year-old machine operator "went into cardiorespiratory arrest and died after being pinned between the back of an industrial robot and a steel safety pole." This robot, like other industrial varieties, resembled an insect more than a human, with its blunt beetle jaws and long needle nose.

Driven by computer-operated motors, it could be programmed for many tasks. Where robots had been used primarily for loading, unloading, and manufacturing large, heavy objects, they more recently have been used in fine assembly work and in service sectors, such as polishing supermarket floors and delivering hospital patients' meals. These newer precision robots have become popular, with thousands being produced and sold annually. There now exists a Robotic Industries Association, based in Ann Arbor, Michigan. Manufacturers have widely praised robots as additions to or replacements for (part of) their human workforces. Unlike humans, robots do not get sick, take vacations, join unions, or criticize management.

Robots rarely pose a physical menace to workers, but often threaten their jobs. Commentators predict "workerless factories" operated by centralized computer systems and incorporating computer-aided design (CAD), computer-aided manufacturing (CAM), and complete automation processes. Many displaced workers would be compelled to seek lower-paying service-sector jobs. Critics are even less optimistic about employees who remain once robots are installed. They contend that robots are designed not merely to replace some workers but also to control others by dictating the pace of operations, and cite General Motors' heavily computerized and automated Saturn division as an apt example. Promoted as an experiment in reinventing the manufacturing process, Saturn avowedly reduced union control over work rules, and linked wages directly to productivity. To these observers, robotics permitted GM to integrate manufacturing in one

Workerless factories remain the goal of some manufacturers. Automation has been especially pronounced in the automobile industry.

location and control the workforce; human workers, ironically, are treated much like robots.

Some evidence exists that such dire projections sometimes miss the mark. A few automotive manufacturers and some industries relying on robots have compensated workers for loss of income and skills by establishing "quality of worklife" programs. Workers share decision-making power with management on not only work processes and materials but also pricing, profits, and plant location. Moreover, as one high-tech proponent observes, "robots can't run factories," and their presence doesn't "eliminate the need for human skill and judgment." Nevertheless, the extent of the shared decision making remains to be seen.

Worker Health and Privacy

Replacement of assembly-line workers with robots did not necessarily decrease worker-related illness. Repetitive stress disorder and carpal tunnel syndrome are products of modern computer word processing as much as they were of old-fashioned meat cutting. Ergonomics, the design of office and other working environments, has become a flourishing specialty. So, too, has the monitoring of work, through computer surveillance superseding scientific management schemes or the more traditional "hands-on" kind.

Manufacturing's New Locus

Redesigned and otherwise "modernized" factories rarely remain in their historic sites. Since World War II, manufacturers have been fleeing America's traditional urban industrial heartland. Stretching from Boston and Baltimore to Chicago and St. Louis, the decline of this region with its traditional concentration of American manufacturing firms and establishments did not engender much comment until the 1960s. By then the industrialized Northeast and Midwest had lost thousands of companies and tens of thousands of jobs to other parts of the country, and especially abroad. The South and West had steadily attracted manufacturing companies through tax incentives, lower living costs, and opposition to organized labor. Western Europe, Latin America, and Asia offered strikingly lower operating costs. Social critics such as Daniel Bell detected the export of manufacturing jobs to foreign lands and decreed that America had entered the "post-industrial era" in which production and distribution of information would replace industrial goods. The nation's new task was service. The preponderance of jobs rested in banking, government service, teaching, fast foods, and the like, not manufacturing. America was becoming "deindustrialized."

The inner-city riots of the middle and late 1960s, the Vietnam War, and the oil crisis of 1973 exacerbated the decline of the "frostbelt," as the urban industrial heartland was called. These three events challenged the long-standing assumption about the limitlessness of American material and human resources, which had seemed to translate into technologically generated plenty and might. The Great Depression, and the atomic bomb with its potential for vast devastation, had provided earlier inklings of the nation's possible limits, but the concern in the 1960s and after was very different. It produced strong new strains of selfishness in a society already infected with individuation; Americans took the perception of limits as a compelling justification to demand and actively to seek what they determined was their proper share of an apparently diminishing pie. President Nixon's New Federalism, which turned federal tax dollars and programs over to the states to use as they wished, was an explicit recognition of America's limitedness, as was California's Proposition 13, which drastically cut taxes and traditional services, and the growth of lawsuits between states over resource questions. Journalist Tom Wolfe's designation, "the me decade," neatly captured the spirit of the 1970s and early 1980s.

Making Factories

In the 1960s, material scientists found ways to increase the strength of metals at least fivefold. Ceramics proved the material of choice in the

1970s, but yielded to the new concrete of the 1980s. This material has a compression strength four times as great (20,000 pounds per square inch) as concrete had in the 1960s. Skyscrapers and large factories are now routinely built without steel I-beams. Reinforced concrete buildings sway less, which reduces nausea. Concrete for these large buildings is pumped through pipe as the constant flow keeps it from setting until it reaches its destination. The new concrete has myriad uses, including for automotive brake linings and indoor furniture. It remains the sole inexpensive material able to hold up under the weight of the largest airplanes.

From Factory to Market

Temporary reduction of the official speed limit on interstate highways from 70 mph to 55 mph (an energy-conservation measure in the wake of the oil embargo) and the rapid rise of petroleum fuel costs did not shake manufacturers' faith in trucks and buses or lead to a rebirth of rail transport. Nor did the federal government's creation in 1975 of Conrail (Consolidated Rail Corporation) out of the Penn Central Railroad and other failing Northeastern freight railroads, and billions in federal loans, stem railroad decline. Those railroads that have remained profitable, such as the Norfolk and Western and Union Pacific, have done so through diversification; freight haulage constitutes only a small and only moderately successful part of their business interests. Any significant profits from freight haulage may ironically depend on forging ties with trucks as well as on computerized information flow among all major railroads. Airline deregulation in the late 1970s further enhanced air transport's long-distance haulage prospects. With marketplace control over fares and routes, stiffer competition and lower fares distinguished popular markets, while airlines cut expenses by reducing or abandoning service in unpopular ones.

From Market to Consumer

Social critic Marshall McLuhan announced that "the medium is the message." That single statement defined television and guided several generations of advertisers. To McLuhan and his followers, the technology of delivering a picture live into a home itself made an impact on viewers. Television's visual emphasis made it a much more potent social force. For that reason, what was shown on television, what came over the airways, took on a new immediacy. Television was among the most powerful stimuli on the individual. The constant bombardment of soap operas and "jiggle TV" (television programs featuring scantily clad men and women) seemed to threaten America. Some argued that contemporary social problems owed their genesis in part to television broadcasts; television's obsession with violence created a sick society. A special national PTA committee targeted television violence. A subsequent committee of the same organization blamed television for the decline in children's reading skills.

Groups such as the Coalition for Better Television and Accuracy in Media broadened the critique. An organization of affiliated fundamentalist religious and conservative citizens groups, including the National Federation for Decency and the Moral Majority, the Coalition disliked television's pandering to sex and profanity, and organized boycotts of sponsors of offending programs. Accuracy in Media noted a pervasive liberal bias in television news and demanded equal time for conservative opinion. Representatives of various minorities and ethnic groups also objected to television's stereotypical or unflattering portrayal of them, claiming that the medium nurtured the seeds of intolerance.

Although most commentators see television as a purveyor of mass culture—much of it lowbrow or explicitly harmful—a handful reverse the indictment and attack television for fostering isolation and alienation. They worry that television viewing (which averages more than seven hours a day per household) decreases time formerly spent developing social skills and relationships, gaining experience, and maintaining familial attachments. The TV generation watches, it does not act, and it watches alone. The multi-television family has become standard as each child now possesses a television in his or her bedroom. The result is passive, alienated individuals, a factor to those expressing such sentiments that seems of major importance to the republic's future. Not surprisingly, some parents have resorted to eliminating television entirely from their homes, while many more restrict and monitor their children's viewing time.

Political elections have become television-dependent; without television money, a candidate is apparently doomed to defeat. But it has been advertisers, more than any other single group, that have best understood television's impact. Commercial budgets for television time far exceed other kinds of advertising. Virtually every business now advertises on television. To this group, television airways allow producers entrance into individual homes to pitch their cases in the manner they deem fit.

Futurecasting

Futurecasting provides the appearance of certainty in an unknowable world. It permits those who employ it to experience a sense of control, of directing the future. As a "change agent," these men and women analyze and plan and receive at least the psychic rewards for those endeavors. Rarely are plans initiated for more than a five-year time frame. Even more disturbing is that the planning cycle on a typical five-year plan generally begins after the second year. Only in that way could a new plan be in place when the old plan ended.

Forecasting of future trends by definition looks only to the future. Although prophecies are probably as old as civilization, "futurecasting" is now a virtual industry in itself. Its mission is not merely to anticipate the future but indeed to shape it. Thanks to computers and other components of the information revolution, forecasting is ever more popular, even in the face of evident weaknesses.

Forecasts of whatever variety reflect at least some dissatisfaction with the present; they are not found in contented, stagnant societies where the citizens hope that the future will resemble the present. Forecasts are by definition intended to instill either hope or concern for the future, and so to spur improvements or prevent problems, or both. Given the increased possibilities of realizing those predictions, the traditional gap between prophecy and fulfillment has narrowed and sometimes disappeared.

Forecasters routinely employ mathematical and social models of growing complexity, and construct elaborate possible scenarios. Many utilize massive data banks as their starting point, then extrapolate specific developments and general trends. "Social indicators" often are used to predict broader changes, as is the "Delphi method" for reaching consensus among various experts; the latter entails mailing anonymous written questionnaires, rather than arranging face-to-face contact, to achieve more objective conclusions free from personality conflicts and group pressures.

The drawbacks of such approaches are: value-laden assumptions and methods; conservative presumptions of continued social stability (lest the forecasts be wholly inaccurate); inability to accommodate radical and unexpected changes; self-fulfilling prophecies; and aversion to nonquantifiable issues and dilemmas. No less important, forecasting is frequently and simply wrong: technological wonders predicted come about sooner than, and in forms other than, those predicted; unanticipated technological advances prove significant; and, not least, impacts of technology on society—and vice versa—differ from that of the forecast. Examples are endless, but the computer, to take a notable one, was not predicted by any of the fifty most prominent American forecasters writing between 1890 and 1940, while the immediate successors of those forecasters expected that a mere handful of computers and operators would suffice for the foreseeable future.

Economic forecasting is particularly problematic. Relatively short-term economic forecasts are *intended* to be revised as the dates to which they apply near. Yet economic forecasters ply their trade with unrestrained determination—not, however, as economist John

Kenneth Galbraith has wryly put it, because they know, but because they're asked. And their forecasts are indeed influential and affect policies in the public and private sectors alike. Forecasters using various models base their predictions primarily on the economy's past behavior, then integrate, with the help of computers, those analyses with visions of future actions by the government and by industry. The limitation of such models is their inability to measure the subsequent changes that do occur because of limitations imposed on their vision by what those groups themselves expect will happen. Paradoxically, then, economic forecasts look too far backward while not looking sufficiently ahead: hence their constant need to be revised.

Lack of Consensus among Forecasters

The president of the World Future Society, a leading professional prognosticator, lamented George Orwell's limited success in predicting the shape of the world in 1984 from the perspective of 1948, when he completed his influential novel *1984*. That Orwell failed to anticipate numerous developments is indeed true, and he does not receive good marks on the scorecard popular with such full-time futurists. But the larger and elementary truth missed by this "expert" is that *1984* was written precisely to prevent its grim story from coming true, and that Orwell had in mind his own day—in England, in the Soviet Union, and in the Socialist movement—as much as 1984. Like all serious utopians or dystopians, Orwell was criticizing his own world more than literally describing ours.

Perhaps most illuminating, however, of the problems confronting modem forecasting is the lack of consensus among alleged experts regarding America's, and the world's, very future. The boundless optimism of a Buckminster Fuller and the stark pessimism of a Jacques Ellul *(The Technological Society)* are repeated not only in other speculative writings but also in the more technical treatises of, say, the upbeat Herman Kahn *(The Next 200 Years* and *The Coming Boom)* and Julian Simon *(The Ultimate Resource),* and the downbeat Club of Rome *(The Limits to Growth)* and *The Global 2000 Report* (to then-President Jimmy Carter). Using presumably the same data, these forecasters disagree completely about such crucial areas as future population growth, food supply, energy sources, and environmental conditions. Indeed, the Club of Rome reversed its pessimistic findings just four years later, and with barely an apology or explanation. The facts, then, fail to speak for themselves, and are themselves in dispute. No Delphi methods, no matter how prolonged, would create any consensus here. What Kahn and Simon together (in *The Resourceful Earth)* say about *The Global 2000 Report* indicates this gap: "The original *Global 2000* is totally wrong in its specific assertions and its general conclusion. It is replete with major factual errors, not just minor blemishes. . . . Many of its arguments are illogical or misleading. . . . Our statements about the future . . . are intended as unconditional predictions. . . . We feel no need to qualify these predictions upon the continuation of current policies, as *Global 2000* claimed to do . . . ."

Such disputes have spurred less technocratic visions, which may be termed "alternative futures." "Appropriate" technology is part of this trend. In general, these visionaries, by contrast to the professional prognosticators like Kahn and the World Future Society, are less elitist and dogmatic about their views and more interested in others' views, and are as concerned with cultural and psychological conditions as with economic and social ones. They do not subscribe to the technological determinism of the professionals or to the accompanying sense of inevitability, as epitomized in Alvin Toffler's writings. They adhere implicitly to the conservationist Sierra Club's motto: "Not blind opposition to progress, but opposition to blind progress."

Growth of the Ideology of Appropriate Technology

The growing acknowledgment, beginning in the mid-1960s, of the various limits to—and costs of—unrestrained technological growth have engendered the concept of "appropriate" or "intermediate" technology. Its leading advocate, E. F. Schumacher, a prominent British economist, was not against technology. Rather, he and his associates throughout the world (not only in the industrialized West) have sought smaller, more personal, and decentralized forms of technology "appropriate" to different societies. Less affluent and less industrialized societies do not necessarily require, and may not benefit from, the same kind of complex and large-scale tools, machines, business enterprises, and management practices that flourish in the United States. For example, inexpensive and easily constructed windmills, water tanks, water pumps, latrines, spinning wheels, solar cookers, and small industries have been successfully introduced in Africa and Asia and have simultaneously raised living standards and preserved existing ways of life. Their comparative cheapness and simplicity are, in engineering terms, their elegance and strength. These devices and processes often have been accompanied by the renewed use of indigenous raw materials, of energy-generating waste products, and of small animal-powered or hand-operated machinery. Such labor-intensive schemes employ local workers and lessen the exodus from the countryside to overcrowded cities.

Unlike earlier academic proponents of "modernization," who believed that vastly different foreign cultures could readily absorb Western

technology—and Western institutions and values—eventually to become model industrial democracies, Schumacher and others recognize
the intrinsic diversity of nations, cultures, and geographic regions.
Smaller-scale, more decentralized technology may appear more "appropriate" to societies less industrialized than the United States, but
even here advocates question the traditional assumption that bigger is
automatically better, and more efficient. The widespread preference in
recent years for smaller, safer, and more fuel-efficient automobiles,
and for solar, wind, water, and even coal energy sources as opposed to
oil and natural gas are examples of appropriate technology at work—
if often for economic more than social or cultural reasons. So, too, are
the increasing demands for improvements in mass-production
processes, particularly group-task alternatives to the monotonous and
unfulfilling single-task assembly-line process—and here not necessarily for economic reasons, given the high wages and generous benefits
of automobile workers, for instance.

Searching for the Good Life

The recent popularity of organic farming and of "natural" foods are
further examples of appropriate technology at work in America.
Spurred by disenchantment with contemporary urban industrial life,
thousands of young Americans, most of them born and raised in cities
and suburbs, became farmers in the late 1960s and 1970s. In search of a
happier, more satisfying daily existence, they eagerly tried their hand
at what two of their heroes, Helen and Scott Nearing, called (in a 1959
book) *Living the Good Life.* Indeed, the Nearings' formerly obscure
work now became a best-selling guide for aspiring agrarians, as did
their complementary *Maple Sugar Book* (1950). Few, however, were as
willing as the Nearings to dispense with the perceived benefits of
modern technology, from machine tools and kitchen appliances to
stereos and televisions. And fewer had the simple, even ascetic, tastes
and firm discipline of the Nearings, who moved from rural Vermont
to coastal Maine in 1952 when the former locale lost its rusticity. Many
of these converted farmers became disillusioned and returned to more
familiar surroundings and occupations.

A great many Americans have become concerned with the harmful effects on their health of chemical and synthetic fertilizers, pesticides, and food additives. They have sought to replace chemical methods of food growth, processing, and preparation with "natural,"
biological ones. In addition to eating low-cholesterol, high-fiber foods
(sometimes avoiding meats altogether) and exercising regularly, they
avoid processed foods like refined sugar and flour. Few produce their
own food, and those who do generally restrict themselves to backyard

gardens. Yet many have become avid readers, if not practitioners, of the organic-gardening techniques especially espoused by Rodale Press, the profits from which have enabled it to establish a farming research center near Emmaus, Pennsylvania, and to manufacture equipment for organic gardeners elsewhere. Some "natural" food enthusiasts also have become severe critics of giant agribusiness corporations. These alternative consumers also recycle newspapers and other household items and often purchase wood-burning heaters. Their practices are usually not, as with the Nearings, alternatives to affluence, but rather its by-products. Growing up in a highly technological society, they, like other practitioners of appropriate technology, wish not to abandon technology but to reform it.

Not all these alternative developments will persist. Their popularity may be temporary, as with solar energy, or may fluctuate, as with compact cars. Moreover, what is appropriate to less-industrialized countries may be utterly inappropriate to "postindustrial" ones like the United States. As a sympathetic critic of appropriate technology observes, "small is not always beautiful, local is not always better, and labor-intensiveness is not always desirable." Indeed, defining appropriateness is perhaps a futile exercise, insofar as the term is both vague and relative.

Substitution of the concept of sustainability in the 1980s worked to broach these questions. Appearing first in agriculture but diffusing through technological discussions in the 1990s, sustainability took a steady-state as its model; it did not necessarily mean smaller or, in corporate parlance, "downsizing" or "right sizing." It permitted the appearance of harmony by eliminating prospects of growth, development, or progress. It sought just to operate at the peak efficiency, with efficiency defined as the maximum that could be undertaken without depletion, without permanent negative change. And it also suggested that the maximum sustainable was the goal. Sustainability promised that virtually nothing would be banked or stored more than necessary to maintain the sustainable quo. A healthy number of jobs would remain and the economy would continue to putter along. Yet despite its proponents' boasts, sustainability ultimately required agreement on what exactly was sustainable and how you achieve it. Each of these answers lies in the eyes of the beholder.

FOR FURTHER READING

(see following Chapter 11)

Private and Public: Technology and Individual Autonomy: The Later 1960s to the 1990s

In 1971, the pocket calculator appeared on the market. At first a high ticket item, its cost soon fell to less than $5. Like the portable radio before it, the pocket calculator introduced consumers to a new form of microelectronics, the programmable chip. The programmable chip calculator enabled everyone to handle rudimentary calculations at unprecedented speeds. The second big programmable chip product, the digital watch, emerged in 1973. By 1980, manufacturers had sold over 100 million digital watches worldwide. Of the two electronic devices, the digital watch has the greater symbolic significance. It reflected a notion of time, a concept of the relationship of past, present, and future new to and congruent with the years after the late 1960s. Unlike earlier watches and clocks, which represented time as a recurring cycle measured in distances before and after the hour and hours as successive units from one to twelve, the digital watch marked time as disembodied points, isolated in space. As depicted by the digital watch, time was neither continuous nor progressive nor cyclical. Each moment was unique.

Technological Thinking and Individuation: New Technologies

Concurrent with the rise of the political idea of rabid individuality were the two major technological innovations of the period, the programmable chip and biotechnology. Each of these revolutionary technologies mimicked the then-contemporary political calculus: they depended on a conception of the fundamental parts as individualized, even isolated. In the case of the chip, all knowledge, all activity was reduced to either on or off (represented as zero or one) while any activity—program—had to be precisely crafted from these individuals to fulfill only whatever task was demanded. In this digitized framework, each transistor junction—each bit of information (or byte)—was as valuable as every other transistor; each spot had a sovereignty of its own. Each line of code, each application, each program was tailor-made from individual bits of information. Individuation was even more obvious in biotechnology. There the organism as a crucial creation ceased to exist. It simply served as a repository of individual genes—some scientists labeled living creatures "genetic bag"—and its outward expression nothing more than a manifestation of those individuals. Species as intellectual constructs no longer seemed meaningful. They had been biological populations gathered around some fixed point. But now individuals could be identically reproduced—cloning—so that each would possess the exact same genetic material or individuals could be particularized, each with its own unique set of genes taken from any number of different animals and plants and therefore have genetic characteristics peculiar only to itself.

The Empowered Individual: The Technology of Social Exchange

The social complement to the individuation/technological thinking nexus has been the disaggregation of individuals, to separate each and to erect barriers to protect each from outside forces. Disjunction must be on the individual's terms, and from that lens technologies are evaluated. Individuals deem technologies empowering because of their perception of a technology's hypothetical ability to isolate and personalize, to remove persons from the tyranny of the social calculus. A technology's reputed capacity to free the individual from the vortex of social forces impinging upon it grants that technology sanction. In this view, control becomes a euphemism for erecting protective barriers around the individual, for encasement, cushioning, insulation.

Emphasis is therefore placed not on the "reality" of a technology, but on an individual's perception of that technology's "power." Technologies that appear useful do so because they seem to help an individual achieve separation, distance. Those who are savvy press their cases for their technologies in those terms, for their alleged genius in assisting individual autonomy. The prospects, for example, of 500 cable TV channels to select from for one's personal home entertainment—a program for virtually every taste and mood—appeals to many.

In this world, authority outside the self is an anathema, a direct assault upon individual autonomy. The idea of expertise is likewise denigrated, yet individuals appreciate that they often rely on others' technical competence. A very difficult situation results. Individuals claim to retain the final say—authority—over those upon whose technical capabilities they nonetheless depend. Hostility sometimes governs this relationship, as does litigation.

A new social convention mitigates the tension. Individuals eschew all trappings and other outward expressions of authority or expertise, even while exercising it. Politicians with their coteries of spin doctors quickly seized and capitalized on the new social sense. Jimmy Carter rejected his more formal name to show his commonness, historically not a desirable trait for a president and leader of the Free World. But politicians as different as Al Gore and Bob Dole, until recently known as Albert Gore, Jr., and Robert Dole respectively, have carried what would have been considered bizarre public behavior a few short decades ago to new heights. In a desperate gambit to position themselves as common, not exceptional, and to shun any mantle of authority, they regularly seek every opportunity to appear as fun-loving guys. These party animals go out of their way to embarrass themselves, doing such things as dancing badly in public or appearing on talk shows to engage in self-deprecating witty repartee (something neither has ever been known for). In this fashion, they aim to humanize themselves, cast off any quality that raises them to special status and therefore achieve a false sense of intimacy with voters. Flaws, even abject and repeated failure, now become ways to curry public favor.

The New NASA

The "David Lettermaning" of politics reflects a trend that has permeated American society. NASA has recently capitulated. For decades its representatives, its media specialists, portrayed the organization as the personification of the expert. All NASA representatives appearing on camera wore white dress shirts, narrow ties, and often white lab coats. They addressed the public; they did not seek to engage it. Astronauts had the "right stuff." Even when disaster loomed, NASA remained utterly professional. "Houston, we have a problem" was the cool manner by which astronaut Jim Lovell announced the fact that Apollo 13

Matt Golombeck became the unlikely spokesman for NASA's Pathfinder mission as the agency shunned its button-down image.

might remain marooned in orbit around the moon and that he and his fellow astronauts would then face imminent death.

In 1997, NASA finally rejected that 1950s and early 1960s approach. It abandoned its button-down look for the "geek" enthusiast persona. Matt Golombeck, project scientist for the Mars Pathfinder mission, dressed in flannels and plaids and never wore a tie.

Golombeck gushed enthusiasm and giggled frequently and awkwardly as he shared his love of space exploration with everyone on the airwaves. No other NASA official represented the agency. The non-threatening, socially pathetic Golombeck was everywhere, almost a regular on all the network morning news shows.

Golombeck connected with his audience, but so too did the agency's new mantra—"better, cheaper, faster." Each press release described the Mars mission in accessible terms. NASA-sponsored web sites sent out live feeds from the Martian surface as the moon rover—often prefaced with the adjectives cute, plucky, and lovable—moved about the terrain. Resembling nothing so much as a familiar LegoLand vehicle, the rover Sojourner surveyed the Martian topography, which quickly acquired NASA-created nicknames. Scooby Doo, Yogi Bear, and Yosemite Sam, NASA names for Martian rocks but also much beloved cartoon characters on earth, and Barnacle Bill, reminiscent of a popular risqué sea chantey, tapped into each person's inner child and welcomed him or her into the exciting field of space exploration.

The Mir Space Station's repeated troubles a few months later ironically bolstered NASA's new human-sized approach. The dangers faced by astronaut Michael Foale and the Russians suggested not NASA incompetence but rather the risks of space travel and just how concerned and caring the agency was and had been. NASA was humanized rather than glorified. The agency no longer was composed of distant experts; NASA was now made up of common men and women.

The agency made a major misstep a short time later. Protesters urged against using highly radioactive Plutonium to power Project Cassini to Saturn. A launch mishap might vaporize the radioactive material and blow the deadly gas into Florida's Disney World and Universal City. Critics demanded a switch to passive solar cells and personalized their crusade by opening an informational web page, gathering signatures on petitions, and picketing the launch site.

NASA reverted and took refuge in expertise. NASA's unwillingness or inability to explain to individual citizens why the mission was necessary or important was particularly telling. Its stiffly formal project manager, Richard Spehalski, accused adversaries of spreading fear, not facts, equating their techniques to "walking into a crowded movie theater and yelling 'Fire.' " Saturn's distance from the sun made solar power impossible; cells would need to exceed the size of football fields. Spehalski then produced a two-foot thick safety analysis and maintained that independent experts had substantiated each aspect. Claiming odds of a disaster approached one in a million, Spehalski asserted that the mission was "demonstrated to be safe."

Manufacturing Consent and Productivity

The market for industrial psychology and social science bromides exploded in the 1970s and after. Having workers operate as manufacturers wanted them to remained the goal, but methods of achieving that aim now stressed individual participation and the absence of hierarchy or authority. Phrases, such as "taking ownership" for the product, wellness programs, and the ubiquitous Total Quality Management blurred in most non-essential matters differences between management and workers and offered workers the appearance of significant freedom and choice in job-related (and many not related) activities as well as insulation from external pressures, such as constraining performance reviews, production quotas, or work standards. Provision of these programs and techniques symbolized that workers mattered, that each individual was a treasured member of what was often called the industrial "family" or "community." Such was the case even as employers cut back on traditional worker benefits and "down"- or "rightsized" their work forces. Appreciation became its own reward.

The Case of Redstone Arsenal

Redstone Arsenal, home of the U.S. Army Aviation and Missile Command, helps the nation remain militarily strong and prepared. Located near Huntsville, Alabama, Redstone has been the nerve center of the Army's missile and rocket program since 1948. It is responsible for missiles, rockets, and supporting equipment, activities that involve research and development, engineering and testing, and procurement and production of materials as well as logistics support.

To that end, Redstone has participated in the Army's "Communities of Excellence" program and has been commended for its efforts since 1992. "At the heart" of Redstone's work on delivery systems for weapons of mass destruction "are individuals committed to the success of this program." The community's ambition has been to "achieve performance excellence everywhere in people, services, and facilities." Essential to reaching these ambitions has been articulation of "a shared vision" and identification of "clearly stated goals." Only those techniques provide "employees with an understanding of their organization's constancy of purpose," which will allow Redstone "to provide continually improved products and services to its customers and a rewarding environment for its employees."

Redstone's vision of what its missile systems are expected to do is rather straightforward and somewhat at odds with the communal, non-competitive sentiment outlined above. The vision's three components are "decisive victory through excellence in missilery," "power projection through superior technology," and "consistently exceeding customers' expectations" (the Army is the sole "customer"), each of which is to be achieved "through an inspired workforce committed to excellence." Its goals are similarly matter-of-fact. It is to "ensure [that] missile systems readiness levels are at or above Army standards through a team effort with soldiers in the field," "achieve world-class customer service," "generate the science and technology to enable America's Army to swiftly achieve decisive victory," and "empower and train the total workforce and provide them with a quality work infrastructure and environment."

These goals and shared vision must be reached in accordance with Redstone's core "values." They include "integrity," "competence," defined as "giving your best, nothing less," and "leadership" through "enabling others to use their talents and resources to excel in all tasks." Other parts of the core are: "loyalty," which is "giving constant support to the organization, its people and its customers," while at the same time giving "respect for the needs and contributions of all"; "commitment," identified as "willingly, consistently carrying out goals of the organization" that is "excellence driven [and] customer focused"; "teamwork" as "empowering people, sharing leadership and cooperating with one another" as well as "respect for all team members"; and "service" that exceeds "our customers' expectation in a professional, pleasant and competent manner."

From Human Potential to TQM

The "human potential movement" of the 1970s began from the laudable goal that each individual had merit and his or her abilities should be "self-actualized" (achieved). This often involved individuals learning how to throw off those restraints that had hampered or stifled individual potential.

"Total Quality Management" became the organizational application of that tenet and its underlying rejection of any sense of comparative merit. TQM emerged from work done by W. Edwards Deming in postwar Japan. A New York University statistician and business professor for over forty-five years, Deming's efforts to instill a new management philosophy into Japanese business—his System of Profound Knowledge—won him considerable notice in America as the Japanese economy boomed in the 1970s and early 1980s. Others elaborated on his work, including Joseph M. Juran, an independent management consultant who had also lectured in postwar Japan, and Philip B. Crosby, an ITT management consultant who pioneered the term "zero defects" and had lectured in Japan in the early 1960s, to create what has become TQM. TQM now reigns as "the management choice of the nineties." To its proponents, TQM "is more than a program; it is a commitment to a new way of life, personally, professionally, and as a world citizen." They define TQM as "a structured system for satisfying internal and external customers and suppliers by integrating the business environment, continuous improvement, and breakthroughs with development, improvement, and maintenance cycles while changing organizational culture."

TQM "underlying" or "core concepts" strike a different chord. There "organizational and personal excellence" comes through accentuation of the individual. "An overall improvement in competitiveness" requires each person to take "universal responsibility." This sentiment places the onus on each individual, but individuals are thought to be up to it. Persons "are experts on their own work; they have a

Total quality management (TQM) has come to dominate American organizations. Here a quality circle considers assessment, strategic planning, implementation, and institutionalization.

deep wish to contribute and be needed; and the more each person knows, the better they perform." In this case, information—explaining to individuals the basis for decision making, often thought mysterious or irrational—impels them to function at their highest level. The totality's success, they argue, "resides in individuals, not in tools or techniques. By developing successful individuals, we develop successful organizations, and successful organizations are essential to America's economic future."

The steps in the TQM informational gambit include "assessment," "strategic planning," "implementation," and "institutionalization." TQM's "essential ingredients" are to its supporters "planning, active listening, team development, conflict resolution, customer service, process orientation and improvement techniques, variation and the tools for measuring variation." Knowledge will maximize each individual and set them all free.

TQM's noble sentiments and platitudes appeal to a broad spectrum of persons. These statements certainly seem like a breath of fresh air to those seemingly victimized by the system. TQM frees those persons from the oversight and control of others and encourages them to erect their own definitions of their blessings. TQM also recognizes them as legitimate and appreciates them for their legitimacy. Put bluntly, TQM permits individuals to cordon themselves off as separate self-defined units. But TQM requires faith. Like New Age, 12-step, and recovery programs, and like cooperative education (a contemporary fad in education colleges), its success depends upon belief, upon the unobstructed, untethered individual doing the "right" thing. The world in which TQM can exist must be non-judgmental, non-threatening, non-competitive, and mutually respecting, and each individual will be self-maximizing. In this closed system all activities occur. Individuals have nothing to solder because there is no group with which to identify.

What about those lacking faith? What about those not buying into the system? In the TQM world, they deserve censure. They violate the non-interference, non-judgmental mandate and thus place themselves outside the community and are not worthy of consideration. Indeed, the religion of TQM as the new corporate or business culture brooks no freedom of religion or belief.

But can, does, or should a world as suggested by TQM exist? Certainly it has appeal to some. Management jettisons sole responsibility, which is replaced by "universal responsibility." TQM's only means of measurement, its "ultimate test," is simply "the quality of service as defined by the customer." Surely this is a gauge that many commercial firms would gladly applaud. What of competition? What of difference in merit? These terms and ideas are not involved in a TQM world. Both denote a comparison between one or more things and both imply essential differences among them. Such comparisons and differences are prohibited.

Technology of Life: Biotechnology

Many of the issues surrounding agricultural chemicals were raised about biotechnology from its genesis in the 1970s through its emergence as a force in the 1990s. But another set of concerns also accompanied it: fear of creating something not found in nature, a threat of Frankensteinian proportions. The risks were not merely physical. To some, possibility of artificial life seemed to place humanity in the role of god.

At its simplest, all biotechnology is based on the discovery by James Watson and Francis Crick and others in the 1950s that the double helix-shaped deoxyribonucleic acid (DNA) carried the genetic code in simple base pairs.

Unraveling the double helix, coupled with requirements that each base would match only its specific base mate, provided rules for how cells divided and replicated themselves, thus passing information on to subsequent generations. The sequence of the base pairs proved a

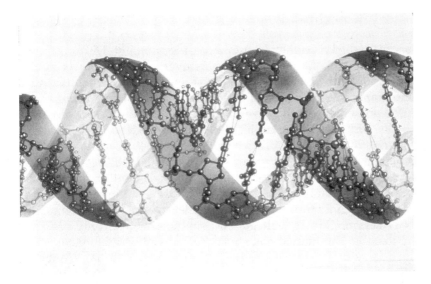

Uncovering the structure of DNA and its method of replication was the first step in what has become a biotechnology boom.

code; each extended sequence was a program to produce a certain substance or do a specific task. What remained was to identify what activity took place at any locus, what the code for that activity was—its program—how to modify or replace that code and therefore that activity and then do it on an industrial scale.

None of those questions was resolved easily. All ignored the organism per se to concentrate on the task. Biotechnology manipulation is simply reprogramming matter. Biotechnologists seek to modify extant programs in living organisms; they learn what series of instructions to write that would produce the desired biology and therefore the desired effect. By the early 1970s, researchers could alter that code by "recombination": cutting a piece of DNA and splicing it with another piece not normally found at that site. The microorganism receives specific qualities, properties, or attributes that may not occur in nature and is therefore called genetic engineering.

Biotechnology virtually removes time from the hereditarian equation. Unlike hybridization, for example, which involves a repetitive life cycle of birth, growth, and propagation for several generations, biotechnology is almost instantaneous and predictive. It eliminates chance errors and other vagaries of reproduction as new individual organisms with distinctive genetic makeup emerge as their creators piece them together on their own timetables.

Classical Biotechnology

It was around classical biotechnology—recombinant DNA technology—that much of the early controversy over genetic engineering occurred. In 1974, soon after Herbert Boyer and Stanley Cohen had first cut and transferred DNA from one bacteria to another, recombinant DNA researchers themselves issued guidelines for their work and possible risky research areas. Under the National Academy of Sciences, they sought voluntary compliance, but limited their focus to the scientific community. Two years later, the National Institutes of Health reaffirmed the researchers' guidelines, focusing attention on whether experimental transfer of DNA molecules from one organism to another posed hazards through accidental release into the environment.

NIH action did not halt genetic engineering but only reduced public debate. The hiatus was short. In September 1978, genetically engineered microbes were producing human insulin. As Congress considered whether to issue biotechnology guidelines, venture capitalists began to invest heavily in biology-based companies. Announcement in 1980 of engineered Interferon, a potentially potent cancer-fighting agent, along with two U.S. Supreme Court decisions the same year, established biotechnology as a major technological force. The first decision allowed Boyer and Cohen to patent their gene splitting and splicing technology. The second permitted the patent office to grant a patent on a genetically engineered "oil-eating" bacterium, a "non-natural man-made microorganism" with "markedly different characteristics from any found in nature."

Receiving patents for reprogrammed life, even simple forms of life, spurred considerable attention and sparked a new biotechnology boom. Shares of the first publicly held genetic engineering company, Genetech, went on sale on October 14, 1980. Even the normally sober *New England Journal of Medicine* gushed that "never has there been a comparable period in the growth in the knowledge of living things." This "geometric progression of information" places us "on the threshold of . . . [a] transformation in health practices, agriculture and industry." NIH quickly relaxed its restrictions of gene-splicing, claiming the years since 1976 had shown the technology to be safe. Universities poured money into biotechnology research—for example, MIT accepted in the early 1980s $125 million from businessman Edwin Whitehead to establish an institute for life-sciences research—as did state governments and private enterprises. Academics, many receiving government grants, were encouraged by governments and universities to become financial as well as research partners in biotechnology firms.

Biotechnology seemed a perfect high-tech solution to the stiff global competition America faced. But national competitiveness at

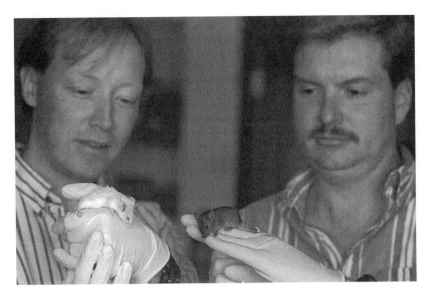

Neither animal is a mouse. Both are "transgenic nonhuman eukaryotic animals." The U.S. Supreme Court ruled in 1988 that individuals could patent mammalian animals that did not occur in nature.

what price? A few municipalities with local biotechnology research facilities, such as Cambridge, Massachusetts, issued guidelines on acceptable practices within city borders. In 1986, the federal government also published guidelines, which conformed to the regulatory-diminishing risk-benefit calculations favored by the Reagan White House, and therefore worked to encourage biotechnology research and application. The policy's first real test came a year later. In 1987, after the courts swept aside the objections of several groups claiming to speak for the environment, the NIH gave final approval to release Ice Minus in crop fields. This genetically altered bacteria protected plants from light frost. Unlike the earlier oil-eating bacterium, which could not sustain itself without a supply of oil to digest, the Ice Minus bacteria could live indefinitely in the soil. A human-made and programmed creature now competed with naturally occurring soil microbes. In the struggle for existence, the engineered microbe could spread, replace the naturally occurring organisms and dramatically change the ecosystem.

As late as 1988, the FDA had approved only five genetically engineered substances. About 200 life forms had been patented. Yet that year marked a major biotechnology boost. The Supreme Court approved a patent for a transgenic mouse. Creating a sophisticated mammal using its naturally occurring genes as well as those from other species—it contained human genes known to make the host exquisitely sensitive to certain types of cancer—and being permitted to patent it as if it were a mechanical device held important economic as well as ethical implications. The terms used to justify patenting the mouse, protecting the "intellectual property rights" of the creators of a "transgenic nonhuman eukaryotic animal," implied that the transgenic mouse was a person's private creation and thus smoothed over the ethical problems of patenting and creating new life forms. And the ability to amend the genetic program of mammals seemed particularly portentous in agriculture and medicine. Insertion of human genes in large non-human creatures promised creation of large supplies of specific chemical agents—vaccines, antibodies, and the like—in medicine, while the manipulation of animals used for human food guaranteed an agricultural boom. In 1988, over forty state governments invested in biotechnology as each labored to spur their home-grown economies. The federal government invested over $1 billion that year.

In the past decade, biotechnology has just begun to bear fruit. Genetically engineered yeast converts lactose into alcohol and disposes of the high-lactose whey, a waste product of cheese processing. Modified Escherichia coli transforms cellulose waste (corn stalks, sawdust, and agricultural by-products) into sugar. In medicine, biotechnologically engineered microbes have produced numerous patentable medical substances. They include: erythropoietin, a hormone that stimulates blood-cell formation; tissue-plasminogen activator, an anticlotting agent used to treat heart attacks; antibody production to fight disease; and vaccines to protect against hepatitis B, herpes simplex I, influenza, and other viruses.

The situation is even clearer in agriculture. Genetic engineers have inserted potato starch genes into corn to change the texture of each kernel and thus to encourage increased human consumption and have introduced similar genes into tomatoes to yield a fruit that can be converted into ketchup with significantly less drying time and therefore less manufacturing expense. Agricultural biotechnologists have engineered a rapeseed plant that produces large quantities of stearic acid for industrial purposes and another that bears no stearic acid, only those oils essential for margarine production. Genetically engineered microorganisms (GEMS) have sparked human-made plagues among economically damaging insects. Plants designed by recombinant DNA technology are virtually immune to specific herbicides so that the noxious chemicals only attack weeds, not cash crops. Others are implanted with genes for resistance to insect pests or common ground viruses. Inserting nitrogen-fixing capabilities into the roots of plants that do not naturally fix nitrogen and therefore eliminate the need for fertilizer eases ground water pollution threats.

Agricultural biotechnologists regularly blur the formerly impenetrable boundary between plants and animals, but transgenic animals have drawn more attention. Engineered sheep excrete insect repellent to produce moth-resistant wool and cows are configured to produce milk that the lactose-intolerant can consume. Transgenic salmon live comfortably in subfreezing seawater, and cows are manufactured to give milk containing red blood cell growth factors to treat pernicious anemia. Transgenic "pharmers" regularly manufacture new genetically manipulated animals to produce pharmaceuticals to fight human ills.

The public response to this individually created, "unnatural" food, fiber, and pharmaceuticals has been muted. The federal government has also been accommodating. As early as 1986, the Office of Science and Technology Policy demanded that the entire government establish a "coordinated framework" and treat biotechnological products no differently than naturally occurring ones, such as hybrids. Specifically, the Office maintained that existing laws and agencies were sufficient to regulate the new engineered products; biotechnology created no new safety issues.

Various government agencies reaffirmed this policy over the next several years. The FDA restricted its focus on food quality, ignoring the manner of production, and therefore did not require engineered food stuffs to go through special premarket clearance procedures or carry special labels. In 1992, Recombinant Bovine Somatotropin (rBST) became the first FDA-approved genetically engineered food product; rBST cows yield about 10 percent more milk than others. Two types of controversies surfaced. Animal rights and human welfare activists complained about engineering's effect on their constituencies. Others wondered about the fate of small dairy farmers and the trend to larger commercial farms. America had a milk surplus; the federal government already bought up and destroyed much of the surplus, which kept prices artificially high. Now it would need to purchase and dump more at the taxpayers' expense.

In contrast, the "Flavr Savr" tomato, approved in 1994, evoked almost no comment. A duplicate copy of the softening gene was inserted in the tomato in reverse orientation from the natural gene. The two genes bound each other, a factor that greatly increased the length of time a tomato could be shipped without refrigeration and retain its flavor. The only dispute surrounding this product was whether to identify it as a genetically engineered food.

Newer Genetic Engineering Forms

Gene Transfer Virtually all marketed biotechnological products have resulted from classic recombinant DNA technology. But industrialists now employ several newer ways to manipulate genetics. Gene transfer identifies desirable genes for a particular act or process and injects them into embryos in culture. The cultured, manipulated embryos are planted in a donor uterus and are born able to produce the desired process or act. Because their genetic material is forever changed, offspring of these founder animals also have their parents' unique abilities.

Gene transfer's medical and agricultural possibilities are profound. Human embryos missing a specific gene and therefore likely to develop some problem later in life could be amended to eliminate the problem for themselves and their progeny. Animals or plants so manipulated can produce substances or acquire characteristics that increase agricultural profitability.

Human Genome Project Genetic manipulation, including gene transfer, depends upon identifying which gene controls what specific act. An effort to map the entire human genome—every gene on all forty-six chromosomes—nears completion. Inspired by the twin admonitions that "for the first time . . . , a living creature understands its origins and can undertake to design its future" and "to know thyself" is "the ultimate commandment," the project is jointly administered by NIH and the Department of Energy, which has been interested in heredity for many years. The discovery in the early 1980s that specific genes—oncogenes—were implicated in many cancers led to calls to map the entire human genome, a project in funding, commitment, and spirit to the program "that led to the conquest of space." The DOE placed the genome project in its budget in 1987. Many biologists voiced opposition, complaining that sequencing was boring and that it sucked off research funding.

Selection of Watson to head the project gave it credibility. It also received boosts from many industrial interests, which claimed that mapping would result in commercially viable products. They also worried about Japanese and European mapping projects getting a head start on marketing products. Senators as far apart politically as Orrin Hatch and Al Gore expressed concern over the project's eugenic possibilities, but their countrymen did not second their distress to any great degree. In 1991, the Human Genome Project became a formal federal program, now scheduled for completion around the year 2000.

Identification of parts of the human genome has led to a profusion of tests to determine an individual's genetic predisposition to a particular malady or condition. In some cases, prophylactic action removes the threat. In others, repeated monitoring enhances the prognosis. In a few instances, such as in a specific type of cystic fibrosis, introduction of engineered material that the individual in question is genetically incapable of producing can keep the person free of the disease's symptoms. But knowing probabilities of certain diseases emerging also has its costs, both financial and psychological. Insurance companies want to factor in this data in rate tables; and not everyone genetically pre-disposed to certain ailments wishes to know whether the ailment will actually occur.

Similar genome projects exist for agricultural animals and plants as diverse as pigs and corn. They raise fewer ethical questions and generate almost no public scrutiny.

Nuclear Transplantation Nuclear transplantation suggests similar possibilities and questions. This genetic engineering form transfers an entire nucleus from one cell to a second cell, which has had its nucleus removed. Much early work has surrounded removing the nuclei of immature animals and planting them in the enucleated eggs of a ma-ture animal of the same species—tadpoles and frogs eggs, for example. But Dolly, the famous cloned sheep of 1996, apparently was created by taking an adult, fully mature nucleus and transplanting that nucleus into an enucleated sheep egg. This process produced a clone, an ani-mal genetically identical to its parent.

Techniques to create a race of mammalian clones are hardly in place. Dolly's creators had over 270 failures before achieving success. Similarly, no other group has managed to replicate the Dolly experi-ment more than a year after its announcement. Nonetheless, some per-sons, such as Richard Seed, a Chicago physicist, confidently promise for the right price to apply the same technology to humans. President Clinton and Congress are pondering calling for a human cloning moratorium.

In addition to ethical issues, human cloning strikes at the very heart of the post-1970s dilemma. Clones are identical genetic replicas of the self. In a world in which each individual seeks uniqueness, iden-tical individuals undercut the idea of specialty. Vanity compels some to be attracted to the idea of cloning, yet repels the same people and others at the notion of a person's reproducibility. Cloning can create an exact tissue match, thereby serving as a store of extra body parts, but raises the issue of one individual's relationship to its genetically identical equal. Cloning suggests the possibilities of immortality but also limits the idea of identity.

Cloning and Contemporary Fertilization Techniques

The other half of the human cloning equation, manipulating fertility in human beings, is an established practice. The first "test tube" baby is now more than 20 years old. Several manipulation methods have be-come standard. Fertility drugs, drugs that cause many human eggs to ripen in a single month, are routinely employed to increase pregnancy chances. The McCaughey septuplets of Iowa, born in 1997, are this process's most famous example. If the female's uterus is unable to carry embryos to term, fertility technologists utilize *in vitro* fertilization—sometimes with direct sperm injection into eggs—and implantation in a donor uterus—a surrogate "mother." Sterile females receive *in vitro* fertilized eggs from a donor and carry the implanted embryo to term. Sperm banks, where semen is quick frozen with liquid nitrogen and dispensed when appropriate, have become a part of the lexicon, but eggs, ovaries, and embryos are also frozen for subsequent use.

These techniques seem more useful than ever. Recent reports suggest that American women increasingly encounter fertility problems, now over 6 percent. American males have declining sperm counts—estimated on average at one half the number of mobile sperm compared to a half-century ago—sometimes thought the product of endocrine-disrupting environmental factors. Since the late 1960s, reproduction has been cast in term of the self. The right and desire to have children, to reproduce part of one's self through progeny, is contrasted with the right and desire to not want to devote the time necessary to having and raising children. More than ever before, that decision has become a personal one, rather than a society-mandated set of mores. More people delay the childbearing decision until after establishing careers; they attempt to control when and whether to procreate. Even abortion has been cast as a matter of personal control. Disputants argue over when control—before or after fertilization—is or is not a matter for social legislation.

But delaying childbearing until the mid-thirties often carries its own decreased fertility risks, thereby increasing medical mediation. It also raises risks of naturally occurring genetic abnormalities, placing an additional premium on use of amniocentesis and other gene-examining technologies. In amniocentesis, technicians withdraw embryonic fluid to inspect fetal cells for missing or grossly deviant chromosomes. New reproductive technologies explored in delayed and other pregnancy decisions include possibilities of transplanting ovaries or testicular tissue and donating cytoplasm from the eggs of younger females to provide extra nutrients and vitality to the eggs—cytoplasm and nucleus—of older women. This last technique would not change the older egg's genetic makeup, but boost a fertilized embryo's survival chance.

Medical Technology

"Non-invasive" marked the medicine of the 1970s and after. Holistic and alternative medicines claimed to leave the site of trauma relatively alone while restoring the entire body to its "proper" or "natural" state and thus enabling it to compensate for the traumatized part. Conventional medicine also adopted "non-invasive" but in reverse, to localize

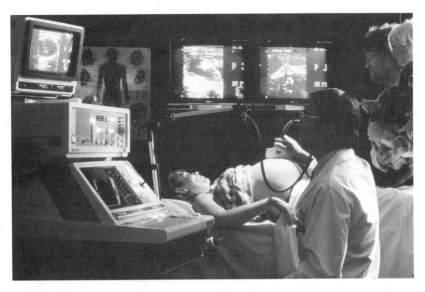

Ultrasound gives doctors a mechanism to check fetal development, and parents an opportunity to see and hear their children before birth.

intervention to the trauma site and therefore not traumatize other body parts.

Preserving the self—the integrity of the unique individual—and placing it beyond any hazard have become modern medicine's goals. Personal health has replaced public health as individuals strive to control what they see as the ultimate personal issue. Demands for new medical technologies and procedures have skyrocketed since the late 1960s. Being well and being healed have become individual expectations, even rights, as Americans incessantly complain about the various socially derived hazards that afflict them. The irony remains that individuals through their personal behavior threaten their own health much more than all socially derived hazards combined. But that persists as an individual, not public, matter.

Diagnosis: Imaging Technologies

New diagnostic technologies also accentuate the "non-invasive." Here ultrasound, Magnetic Resonance Imaging (MRI), and Computed Axial Tomography (CAT Scanning) are boosted for limiting trauma or disruption to the site examined.

Each permits a three-dimensional portrait, enabling technologists to peer into the body without opening it. Yet while these newer diagnostics embrace a sense of passivity, they each treat the body as a series of discrete, disaggregated units. In short, the technologies are predicated upon assumptions very much in concert with the individuation undergirding biotechnology and digitization. Ultrasound, MRI, and CAT reduce the body respectively to a series of textures, a series of atoms, and a series of points or planes. The recombination of these textures, atoms, points, or planes on a two-dimensional medium constitutes the three-dimensional portrait. The portrait is a unique picture of a unique site in a unique individual, a personal profile rather than a group or statistical norm. Computers are essential to the recombination task in MRI, CAT scans, and ultrasound.

Ultrasound, CAT, and MRI each subject the individual to high radiation levels. Yet few investigate its safety. Persistence of this informational void without arousing concern or debate suggests the private matter of personal diagnosis overwhelms the public issue of subjecting populations to abnormally great amounts of radiation. After about 1970, private trumps public.

Ultrasound

Ultrasound diagnosis dated to the 1950s, when doctors in America and Europe passed high frequency sound waves through human brains to detect differences in textures, which might suggest tumors. But this point-to-point transmission quickly gave way to the pulse-echo approach. Here the situation was more akin to radar, where a single transducer served as transmitter and receiver of the reflected sound. The University of Minnesota's John Wild recognized that different tissues possessed different textures and that those textures reflected sound waves at different rates and intensities. Rather than focus on the possibilities of a realistic portrait, Wild was expressly concerned with the existence of a solid mass—a tumor—in a place it did not belong, especially the brain. Others refused to adopt or modify Wild's technique because concentrated sound waves could generate heat. Ultrasound was potentially dangerous, requiring investigators to prove harmlessness before using it in human medicine.

Such an occurrence took considerable time and money. As late as 1968, ultrasound found use only in the most serious cases. Not until the mid-1970s did it become an inexpensive and potent diagnostic tool. Computer-adept technicians reduced each pass to a series of points and took repeated passes from slightly different perspectives and at slightly different times. When this data was assembled, it created a three-dimensional composite representation. Pioneering work at the University of Washington on the Doppler effect and ultrasound now paid off. Enhanced three-dimensional images, such as in fetal monitoring, made that practice the most extensive ultrasound medical use, although it became commonplace only after about 1980. Doppler also permitted measurements of movement of body fluids. Echocardiograms—the second most common ultrasound usage—of the blood coursing through the heart and arteries helped detect occluded or otherwise diminished pathways and structures. By the mid-1980s, the echocardiogram became a medical diagnostic staple.

Industry adopted ultrasound in much the same way. As part of the growing area of non-destructive evaluation, technicians used ultrasound to detect flaws in solids, including stress fissure in airplane wings and blowholes in cast metals. Ultrasonic vibrations cleanse industrial materials to facilitate soldering and welding, pulverize kidney and gall stones, and remove tartar from teeth.

But the most noted ultrasound use has little to do with industrial processes or medical care. Many parents expect to hear a fetus's heartbeat in the mother's womb and to secure a picture of the blessed creation. These pictures and sounds inspire all sorts of personal emotions but ignore one important fact: There has never been a systematic attempt to determine if and when ultrasound vibrations are safe for fetal tissue. Persons complain about electromotive force and its potential consequence. Yet in their pursuit of immediate personal gratification, they willingly and willfully demand unnecessary sonograms without any evidence of risk or safety.

Computed Axial Tomography

CAT scans depend on gamma rays, which, unlike ultrasonic waves, are not reflected by most soft tissue structures. Emissions pass through a body and are received and recorded on the other side. Technicians repeat scanning from slightly different angles, each providing digitized coordinates. Computers store each minutely dissimilar scan until several hundred passes have been made and the session is completed. Computer programs then accomplish the laborious task of comparing and measuring the scans and removing duplicate information. A series of estimates, with each estimate compared to data and the resulting dichotomy the basis for the next estimate, generates an increasingly realistic numerical projection of certain tissue structures. The pixel-by-pixel recreation of that numerical estimation becomes the three-dimensional portrait, which can be colorized.

Like ultrasound, CAT scanning required powerful computers to create portraiture. And like ultrasound, university-based scientists in the 1950s and 1960s achieved the pioneering work. But unlike that sonic device, CAT scanning was expensive. Nonetheless, the speed at which these nearly half-million-dollar devices penetrated American hospitals in the early 1970s was astounding. Patients proved willing to pay higher hospital or insurance rates to have immediate access to a CAT scan. As important, owning a CAT scanner became an almost necessary prerequisite to attract patients to a medical facility. Yet by 1976, Joseph Califano, HEW Secretary, complained that every hospital needed a CAT scanner no more than every garage needed a Cadillac.

Locating CAT scanners everywhere encouraged hospitals to justify their steep investment. Frequent and often questionable use led to patients receiving considerable doses of radiation. Yet that potential menace drew little attention as individuals continued to demand at least one CAT scanner at the nearest medical facility.

Magnetic Resonance Imaging

Magnetic Resonance Imaging machines proved nearly three times as expensive as CAT scanners. They quickly became hospital staples in the mid-1980s, as persons demanded that their health care institutions own them. FDA approval in 1985 of MRI as a valid diagnostic tool made costs reimbursable through Medicare as well as most private insurance plans and further stimulated MRI purchases. Yet MRI employs massive magnets that subject individuals to magnetic fields some 80,000 times more powerful than what is normal. The FDA has warned physicians not to use MRI on pregnant women and mandated a lower exposure for children. These safety precautions may be prudent, but they certainly are arbitrary. No evidence beyond the anecdotal exists on the impact of extremely strong magnetic fields on fetuses, children, or even adults.

MRI stemmed from the phenomenon of nuclear magnetic resonance (NMR), identified in the 1920s and 1930s and established to analyze chemical substance in the 1950s. Atomic nuclei with odd numbers of protons or neutrons align themselves when subjected to a strong magnetic field. A radio signal at the right frequency will cause atoms that resonate to that frequency to absorb energy. When the radio signal is discontinued, the energy is released. Two dissimilar measurements can be taken of the release. Similar elements in different compounds have different frequencies, and these different frequencies can be measured to suggest molecular structure, the atom's position, and type of bonding in the molecule.

Not until 1973 did Paul Lauterbur, a chemist at the State University of New York at Stony Brook, conceive of using NMR to create an image. He superimposed a second magnetic field on the basic magnetic field. This converted the specimen to a series of grids with different magnetic fields, which would respond to different resonance frequencies. Signals would now come from locations within samples, not samples themselves. But Lauterbur went a step further. He recognized that if you rotated the second gradient about the test object/sample you would reduce the entire sample to a series of coordinates—points. If each measurement during the rotation were combined by computer using a CAT scan-like algorithm, then a three-dimensional portrait could be achieved.

Huge supercooled superconducting magnets provided the fields necessary for MRI. Their cost and upkeep warned medical facilities off MRI quite early. Iron objects, even desk-size objects, become airborne, drawn by the magnets. Separate facilities or significant shielding was required to protect workers and instruments. But MRI diagnoses exceptionally well certain kinds of tumors and soft tissue damage, such as injuries encountered by athletes. It virtually disregards bone to focus instead on the soft tissues, difficult or impossible to detect by other means. When combined with ultrasound and CAT scans, MRI has made exploratory surgery almost non-existent.

Treatment: Surgery

Newest surgical techniques also attempt to preserve the sanctity of the self. Almost all techniques are site specific, limiting trauma to the area requiring maintenance. Pain, rehabilitation, and healing of collateral structures all have been lessened.

Angioplasty and arthroscopy closely approach the ideal. Angioplasty replaces the arterial by-pass, which entailed breaking the patient's breastbone, retracting the ribs, excising and removing the clogged arteries, and grafting on veins (usually from the legs) to take their place. In angioplasty, thin, ballooned-tipped catheters are guided by fluoroscopy from a tiny incision near the thigh to the arteries near the heart. Once in place, balloons are inflated to force through and clear the blockage. A mesh inserted in the same manner protects the weakened spot. A hospital stay may be measured in hours, with virtually no recovery time, compared to the month-long by-pass course.

Arthroscopy gained its surgical vision through fiber optics, not x-rays. Thin superclean, glass-like silica filaments spatially aligned from end to end carry light from a strong laser into the body by refracting the light within the filament bundle; a minuscule camera projects the surgical site on a large television-like screen. Arthroscopy is used for gall bladder removals and other body cavity operations, but its most common use is in joint repair. Joint injuries had almost always been debilitating, marked by extensive recovery times and a year or more of painful rehabilitation. Surgeons often needed to cut through healthy muscles, tendons, and other joint-surrounding bodies to expose the reparation site. Arthroscopy requires only three

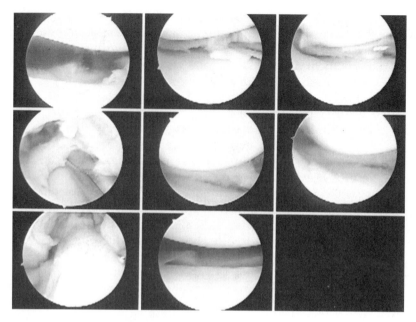

Arthroscopy enables surgeons to view and repair
internal structures with minimal trauma. These six
photos document the condition of a knee before and
after the repair of the medial meniscus.

small incisions for most operations. Surgeons inject fluid in one hole to swell the joint and to make it easier to maneuver within. The fiber optic light/camera assembly is inserted in the second hole and the third is for instruments—shavers, snipers, sutures. Surgeons can do operations as complex as total knee replacements arthroscopically. They replace the load-bearing parts of the knee without disrupting or severing the tendons and ligaments. Small mechanical jigs guide saws to make bone surfaces perfectly flat. High-density polyethylene is cemented on the sawed-down tibia top and a cobalt-chromium alloy (or titanium) covers the head of the femur.

Consumer Products

Kitchen After 1970, a slew of new appliances particularized kitchen work. The microwave, available much earlier, became a kitchen staple after about 1980 and offered almost instant access to certain foods. Manufacturers quickly produced new product lines of microwavable foods and containers. But while the microwave may be the most significant new piece of kitchenware, it was just one of many. Each allowed food preparers to manipulate food more easily or in a different fashion. Food processors, celebrated as the Cuisinart, replaced block graters, blenders, and other devices. Oven ranges with grill and griddle capabilities enabled home chefs to prepare food in ways previously available only at restaurants, and toaster ovens fulfilled similar ambitions. Individual bread makers and coffee grinders and makers further freed the individual from commercial enterprises.

Reducing the workload per task while increasing choice has been a dominant theme. Teflon and other non-stick substances now coat virtually all cookware, making washing less onerous. Ranges now seal burners under a clear polyurethane substance so they can be wiped clean quickly. Coatings on no-wax floor tiles or linoleum end the misery of weekly floor waxing and stripping. Metallic wires covered with paper (often called "twist ties") and, finally, self-seal reclosable plastic bags hold foods in portions of whatever size and end cleaning after transfer.

Introduction of timers and other automated starting and stopping mechanisms as well as servomechanisms often with microprocessors may have been the most important kitchen innovations. Battery-powered smoke detectors became ubiquitous, but most of the new automated or servomechanisms involved food preparation and cooking. In general, they accomplished two things: deskilled food preparation so that a much wider segment of society could manufacture a suitable repast; and enabled food preparers to leave the home during cooking. Memorialized perhaps most exquisitely in the crock pot, a phenomenon of the late 1970s, these new devices permitted would-be home chefs to set up dinner before they left for the day and to return to a fully cooked meal.

Electronics Home entertainment centers were all the rage in the 1980s and, the idea has been institutionalized in American households even as almost all of the machines are manufactured in Japan.

Sales of consumer electronics products topped $75 billion in 1998. Audiotape players sit atop compact disc players and videodisc machines and next to videocassette recorders. Output from the VCR and videodisc machine is funneled through a big screen television or a more modest viewer, which also receives signals from a cable TV company or directly from a satellite dish. Digital Versatile Discs (DVD) introduced in 1996 have begun to penetrate American households at an unprecedented rate. Americans purchased 200,000 DVDs the first year; by contrast, it took three years to sell a similar number of VCRs.

Americans surely misuse and underuse this technology. But the inability of Americans to program their VCRs has not dissuaded them from purchasing and placing these devices in their households. Even in the limited manner in which some use them, these consumer electronic

Couch potatoes have been an offshoot of consumer electronics. Big screen televisions, VCRs, and digital surround sound are musts for modern homes.

devices seem to increase individual control and ability to manipulate life free from social interactions. The VCR, for instance, allows persons to play movies and to free themselves from movie theaters. They view a tape when they please in the comfort and security of their home. Taping a television program provides similar freedom, but viewers can also fast forward through and eliminate the constant commercial bombardment. VCRs also stretch time. Without commercial interruption, an hour-long program now runs forty-eight minutes.

Digital video cameras, first introduced in America by Sony in June 1980, and cordless telephones offer similar freedoms. Microcircuitry is critical in both. Videocams use metal tapes rather than the conventional metallic oxide tapes because powdered and evaporated metals produce less interference—less snow—and more digitized information in a smaller tape area. Personal videocams enable anyone to document family history or record any event. Cordless phones remove the requirement that one stand within a few feet of the phone. Phone conversations have become the second thing people do; the first is what they were doing—and continue to do—when the phone rang.

VCRs Personal VCRs are descendants of the videotape machines of the 1950s and early 1960s. In fact, Ampex opened a consumer division in 1963 and offered for home use its standard home reel-to-reel videotape machine, which the merchandising giant Neiman-Marcus listed in its Christmas catalogue for approximately $30,000. The next year its advertising copy claimed that the home device would "change the whole concept of prime time television . . . because any time will be prime time."

But the actual devices that now populate homes are based not on transverse heads but on a helical loop of tape flowing past a single-recording/reading head. Ampex in America and Toshiba and Sony each opted to explore the helical scan as early as the late 1950s to reduce cost. Ampex never produced a workable device, but Toshiba and Sony, sacrificing quality for cost, managed devices in the early 1960s. Toshiba's became the standard for Japanese television broadcasting, while Sony, which entered into a patent/licensing agreement for Ampex's technologies, marketed in America the first home video-recorders in 1966. These reel-to-reel machines sold for about $10,000, far in excess of most family budgets. Sony reduced tape width to 3/4 inch and line resolution and introduced in 1969 the first mass market videotape recorder. The company again reduced tape width by 1/3 in 1975 and turned from standard to ultrathin magnetic tape. Sony also encapsulated the tape and dramatically slowed tape speed, which lowered cost and improved quality, to produce a reliable, simple-to-operate, full color, two-head cassette videorecorder. Marketing the $1,300 VCR as a "time-shift machine" and a device to "free us of time tyranny," Sony's Betamax line quickly signed up licensees. By 1983, thirty-one firms made the Sony-based machine.

But Beta did not have the field to itself. In 1976, JVC promoted its own 1/2-inch videocassette machine standard, the VHS. VHS recorded less well than Beta, but RCA in America sought to derail Sony and threw its resources behind the VHS. The VHS used a slower tape speed, which produced a theoretically worse picture, but it was the first programmable VCR, which proved a crucial market incentive. Sony did not offer a programmable VCR until 1980, by then quite late. Early VCR enthusiasts were hardly representative of the American population. These persons were generally technophiles, geeks in training, and ability to manipulate technology was considered quite desirable. Sony never did catch up. In 1981, Zenith, Sony's first licensee, abandoned the Beta for VHS. Dolby offered its surround sound processing for VHS videotapes in 1982, making it possible to enjoy multichannel movie soundtracks at home. The company's Pro Logic processing, introduced in 1987 for VHS, popularized home theater among enthusiasts and hammered the final nail in the Betamax coffin. By 1988, VHSs outnumbered Beta machines four to one. VHS owners purchased 325 million blank videocassette tapes in that year.

Videodiscs and Optical Scanners Videodisc technology entered the American marketplace after VCRs were established. These mass marketed devices were considerably different from the first video-discs, which were magnetic and operated like magnetic tape. Ampex and others produced these machines from the mid-1960s. They did poorly, as did attempts to use metallic styluses to etch mechanically encoded sound and video into plastic discs. Similar to photographic records, this method produced relatively poor quality images with significant distortion.

Around 1980 the shift from magnetic to optical scanning occurred. This laser-based technology is the same technology used in compact discs, which record audio, and in CD-ROMs, multimedia, or storage usually associated with computers. Any form of digitized information can be encoded and stored in this fashion, and such important data as playing time is stored on otherwise all-audio compact discs. In audio discs, natural sound, a continuum and panoply of tones, is sampled, and reduced to digital information (digitally remastered ones and ze-roes), which substitutes clarity of digital reduction for the range, sub-tlety, and complexity of raw sound. Compact disc players became popular around 1983, while CD-ROMs did not reach mass market sta-tus until around 1990. In each as with videodiscs, input—in the case of videodiscs, sound, and pictures—are encoded on a disc as high-pow-ered lasers record those impulses by gouging out a series of minuscule pits at varying depths in an outward spiral. Nothing but focused light actually touches these masters, which are generally metallic but some-times hard plastic. After coding, the disc is dipped into an etching chemical, which removes the laser-beamed areas to produce the actual pits. The master is electroplated and molded plastic copies are stamped out, exposed to vaporized aluminum or silver, and sealed in acrylic.

Playing back a disc also requires lasers. Weaker beams are focused on a small disc sector and the encoded pits alternatively reflect and scatter the light. An optical sensor reads the scattering patterns and converts them into sound, video, or whatever. Again, nothing but light touches the surface of the disc, causing no damage or deterioration.

RCA confidently predicted in 1981 that videodiscs "would make home movie-watching as common as listening to rock records." But videodiscs proved an economic disaster. VCRs played back *and* recorded, an option videodiscs did not overcome. In 1984, RCA with-drew from the videodisc market.

Cable TV In 1972, Home Box Office created the first national cable net-work. Operating at microwave frequencies, HBO sent out its broadcast signal, which was collected by a separate receiver every couple of miles, and then rebroadcast to the next receiving center a few miles distant. By linking together some hundreds of such receiving and re-transmitting stations, HBO could broadcast signals across America.

From each of these stations coaxial cables—wires surrounded by insulating layers and finally a metal jacket to decrease tellurian and other interference—carried signals to individual subscribers.

But the HBO-initiated system was hardly new. From about 1953, difficult-to-reach areas unable to receive television signals from stations that normally broadcast in the open air had used a similar strategy. Community Antenna Television (CATV) had sent shows available in densely populated places throughout the countryside, and by 1959, 560 CATV systems served over half a million customers. What distinguished the 1972 HBO effort was that it offered at premium prices a series of shows unavailable elsewhere.

This for-pay alternative to free network television received a boost in 1975 when satellite communication erased the need to boost microwave transmission every few miles. A focused signal was beamed from a central source to a satellite, which beamed that signal to any of a number of regional or local delivery systems, which received the signal and transmitted it by cable to individual subscribers' households. For a price, HBO freed persons from the "tyranny" of open air broadcast network TV. Because subscribers paid for the service and because its material was not accessible in homes that did not want it, HBO could broadcast whatever the market might bear. Individuals making individual decisions could accept HBO programming.

HBO's tremendous success inspired imitators. Each designed its network to cater to a particular coterie of individuals. Sports teams were an early draw. Ted Turner used the Atlanta Braves to transform his local Atlanta station into the nation's first "superstation" and his Braves into America's team. Now, in addition to ESPN, there is a 24-hour golf network that presumably finds a market niche. MTV, CNN, A&E, and the Weather Channel are among the more popular networks that appeal to individual tastes. In 1994, 63.4 percent of United States homes had cable and 95 percent of cable customers received over thirty channels. Subscription services offering direct home reception from communications satellites in stationary orbits through backyard satellite dishes have further multiplied choices by offering over 200 channels per household.

Television has become almost infinitely plastic and personally moldable. In addition to a cornucopia of channels catering to virtually every taste, infrared remotes and other electronic devices send light waves to sensors and permit users to go channel surfing while remaining in easy chairs. Couch potatoes need not rise to avoid commercials. Web TV grants immediate access to the Internet. Interactive TV allows viewers to register individual preferences and choices, as do dial-up systems for selecting movies and other fare (including when they start). The promised V-chip as well as the more widespread individual TV channel lock offers further personal control.

Programmable Chips Kilby's and Noyce's integrated circuit technology enabled manufacturers to miniaturize electronic devices by reducing if not eliminating vacuum tubes. Integrated circuit-based electronics proved more dependable and longer lasting than vacuum tube technology, which also made the new technology cheaper once manufacturers overcame the steep initial investment in circuit-making materials and techniques. NASA and to a lesser extent the military provided the funding to accomplish the transformation. The spatial concerns related to Cold War weaponry and moon landing rocketry made cost virtually insignificant.

Computers and other machines using thousands of vacuum tubes became the next technology to accept integrated circuits. As late as the mid-1960s, businesses defrayed computer expense by sharing time on a centrally located vacuum tube machine. But the relative inexpensive transistor-based integrated circuit technology—computers were roughly 1/10th as expensive—led many firms to order their own smaller but no less powerful personal machines before decade's end. Manufacturers also tapped the consumer market by demanding an integrated circuit designed for portable calculators, a computation-like device. Such a chip would reduce calculators to mere handheld machines. Portable calculators would likely have extensive acceptance within the scientific and university communities.

Japanese firms initially recognized the market potential, but they relied on American chip makers. Ted Hoff, an Intel engineer, received the task of designing a calculator chip for a Japanese firm but instead created a general purpose memory chip. Hoff's chip, the 4004, measured one-eighth inch wide and one-sixth inch long, contained about 2,300 transistors, and included input and output circuits, memory, and a central processor to manipulate data. It packed as much power as had the room-sized ENIAC and sold for only $200. As significant, it was potentially programmable; it could function as a memory chip in calculators or be reprogrammed as memory for other applications. Intel quickly understood what it had and announced the device in November 1971 as initiating "a new era of integrated electronics." This device was nothing less than "a microprogrammable computer on a chip." Two Texas Instruments engineers, Gary Boone and Michael Cochran, improved on Hoff's device. An impressive array of consumer electronic products were possible with this chip, especially when combined with a transducer to convert electrical energy into light. Portable calculators and digital watches were simply the most successful.

Yet the 4004 was a 4-bit chip; it could handle only four binary digits at a time, too few to serve for more than memory. The 4004's 8-bit successor, the 8008 chip, first sold in 1972 but also was limited to memory. It remained until 1974 for Intel to introduce the 8080, the world's first general-purpose microprocessor. An 8-bit microprocessor, the 8080 contained nearly 5,000 transistors and could be programmed for virtually any function, not simply memory.

Revenge of the Nerds

The new world of microelectronics depended on Intel, Texas Instruments, and other large manufacturers for its products, but geeks supplied inspiration. Unsocialized, independent, awkward young white males from moderately well-to-do homes gravitated to the new technology. These teenage boys or young men were bright and creative but rarely successful in structured environments. They were essentially operating outside of society; in that sense, they themselves were digits, monads. Yet they brought their passion—some would say dysfunction—to personal manipulation of the new technology. Their numbers were legion, but few received acknowledgment in the public pantheon. The mass marketing of their ideas and inventions is remembered, not their specific contributions. Only those fortunate or savvy enough to remain or become the leaders of successful corporate ventures persist in the public imagination.

Nolan Bushnell Pocket calculators and digital watches are utilitarian devices, fulfilling some established purpose. Use of microprocessors in frivolous activities helped demystify that technology. It prepared Americans to accept products based on the new chips, which in turn created potential new markets.

Video games were one early activity, and no one deserves recognition more than Nolan Bushnell. Neither Bushnell nor any one else involved in early video game history considered themselves a conduit to introduce the new high tech into American households. But video games catered to the young, the potential market of the future. Bushnell's childhood gave no promise that he would be of consequence. An awkward child who fixed radios and washing machines for fun, Bushnell studied engineering at the University of Utah but spent most of his time playing a game called Spacewar on the huge campus computer. His postgraduate goals were equally modest. He had worked in an amusement park during the summer and hoped to land a permanent job at Disneyland.

When he failed to catch on at Disney, Bushnell joined Ampex in 1969, but his real love remained Spacewar. In 1971, he decided to join two of his passions, Spacewar and bars. Bushnell took advantage of the new microprocessors, hooked them to transducers, and ran the output through video terminals as he labored to convert his beloved Spacewar into a game tavern patrons might play. Finding the game, coupled with liquor, much too confusing, Bushnell's plan flopped.

But the next year he was at it again. This time he simplified. His new game was just a white dot on a green screen that seemed to bounce between two white lines, each of which could be controlled by a patron. He added sound effects to more nearly approximate a game of Ping-Pong.

The approachable, almost hypnotic, escapist Pong became an immediate hit. Before its success was assured, however, Bushnell took $250, parlayed it with a like amount from a friend, and created Atari to market these machines to bars. By the end of 1973, Atari had sold nearly 10,000 machines.

Atari moved from the bar to the home in 1974 and 1975. Not the first home video game—the Odyssey 100 beat it by two years—but the first successful venture of its type, Home Pong could be played on the family television and proved the largest selling item for Christmas 1975. Well before that date, Bushnell's Atari had planned for the future. He moved his offices out of his daughter's bedroom and into a rented facility. Always the outsider, Bushnell's Atari helped create a new form of business culture, "geek chic." Blue jeans served as corporate uniforms. Rock music was piped into the workplace and several marathon brainstorming sessions/parties, reportedly complete with beer and illegal drugs, punctuated the workweek. The company even helped its employees to mellow out by purchasing hot tubs, which it nicknamed "think tanks."

Home Pong's success stimulated numerous competitors. Over seventy different companies entered the video game industry in 1976. Rather than continue to pilot his company, Bushnell sold out to the megapublishing giant Warner, which rode the video game boom. The game Space Invaders in the later 1970s mesmerized a second generation of teenage boys, while Atari's introduction of the cute Pac-Man in 1981 proved a great hit with both sexes. Ms. Pac-Man soon followed. Video games today gross over $4 billion. Bushnell started over a dozen other technology-dependent amusement businesses after leaving Atari. His Chuck E. Cheese Pizza Time Theater, a pizza parlor/ video game arcade featuring large talking animals, has about 300 outlets in the United States.

Bill Gates William Henry Gates III was born into a prominent Seattle family. His parents quickly placed him in a local prep academy, the Lakeside School. There Gates mingled with others equally adept at studies and equally inept at social relations. To engage and stimulate these awkward yet brilliant youths, Lakeside bought computer time in 1968. The 13-year-old Gates, Paul Allen, and a few other Lakesiders became inseparable from the computer. They stayed in the computer room day and night, learned BASIC to write programs, and read computer literature. Their school work suffered. Gates and the others did little homework, skipping class to play with the machine. Rather than end the computer experiment as hampering traditional work, the non-traditional school expanded it. Lakeside got access to the computer of a new Seattle company, Computer Center Corporation. Gates and his compatriots crashed the machine several times and broke through its security system. They even erased the files that recorded how much computer time they had used.

Computer Center Corporation responded not by banning the children but by hiring them to find flaws in programs and weaknesses in computer security. Unlimited computer time was their payment. But when the company went bankrupt in 1970, Gates and the others got their first real jobs, making a payroll program for Information Services, Inc., which also granted them computer time. Lure of time and money proved powerful to Gates and Allen, and they branched out by starting their own company, Traf-O-Data. Using the 8-bit 8008 as the basis for a small computer in 1972 and hiring a Boeing engineer to design the supporting electronic paraphernalia, the two boys designed a simple program to read data gathered directly from street corners and expressed on paper tape about traffic patterns in south Seattle and to translate that data into computer form. They then sold several of their devices to other cities. Their success brought them to the attention of the huge defense contractor, TRW, where as a junior in prep school Gates, with Allen's assistance, located flaws in the company's computer programs and repaired them.

Gates went to Harvard in 1973. He immediately discounted his studies and skipped classes for the computer world. During Gates's sophomore year, Intel released its 8080 microprocessor and MITS company created the Altair 8800, the "world's first microcomputer kit to rival commercial models." For the first time, every electronics aficionado could own a personal computer—cost was less than $400—that approached in power much larger and more expensive machines. To Gates and Allen, computers had become personalized. The boys believed a significant market was about to burst open. Furthermore, they understood that software—programs—were required for the new machines. Once the technology existed (and the Altair had no keyboard, monitor, or permanent memory), individuals would demand ways to employ the machine. Canned programs or at least the ability to program the device in a relatively straightforward computer language could stand as a potential moneymaker.

So Allen and Gates used their Traf-O-Data letterhead stationery and wrote MITS claiming to have created a version of BASIC to run on the 8800. No such thing was the case, however, and in the month before their meeting with the MITS staff at its Albuquerque facility they labored to make the language. When they succeeded, Gates dropped out of Harvard and both boys moved to New Mexico. They permitted

MITS to sell their BASIC with the machines, but they also retained rights to modify the essential program for other personal computers. They even established a new company to produce and market the new microcomputer software, Microsoft.

Steve Jobs Altair enthusiasts gathered near their homes to examine the new machines. One such enthusiastic individual was Steve Jobs. Even as a teenager, Jobs had had a passion for technology, attending Hewlett-Packard lectures after high school classes. But as a tactless, pretentious loner, Jobs had few friends. His parents even moved to a different school district in hopes of improving his social and scholarly life. After a brief tenure working as a woodland creature in the local shopping mall, Jobs got a summer job with Hewlett-Packard, where he met Steve Wozniak, four years his senior. Wozniak matched Jobs' enthusiasm for electronics and his social awkwardness. Almost immediately the two Steves began to toy with blue boxes, devices that emitted electronic-generated tones that would permit free access to long distance telephone service. Apparently the boys hacked telephones for sport, not profit. They even called the Pope pretending they were Henry Kissinger.

The boys separated in 1972 when Jobs graduated from Homestead High and attended Reed College in Oregon. There Jobs rejected formal education he dropped out after the first semester—but stayed in Portland to study philosophy, physics, literature, and poetry on his own. He also experimented with drugs, took up Eastern religions, bought a Volkswagen micromininbus, grew his hair long, wore a beard and sandals, and even took a trip to India as part of his spiritual quest. By 1974, he moved back to California and got a job with the one company that would match his lifestyle, Atari, where he designed video games. Jobs hooked up again with Wozniak—they worked on the classic game Breakout—and the two Steves attended the Homebrew Computer Club, a local assembly of hobbyists interested in the new technology.

Wozniak had begun to design possible computers before Altair 8800 was announced, but that kit further triggered his interest and resolve. Unable to afford the Altair's chip, the Intel 8080, he looked for other cheaper chips as numerous competitors sought to capitalize on the market Intel had pioneered. A knock-off version of the Motorola 6800 chip, the MOS 6502 could be had for a mere $25, and Wozniak not only designed a computer around that chip but also wrote a version of BASIC specially for it. He established simplicity and personal convenience as core design values; Wozniak decided that a keyboard would prove the most suitable input method, and he hooked his computer up to a television as a video terminal. He also established an internal program—a read-only memory (ROM)—that undertook certain

Apple decided quite early that selectively donating Apple II computers to public schools would help the corporation capture the educational market.

fundamental tasks, the programming for which would not have to be replicated whenever the machine was in use. Wozniak repeatedly took the computer to the biweekly Homebrew meetings, where he received suggestions for improvements.

Jobs was particularly aggressive. He saw a potential market for this device and he urged Wozniak to quit his job at Hewlett-Packard and manufacture his device full-time. After some initial hesitancy, Wozniak and Jobs pooled their limited resources—Jobs sold his minibus and Wozniak his HP calculators—to form Apple Computer Company on April 1, 1976. The vegetarian Jobs—at this point in his life he would only eat fruit—had recently worked at an organic apple orchard and had become convinced that apples were the perfect food because of their high nutritional content, appealing packaging, and ability to withstand damage. He hoped the new company would approach the fruit's perfection. Jobs apparently was able to sell others his vision. With his beard, long hair, and sandals, he made his way through northern California's staid venture capitalists, finally convincing Mike Markkula, a former Intel manager, to help support the fledging company.

Apple's initial computer, the Apple I, was followed in quick succession by the Apple II. It competed for an ever-growing market, the personal computer market, as these new devices made their way to the general public. Its advertisements catered to this new clientele. Apple soothed worries and fears, slowly walking even the most backward persons through the ABCs of personal computing. It accentuated being user-friendly. One Apple ad read, "the home computer that's ready to work, play and grow with you. . . . You'll be able to organize, index and store data on household finances, income taxes, recipes, your biorhythms, balance your checking account, even control your home environment." The Apple II was to be anything a person wanted to make it. Apple continued its advertising blitz by giving computers to schools or selling them at deeply discounted prices. By hooking the young on computers, Apple thought it ensured itself the market of the future.

The giant business machine company, IBM, viewed popularity of personal computing with considerable interest. Apple had sold over $100 million worth of Apple IIs in 1980, and Big Blue saw a vast business market for computing. In the years prior to 1980, spreadsheet, word processor, and database software were created. IBM initially hoped to enter this arena by purchasing Atari's computer efforts but decided instead to make its own. It made two fateful decisions. First, it mimicked in style those who had pioneered personal computers. Rather than assign design to a button-down IBM team, the computer giant took its "wild ducks"—its renegades—and gave them the task. But in the hidebound IBM, even its renegades proved too tame. To provide additional inspiration, it asked Microsoft's Gates to explain to them what a state-of-the-art personal computer required. Running a still small company heavily dependent on writing software for the Apple II and other computers, Gates offered his advice and IBM contracted with his company to program the ROMs with a special version of BASIC. It looked elsewhere for its operating system, but after a plan fell through, Big Blue returned to Microsoft and contracted with that company to provide a system.

Microsoft had no experience in that area, but it knew Seattle Computer Products was working on a suitable system. Microsoft purchased QDOS—Quick and Dirty Operating System—and entered into an agreement with IBM that permitted Microsoft to market its new system separate from IBM's new personal computer. It then madly adapted the QDOS to create MS-DOS (Microsoft Disk Operating System).

IBM introduced its PC on August 12, 1981. Predictably, the IBM venture failed to do some things that Gates suggested. It had monochromatic graphics, used a relatively slow chip to save money, and had a cassette tape interface with optional five-inch floppy drive. Despite these design flaws, the IBM PC proved a major success. Its advertisements concentrated on the machine's familiarity. To that end, they co-opted Charlie Chaplin's Little Tramp. Picturing the tramp working at an IBM PC in a pleasant environment made the device appear approachable, certainly the antithesis of the factory in the classic *Modern Times*, and the giant IBM anything but aloof. The promise of Big Blue dominating an ever increasing market led software vendors and others to produce new applications and continually to offer upgrades. As early as 1983, *Business Week* declared IBM the victor in the personal computing war.

Old Ideas in New Bottles

In the earliest days of computing, Xerox, the giant copying company, had put together a team to design a personal computer. The Alto, created in 1972 at the company's Palo Alto Research Center, was its first effort, and the group continued to improve on its concepts throughout the decade. Xerox never chose to become involved in personal computing per se, but in 1979 it purchased $1 million in Apple stock and, as a stockholder, permitted Jobs and a few others at Apple to tour its facility. Jobs immediately recognized the future of computing. Xerox prototypes incorporated Graphical User Interface with icons (GUI), a handheld mouse, a desktop metaphor suggesting the computer as the office of the future, plug and play architecture, object oriented programming, networking among machines, desktop publishing, and laser printing. Overwhelmed by this technology, the Jobs-controlled Apple set its sights on translating it to personal computer reality. Apple's close associate, Gates, got a Xerox tour the next year and pronounced himself suitably impressed.

Even as the IBM PC captured a large market Apple worked feverishly on its radically different machines. Its first effort, the Lisa, sold for over $10,000, nearly three times the cost of the IBM PC. At that price it proved an unmitigated disaster. Many commentators admitted they admired the technology but deemed the cost far too high. The company's Apple III was even less well received. Undeterred, Apple rededicated itself to pushing its image as an independent individual in a world dominated by constraint, in this case the overwhelming constraint of corporate America in the guise of Big Blue. Its scaled-down, moderately priced yet technologically more sophisticated version of the Lisa became the machine around which the company confirmed its individuality. Even the initial announcement of the device took on an air of mystery. It picked the 1984 Super Bowl to unleash this visual image. The ad began by showing "a roomful of gaunt, zombie-like drones with shaved heads, dressed in pajamas like those worn by concentration camp prisoners, watching a huge viewing screen as big brother intoned about the great accomplishments of the computer age. The scene was stark, in dull, gray tones. Suddenly, a tanned and beautiful young woman wearing bright red track clothes sprinted into the room and hurled a sledgehammer into the screen, which exploded into blackness. Then a message appeared: 'On January 24, Apple Computer will introduce the Macintosh. And you'll see why 1984 won't be like *1984.'* " In case anyone deemed the 1984 commercial too subtle in its attack on the IBM mentality, Apple followed it up at the next Super Bowl with an ad known as "Lemmings." It featured a series of blindfolded, nearly identical, dark suited, briefcase-toting corporate types, each with a hand upon the shoulder of the person ahead, who one by one walked off the edge of a cliff like lemmings in a suicidal version of follow-the-leader. Finally, the last person in line, a Macintosh user, refused to be part of the crowd. He lifted his blindfold and walked away from the precipice to chart his own personal course.

The Mac incorporated virtually all of Xerox's innovations. This all-in-one-case machine did away with separate terminals, numerous cables, and other inconveniences. A single mouse click made any series of baroque commands obsolete. The Mac became a striking success, especially in education, art, and publishing, where it offered competitive advantages. But it also did well as a personal and business computer in part because an extensive set of software existed before its introduction. Microsoft had been privy to the Mac from early 1981 and worked up a number of programs for the new platform. Having a virtual monopoly of Mac applications provided Microsoft with a constant revenue stream while shielding it from the highly competitive PC software arena. Microsoft learned to take those applications that proved popular with Macs and prepared versions for the increasingly stiff PC market. IBM's entry into computing in 1981 had created a de facto standard. With the notable exception of the Mac, the vast majority of firms producing computers after IBM based their machines on Big Blue's chip and MS-DOS. After all, these other firms wanted to run the vast store of IBM PC software. The competitive advantage of these "clones" had to be cost or efficiency. Even so, Microsoft remained heavily dependent on Apple. Until 1988, over half of Microsoft's revenue came from Macintosh software.

Nor was Microsoft idle in translating a version of the Xerox computer into new software. As early as late 1984 the company announced the first copy of Windows, but the Intel chips presently in use were much too underpowered to provide the graphical user interface that would make the machine appear "user-friendly." Not until 1986, when Intel issued its 80386 chip, could Windows work even marginally well. But the 80486 microprocessor, introduced in 1989, really made Windows acceptable. Gates announced in 1990 that now Windows "puts the personal back into millions of MS-DOS-based computers." Microsoft sought quickly to saturate the market with the new software. It included Windows with every copy of MS-DOS it sold. In this manner, it hoped to create a Windows-literate and -dependent public. By 1993, Windows 3.0 and its subsequent versions were selling at a rate of 1 million copies each month.

Chips: Size Matters?

By the later 1980s, computing's basic form had taken shape. To be sure, chips became more powerful and included more transistors. Intel's Moore posited a pre-chip relationship in 1964 that remains roughly true: computing power doubles in capacity every 18 months and the number of transistors increases four-fold. Despite increased power, chip prices are stable. Competition, coupled with economies of scale and the farming out of chip production to sites in the third and fourth world, enable manufacturers to keep costs low. Recent technological breakthroughs assure continuation of the low-cost trend. IBM now makes copper conductors to replace aluminum leads, which, in the range of 25 microns, fails for chip technology. Copper conductors work down to the range of .05 microns, 20,000 times thinner than a human hair. Intel's new flash chip technologies now crams two bits of digital information on a single chip, doubling (at least for memory) every device's capabilities. Theorists persist in dreaming of a quantum computer in which each atom becomes a de facto transistor. Deposited one at a time on a surface, charges would be transferred by light, by changing an atom's quantum state. Quantum computers would transmit and exchange information literally at the speed of light.

More and more computing power need not require a bigger, faster chip. The first huge supercomputers in about 1970 accomplished about 80 million operations per second. They have been superseded by what is called "massively parallel computers," which take numerous smaller chips and array them to process in parallel at a small fraction of the cost and with much greater speed. A recent supercomputer was constructed by putting together 9,072 Pentium Pros. This device had over 2 trillion bytes of disk space, 600 gigabytes of memory, and performed 1.8 trillion operations/second. Using standard chips and placing them in parallel also permits extant software to be easily modified to fit the new configurations. Rather than write entire new programs from scratch, these supermachines have used established programs to determine how proteins interact, predict the weather, help design cars likely to sustain less crash damage, and simulate nuclear weapons tests and weapons degradation, the last funded by the Department of Defense and the National Science Foundation.

Although supercomputer design equals in elegance the automated chip manufacture in America and other industrialized countries, assembling chip-dependent technologies is decidedly low tech. Putting together devices from components generally occurs in Southeast Asia and requires extensive labor, frequently female. These workers use microscopes, which cause eyestrain, and are exposed repeatedly to caustic and toxic chemicals. Workers cut the silicon wafers into individual chips, discard the nonworking chips, bond the working chips, and solder them to printed circuit boards according to templates. The finished circuit boards are then sealed in protective ceramic or plastic coatings.

Peripherals During the last decade, microprocessing chips have been fully integrated into the American scene. Interactive TV, video servers, cellular phones, ATM machines, and other banking services including electronic payment are now facts of life for most Americans. Introduction of a series of peripherals—modems, cable modems (which provide high speed connections through local cable companies' coaxial cables), networking software, digitized satellite communication, magnetic floppy and larger disk drives and optical storage, such as CD-ROMs—marked the past decade of computer technology. Each innovation seeks to accentuate the computer's accessibility or convenience, to empower the individual by granting him or her dominion over tasks previously dependent on society and its institutions. Personal Digital Assistants, for example, serve as electronic pocket-size appointment booklets that store telephone numbers, important documents for business dealings, business cards, dictionaries, and other frequently needed sources of data. They make telephone calls using radio waves and send and receive faxes, eliminating fax machines and secretaries. Portable computers enable businesspersons to carry their offices with them, and children to entertain themselves on trips.

Fiber Optics

Fiber optics' growth is worth noting. Dependent upon lasers (as is satellite communication because light carries more data more coherently

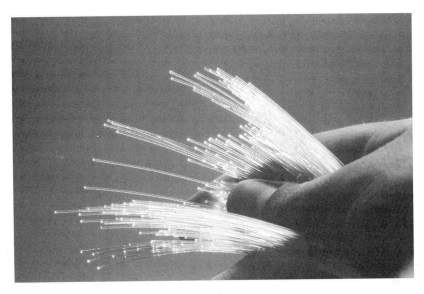

Fiber optic cables now gird the world. They carry a much greater load of electronic signals than conventional cables do and at greater speed and lower cost.

than microwaves), optical fibers replace cables for the long-distance transmission of digitized information.

Elias Snitzer of the American Optical Company of Southbridge, Massachusetts, did the pioneering work in the early 1960s; investigators in England also contributed. Glass quality posed initial limitations. Although Snitzer and others demonstrated that thin pieces of drawn glass could transmit signals over distance, fiber made from ordinary glass is so dirty that impurities reduce signal intensity by a factor of 1 million in only about fifteen feet of fiber. Not until the late 1970s did technologists at Bell Labs and elsewhere develop fiber drawing and glass purification techniques sufficient to make communication-quality fiber. These fibers, really ultrapure fused silica, carry a much greater load than conventional metallic cables, and at much greater speed and much lower cost. Signal degradation is also considerably reduced, as is interference from extraneous electrical fields. Introduced commercially in the early 1980s, optical communication fibers joined many American cities by 1985; each fiber has a glass transportation core and a glass cladding with a higher refractive index to serve as a barrier to prevent the signal from escaping. By 1990 cables were laid under the Atlantic and Pacific Oceans.

The Internet

The Internet links together an extraordinary number of individuals, vendors, and institutions. In many ways, its progenitors conceived of it much as persons now do supercomputers. Each site, each individual operator or resource center, would contribute its knowledge or processing power, thereby enabling each user to benefit from the knowledge or power of all others without expending the space and moneys necessary to build repositories or facilities locally. Each computer could deal with a section or portion of a larger problem, the results reintegrated in yet another machine and sent out to all network participants.

That such a project originated from a Cold War-era, defense-related government agency ought not to surprise. ARPA had the funding and mandate necessary to encourage cooperation among its members. When it was conceived in 1963, ARPANET was to join together ARPA computers (there was but a handful of these monstrous machines) primarily on the East and West coasts. When it initially began transmission in 1970, it connected only four places, three in California and the other in Utah. By that time, it had already established a transmission protocol—it sent packets of information, which meant that the computers received information in discrete, manageable units rather than as a continual stream—and had decided not to hook each computer up to one another but rather establish regional nodes—not unlike the present idea of regional hubs for airlines—to collect messages from other nodes and to distribute the messages to the appropriate individual computers in its region. In that way, each node was connected to every other node but individual computers in a region were only connected to the node. This reduced exponentially the number of connections necessary to link together all networked computers.

As late as 1974, ARPANET connected only 111 computers. But announcement of the Altair 8800 changed matters. Yet it was not simply the number of computers that encouraged ARPANET use. A new application was found for the network, electronic mail. Invented in 1972 by Ray Tomlinson, an ARPANET pioneer, e-mail made it convenient and cheap to transmit messages over the network and, by late 1975, e-mail traffic dwarfed all other ARPANET functions. Quickly users outside of the government combine recognized e-mail's virtues and established networks of their own. USENET was created in 1978 by colleges and universities excluded from ARPANET. In addition to e-mail, it offered news groups, literally fixed titled places where any network member could post a contribution. The ARPANET/USENET model was followed in the late 1970s and early 1980s in business with TELNET and TYMNET, in non-defense-related governmental sectors such as NASANET and the NSFNET and elsewhere. Each new system took packet/node as its archetype but developed its own connectivity protocols.

Each network's members could e-mail everyone else on that network but no one on another network. Attempts to create a method of internetworking culminated in the INTERNET. An ARPANET devised protocol, Transmission Control Protocol/Internet Protocol (TCP/IP), which was first proposed in a 1974 memo where the term "Internet" was initially used, soon became the de facto Internet standard. Yet the great growth of the Internet began only after 1983. Up to that point, only 500 nodes existed. Six years later there were over 100,000. Then Internet traffic began to change. Persons in significant numbers started to exchange and offer conversation and data, not just mail. Special protocols for conversation, Internet Relay Chat (IRC) and Multiple User Dungeons (MUD), for instance, were established. And a special protocol was adapted for information exchange—hypertext markup language, which permitted sound and graphics as well as a simple click here routing system—and in 1990 the World Wide Web was born. Addresses and the idea of domain names, such as .net, .com, .edu, and .org, to denote the type of site followed.

As the number of home computers grew dramatically, companies sought to tap the market of persons without government or education access to the Internet. CompuServe, America Online, and other for-profit servers permitted members to exchange e-mail, to engage in their own discussion groups, and eventually, allow full Internet access for a monthly charge. By 1997, the number of Internet hosts providing some sort of information broke 16 billion.

Cup of Java

From the earliest days of computing, each computer needed an operating system and software to run on that operating system. Emergence of the Internet in the 1990s has promised to end that dependence. Java, the brainchild of Sun Microsystems, which created that protocol between about 1992 and 1995, does away with the need for conventional software while on the Internet. Small programs in that language are stored on the Internet. Persons access those programs, called applets, with a Java-savvy browser while on the Internet, and they disappear as soon as the connection is severed. The network, in effect, becomes the computer, and only terminals, which are much less costly than microprocessors, hard drives, and specific program licenses, are required locally. An extraordinary number of programs could be made available for an extraordinary number of tasks. Terminals could be placed in hotels, supermarkets, and virtually any other place. Java programs could operate appliances, a single click could tell your VCR to record a specific program—rendering VCR programming a thing of the past—recommend recipes, or regulate air conditioning. Java applets enable any person to establish a chat room for whatever topic that person wishes. Each individual selects what unique applications he or she wants. What Java does is simply provide each person an almost unlimited supply of choices; it does not bind individuals together.

Software vendors oppose Java as threatening their businesses, and no company has been more aggressive than Microsoft. One of the seventeen initial Java licensees, Microsoft modified the language to render Java incompatible with anything other than a Microsoft platform—either Windows or MS-DOS—and shipped it as Java on all Microsoft web browsers. Sun sued for contract (and trademark) infringement in 1997, claiming that Microsoft needed to comply with the portion of the contract that dictated cross platform compatibility to use the Java name.

But the software giant also ran afoul of the Justice Department that year. Justice claimed that Microsoft, which had revenues of over $4 billion in 1994, violated an agreement to stop forcing hardware vendors to distribute other Microsoft products, especially its web browser, as part of its licensing of Windows software. Microsoft maintained that the web browser was an integral part of Windows and that to remove the browser would render the entire system non-functional. Ralph Nader agreed with Justice and pronounced Microsoft "a looming monopolistic giant trying to control the information highway through bundling and predatory pricing." The two matters remain unresolved as of this writing.

Whither the Internet?

Among its earliest partisans, the Internet promised to put everyone in touch with everybody else and convert the world's people to Netizens, ending the tyranny of the nation-state and the global conflicts they engendered. Empowerment through technology alone was their cry and universal access a non-negotiable demand. The Internet's social benefits were to be similar to the printing press; a Renaissance would blossom. They spoke, for example, of telemedicine as the norm. Long-distance diagnosis would be de rigueur and long distance, robot-performed microsurgery would become commonplace.

Despite continued promises and predictions, little has actually transpired. Virtually no gain in productivity has taken place. Optimists claim that when more people operate with facility on the Internet, dramatic shifts in productivity will occur, and those shifts are right around the corner. Pessimists find little reason to expect increases anytime soon. They reason that word processing—using the computer as if it were a typewriter or pencil—now stands as the single largest application of computer power in America. Entertainment—playing a game—and information seeking—surfing the World Wide Web or subscribing to an on-line service—monopolize most computer time. These are hardly the sorts of enterprises likely to convert persons into global citizens or lead to worker productivity increases. Market forces have been introduced into the equation. President Clinton and Vice President Gore called in their 1992 election campaign for a National Information Infrastructure as a fundamental piece of the "bridge to the 21st century," and other politicians call for a computer on every school desk, but much of the supporting technology for the Internet in America was privatized in 1995, thereby reducing access and increasing expense. Present plans are for the government to reduce significantly, if not eliminate, its role in Internet management and oversight by the year 2000.

To be sure, for those persons differently abled—wheelchair-bound and the elderly, for example—the Internet is a godsend. They can communicate 24/7 (twenty-four hours a day, seven days a week, in Internet-speak) and make purchases, although merchandise and services on the Internet have grown glacially. But rather than empowering persons, others detect the Internet as a threat to the health and well-being of Americans. A portion of the critique is reminiscent of the earlier critique about computers: physical (excessive sedentary posture, eye strain, exposure to dangerous rays) maladies; invasions of privacy; transfer, scrambling or destruction of military, financial, legal, medical, and other confidential records by "hackers;" and above all, computer dependence or domination.

Yet another subtler thread also exists. At its most basic level, those who reflect on the decentralizing abilities of computers and the Internet, especially the decline of a central office or workplace, and wonder if this physical isolation will result in alienation, anti-social actions, or new social pathology. Others worry less about isolation and more about shallowness. They maintain that "the Internet has the potential of leading you to increasingly superficial interactions with more and more people"; it trivializes human relationships, which fosters ennui. Still others complain about its proponents' confusion between knowledge and access and the substitution of the latter for the former. With more and more persons placing their material on the web, how is an individual to determine what is true or even valid? (Or even find it because automated web engines lack sophistication.) Guillermo Gomez-Pena, a noted performance artist who regularly surfs the web, argues that the net is nothing but performance. On the web, you "hide your gender, race, social class, accent." What emerges is pure unfettered individualism, stripped of any social convention and any sense of decorum. But this individualism is pure only in the

Hobbesian sense. Individuals allowed to run free and act on their passions without social constraint make life "solitary, poor, nasty, brutish, and short." In place of a social contract individuals find solace in "cybertribes," "virtual communities" that grant them the self-gratification that they lust for.

Even as these questions are raised, efforts are underway to replace the Internet with a far faster, more powerful data network. Scientists have long claimed that "civilian" traffic clogs up the net, making large-scale simulations impossible. To that end, the NSF has funded a scientists-only computer network, the vBNS (very high speed Backbone Network System). Formed in 1995 and operating sixty times faster than the Internet, the vBNS incorporates fiber optics technology and evokes those questions of exclusivity that have plagued the computer revolution since its beginnings. Although everyone on the net is equal, some persons may be more equal than others, especially those with enhanced access. Rather than produce a new era of freedom, many argue that these technologies merely perpetuate the unequal status quo.

High-Tech Operations: The Forgotten Laser

Microelectronics—computers and chips—and fiber optics have come to signify high-tech operations, but lasers find an extraordinary number of applications. The military first committed heavily to laser technologies in about 1970. These devices now find the range for and guide conventional weaponry as well as antiballistic missile and antisatellite defenses. Lasers fuel guidance systems for both military and civilian aircraft. Heat-producing lasers open clogged arteries, vaporize tumors, seal capillaries, and cauterize ulcers in medicine. Brief bursts of laser light kill certain germs and are used to sterilize some commodities, such as wine, without changing the taste. Lasers fix toner to paper in laser printing and in copying, weld together metallic components on large and small scale, and bore neat, discrete holes through otherwise difficult-to-cut substances. Glass etching and photolithography have become laser-driven, as has surveying both on earth and on the moon. Identification of compounds resonating with specific laser frequencies facilitates isotopic separation.

The situation is no different in the commercial world. From the mid-1980s, lasers have scanned Universal Product Code seals. Originally agreed to by five supermarket chains in 1971, UPC seals enable supermarkets and retailers everywhere to regulate stock, ordering, and pricing. Similar technology regulates factory inventories and has helped create the digital office. Simplification of office tasks itself proved a benison. Americans made 522 billion photocopies in 1986, a prodigious waste of natural resources.

High-Tech Happenings: The Rise of Silicon Valley

Creation of "geek chic" in the early 1970s paralleled the rise of California's Silicon Valley, which became the world's densest concentration of high-tech enterprises. Large corporations such as General Electric and Kaiser set up branch manufacturing plants in the area, and they and others, such as IBM and ITT, also established research centers at Stanford's Industrial Park and elsewhere. The Park leased space only to high-tech firms beneficial financially and intellectually to the university, and provided a model of both landscaping and architecture for later industrial parks: low-lying, clean, attractive campus-like settings antithetical to the huge ugly factories and sooty smokestacks of traditional big industries. As the complexity of semiconductor research and development grew, and as the need arose for custom-made integrated circuits for major defense contractors, Silicon Valley's critical role as military and aerospace subcontractor expanded. So, too, did the number and size of companies producing materials and equipment for manufacturing semiconductors. Not surprisingly, no other part of the country obtained so many defense contracts.

Many of the initiatives that have come to define modern corporate practice first found expression in Silicon Valley. "Campuses" replaced factories and office buildings. Child care and flex time were further attempts to personalize business, to encourage employees to produce their best work.

High-Tech Business Expansion and the Quality of Life

Silicon Valley's virtual monopoly of high-tech businesses was a casualty of federal, state, and local policies. Carter's emphasis on commercializing the products of nationally funded science, coupled with his successors' dramatic tax and other initiatives in that direction, sparked a whole series of high-tech sites across America. The "sunbelt"—states in the South and Southwest—was an early winner, welcoming hundreds of thousands of manufacturing jobs and millions of "frostbelt" refugees. But hard-hit states, such as Massachusetts and Michigan, soon counterattacked by moving aggressively toward what seemed a panacea. State legislatures offered their own sweetheart deals to encourage new high-tech industries, such as manufacturers of office and personal computers, fiber optics, lasers, video equipment, robotics, machine-vision systems, and genetic-engineering firms.

High-tech industries have brought new jobs to frostbelt economies, and unemployment rates have consequently declined. Massachusetts was an early example of this turnabout in economic fortunes, and its city of Lowell exemplified that trend: from one of the nation's highest urban unemployment rates, dating back to the decline of the nineteenth-century textile mills that made the community famous, to one of the nation's lowest, thanks to Wang Laboratories and other high-tech local industries. Other states did not enjoy the educational and cultural climate that, in part, had made Massachusetts so attractive; nor did other states enjoy its diversity of high-tech industries—as exemplified by those along Route 128, a freeway running through suburbs ten miles from Boston. Still, the eventual bankruptcy and severe downsizing of Wang, and the ultimate failure of Route 128 to rival Silicon Valley's success, demonstrated that high-tech-based economic turnabouts could be as short-lived as those based on earlier technologies.

Yet each state and city defined itself to capitalize on its manifest advantages. To do otherwise would condemn it to marginal status as a loser in the politics of personal enhancement. Many governmental entities proved extremely successful. For example, cities in agricultural states and the states themselves often concentrated on establishing agricultural biotechnology firms and worked municipal tax breaks and land grants as well as state law to make them especially attractive. Rust Belt cities promoted cultural and other, non-weather-related quality of life advantages. Tickets to home games of professional sports teams became an essential part of every major company's business practice, replacing the three-martini lunch. Every place now touts its uniqueness and its ability to provide businesses and their employees some benefit or inducement not found elsewhere. Now more than ever, high-tech businesses are defused throughout America and have come to define American enterprise.

Crossing Over: Americans and Their Technologies

Reduction of living things to their fundamental elements—genes—and reducing machines to binary codes—zeroes and ones—and then using these fundamental parts to construct or reconstruct entire organisms or machines presents the real possibility of blurring the distinction between living being and machine. This heretofore impenetrable divide regularly is broached. For example, biomechanical limbs and other prosthetic devices offer humans mechanical replacements for lost or non-functioning human parts. Sometimes it is symbolic, as in the case of persons walking and running while tethered to a personal stereo, such as the original Sony Walkman that was first offered in 1979, or the more contemporary digital pets, which just like truly organic creatures require care or die. Or perhaps it is television's Star Trek, where the Borg, a lifeless but living, ruthlessly efficient race of beings/machines, represent a particularly distasteful combination, especially when they utter the chilling admonition that "resistance is futile." Here the computer becomes the second self, an extension of the operator's unique personality, and the ubiquitous mouse a mechanical hand. Or sometimes it is the attempt to develop a computer program that accomplishes human activities. The mania for creating artificial intelligence (AI) in machines neatly dovetails with IBM's Deep Blue playing world class chess against human world champion Gary Kasporov. Other efforts include attempting to digitize artistic expression, to reduce artistic creativity to a program of places and spaces.

Humans sometimes adopt the other approach, seeking to convert humanity into machine. The music of artists beginning with John Cage seeks to program music, to deconstruct or disassemble it into units rather than patterns. And theories of human behavior, especially sociobiology and its descendants, take life as programmed matter and genes as engines of selfishness that eat, drink, and breathe. Hyperfiction and cyberfiction, two distinct literary styles, also fit the bill. Hyperfiction is ephemeral and intensely personal. Each author/reader creates his or her own personal story on magnetic media and ships it to the next living node on the line. Cyberfiction postulates an entire world in which distinctions between organic life and machine life have disappeared. Nanotechnology regularly courses through veins and persons reduce themselves to a series of atoms to recombinate elsewhere.

Cross-over activity is consistent with an individuated, digitized, programmable world, one in which the traditional question of a particular technology's impact upon society has been rendered meaningless. And it helps account for the unprecedented American ambivalence toward technology. On the one hand, anything that seems to enhance individual sanctity is cherished but, on the other, those things that appear to circumscribe individuals through imposition from the outside merit condemnation. In that sense, technology seems at once to victimize and to empower. Which it does in any particular case is seen through the measure of individual inviolability. And each individual measures for itself.

FOR FURTHER READING

Almond, Gabriel A., Marvin Chodorow, and Roy Harvey Pearce, eds. *Progress and Its Discontents* (1982).

Arrow, Kenneth J., ed. *Education in a Research University* (1996).

Bell, Daniel. *The Coming of Post-Industrial Society* (1973).

Blume, Stuart S. *Insight and Industry: On the Dynamics of Technological Change in Medicine* (1992).

Bormann, F. Herbert, Diana Balmori, and Gordon T. Geballe. *Redesigning the American Lawn* (1993).

Boroush, Mark A., Kan Chen, and Alexander N. Christakis, eds. *Technology Assessment* (1980).

Bud, Robert. *The Uses of Life. A History of Biotechnology* (1993).

Campbell-Kelly, Martin, and William Aspray, *Computer: A History of the Information Machine* (1996).

Cantelon, Phillip L., and Robert C. Williams. *Crisis Contained: The Department of Energy at Three Mile Island* (1982).

Chaffee, C. David. *The Rewiring of America: The Fiber Optics Revolution* (1988).

Doyle, Jack. *Altered Harvest: Agriculture, Genetics, and the Fate of the World's Food Supply* (1985).

Duderstadt, James J., and Chihiro Kikuchi. *Nuclear Power: Technology on Trial* (1979).

Dunlap, Thomas R. *DDT: Scientists, Citizens, and Public Policy* (1981).

Ezrahi, Yaron, Everett Mendelsohn, and Howard Segal, eds. *Technology, Pessimism, and Postmodernism* (1994).

Fuller, R. Buckminster. *Utopia or Oblivion* (1969).

Gall, Sarah, ed. *NASA Spinoffs* (1992).

Gibson, James William. *The Perfect War: Technowar in Vietnam* (1986).

Graham, Frank, Jr. *Since "Silent Spring"* (1970).

Hauben, Michael and Robin. *Netizens: On the History and Impact of Usenet and the Internet* (1997).

Henderson, Hazel. *Creating Alternative Futures* (1978).

Hirschhorn, Larry. *Beyond Mechanization: Work and Technology in a Postindustrial Age* (1984).

Hoos, Ida R. *Systems Analysis in Public Policy*, rev. ed. (1983).

Howard, Robert. *Brave New Workplace* (1985).

Ichbiah, Daniel, and Susan L. Knepper. *The Making of Microsoft* (1991).

Kevles, Bettyann Holtzmann. *Naked to the Bone: Medical Imaging in the Twentieth Century* (1997).

Kevles, Daniel J., and Leroy Hood, eds., *The Code of Codes* (1992).

Krimsky, Sheldon and Roger Wrubel. *Agricultural Biotechnology and the Environment* (1996).

Kuhns, William. *The Post-Industrial Prophets* (1971).

Lappe, Mark. *Broken Code: The Exploitation of DNA* (1984).

Lyons, Nick. *The Sony Vision* (1976).

Matthewson, David. *Revolutionary Technology: An Introduction to the Video and Digital Audio Disc* (1983).

McDougall, Walter A. *The Heavens and the Earth: A Political History of the Space Age* (1985).

McLuhan, Marshall, and Quentin Fiore. *War and Peace in the Global Village* (1968).

Mahon, Thomas. *Charged Bodies: People, Power, and Paradox in Silicon Valley* (1985).

Malone, Michael S. *The Big Score: The Billion-Dollar Story of Silicon Valley* (1985).

Marcus, Alan I. *Cancer From Beef: DES, Federal Food Regulation, and Consumer Confidence* (1994).

Marcus, Alan I, and Hamilton Cravens. *Health Care Policy in Contemporary America* (1997).

Mazlish, Bruce, ed. *The Railroad and the Space Program: An Exploration in Historical Analogy* (1965).

Norberg, Arthur I., and Judy E. O'Neill. *Transforming Computer Technology* (1998).

O'Neill, Gerard K. *The High Frontier: Human Colonies in Space* (1982).

Reid, T. R. *The Chip* (1984).

Rose, Mark H. *Interstate: Express Highway Politics, 1941–1956* (1979).

Roszak, Theodore. *The Cult of Information* (1986).

Rybczynski, Witold. *Paper Heroes* (1980).

Schumacher, E. F. *Small Is Beautiful* (1973).

Segal, Howard P. *Future Imperfect: The Mixed Blessings of Technology in America* (1994).

Smith, Douglas K., and Robert C. Alexander. *Fumbling the Future: How Xerox Invented, Then Ignored, the First Personal Computer* (1988).

Stares, Paul B. *The Militarization of Space* (1985).

Toffler, Alvin. *The Third Wave* (1980).

Turkle, Sherry. *The Second Self: Computers and the Human Spirit* (1984).

Waring, Stephen P. *Taylorism Transformed: Scientific Management Theory Since 1945* (1991).

Yoxen, Edward. *The Gene Business* (1984).

PHOTO CREDITS

INDEX

F

G

T

videotape recorders, 281-83
Vietnam War, 294, 317
Viking rocket, 256
village industries, 222-24
Vincent, J. G., 202
Virginia Company of London, 18
Von Neumann, John, 243
Vostok I (1961), 296

W

wagon,
    Conestoga, 30-31
        (photo), 31
Waksman, Selman A., 252-53
Walker, Timothy, 67-68
Wallace, Henry A., 228
Wang Laboratories, 380
War Games (1983), 310
War Industries Board, 199
War of 1812, 57
washing machine, 176-77
Washington, Bushrod, 63
Washington, George, 24, 31-32, 34
watch, digital, 334
Water Resource Planning Act (1965),
    314
waterwheel, 4, 8-9
    (*see also mills*)
Watson, James, 342
Watson, Thomas A., 127
Watson, Tom, 279-80
Watson-Watt, Robert, 248
Watt engine, 33
WEAF (New York City), 235
wealth, 5
weapons, 200-202, 339
    flintlock, 27
    intercontinental ballistic missile
        (ICBM), 310
    Maxim, Hiram S., 200
    napalm, 294
        (photo), 294
    nuclear, 295-96
    Pennsylvania long rifle, 27
    proximity fuse, 250
    Robbins and Lawrence rifle, 104
    (*see also atomic bomb*)
weaving, 14
    linen, 14
    wool, 14

Webster, Daniel, 68, 104
West, Benjamin, 81
Western Electric, 128, 129, 210, 211,
    212
Western Union, 83, 84, 106
    telephones, 128
Westinghouse, 132
Westinghouse air brake, 120
Westinghouse, George, 120, 125
    Niagara Falls Project, 126
Westinghouse Lighting Company,
    120, 124, 125
Weston, Edward, 117, 118
Weston Electric Light Company, 117
Wheeler & Wilson Manufacturing, 90
Whitney, Eli, 62, 63
Whitney, Willis, 140
Whyte, William H., Jr., *The
    Organization Man* (1956),
    262-63
Wild, John, 352
Wild and Scenic Rivers Act (1968),
    314
Wilson, Allen B., 90
Wilson, Sloan, *Man in the Gray
    Flannel Suit* (1955), 263
Wilson, Woodrow, 179, 199
Winthrop, John, Jr., 18
Wolcott, Alexander, 76
Wolfe, Tom, 326
Woodward, C. M., 196
wool
    processing, 13-14, 15
    weaving, 14
workingmen-s parties, 61-62
Works Progress Administration,
    240
World Future Society, 330, 331
World War I, 132, 198-205
    air technology, 201-2, 203
    land technology, 200
    munitions, 200, 203-4
    resources for, 199
    sea technology, 200-201
World War II
    atomic bomb, 246-48, 251
        (photo), 252
    aviation, 250-51
    proximity fuse, 250
    radar, 248-49
    sonar, 249-50
    technology during, 244-53
Wozniak, Steve, 366-68